Newnes MS-DOS 6.0 Pocket Book

Newnes MS-DOS 6.0 Pocket Book

Ian Sinclair

NEWNES

Newnes
An imprint of Butterworth-Heinemann Ltd
Linacre House, Jordan Hill, Oxford OX2 8DP

A member of the Reed Elsevier group

OXFORD LONDON BOSTON
MUNICH NEW DELHI SINGAPORE SYDNEY
TOKYO TORONTO WELLINGTON

First published 1993

British Library Cataloguing in Publication Data
A catalogue record for this book is available from the British Library.

Library of Congress Cataloguing in Publication Data
A catalogue record for this book is available from the Library of Congress.

ISBN 0 7506 0999 0

Typeset by P K McBride, Southampton
Printed and bound in Great Britain

Contents

Contents

Preface

The aim of this book is to provide in an easily portable form a useful and comprehensive guide to the MS-DOS 6.0 operating system and its successors for computers of the PC class using the 80386 or 80486 chips. Unlike books dealing with earlier versions of MS-DOS, this book assumes the use of a modern fast machine, a hard disk, and adequate RAM (at least 2 Mb and preferably 5 Mb or more). It also deals with the considerable enhancements made to MS-DOS in Version 5.0 as well as in 6.0, and deals in detail with the DOSSHELL, since many users may prefer this to the use of Windows when true multi-tasking is not needed.

It would be possible to reduce the essentials of MS-DOS commands to a few lines for each command, but the aim here has been to provide rather more, enough information to ensure that you can be confident in your use of a command even if you have never used that command previously, though not as much as would be provided in an exhaustive text, nor as much as would be required by an assembly-language programmer using MS-DOS routines.

In addition, some background information on the origins of MS-DOS has been included, because, to use the famous phrase, it's easier to tell where you are going if you know where you have been. The bulk of this book concerns the **user** of the most recent version of DOS, assisting with the day to day control of the loading and saving of programs and data, backing up files, checking files and disks and the integrity of data. Commands that have by now fallen into disuse and which are present only for the sake of compatibility with early versions are dealt with only cursorily. Some of these older commands are no longer present in MS-DOS 6.0.

The book is concerned not only with the commands of DOS, but with how the computer is set up, using the AUTOEXEC.BAT file and the CONFIG.SYS file, since these important parts of the set-up are often omitted in books that cover MS-DOS. The emphasis is on the use of a machine with a hard disk, but users of single/double floppy machines will also find much that is applicable. The aim is to provide a reference guide for the user that will be **used** and carried about rather than gather dust on a shelf.

This book deals in detail with the enhancements that has been made to MS-DOS since Version 5.0, notably the Double-Space disk compression software (which can be used on floppy disks as well as on a hard drive), the MemMaker for optimising the use of memory on 386 (upwards) machines, the new Backup and Restore utilities that can be configured for the machine in which they are working, ending a long history of confusion about these commands, the Anti-Virus software, Diagnostics, and the Interlnk system for creating a simple network. In addition, the smaller points such as the enhanced menu system, Undelete, disk defragmenter, menu choice in CONFIG.SYS files and AUTOEXEC.BAT, new Smartdrive, Power command for laptop machines and a menu command for batch files will all make a considerable difference to the overall usefulness of this DOS.

I am most grateful to Mike Cash of Butterworth-Heinemann Ltd. for suggesting this title, and to Microsoft Inc. and PR Text 100 for the information that they have so willingly supplied, particularly in the provision of a late beta-test version of the program.

Ian Sinclair, Spring 1993.

NOTE: Throughout this book the key which is marked with the return arrow in the form [↵] will be referred to as the ENTER key. On a few computers this is marked RETURN, so that the phrase RETURN/ENTER is used at some points to emphasise that this is the same key.

1 Beginnings and Fundamentals

DOS History

When micro-computers started to be used seriously for business purposes, many manufacturers devised their own operating systems. The operating system is a program that either exists in the computer in the form of a chip (a ROM or Read Only Memory system, used now mainly for portable machines) or which can be loaded in from a disk, using a very small loader program held in ROM. The aim of the operating system is to provide, at the very least, the essential routines that allow the computer to make use of the screen, the keyboard and the disk drive(s), managing files and loading and running programs. Without program routines that attend to these tasks, the computer is usable only if each program that is to be run attends to all of these actions for itself. This would be a wasteful duplication, so that the operating system is just as important as all the hardware of the computer.

The use of different operating systems by different manufacturers, however, makes it virtually impossible to set standards that will allow one computer to run a program that works on another computer from a different manufacturer. When all computers were mainframes, with one computer to one company, with programs specially written for each machine, inter-changeability of programs was of no importance. The prospect that each user of a computer might eventually be working with a separate machine came only with the development of microcomputers, and only when corporate users started to take microcomputers seriously. To see what the attitude of corporate users was to microcomputers, it is interesting to look at some of the textbooks of Computer Science which are still used in schools, some of which seem almost intended to discourage computing as a career.

One solution to the problem of interchangeability came about in the very early days of the development of microcomputers, in the form of CP/M. This was a system to control, program and monitor (hence the initials) the operation of these early microcomputers, and it was devised by Gary Kildall in or around 1973, before microcomputers were a commercial proposition. At that time, the idea of a standardised operating system was not new because Unix was already under development for mainframe machines, but the idea of a standard operating system for micro-computers was certainly new. Today only a very few portable machines, such as the Amstrad NC100, use their own operating systems.

The Intel 8080 microprocessor, around which many early microcomputers for business use were designed, first appeared in 1975, and CP/M was quickly adapted to it. Though some of the machines which made most of the running in these early days, such as Apple-2, Commodore PET and Tandy TRS-80, used their own operating systems, the advantages of a standard system were recognised by many other manufacturers who were able to market machines for business use which could interchange programs and data, provided that their disk formats were compatible. The format for 8" floppy disks had been standardised by IBM, but, unfortunately, no standard for 5.25" disk formats existed at that time. The advantages of using CP/M were therefore often diminished by the inability to exchange disks other than 8" floppies directly, though programs and data could be exchanged by way of the serial ports (which were, of course, controlled by CP/M), and by programs which could be used to allow a machine to read a disk that had been formatted in a different way.

One particularly valuable feature of CP/M was that it came along with a set of utility programs that allowed the user to carry out tasks like file copying, file checking, program modification, disk verification and all of the other housekeeping actions that are now so familiar. Some of these programs had been devised in the very early days of micro-computer use, and were intended for the programmer rather than the user. In these days microcomputers were bought in the main by people who understood computer programming, or who were determined to learn, so that these utilities were welcomed even though their use was by no means easy. The idea of a program being user-friendly was a few years away, as was the idea of really widespread use of computers.

The IBM PC

The start of serious small-scale computing as we know it today was with the IBM PC machine, which was released in 1981. The original PC machine was designed around a new microprocessor chip, the Intel 8088, which allowed data to be handled internally in 16-bit form rather than the 8-bit form that had been standard in the CP/M machines (which used the 8080 or Z-80 chips). Data was, however, read and written in 8-bit form, in contrast to the companion Intel chip the 8086. The 8088 was chosen for the IBM PC because at the time the 8086 chip was difficult to mass-produce, but later PC-compatible machines have taken advantage of falling chip prices to use the superior 8086 rather than the simpler 8088.

Both of these chips, however, have a structure which was very much a development of the older 8-bit 8080 chip (also by Intel), so that it was possible to revise programs that had worked on the earlier CP/M machines so as to run on the new IBM PC. Before the machine could be released, however, it needed an operating system, one that would provide the facilities of CP/M on an extended scale for a complete new generation of 16-bit machines.

Digital Research, the company that had been set up to market and develop CP/M, offered a new version, CP/M-86, which could be used on the PC type of machine. At the same time, however, the rival software house Microsoft were using a 16-bit operating system which had been developed by a smaller firm, Seattle Computer Products in 1980, and which at one time was termed QDOS, with the QD meaning Quick and Dirty. This was renamed 86-DOS and with intensive effort was developed into a powerful operating system which was offered to IBM at a price that considerably undercut CP/M-86. The system as used on the PC was known as PC-DOS, and a virtually identical version was available for any other manufacturers of machines using the Intel chips, using the name MS-DOS. This has progressed through many versions as the demands for new facilities has expanded; the main changes in the later versions have been to allow for networking use and for use with the 80386 and 80486 types of machine in which the memory limitations of earlier versions are overcome.

Chip Development

The first IBM PC machine used only 16 Kbyte of RAM, and in its standard form used cassette tape rather than disks. Disk drives could be added, however, with a memory extension to 64 Kbyte, which seemed adequate at the time, since all of the standard business programs (such as WordStar, SuperCalc, dBase-2) ran under CP/M in this amount of memory space on the CP/M machines and could be converted to run in the same amount of space on the new machine. The 8088 chip and its stable-mate the 8086 allowed up to 1 Mbyte of memory to be used, however, so that pressure soon built up for the use of more memory.

The Intel chips have always been designed to offer a complete set of computing actions along with quite exceptional compatibility, and the history of MS-DOS closely parallels the work that has been done in the development of these chips. Though there are versions of MS-DOS that run as 'simulations' on machines with a different chip set, the use of MS-DOS has always been aimed at the Intel chips. This, in particular, affects the way that memory can be extended and used.

In particular, decisions that were taken a long time ago still affect what is easily possible. When the Intel 8088/8086 chips were being designed in 1979 the price and performance of RAM was such that no-one envisaged more than 1 Mbyte of total memory ever being used, and the simplest way of retaining the compatibility between the new chips and the old was to manage memory in 64 Kbyte pieces, each piece being called a *segment*. This allowed several important advantages, not least of which was that the new chips could use many of the design features of the old ones.

One important point was that the registers (small memory units within the processor chip) that controlled the use of a segment of memory could be identical to the registers that were used in the 8-bit chips, and the choice of different segments could be achieved by placing a segment number into another register. This, in turn, allowed for the possibility of using programs that would run in a 64 Kbyte segment, with a different program in each segment, or as an alternative, the use of programs which would take up more than one segment, like the bloated monsters of 360 Kbyte and more that we are familiar with today. This also allowed older programs that ran under CP/M to be updated comparatively easily, and was the start of the trend to compatibility that has become the main selling attraction for PC machines. Considering that the value of software can be ten times the value of the computer on which it runs, compatibility is a feature that manufacturers neglect at their cost.

MS-DOS Development

As the demand for the PC grew, and the disk system was standardised to the familiar, but now obsolete, 5.25" 40-track double-sided double-density 360 Kbyte format, MS-DOS was being steadily developed to cope with new needs. One restriction that has remained on MS-DOS throughout is that of memory management. MS-DOS was originally written to cater for a maximum of ten 64 Kbyte segments of RAM, corresponding to 640 Kbyte, and this has to date never changed, though versions 4.0 onwards allowed for some restricted use of extended or expanded memory (see later for explanation). The limit was originally fixed by the use of a 1 Mbyte address limit on the original 8088/8086 chips, which both used a 20-line address bus, so that the address range covers 2^{20} addresses. This number is 1,048,576, which is one megabyte (1 Mbyte), allowing 640 Kbyte for RAM and the remaining 384 Kbyte for ROM and for access to the RAM that is used for the screen display (video RAM), all placed in the *higher* addresses.

The development of higher-resolution screen displays from the original text-only type, through monochrome graphics to the colour graphics of the GCA, VGA and EGA variety, has made increasing inroads into the memory allowance which was set aside within the original 1 Mbyte space, and a further piece is taken on XT machines by the hard-disk ROM (whether the hard disk is built in or added as a card). The later 80286 chip was constructed in a way that allowed it to handle up to 16 Mbyte of memory - but only when running a different operating system such as Xenix or Unix, and it retained the 1 Mbyte limit for MS-DOS. Only the 80386 and 80486 chips, of those announced and being delivered to date, overcome the problems of 64 Kbyte segments and the 1 Mbyte memory limit - but MS-DOS has not adapted fully to this freedom even in Version 6.0 because of the incompatibilities that would result.

It is true that the versions from MS-DOS 3.0 onwards have provided for using add-on memory, the type called *expanded* memory which is added in the form of a card, and switched into circuit as required. This should not be confused with *extended* memory which can be added to 80286, 80386 and 80486 machines, provided for in versions 4.0 onwards. These machines use a 24 or 32-line address bus so that at least 16 Mbyte can be addressed, and memory that is installed beyond the original 1 Mbyte limit on such machine is *extended* memory, which can be used only by programs that have been written to do so. The differences between these types of added memory have often caused confusion in the past, so that an explanation may be useful here. The important point is that all modern 386 or 486 machines should use extended memory, whether they are running MS-DOS alone or with Windows (see later).

The limitation caused by the early chip designs, 8088 and 8086, was that only 1 Mbyte of memory *address numbers* were available. The use of memory by the processor depends on each byte of memory being allocated an address number which can be used as a reference in the way that the address of a house allows for the delivery of mail. Adding memory chips to such machines was therefore pointless because the address numbers that such memory would need were not available.

Expanded memory solved this problem by making use of some address numbers more than once. The addresses in the higher 384 Kbyte of memory are not completely taken up by ROM, so that there is usually a substantial number of spare addresses that do not correspond to any connection to memory. By using software described as *EMS drivers*, it is possible to make use of, typically, 64 Kbyte of these address numbers and to allocate them to different pieces of added memory. This limits the use of such memory to 64 Kbyte at a time, but since this corresponds to the size of a segment in conventional memory the limitation is not serious, though the time taken to access such memory is a limitation. Another time problem is that an expanded memory board fits into an expansion slot, and an expansion slot operates at a slower speed than the motherboard of the computer.

Expanded memory is, however, only a dodge that allowed these early chips to make use of added memory. All of the later chips have been provided with sufficient connections to be able to address much more memory, 16 Mbyte for the 80286 and several Gbyte (1 Gbyte = 1024 Mbyte) for the 80386 and 80486 (though the 80386SX is limited to 16 Mb). The construction of these chips allows memory to be added directly to the motherboard of the computer and used directly by the chip without any limitation on using 64 Kbyte pieces addressed by way of numbers that correspond to the upper part of the original 1 Mbyte limit. This type of added memory is referred to as extended memory.

■ This is a novelty only for the PC type of machine. The machines which use the rival Motorola type of 68000 chip have always used memory in this way, with no segment divisions or 1 Mbyte limits. Unfortunately, no standard operating system has been developed, so that the 68000 chip machines from Apple (Mac), Commodore (Amiga) and Atari (ST) are all incompatible with the PC and with each other.

Extended memory presents no hardware snags, it does not require any special (and expensive) plug-in boards as expanded memory does; instead, the chips are plugged in directly, usually in the form of SIMM (Single in-line memory module) groups which add either 1 Mbyte or 4 Mbyte per unit (16 Mbyte SIMM modules are also available). Unfortunately, software has not advanced so rapidly because of the need to preserve compatibility with older versions of MS-DOS and with older machines.

In other words, if your 80386 machine contains 4 Mbyte of RAM, MS-DOS can use only 640 Kbyte of it for programs, and the rest, if it is used at all, can be used only for cache memory or RAMdisk. This is clearly unsatisfactory, but until there is no need for programs to run on 8088, 8086 and 80286 machines it is difficult to avoid. Windows 3.1 is one way out - it allows full use of extended memory for the programs which are intended to run under Windows 3.1 control, and it makes no concessions to 8088 and 8086 machines - Windows 3.1 cannot be used on such machines. Programs written for such machines can, however, be run by a machine that uses Windows.

At present the situation is that expanded memory is obsolescent, used only on a dwindling band of older machines. Extended memory is the norm and is essential for any machine running Windows - see the Windows 3/3.1 Pocket Book for details. Currently, MS-DOS can make use of extended memory only by way of an additional driver, HIMEM.SYS which is installed using the CONFIG.SYS file (see Chapter 2).

MS-DOS therefore does not provide for multi-tasking, meaning that two or more programs can be run in the memory at the same time, when this 640 Kbyte requirement would be exceeded. The MS Windows 3.1 system allows for more than one program to be present, and for switching easily between programs, making use of extended memory to store a program and data while the use of the program is suspended. The use of Windows, which is not an operating system in its own right, allows the 640 Kbyte memory barrier to be broken.

Windows 3.1 allows for true multi-tasking on the 80386 and 80486 types of machine, and the 640 Kbyte barrier is also broken by the later operating system, OS-2, from IBM, rather than by MS-DOS itself. However, OS-2 requires very much more memory for its own purposes, and is intended for machines with many Mbyte of RAM memory, as also is the Microsoft NT system, the main competitor for OS-2. At one time, it was fashionable to speculate that Unix would become the standard operating system for PC machines, but this seems most unlikely in the light of NT and the later revisions of OS/2. It seems unlikely, in fact, that any really standard version of Unix will ever exist.

DOS Versions

The original versions of MS-DOS were 1.0 and 1.1. These were suited to the older version of the PC, and V.1.0 could be used only with single-sided disk drives. V.1.1, which allowed the use of the familiar double-sided disk, was released in 1982. These early versions were rare in Europe, where the PC type of machine was not outstandingly popular at first because of its high cost and a specification that looked rather restricted compared to many CP/M machines.

Versions 2.0 and 2.1 were written to expand the use of MS-DOS very considerably when the PC was almost universally supplied with a disk system and more memory, often with 360 Kbyte or more. At this time, clones of the PC began to appear, some of which provided as standard many of the facilities that had been available on the original machine only by way of plug-in cards. The most important of the additions that were made to MS-DOS at that time were to cope with TSR programs, country-variables, hard disk use, and file handling.

A Terminate-and-stay-resident program (TSR) is one that can be loaded into a segment and which will then stay in that segment, being activated and deactivated as needed within a computing session without the need to be re-loaded. The use of such programs involves the allocation of memory and the protection of that memory in order to make sure that no other program is loaded over the TSR program.

There also must be provision for 'hot-key' use, so that a key combination, such as Alt-Shift, can start or stop the TSR program. What is not usually provided for is the removal of a TSR program cleanly from the memory so that the memory can be released for other use. This often means that loading in a large program, such as a desktop publishing package or a large program like Lotus Agenda or Symphony can lead to Out of memory messages, and the program can be run successfully only if the machine is re-booted first. There are utilities, such as MARK and RELEASE, for freeing memory, but they do not appear to be widely known. MS-DOS 6.0 provides for some of its memory-resident utilities to be released from memory though, as with MARK and RELEASE, some care has to be taken that others are not also released at the same time.

Country variables refer to the keyboard and screen characters that will appear in versions of MS-DOS that run on machines which are used with a character set other than the standard US one. This is provided for in DOS versions from 2.0 on, but versions 2.0 and 2.1 provide only for getting this information, not for easily changing it. The ability to view and modify the country variables was completely implemented in version 3.0. The provision for hard disk drives was a particularly important step forward. This was made necessary because of the fast rate of development of miniature hard disks from the 8" size to 5.25" and then to 3.5", making it possible to have a hard disk in the physical space of a floppy drive, or even on a card that would fit into one of the slots inside the computer. The familiar commands that were added at this time include MKDIR (or MD) to make a disk directory, CHDIR (or CD) to switch to a named directory, and RMDIR (or RD) to remove a directory. The drive memory limit was set at 32 Mbyte, after which the disk drive had to be *partitioned* as if it were more than one drive. The commands such as ASSIGN, JOIN and SUBST were added at this time so as to allow hard-disk directories to be used as if they were floppy drives. This was done so that older programs which did not provide for the use of hard disk directories could still be used. These commands should nowadays be regarded as obsolete, because the programs which required them are now obsolete. They are not part of MS-DOS 6.0.

At the same time, MS-DOS 2.0 added a large number of routines for handling files, most of which are not accessible directly through command names but which can be used by programmers working in assembly language or in some higher level languages, notably C. The EXIT command was also added, which makes it possible to jump out of a program (the *parent* program) to use DOS (as a *child* program), and then (by typing EXIT and then pressing the ENTER key) to return to the program. Not all programs are written in order to take advantage of this, a process described as **shelling-out to DOS.**

Another major addition was a supplementary way of controlling files. The earlier versions of MS-DOS had used the same method of keeping track of files as CP/M, a method called file control blocks (FCB). With MS-DOS 2.0, this older method was supplemented by a set of new routines which could use a much simpler method, a file handle. Without going into detail, using a file control block (FCB) meant that a set of bytes in memory had to be used to hold, in correct order, all the details of a file, and this form of memory block had to be set up for each file.

The file handle method allowed a simple string of ASCII characters, consisting of drive letter and full filename, to be used as a file control by assigning a 16-bit code number, with all the rest of the work performed by the operating system. The file-handle system also allowed peripherals like the printer and the serial port to be used as if they were files, with names such as PRN and AUX1, so that a file could be copied to a device name as easily as to a directory name. Programs could still be written using the older method, because it was still available on DOS 2.0 and beyond, but the file handle method is so much easier to use that most programmers have taken advantage of it. Commands that involve file control blocks are now obsolete.

There were also some useful minor additions in MS-DOS 2.0, such as the ability to control the use of the Break key, and the ability to rename a file and to label a file with date and time. Also added was the information on the space remaining on a disk (following the disk directory) and the VER command to get the MS-DOS version number.

The large changes between versions 1.1 and 2.0 or 2.1 meant that programs that were written to take full advantage of version 2.0 or 2.1 could not be used with 1.0 or 1.1. This incompatibility was less serious that it seemed, because the major changes that had taken place in the requirements for DOS, such as hard disk use, made it pointless to write programs that would use the older version, and it was still possible to run programs that had run under the older versions. The changes that were made from version 2.1 to version 3.0 (followed in quick succession by 3.1, 3.2, 3.3 and 3.4) were not so dramatic from the point of view of the user of a single machine, but they added significant extensions. Very few modern programs will run on MS-DOS versions earlier than 3.0 and many demand at least version 4.01. The main extensions concerned the use of programs by computers that were part of a network. Networking requires changes to the operating system in order to make certain that one computer does not, without permission, alter the files that belong to another, and quite extensive additions to MS-DOS had to be made in order to satisfy the requirements. For users of solo machines, however, these had no impact, but the addition of pipes and filters did.

The principles of pipes and filters had existed for a considerable time in the many versions of the Unix operating system for mainframe computers, but they had not previously been implemented in an operating system for a microcomputer. A pipe implies that a command symbol will allow data to the channelled from the output of one program to the input of another, or from a program to a different outlet (to printer, for example, rather than to screen). A filter means that a program which can modify data can be placed in the way of data that is being transferred. For example, data that is to be shown on the screen can have a filter inserted that will ensure that it appears in alphabetical order, or it can be arranged to appear 24 lines at a time so that the user has time to look at one screen before seeing the next 24 lines. Redirection of this type was the main step forward in version 3.0 as far as the single user was concerned.

The introduction of the PC/AT in 1984 required the DOS to be able to cater for the high-density 5.25" disk system, 1.2 Mbyte rather than the 360 Kbyte of the earlier disks. In addition, the drives were able to sense the disk working density and could read 360 Kbyte disks as well as the 1.2 Mbyte type. Unfortunately, it was not possible for the high-density 5.25" drives to write to 360 Kbyte disks, and this deficiency has never been remedied. The replacement of 5.25" drives by the more modern 3.5" drives means that the larger size of disk is now obsolescent, though it is still used in enormous numbers.

As a more minor change, the country variables could now be set by the use of KEYB files, such as KEYB UK which sets the keyboard for the UK character set, with the pound sign, and with the single and double quote marks in positions that are transposed in comparison to the US keyboard.

Version 3.2 also introduced support for 3.5" disk drives, allowing a change to this size of disk. This was rather belated as far as the PC was concerned, because machines such as the Apple Macintosh, Amiga and Atari ST had shown the advantages of the smaller and better-protected disks. The first generation of 3.5" disks were of 720 Kbyte capacity, but by the 1990s the 1.4 Mbyte form of 3.5" disk was fitted almost universally to machines in the 80386 and 80486 class, and MS-DOS 5.0 provided for the use of 2.8 Mbyte disks of this diameter, though the drives have taken some time to appear and disks have taken longer. More recently, it has been possible to buy Floptical 3.5" drives (from the Insite Corp., sold in the UK by Panorama) which can use either the conventional magnetic floppies or a read/ write form of optical disk of 21 Mbyte capacity (some types cater for 128 Mbyte disks). Read/write optical disks of 128 Mbyte capacity, using a different drive, have also appeared, and it may take some time before standards are established. Other recent developments are the Canon drive that can accept either 3.5" or 5.25" disks and the Verbatim 24Mbyte magnetic drive.

Versions 4.0 and 4.01

Version 4.0 became available in 1988, and seems to have been intended as a way of preparing users for the use of OS/2 (which had been long delayed). The 32 Mbyte limit on the hard disk drive was removed, so that partitioning was no longer needed, and at last there was some use of memory above the 640 Kbyte limit. The release of V.4.0 was, however, accompanied by many problems, not least the amount of memory that the operating system required, which made it impossible to run some of the larger programs such as Aldus Pagemaker. A hurried modification, V.4.01, was released, but many users clung to V.3.3 rather than updating. This situation did not change until the release of MS-DOS 5.0 in 1991.

MS-DOS 5.0

The principles embodied into MS-DOS 5.0, some of which were carried over from V.4.01, represented a considerable change as compared to versions 3.x, and an immense improvement on V.4.0. For the first time, the installation of a new version of MS-DOS on to an existing hard disk (without requiring re-formatting) was made easy due to the use of an automatic setup routine.

For almost all users of MS-DOS, the upgrade was very attractive and strongly recommended. If the upgrade was carried out and there was a need to revert to the older version, there was provision for an UNINSTALL routine to be run. Note that the use of a hard disk was assumed for V.5.0 - the main benefits of V.5.0 were apparent only to users of machines with some extended memory, 80286 and higher. The operating system could be used by floppy-only machines, but these could not make such easy use of all the accessories that were offered because of the space limitations of the floppy disk. The full set of files (most of which were utilities, as in previous versions), needed some 2.13 Mbyte of disk space.

The greatest advantages were felt by users of 386 and 486 machines, through much better management of the memory above the old 640 Kbyte limit. Users of 286 machines could also benefit from some of these improvements, which allow the use of the extended memory for loading MS-DOS itself. Users of old 8088 and 8086 machines did not experience any memory benefits unless they had been using MS-DOS 4.0 or 4.01; MS-DOS 5.0 took up rather less memory than 4.0 or 4.01, but slightly more than V.3.3. Even on the older machines, however, the transformed ease of use of MS-DOS 5.0 makes the change worthwhile. An outstanding feature of V.5.0 is that it can be easily installed even on a hard disk which is already well-packed with files, and the installation no longer puts existing files in danger though, as always, it is prudent to keep a full backup of all files. The other new features of MS-DOS 5.0 included:

- A new HELP command which lists all commands, together with on-line help (using the /? keys following the command name) for individual commands.
- A Shell system, the DOSSHELL, which allows all MS-DOS actions to be selected by mouse and permits switching between programs (one active, others suspended).
- A new set of selection letters for the DIR command which allow subdirectory search, sort order, selection by attribute, abbreviated listing (file names only) and lowercase display.
- A safe format (allowing unformatting) and an undelete utility. There is also a quick format option for previously-formatted disks, and an unconditional format which will completely erase a floppy (a file-shredding option).

- Provision for recalling commands and assigning commands to keys (key macros).
- A full-screen editor to replace the old EDLIN.
- Greatly improved provision for large disk drives, ending the 32 Mbyte limit. The 2.88 Mbyte 3.5" floppy drive is supported.
- There are changes to ATTRIB and other commands, the ability to nominate a file for pipe actions, renaming of directories, and a case-insensitive option for the FIND command.
- In addition, the documentation of MS-DOS 5.0 is much improved, and a new BASIC interpreter, QBI, has replaced the older GW-BASIC.
- The utilities are stored in compressed form and are expanded only when they are transferred to the hard disk by the installation program. This form of compression paved the way for the compression utility built into MS-DOS 6.0.

Version 6.0 extensions

Version 6.0 has added a considerable number of new utilities to MS-DOS 5.0, including:

1. A disk-space compressor called DBLSPACE. This allows, for example, a 40 Mbyte hard disk to be used as if it could hold 60 - 80 Mbyte (depending on file type), and even floppy disks can be used to hold more than is normally available. Unlike disk-space utilities from other suppliers, DBLSPACE is integrated into the MS-DOS system so that it could potentially be used to allow distribution of files on compressed floppy disks, rather in the way that MS-DOS 6.0 itself is distributed.

2. MEMMAKER is a utility aimed at 386, 486 (and upwards) machines on which memory management is important in order to gain the advantages that these chips can supply. MEMMAKER will set up the memory manager utilities (HIMEM and EMM386) so as to provide the optimum use of memory, something that requires considerable knowledge to carry out manually.

3. The UNDELETE program of MS-DOS 5 has been considerably extended to allow three levels of recovery action for accidentally deleted files, classifying such files as Perfect, Good, Poor or Destroyed. The SENTRY system replaces the MIRROR used on MS-DOS 5.0.

4. A totally new Backup and Restore system allows for configuration to an individual machine and a testing routine that ensures that backing up can be relied upon.

This is a very considerable improvement on the system used in older versions of MS-DOS.

5. There is now an Anti-Virus set of utilities. In one form, this can scan your hard or floppy disks for any trace of a known virus, reporting on what it finds. There is also a memory-resident form that can be loaded in when the computer is switched on, and which will report any attempt to use routines which might indicate a virus action.

6. There are Windows versions of Undelete, Backup and Restore, and Anti-Virus which can be placed in a separate MicroSoft Tools group within Windows.

7. There is a simplified networking system, Interlnk, which is intended mainly to allow a laptop and a desktop machine to share printers and files.

8. The diagnostic program MSD allows you to obtain and print a complete technical report about your computer.

In addition, there are many minor enhancements including:

- An updated EMM386 driver which offers better control over extended memory and allows expanded memory to be simulated if needed.
- A DELTREE command which will delete a directory and all its files and sub-directories in one step.
- An enhanced MEM command to provide a technical description about the use of memory
- Better LOADHIGH and DEVICEHIGH commands for loading programs into specified parts of memory.
- A Disk Defragmenter for reorganising the files on a hard disk, allowing the disk to be used more efficiently.
- A new version of the SmartDrive cache program which offer both read and write caching
- A new CHOICE batch command that allows a menu selection within a batch file.
- The ability to start the machine either bypassing the CONFIG.SYS and AUTOEXEC.BAT files, or selecting commands in the CONFIG.SYS file and opting whether or not to run AUTOEXEC.BAT
- The ability to write CONFIG.SYS files that offer options at the time when the machine is switched on, and the ability to run different versions of AUTOEXEC.BAT depending on the choices made in the CONFIG.SYS file.

- The ability to use power-saving on any laptop computer whose BIOS chip contains power-managing routines.

The full set of utilities for MS-DOS 6.0 needs around 5 Mbyte of disk space.

Practical points - COM and EXE files

MS-DOS can run two types of machine-code program which use the extension filenames of COM and EXE respectively. A COM file is constructed almost identically to a CP/M file (which would also carry the COM extension), and the entire program, along with all of its data and other use of memory, is contained in a single 64 Kbyte segment. MS-DOS will decide which segment is selected (always the lowest-numbered available part of the memory), and because all of the program is contained within a 64 Kbyte address space the address numbers can use single-word (16-bit) registers. This makes it possible to design and use short and memory-efficient programs, and also to have several such programs present in memory at any given time.

The alternative is the EXE type of program which will usually make use of more than one segment. In addition, such a program can be relocated anywhere in the memory (subject to rules about where it would start in a given segment) and will still run. This is the method that must be followed for larger programs, or programs in which data needs a separate segment. When an EXE program is loaded, MS-DOS will place it wherever it can be put.

The organisation of memory in the PC type of machine is illustrated here in Figure 1.1, with addresses up to 1 Mbyte in hex (00000H to FFFFFH). On the 8088/8086 machines, this upper memory limit is determined by the number of address lines, but on the 80286 and 80386/80486 machines the limit is more usually determined by MS-DOS itself. The 80386 machines were replaced as 'leading-edge' technology in a remarkably short time and by 1992 any machine lower than 80386 was regarded as obsolete, with the 80386 considered as the introductory machine and the 80486 the 'leading edge'. For many users the 80386 will be satisfactory for a long time (as was the XT machine, millions of which are still in use).

The normal amount of RAM memory, the base memory, is still in the 640 Kbyte range, and of this DOS typically takes 70 Kbyte or less, depending to what extent the extended memory is used. At the time of writing it is fairly normal for a machine to carry 4 Mbyte of extended RAM as standard, and many users who intend to use Windows will opt for 8 Mb or more.

Figure 1.1

The organisation for the first megabyte of memory in any PC type of machine. The 640Kb restriction would not have existed if the RAM area had started at A0000H, with ROM at 00000H.

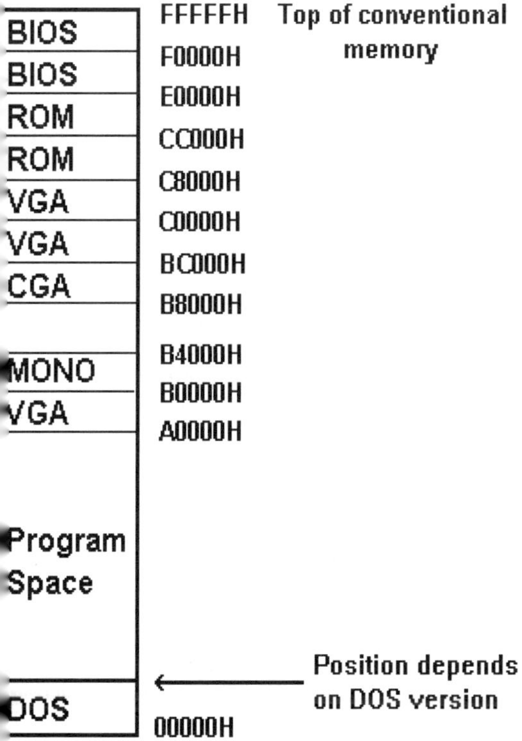

The utilities

Early versions of MS-DOS were supplied with a set of utilities of which the most used were those which attended to disk needs, such as formatting floppies, copying and deleting files, and showing file directories. Some utilities have been carried over from the oldest versions and are by this time seldom used and are present only for the sake of compatibility.

The advent of MS-DOS 5.0 saw the first set of hard-disk recovery utilities built into the operating system itself. Hard disk users know that in the lifetime of a disk, files are added and deleted many times over. Each time a file is deleted, its space on the disk is released, and saving a new file will make use of released space. A large file, however, may make use of many small amounts of space released by the deletion of many smaller files. This 'fragmentation' results in much slower access times for such files, because of the number of times that the head of the disk drive has to be moved in order to read all the portions of a file.

Before MS-DOS 5.0, users would be required to buy some form of hard-disk 'toolkit' program, such as Norton Utilities or PC-Tools (see my book *Using Disk and Ram Utilities*, Heinemann Newtech). MS-DOS 5.0 introduced the disk recovery system of PC-Tools, licensed from Central Point Software, providing a considerable step forward in security for hard disk users. The UNDELETE command introduced in MS-DOS 5.0 allows files that have been unintentionally deleted to be recovered either by reference to the MS-DOS directory system, or by the use of an 'undelete file'. This latter method, which is faster and more certain, is performed by using a utility called MIRROR which has to be run each time the machine is switched on. MS-DOS 6.0 has extended this with the SENTRY system, and has added the DEFRAG file utility, reducing the need to depend on any other disk utilities.

The MS-DOS main files

MS-DOS relies on several files to achieve its effects. One of these files is normally held in a ROM chip, and is known as the BIOS, meaning Basic Input-Output System. This part of the operating system is provided by the manufacturer of the computer, who is therefore responsible for its contents and its correct interaction with the rest of the system. For the IBM PC and several of its clones, the ROM BIOS is the IBM version.

Other manufacturers, such as Amstrad, will have their own names and copyright information coded into the ROM BIOS, but there are a few examples in circulation of machines whose makers deny any connection with IBM but whose BIOS chips carry the IBM copyright notice.

Irrespective of its design, the BIOS in ROM must carry out the elementary input and output actions, and it must do so using certain fixed starting addresses that will be used by MS-DOS. Any manufacturer can therefore design a BIOS chip, and a licence from IBM is necessary only if that particular chip is duplicated, or so closely copied as to make it a duplicate in all but name. Some early copies were detected because they copied the known errors in the BIOS chip as well as all of the standard routines.

The BIOS address area is at the top of the memory, and a lot more space is reserved than is normally needed, so allowing for additional BIOS ROMs to be used. For example, the Amstrad version of BIOS, called ROS (Resident Operating System) occupies only 16 Kbyte of the 128 Kbyte which is reserved for BIOS use. There is an additional 128 Kbyte allocation of memory lying under the BIOS region which is also reserved for expansion ROMs, and when a hard disk drive is fitted to the older XT type of machine, the ROM that is on the hard-disk driver card will use some 16 Kbyte of this space, leaving plenty of room for another hard disk unit to be used. In some computers, you will find more than one copy of the BIOS in the reserved addresses.

The system files

The rest of the work is done by files that are read in from the disk, and one of the tasks of the BIOS in ROM is to allow the other files to be read, put them into the correct places in the memory (at the lowest end of the memory) and to start them running. The names of these files depend on the software that has been supplied with the machine. On the IBM machine, these files are called IBMBIO.SYS and IBMDOS.SYS, but on most other machines they will have other names, typically IO.SYS and MSDOS.SYS. The first of these is an addition to the input/output facilities of the BIOS in ROM, and the second is used to carry out some of the MS-DOS (or PC-DOS) actions. These files should be the first two files stored on the disk, and if they are not found the system will halt and issue the error message:

```
Non-System disk or disk error
Replace and strike any key when ready
```

The floppy drive A is **always** checked first for these files, and even if you always start the machine from a hard disk, you will get this error message and a hang-up if there is a disk without system tracks in drive A. The remedy if you use a hard disk is always to start the machine with drive A empty.

- More recent machines using the AMI (and similar) BIOS chips will allow you to set up a fast-boot option, in which the A: drive is never used during booting. This is a very attractive option, though it will have to be switched off if you ever need to boot from a floppy (for example, if a new line in the AUTOEXEC.BAT file causes the machine to lock up).

If the system tracks are found, the IO.SYS and MSDOS.SYS files are read and placed at the lowest end of the memory. The IO.SYS program starts to run, and calls the MSDOS.SYS program. It is during this time that the memory of the machine is checked. When the IO.SYS program starts running again, it will configure the machine according to the lines in the CONFIG.SYS file (see Chapter 2).

In addition, there is a file called COMMAND.COM, which is used for most of the built-in commands of MS-DOS, the actions which are carried out when a word is typed and the RETURN/ENTER key pressed. The COMMAND.COM file is loaded by a routine in MS-DOS, and it is arranged so that part of it is retained in the memory so that essential actions (the internal commands) are available when needed, but the other part of COMMAND.COM can be (and often is) wiped out by parts of other programs.

This is because this *transient* part of COMMAND.COM is loaded into the top end of memory, and since MS-DOS will allocate the whole of the memory to a program unless instructed otherwise, it is quite usual for this part of COMMAND.COM to be replaced. When this has happened, users of floppy disk machines will get a message:

```
Insert disk with COMMAND.COM into Drive A
```

so that the missing part of the file can be restored. Users of a hard disk that has been correctly set up with a path (see Chapter 2) to COMMAND.COM will never see this message, because the re-loading is automatic.

Of all the files that make up MS-DOS, COMMAND.COM is the most visible in the sense that it appears in the disk directory and is the subject of the message when floppy disks are being used. The other two files in RAM are *hidden* files, meaning that they do not appear in a conventional listing using the DIR command. This is done deliberately, along with making the files read-only and delete-protected, to prevent you from working on these files, perhaps deleting them accidentally with a command that would wipe all of the files from the disk.

The presence of these files, along with COMMAND.COM, makes the difference between a *system* floppy disk and a *data* floppy disk. For example, using MS-DOS 6.0, on a 1.4 Mb disk that has been formatted for data 1457664 bytes are free for use, but on a system disk you will find only 1325568 free. The difference of 132096 is due to the MS-DOS system files. The precise size of the various files changes in each new issue of MS-DOS, so that these figures are for Version 6.0 only; earlier versions used much less space for system files (typically 70 Kbyte or so). The size of the later files reflects the enhanced abilities of the later versions.

COMMAND.COM

The COMMAND.COM file is used along with the hidden files to implement MS-DOS, and it is important to ensure that you use the correct version of COMMAND.COM. As various versions of MS-DOS have appeared, COMMAND.COM has changed also, so that if you use, for example, a COMMAND.COM from MS-DOS V.3.3 along with the hidden files from MS-DOS V.3.2, then at some stage you will get an error message to the effect that COMMAND.COM is not present, or that the wrong version is present. Use of the wrong version is particularly easy if you use a hard-disk system with COMMAND.COM in the root directory. If you then carelessly copy to your hard disk a floppy disk which is a system disk, the COMMAND.COM file from that disk will replace the COMMAND.COM on the hard disk, and you will from then on use the new COMMAND.COM. No harm will come of this if the new COMMAND.COM is identical to the old value, but if it is not, then there will inevitably be problems. See Chapter 9 for notes on virus infection of COMMAND.COM.

Filenames

MS-DOS in use will require you to specify names for your files, and all MS-DOS versions follow, as far as floppy-disk users are concerned, the same requirements as CP/M. In addition, any programs that make use of the DOS (and practically all do, including Windows) will impose the same rules on filenames, so you need to be familiar with what is required. To start with, there are names that you cannot and must not use. You cannot use any of the names that appear on the Master Disk, because these are reserved for the programs that bear these names.

In addition, there are 'internal' commands, stored in the memory, whose names you must not use. These are:

BREAK	CD	CHCP	CHDIR	CLS
COPY	CTTY	DATE	DEL	DIR
ECHO	ERASE	EXIT	FILES	FOR
GOTO	IF	MKDIR	MD	PATH
PAUSE	PROMPT	RENAME	REM	RMDIR
RD	SET	SHIFT	TIME	TYPE
VER	VERIFY	VOL		

Any attempt to use these names other than for the actions that they represent will cause problems.

Various programs that you use will also have their own prohibitions, all designed to prevent you from damaging essential files on the disks. In general, a suitable filename will consist of up to eight characters, the first of which *must* be a letter. The other characters can be letters, or you can use the digits 0 to 9, or the symbols:

$ # & @ ! % ( ) - _ { } ' ~ ^`

The following characters *must not* be used:

* + = [ ] ; : , . / ?

nor can you use:

the space
the tab
the Ctrl character

Unless it's particularly important to you to use the permitted symbols, they are best avoided, particularly symbols like the single inverted quotes, which are easily confused or overlooked. A good rule is to use words with a digit or pair of digits used at the end to express versions, like TEXT001, TEXT002...TEXT015 and so on. Allowing up to eight characters means that you may have to abbreviate names that you would want to use, such as ACCREC1 or BOTLEDG1, but it should be possible to provide a name that conveys to you what the file is all about. Whether you use lower-case or upper-case characters, MS-DOS will convert all filename to upper-case.

Drive letter

The eight-character (or less) main name for a file is essential, but there are two other parts to a file name that are optional. One of these is the drive letter. The PC type of machine labels its main drives as A (the only *physical* drive in a single-drive machine), B (second drive in a twin-floppy machine, or an alternative drive letter on a single-floppy machine) and C. The C-drive on a machine that uses only floppy disk(s) can be a RAM-drive or a network drive. On a machine that uses a hard disk, the C-drive is normally the main hard disk, and the letter D will be used for a RAM-drive or for a second hard disk. Additional drive letters will appear on networked machines, and when MS-DOS 6.0 is being used, in conjunction with INTERLNK (see Chapter 11) and DBLSPACE (See Chapter 4).

RAM-drive simply means that part of the memory is set aside and used like a disk, so that disk commands will store data to this memory or read data from it. This is useful for storing files that programs often make use of, like the dictionary of a spelling-checker. MS-DOS contains methods of setting aside memory for a RAM-DRIVE, and a particularly useful provision is for extended memory to be used in this way. RAMDrive, however, is virtually obsolete because its actions can often be better carried out by using a read/write cache, see Chapter 4.

If you have only a single floppy drive and no hard disk, then you can ignore a lot of the information about drive letters, because only the A drive will physically be used; and possibly the letter C for RAM-drive or network drive. Nowadays, a machine with no hard drive is generally used only in a network with the server machine containing the hard drive for the whole set of machines.

There is an important distinction, however, between a *physical* drive, meaning one that is physically present, and a *logical* drive. MS-DOS will, on a single floppy machine, assign the logical drive letters A and B for the single floppy drive.

This allows you to call up programs such as:

B:callit

and get the message:

Insert the disk for Drive B: in the drive

so that you can make use of a single-drive system as if two drives were present.

For the user of twin floppies, specifying a filename such as B:PROG, means that you are stipulating that the file will make use of the disk in drive B. The drive letter precedes the main part of the filename, and is separated from it (very important) with a colon. If no drive letter is used, of course, the colon is not needed. The machine will then use the default drive, whatever drive was last in use, or the A: drive if you have just switched a floppy-drive machine on. This use of a drive letter applies whether you want to load the program from the disk or record (save) it on to the disk. Similarly, using C:PROG will specify the use of the C drive, usually the hard disk.

Using a drive letter in a filename in this way specifies the drive only for the duration of the command that is used with the filename. In other words, if you have specified that you want to run a program B:TESTIT, then the program is loaded from drive B, but whenever the program has been loaded, the normal drive will be the one that was in use previously. This normally means that the program loads from drive B, and from then on, any use of disks will make use of the A drive again. If no change is made (using the command B:, for example) then the normal default drive is the A drive on a floppy-only machine, or the C: drive on a machine equipped with a hard disk or network. MS-DOS has a set of commands that are particularly aimed at the hard disk user. These are dealt with later.

Extension

As well as the drive letter, which is always a single letter placed ahead of the file name and separated by a colon, the complete filename can contain an 'extension'. The extension is a set of up to three letters that are added to the end of the filename, separated by a dot. Any letters following three will be ignored when the file name is typed. Like the disk drive letter, the extension is optional, and if it is not used, then the dot is not needed.

■ This is why the use of the colon or the dot is prohibited within an 8-character main filename.

The purpose of the extension is to convey some extra information about the type of file, though you can make whatever use of it suits your own purposes, within limits. Just as there are forbidden filenames, there are also forbidden extensions, and in particular you should not make use of the extensions .EXE, .BAK, .HEX, .COM or .OBJ for your files, because these are extensions that are used with special meanings. The list following shows a few 'standard' extension letters and their uses, and you should, if you use extensions at all, either keep to some of these or use some entirely different codes of your own.

BAK	A back-up file.
BAS	A program that cannot be run unless BASIC has been loaded first.
BAT	A batch file of commands to the DOS.
COM	A program that can be loaded and run by typing its (main) name.
DOC	A text file of documentation for a program.
EXE	As for COM, but a longer program.
MSG	A text file of instructions.
SYS	A file that is used by the operating system.
TMP	A file that is created temporarily and wiped later.
$$$	Also a temporary file.

Particularly useful extensions for you to use are .TXT for files of text, as from a word processor, and .DAT for files of data as might be used in accounts programs. You will find that many programs that you will use will generate their own extensions for data that they save to disk, and you should not use these extensions for other files. It's particularly important to know at this point that any file with the extension of .BAK is a file that has been replaced with a more recent version with the same main filename. Some programs will not allow you to save a file with the same name as one that already exists on the disk. Others will automatically rename the existing file as a BAK file, and save your new file with a different extension. Many programs, however, will delete an old file that has the same name as one you are saving.

Wildcards in filenames

The term 'wildcard' sounds very fanciful when applied to computing, but it's a useful feature of most disk operating systems. The wild card is a character, usually ? which can be used as a substitute for a character or * for a group of characters. When you use the asterisk wild-card you are saying, in effect, that you don't care what that part of a name is.

For example, if you type

```
DIR *.COM
```

and press ENTER, you will get a listing of any files that have the extension letters of COM, whatever the main part of the filename happens to be. If you type:

```
DIR MA*.TXT
```

then (if the disk contains them) you will get names such as MAINONE.TXT, MANALIVE.TXT, MARTIN.TXT, MALLARD.TXT and so on. The ? wildcard is more selective, because it allows the substitution of one character only, so that using WORK?.TXT would allow files WORK0.TXT, WORK1.TXT, and so on up to WORK9.TXT to be used, but not WORK10.TXT or higher numbers.

The use of wildcards can be very convenient, allowing a lot of actions to be carried out with just one command. It can also be very inconvenient, causing you to delete a file accidentally just because you were deleting a group that happened to have similar names, for example. The asterisk is the wild card that is most often used, because it's so convenient to be able to substitute for any number of characters. Not all commands allow the use of wildcards, and in some cases the use of wildcards can have unexpected results, so that in the following Chapters, instructions that do not permit the use of a wildcard are noted. Such instructions can be 'converted' to wildcard use by a batch file that contains the FOR..IN..DO command, see Chapter 6.

2 Installation, Configuration and assorted actions

This book is aimed at users of 386 and 486 machines; if you are using a machine based on the older chips you may not feel that there is much point in upgrading, and the Newnes MS-DOS Pocket Book, dealing with versions up to 5.0 is probably more appropriate for your uses. An outstanding feature of V.6.0, carried over from V.5.0, is that it can be easily installed even on a hard disk which is already well-packed with files, and the installation no longer puts the existing files in danger though, as always, it is prudent to keep a complete backup of all files.

In connection with setting up MS-DOS 6.0, and in many other contexts, you will see the term *reboot* used. Booting is the action of switching on a machine so that MS-DOS is started running, and rebooting means restarting the machine. This can be done either:

- by pressing the Ctrl, Alt and Del keys together (using the Del key on the keypad at the right hand side, not the one in the set of six keys next to the ENTER key.
- by pressing a RESET button on the main casing of the computer if this button is fitted.
- by switching the computer off and, after an interval of about 30 seconds, on again.

The new features of MS-DOS 6.0 as compared to V5.0 have been noted in Chapter 1 and in this and the following Chapters the use of MS-DOS 6.0 will be dealt with fully, without reference to older versions.

Installing MS-DOS 6.0

Installation of MS-DOS 6.0 should start by making certain that valuable files on the hard disk are backed up by normal copies (NOT by using the BACKUP command of older versions of DOS). By valuable files I mean files of text, worksheets, graphics etc. that you have created and which are therefore irreplaceable, not program files which will still be available to you on their original disks. You should hold backups of all your own files in any case, but it is important to check for backups when you carry out any modification to an operating system. Make sure that you have backups of a tree diagram to remind you of the directory structure, and of the AUTOEXEC.BAT, CONFIG.SYS and any INI files.

- MicroSoft claims that some actions will survive even a power-cut without loss of data, but it is still prudent to maintain a full backup.

During the course of installation, the old system files will be placed on to a disk or disks in the A: drive that will be labelled as Uninstall disks. If the A: drive is high density (1.2 Mbyte or 1.44 Mbyte), one blank formatted disk will be needed; if the drive uses 360 Kbyte or 720 Kbyte floppies, two blank formatted disks will be used. You should make sure that you print out and read any README.TXT file, and any other TXT files on the MS-DOS 6.0 distribution disks, particularly if you use MS-DOS over a network. Make sure to note any points in these files that particularly affect you - this applies particularly if you are using a network, upper memory blocks on a 386/486 machine, some types of hardware, or software which is known to present problems. The README.TXT file is likely to change at frequent intervals, but on the early versions of MS-DOS 6.0 the software that was likely to cause problems was either not readily available in the UK or could be upgraded.

- It is important to realise that you cannot install MS-DOS 6.0 simply by copying files to your hard disk, because files are stored in compressed form, and the SETUP utility should normally be used to expand and place these files, though they can be manually expanded and copied if required. The compressed files are marked by using an extension that ends with an underscore, such as MSDOS.SY_ or UNINSTAL.EX_.
- Many actions in DOSSHELL are easier with a mouse, using a single click (press and release) to select and double-click (press and release twice in quick succession) to run or open a file. The left-hand mouse button is used exclusively. If your computer contains no mouse-port, you can fit a serial mouse (which can be remarkably inexpensive if you opt for the Genius mouse) or a Bus mouse which is packed along with an interface card.

Note that when a pause is used during installation to allow you to read a notice, the RETURN/ENTER key is used to continue installation, the F1 key to obtain help, and the F3 key to exit.

- Note that the following description is for a 386 machine which was equipped with Windows 3.1. A 286 or 386 machine without Windows would trigger some different messages, and there is a slight difference between monochrome and colour screen PCs.

The installation procedure is then as follows:

1. Insert the first MS-DOS distribution disk into Drive A:. Switch to this drive by typing A: (press ENTER), and then type SETUP (ENTER). The system will be checked, and you are reminded to have one or two UNINSTALL disk(s) ready. Remember that these must be placed into the A: drive when needed.

2. Wait until any message about diagnostic reports are completed.

3. Setup will check the complete computer system. If some old MS-DOS files are found on the root directory of the hard disk you will be asked to leave SETUP and remove these files. See the note at the end of this Section for removal of old DOS files.

4. You are then given the opportunity to continue with SETUP (press ENTER key), to learn more (press F1) or to abandon SETUP (F3).

5. You are reminded of the need to format and label a 3.5" 1.4 Mbyte or 5.25" 1.2 Mbyte disk as an UNINSTALL disk. If your A: drive uses a 360 Kbyte or 720 Kbyte drive, prepare two disks. The UNINSTALL set contains files that allow the old version of MS-DOS to be replaced if any difficulties arise. Press the ENTER key to continue with SETUP.

6. You are shown the existing operating system software and video hardware configuration which you can confirm or change as required.

7. You are shown the options of Backup, Undelete and Anti-Virus and asked which program options you want to install. By placing the cursor on any of these options you can obtain the further choices of Windows version, MS-DOS version, or both. You will probably want to install all three of these options in one version at least. Note that the disk space required for all three options in their Windows versions is 6,936,128 bytes, considerably more than was needed for MS-DOS 5.0. Note that the options that are presented depend on whether or not Windows is present in your computer. If your machine has Windows, only the Windows versions of the options are shown.

■ By using DBLSPACE (Chapter 4) you can obtain more hard disk space despite this extra requirement.

8. The WINDOWS directory will be shown if Windows is installed - you are asked to confirm (or change in the unlikely chance that the wrong directory is shown).

9. You are reminded that SETUP should not be interrupted from this point onwards, and are given a final chance to leave (F3) or to proceed (Y key).
10. From this point the process is automated. You will be asked to change disks at times. The first of these times occurs when you are asked to place the UNINSTALL (or UNINSTALL #1 if there are two) disk into the A: drive and press ENTER to notify this.
11. The progress of installation is marked by a display which shows a yellow bar (on a blue background) which lengthens to indicate the extent of installation. Several messages appear in the course of installation to remind you of facilities that will be available when MS-DOS 6.0 is installed. When UNINSTALL is complete, you are asked to return to the first SETUP disk and press ENTER.
12. The second disk of the 1.4 Mbyte set is requested after about 33% of installation has been completed. You will see a note about the use of MEMMAKER while this disk is being used. The other disks will be requested in turn.
13. When the last disk has been read, you are asked to remove all floppy disks and press the ENTER key. You are reminded that MS-DOS 6.0 is installed, and that old file versions have been saved on the UNINSTALL disk(s). Pressing the ENTER key again will restart the machine running MS-DOS 6.0 (it has been running the old DOS up to this point).
14. You should see the screen prompt now appearing as **C:\>**. Examine the CONFIG.SYS and AUTOEXEC.BAT files to see what alterations, if any, have been made. If you had to clear files from the root directory you can restore your original versions now.

- If you had to clear the C:\ root directory to allow SETUP to proceed, your original AUTOEXEC.BAT and CONFIG.SYS files will not be on the UNINSTALL disk but on the backup disk that you used to hold the files, see *Removal of Old Disk Files*, below. In any event, always check the CONFIG.SYS and AUTOEXEC.BAT file to make certain that they still include lines that you placed there in your previous version of MS-DOS.

14. The partitioning of your hard disk, if any, is unaltered by the installation of MS-DOS 6.0, so that if you were running, for example, a 42 Mbyte hard disk partitioned into 32 Mbyte drive C and 10 Mbyte drive D, this arrangement will remain unchanged. If you want to re-partition so that the entire disk is available as one drive, you will have to use the FDISK version in MS-DOS 6.0, remembering that this WILL ERASE ALL OF YOUR FILES, see Chapter 4.

- Disk partitioning in MS-DOS 6.0 is neither necessary nor desirable, particularly if you intend to use the DBLSPACE option, see Chapter 4
- The new MS-DOS files will carry a date in December 1992 or later.
- You should at this stage, if you previously used MS-DOS 5.0, copy the file called DOSSHELL.INI which should be among your DOS files. Copy this to a floppy disk so as to avoid having to re-install the Shell program if you should alter settings unintentionally.
- It is also important to make several SYSTEM floppy disks from which you can boot the computer if there is at any time a failure of the hard disk, and these copies should include the COMMAND.COM, CONFIG.SYS and AUTOEXEC.BAT files also. These will be particularly useful in conjunction with MIRROR and REBUILD, see later. These disks can be made by using the FORMAT /S command from the hard disk.

Removal of old DOS files

If SETUP requested you to remove old DOS files from the C:\ root drive, this is most easily done, if you currently use MS-DOS 5, by selecting the files using DOSSHELL, copying all root directory files to a floppy, and the deleting from the hard disk all root files except IO.SYS and MSDOS.SYS. Otherwise you need to proceed as follows:

1. Ensure that you are in the C:\root directory by typing

CD\ (press ENTER)

2. Type DIR (ENTER) to get a listing.

3. Place a formatted blank floppy into the A: drive. Type:

COPY C:*.* A:

to copy all the files on the hard disk root directory to the floppy. You should never have so many files on the root directory that they would need more than one 1.4 Mbyte floppy.

4. For each MS-DOS file that has been copied, type DEL followed by the filename and press the ENTER key to delete.

The filenames you are looking for are old versions of some COM and SYS files that are part of an older MS-DOS version. If you cannot recognise them, simply delete all files except IO.SYS and MSDOS.SYS.

When you run SETUP again, you may be asked to delete the MSF file, but this can be done by using an option presented to you in SETUP.

- When MS-DOS 6.0 is installed and running, it will use the CONFIG.SYS and AUTOEXEC.BAT files that were originally present, unmodified. If anything alters these files, you can restore your original AUTOEXEC.BAT and CONFIG.SYS files from your backup disk, along with any other SYS files which are not part of the MS-DOS system (such as SYS files for running scanners and other equipment)

The CONFIG.SYS file

The CONFIG.SYS file is a set of lines of commands written as text (not coded), and is used when the computer is started up. Figure 2.1 shows a typical CONFIG.SYS file from a 80386 machine. This use of CONFIG.SYS isautomatic when the system is started (booted), and the CONFIG.SYS file cannot be run on its own.

```
DEVICE=\MSDOS\SETVER.EXE
device=C:\WINDOWS\HIMEM.SYS
device=C:\WINDOWS\EMM386.EXE L=3000 ram
files=30
buffers=20
country=044,850,\country.sys
SHELL=\MSDOS\COMMAND.COM
C:\MSDOS\  /p DOS=HIGH,umb
STACKS=9,512
device=c:\hhscand.sys/a=280/i=3/d=1/h=4:8&:12:16/w=103/t
```

Figure 2.1
A typical CONFIG.SYS file. Your CONFIG.SYS will not necessarily be identical because the file controls the machine configuration, which will not be identical for any two machines.

A few commands can be used either in the CONFIG.SYS file or the AUTOEXEC.BAT file (see later, this Chapter), but most of the CONFIG.SYS commands can be used only within the CONFIG.SYS file. The most important feature of the CONFIG.SYS file is that it allows you to set up several important features of MS-DOS use, such as files and buffers, along with installing device drivers, files which allow specific devices to be used. This means that no two CONFIG.SYS files will be identical, because each PC user will have differing requirements.

A simple CONFIG.SYS file for a PC might consist of the lines:

```
files=20
buffers=5
country=044
```

and it's likely that you would want to use at least this number of lines, probably many more, and probably with different entries for a different machine, particularly when memory has to be organised on a 386 or 486 type of machine. The most complicated command form of CONFIG.SYS is DEVICE, so that the DEVICE command will be considered last in this list.

- NOTE that changes to a CONFIG.SYS file have no effect until the machine has been rebooted with the new version of the file.
- The use of the = sign is important. There must be no space on either side of the equals sign in any CONFIG.SYS line.

Working with the CONFIG.SYS file

The CONFIG.SYS file is a set of lines of commands written as text (ASCII code). The use of CONFIG.SYS by the computer is automatic, and the CONFIG.SYS file cannot be run on its own by typing CONFIG, for example. Most of the CONFIG.SYS commands can be used only within the CONFIG.SYS file, though a few exist in alternative versions that can be used on their own. The most important feature of the CONFIG.SYS file is that it allows you to set up several important features of MS-DOS use, such as installing keyboard and mouse driver programs and specifying how many files and buffers can be used with programs. Of all the items that occur in a CONFIG.SYS file, the DEVICE item is by far the most important, because its omission will make it impossible to use some types of devices. Remember that changes to a CONFIG.SYS file have no effect until the machine has been re-started with the new version of the file.

The form of a DEVICE line, of which more than one can be used in a CONFIG.SYS file, is:

DEVICE=filename

in which a full filename with path and extension can be used if needed. There must be no space either side of the equality sign. In general, the filenames that will be used have the extension SYS, and not all of the possible program files will be included on your MS-DOS distribution disk. You can buy additional SYS files for use in the DEVICE command, and there are several public domain device files available.

One of the most important filenames involved in a DEVICE line is DRIVER.SYS. This is the program file which allows floppy disk drives to be set up, and is particularly useful if you alter the pattern of disk drives on a machine by adding an external drive or by replacing one kind of internal drive by another (such as replacing a 5.25" PC/XT drive by a 3.5" drive). Old versions of DRIVER.SYS allowed hard drives to be set up also, but this provided all sorts of possibilities for error and the MS-DOS 6.0 version allows only for floppy disks.

The command allows you to select a number (the physical drive number) and a letter (the logical drive letter). The difference between these two is that the number has to correspond to an actual piece of hardware; but the letter can be assigned to a RAMdrive, or as another letter affecting an existing drive. You could, for example have letters A, B, F, and G referring to the same floppy drive if you wanted this.

During the startup procedure, before the CONFIG.SYS file is read, the standard set-up of drives A, B and C is carried out. On a single floppy drive, both A and B are assigned to Drive 0, the floppy drive. This is how you can use the single drive to copy disks with the message about changing to the disk for the B: drive appearing. The C letter is reserved for the hard disk, but can be assigned to RAMdisk on a floppy-only machine.

In a DRIVER.SYS line, you can specify variations by using the slash mark / followed by a letter:

/D:, the drive number, using 0 to 127 for floppy disks.

/T: the number of tracks per side, 1 to 999, default 80.

/S: the number of sectors per track, 1 to 99, default 9.

/H: the number of heads (maximum), 1 to 99, default 2.

/C - detection for drive door open.

/N - a fixed disk.

/F: type of device as:

/F:0 - floppy of 160 Kbyte to 360 Kbyte
/F:1 - floppy of 1.2 Mbyte
/F:2 - floppy of 720 Kbyte (default)
/F:7 - floppy of 1.4 Mbyte
/F:9 - floppy of 2.8 Mbyte

For example, the line:

```
DEVICE = DRIVER.SYS /D:2 /F:2
```

will allow the software to recognise an external floppy disk, drive 2, with 720 Kbyte capacity (this would be a 3.5" disk). The system will allocate a letter, probably E, for this drive which must, of course, be physically present.

Most computers will allow drive letters up to E to be used but will not allow any further additions. This can be overcome by using the LASTDRIVE command *ahead of the DEVICE line* in the CONFIG.SYS file. For example:

```
LASTDRIVE=H
```

will allow drive letters up to H to be used. MS-DOS 6.0 will assign drive letters beyond the limit set by LASTDRIVE when it uses INTERLNK or DBLSPACE.

The line:

```
DEVICE=MOUSE.SYS
```

can be used to install a mouse, and this is one of the CONFIG.SYS lines that can be carried out by an alternative method. To operate in this way, the MOUSE.SYS program must be present in the root directory (on in a searched path). The alternative, more commonly used, is to use MOUSE.COM and place the MOUSE command in the AUTOEXEC.BAT file, see later this Chapter. A common mistake is to use MOUSE.SYS in the CONFIG.SYS file but to have only MOUSE.COM on the disk, or to call MOUSE in the AUTOEXEC.BAT file but have only MOUSE.SYS available on the disk. The two are not interchangeable.

CONFIG.SYS lines are also available to set up a RAMdrive, a section of memory that can be used as if it were a disk, with the important difference that the data on a RAMdrive is lost whenever the machine is switched off. RAMdrive is useful for items such as the dictionaries of spelling checkers which are loaded into the RAMdrive from disk. Using RAMdrive in this way speeds up spell-checking because memory access is much more rapid than disk access. The snag is that in the ordinary PC machine, the 640 Kbyte RAM limit does not allow enough space to set up a RAMdisk of reasonable size and still run the sort of program that can make effective use of it. The remedy is to have expanded or extended memory (see Chapter 4) and to set the RAMdisk into this space.

Setting up a RAMdisk requires the use of VDISK.SYS or RAMDISK.SYS, depending on the version of MSDOS you are using. A typical line is

```
device=ramdrive.sys 360 128 64 /e
```

which sets up a 360 Kbyte RAMdisk using 128 byte 'sectors' and providing for up to 64 directory entries, with the extended memory (on an AT machine) used. If none of the parameters is supplied, a 64 Kbyte RAMdisk will be set up in the conventional memory, reducing space for programs and providing little useful RAMdisk room. In general, if you have memory space for a RAMdisk of reasonable size (1 Mbyte or more) you would be better advised to use SmartDrive - unless you already use SmartDrive in 2 Mbyte or RAM and still have extended memory left over for RAMdrive.

Other lines in the CONFIG.SYS file control aspects of use of programs and the operating system of the machine. Adding the line

```
BREAK=ON
```

will allow disk operations, which are not usually interruptible, to be broken off when the Break key is pressed. This has the disadvantage that it slows down the action of the computer because of the time that is spent in checking for this key being used, but it can be useful if you need to be able to break out of disk saving or loading operations.

A more common provision is a line such as

```
BUFFERS=15
```

which specifies the number of memory buffers (temporary resting places for data being loaded or saved) that MS-DOS can use. The default on versions of MS-DOS prior to 3.3 was only 2 buffers, but on V.3.3, the number of default buffers is made proportional to the amount of RAM installed. If you do not use any memory-cache type of program, it can be an advantage to use a large number of buffers. Up to 99 buffers can be specified in a BUFFERS=nn type of line. Each buffer requires 528 bytes of memory to set up, and for programs that do not use a lot of random-access filing, two buffers is often adequate. Program manuals will usually indicate if they require a special BUFFERS setting, so that you should set your CONFIG.SYS file to a BUFFERS number that will suit the most demanding program.

In DOS 3.0 onwards the COUNTRY command line in CONFIG.SYS used the form, shown here for the UK:

```
COUNTRY=044
```

in which the code number 044 is simply the international telephone dialling number for dialling into the UK. By specifying this number, the date, time and currency conventions for the UK can be used in MS-DOS and in programs that make use of MS-DOS. MS-DOS V3.3 and later used in addition a more complicated system of Code Pages (there are two code pages for each country) and a country information file. If nothing is specified, the defaults are Code Page 437 and file COUNTRY.SYS. The use of Code Pages is restricted to a few printers (such as the IBM 4201 and 5202) and the display systems (VGA, EGA and LCD) that support the system. When this latter system is used there has to be a copy of COUNTRY.SYS in the current directory. The DISPLAY.SYS command is also used on V3.3 onwards to allow code page switching on EGA and LCD screen types. Code pages are of little interest to the majority of users.

The other line that is often required in order to run some types of program is typically

```
FILES=20
```

which, in this example, allows 20 files to be manipulated at any one time. For each file that has been opened, MS-DOS allocates a 16-bit number, called the file handle. The default is 8, but some programs, particularly word-processors, require more files to be worked (because they set up several temporary files that you do not normally see in the disk directory), and if no additional file handles are available, the message:

```
No free file handles
```

will be delivered, causing restrictions on what can be done. By using a line such as FILES=20, the number of file handles can be increased, with very little expense in the amount of memory used, only 39 bytes for each file handle above the statutory 8.

- When a DEVICE line has to be added to your CONFIG.SYS file, it is now common for the software that requires this line to add it in the course of an INSTALL or SETUP program. This relieves you of the need to edit the CONFIG.SYS file you yourself, but you still need to check the file following the installation of a new program. In some cases, the addition of a new DEVICE line can cause problems with other DEVICE lines, and such conflicts are usually resolved by shifting the new DEVICE line to another position in the file. This has to be done with some care, because there are lines for installing devices such as HIMEM.SYS and EMM386.SYS which must be placed at the start of the CONFIG.SYS file, and some device lines must be placed as close as possible to the end.

Summary of CONFIG.SYS commands

The commands of the CONFIG.SYS file are summarised here.

BREAK

This is used along with ON or OFF in the form:

```
BREAK=ON
```

in the CONFIG.SYS file. The BREAK command can also be used as an internal command (it can be typed at the keyboard), and can be included in the AUTOEXEC.BAT file. The effect of BREAK=ON is to extend checks of the keyboard for the use of the Ctrl-Break keys, allowing disk operations to be broken off, but slowing the action of the computer. The BREAK command is internal, so that no system disk or MS-DOS files need be present to implement BREAK.

BUFFERS

By using a line such as

```
BUFFERS=5
```

the number of 512-byte memory buffers that MS-DOS can use is made equal to 5. The number of default buffers is made proportional to the amount of RAM installed. Some disk-caching programs (such as SpeedRead, supplied with the Western Digital filecards) create additional buffers, and allow you to use a small number of buffers, such as 5, in the CONFIG.SYS file. See page 37.)

COUNTRY

is used to read a file which sets up standards for showing time and date, currency, case conversions and the decimal point or comma use. COUNTRY can take two additional options of a code page number (there are two code pages for each country) and a country information file. If nothing is specified, the defaults are Code Page 437 and file COUNTRY.SYS. The use of Code Pages is restricted to a few IBM printers and the display systems (VGA, EGA and LCD) that support the system.

■ If you do not use these printers or screen types, you can ignore code pages entirely, and even if you use a VGA screen and an IBM printer it does not follow that you will ever need Code pages. See Chapter 11 for details.

Note that COUNTRY is an external program, so that if it appears in the CONFIG.SYS file, there has to be a copy of COUNTRY.SYS in the current directory. You cannot make use of a PATH command in the AUTOEXEC.BAT file, because CONFIG.SYS is run before AUTOEXEC.BAT is read.

Example:

COUNTRY = 044,850,C:\MSDOS\COUNTRY.SYS

- establishes the country code number as 044 (the UK), and the code page (for suitable printers and screens) as 850. The file path to COUNTRY.SYS is given, since no PATH command can be used at the time when this command runs. If no code page is specified, as is normal, the commas must still be used, as in:

COUNTRY = 044,,C:\MSDOS\COUNTRY.SYS

■ If you specify a page number which cannot be used (because it is not prepared, see Chapter 11) it will be ignored. The COUNTRY code number affects TIME and DATE configurations.

DEVICEHIGH

is used within the CONFIG.SYS file in order to put a device driver (such as a mouse or scanner driver) into the reserved memory of a 386 machine. It is not applicable to an 8088, 8086 or 80286 machine, and can be used on a 386 or 486 machine only if the EMM386 device driver has already been used in the CONFIG.SYS file, along with the DOS=UMB line. All of this will probably have been installed by the SETUP of MS-DOS 6.0 and MEMMAKER (see Chapter 4) if your computer is a 386 or 486 type, so that you are unlikely to need to use this command explicitly.

DOS

is used within the CONFIG.SYS file in the forms:

DOS=UMB
or DOS=NOUMB,
or DOS=HIGH
or DOS=LOW

in order to place the main part of MS-DOS 6.0 into different parts of memory. If your machine uses the 80286 processor, the DOS=HIGH line will have been put into CONFIG.SYS by SETUP to put DOS into the extended memory; on a 386 or 486 machine the DOS=UMB line can be used to put DOS into the Reserved Memory provided that a suitable driver for this memory region (such as EMM386.SYS has been used). The DOS=NOUMB or DOS=LOW can be used to prevent this use of memory beyond the 640 Kbyte limit.

DRIVEPARM

DRIVEPARM allows one drive to be configured so that it differs from the normal specification (for the other drive in a twin-drive machine, for example). The form of the command is:

DRIVEPARM=/D:2/F:2/T:80

-and this example is typical if you are converting a twin 5.25" machine to use one 3.5" drive in place of the B: drive. The option letters are shown below, using the same numbers for /D as DRIVER.SYS with n used to mean a single digit:

/T:nnn	Tracks per side, 1 to 999
/S:nn	Sectors per side, 1 to 99
/H:nn	Maximum head number, 1 to 99
/C	Doorlock support needed
/N	Non-removable block device

/F:n Form factor, 0 to 9 using:

0 = 5.25"
1 = 5.25" 1.2 Mbyte capacity
2 = 3.5" 720 Kbyte
5 = Hard disk
6 = Tape drive
7 = 3.5" 1.4 Mbyte disk
8 = Read/write optical disk
9 = 3.5" 2.8 Mbyte disk

Note: numbers 3 and 4 were originally used for 8" disk drives. Note the wider range of devices than is provided for DRIVER.SYS.

FCBS

is important only if you are using programs that were written for a very old version of MS-DOS. The form of this obsolete command, which can be used only in the CONFIG.SYS file, is:

```
FCBS=12
```

meaning that up to 12 files can be manipulated at once. Modern versions of MS-DOS use FILES in place of FCBS.

FILES

The line FILES=20 allows 20 files to be manipulated at any one time. For each file that has been opened, MS-DOS allocates a 16-bit number, called the file handle. The default is 8, but some programs, particularly word-processors, require more files to be worked, and if no additional file handles are available, the message:

```
No free file handles
```

will be delivered, causing restrictions on what can be done. By using a line such as FILES=20, the number of file handles can be increased, with very little expense in the amount of memory used, only 39 bytes for each file handle above the statutory 8.

HIMEM.SYS

is the extended memory manager of MS-DOS 6.0 (and of earlier versions). For details of this driver which is essential for the use of extended memory, see Chapter 3.

INSTALL

is used in the CONFIG.SYS file for a few specialised applications, to load some programs which otherwise would be loaded by AUTOEXEC.BAT. The advantage of using CONFIG.SYS is that in a 386 or 486 machine, the loading can be into reserved memory. INSTALL is used for FASTOPEN, KEYB, NLSFUNC or SHARE, but for no other commands, in the form:

```
INSTALL=FASTOPEN.EXE
```

in which the command can take whatever parameters are needed following the command name.

LASTDRIVE

is used to declare the letter that will be used for the last logical drive. This is normally E, but if you want to use the SUBST command (despite all of the warnings) then you can allocate more letters for drives, up to Z, with a command such as:

LASTDRIVE=K

LASTDRIVE can also be very useful if you want to partition a hard disk in several sections (see FDISK, Section 5), or make use of expanded memory to set up a RAMdisk or more than one RAMdisk.

NUMLOCK

is used to determine whether the NumLock key on the keyboard will be on or off when the computer is switched on. The default is to have this key on. The command is used in the forms:

NUMLOCK=ON or NUMLOCK=OFF

This command was not available in earlier versions of MS-DOS, and it is part of a set that includes MENUCOLOR, MENUITEM, MENUDEFAULT, SUBMENU, and INCLUDE, all noted later in this Chapter.

RAMDRIVE.SYS

-a RAMdisk device drive is used to organise a section of memory, usually extended memory, so that it can be used as if it were a disk drive. Such a 'drive' does not retain data when the machine is switched off, but allows very fast access both for reading and writing. This is useful for such applications as the speller dictionary of a word-processor. More than one RAMdrive can be set up by using more than one line in CONFIG.SYS. For details, see Chapter 3.

■ The use of RAMDRIVE is made unnecessary when SmartDrive is in use.

REM

can be used on the CONFIG.SYS file to mark a comment or to ensure that a command line is not obeyed (remmed out). Note that this use of REM was not available in CONFIG.SYS before MS-DOS 5.0. The semicolon ; can also be used for this purpose.

SET see later.

SHELL

is very unlikely to be needed unless you have very specialised interests. It allows the COMMAND.COM program to be by-passed in favour of another form of command processor, and the form of the command is:

SHELL=MYCOM.COM

assuming that a program called MYCOM.COM is available for use in this way. A SHELL line will be installed for you with MSDOS 6.0

STACKS

determines the number and size of pieces of memory, the stacks, which are used for temporary storage. Machines which use MS-DOS only do not generally need this, or can use the line:

STACKS=0,0

but machines running Windows will generally require the line:

STACKS=9,512

SWITCHES

is used in the form

SWITCHES=/k

in CONFIG.SYS to allow the use of 101/102 key keyboards along with older application programs which assume the use of the older type of keyboard. This form of the command is obsolescent, since all modern machines use the 101/102 key keyboard. The other options are:

- **/W** to specify the position of the WINA20.386 file for Windows 3.0. This is needed only if you use Windows 3.0 and have moved the WINA20.386 file - both unlikely.
- **/N** Prevents the F5, F8 or SHIFT keys from affecting the running of the CONFIG.SYS file.
- **/F** Removes the 2-second delay in which the message Starting MSDOS is displayed.

The marks **@ ?** and **;** also have special significance in a CONFIG.SYS file. The semicolon ; has the same effect as REM, to ensure that whatever follows the mark (up to the point where the ENTER key was pressed) is ignored. The @ mark prevents the words of a CONFIG.SYS line that starts with this mark from appearing on the screen. To prevent any CONFIG.SYS lines from appearing, use ECHO OFF at the start of the CONFIG.SYS file. The ? mark is used to ensure that a CONFIG.SYS action has to be confirmed from the keyboard before it is executed. For example:

```
FILES?=20
```

will cause the CONFIG.SYS file to pause so that you can answer Y or N to this step being carried out.

- If you press the F5 key (or the SHIFT key) just after switch-on when the Starting MSDOS... message appears on the screen, the CONFIG.SYS and AUTOEXEC.BAT files will be ignored. If you press the F8 key at that time, each line in the CONFIG.SYS file will be queried for confirmation, and you will be asked whether you want to run the AUTOEXEC.BAT file or not (you cannot opt to confirm each line in the AUTOEXEC.BAT file).
- Use the line SWITCHES /F to prevent the 2-second delay for the Starting MSDOS message. Use SWITCHES /N to prevent the use of the SHIFT, F5 or F8 keys as described above. You can combine these into SWITCHES /F /N

Menu-driven CONFIG.SYS

This section is rather more advanced than the preceding information on CONFIG.SYS, and you should make use of it only if your requirements call for using one machine with a variety of different set-ups. This is not particularly common, but in the past it would have required you to start the machine, edit the CONFIG.SYS file, and then re-start the machine. The menu system introduced with MS-DOS 6.0 allows you to prepare a CONFIG.SYS file that caters for more than one possible setup (multiple configurations).

This is done by starting the CONFIG.SYS file with a menu block which contains words that refer to the options. This block is headed by the word [menu] and ended with a blank line. For example:

```
[menu]
menuitem=windows
menuitem=dos
```

when run, would result in the display:

```
MS-DOS 6 Startup Menu
=====================
   1. windows
   2. dos
Enter a choice: 1
```

- allowing you to enter a number and press ENTER to allow the choice to be made. The menuitem command is used to name the alternatives, and you can follow the name with a description, using a comma to separate the sections, as, for example,

```
menuitem=windows,Windows configuration
menuitem=dos,MS-DOS configuration
```

- the description will assist you in making the choice. The next part of the exercise is to write alternative CONFIG.SYS files to deal with each choice. Each file has to start with the name that has been assigned above, so that the CONFIG.SYS file for windows will start:

```
[windows]
stacks=9,512
files=20
buffers=30
```

and so on. The dos section will start possibly as:

```
[dos] stacks=0,0
files=15
buffers=20
```

and so on.

In some cases, only a few items need be different. In this case, these menu lines can be placed at the start of the CONFIG.SYS file, and the remainder of the file that needs to be executed for either choice is placed following the marker [common]. For example, using:

```
[windows]
stacks=9,512
[dos]
stacks=0,0
[common]
files=20
buffers=30
........
```

allows all the lines following the [common] mark to be carried out irrespective of which choice is made earlier.

■ Even if you do not have any common lines at present, you should place the [common] mark at the end of the CONFIG.SYS file. This will allow and alterations to the file that may be made by a SETUP or INSTALL program to be placed into the common section. You can place a [common] set of lines anywhere in the CONFIG.SYS file, before or after menu choices, as long as each section is marked out with the [common] start line and a blank line to mark the end.

You can specify colours and a default choice by using commands that are in standard CONFIG.SYS form. For example,

```
menucolor=14,1
```

specifies that the menu should use bright yellow text (colour 14) on a blue background (colour 1). These colour numbers are:

0 Black	8 Grey
1 Blue	9 Bright blue
2 Green	10 Bright green
3 Cyan	11 Bright cyan
4 Red	12 Bright red
5 Magenta	13 Bright magenta
6 Brown	14 Yellow
7 White	15 Bright white

Note the order of menucolor. If the background colour number is omitted, black will be used.

The menudefault line is used to specify a default block of commands (other than common) and a time after which this set will be carried out. This prevents the machine from hanging if there is no reply to the menu. For example, using:

```
menudefault=dos,30
```

will run the [dos] lines of the earlier example after a delay of 30 seconds.

The include command is also in normal CONFIG.SYS format, and is used when a menu might contain an option that includes more than one set of other options. For example, if your menu contains the items:

```
[text]
[graphics]
[both]
```

you can use the lines:

```
[both]
include=graphics
include=text
```

to ensure that the [both] item would run both sets of lines without the need to re-type them all.

The submenu command allows you to use a menu item that leads to another menu. You might, for example, want to use a selection of graphics programs, one of which needed extended memory and the other needed expanded memory,or you might want to select [Network] on the first menu and get the option of one or the other of two networks. By using in your main menu a line that starts with submenu you can specify the name of the submenu that will carry out the actions.

For example, using:

```
[menu]
menuitem text
submenu graphixmenu
[grafixmenu]
menuitem pixit
menuitem drawit
```

you can force the choice of graphixmenu to lead you to another choice of two items - only the menu choice lines have been shown here.

These menu lines allow you to set up your computer according to what is required - one very common example is use on a network or independently. Note that the choices that are made in the CONFIG.SYS menu can be carried over into the AUTOEXEC.BAT file, see later, this Chapter and Chapter 6.

The AUTOEXEC.BAT file

The AUTOEXEC.BAT file is unique in being the only batch file (see Chapter 6 for details of batch files and AUTOEXEC.BAT) which is run automatically. This is done when the computer has loaded up the MS-DOS operating system and run CONFIG.SYS. The AUTOEXEC.BAT file will also contain commands that configure the whole computer system to the way you want it.

- Note that some configuration actions are carried out prior to running AUTOEXEC.BAT by the CONFIG.SYS file. Unlike AUTOEXEC.BAT, CONFIG.SYS can be used only by re-starting the computer or switching on.
- You can run AUTOEXEC.BAT at any time while the computer is running simply by typing AUTOEXEC (press ENTER).

No two AUTOEXEC.BAT files will be identical, because both computers and computer-users have different requirements. What follows is a list of some typical lines that are likely to be found in the AUTOEXEC.BAT files of machines running MS-DOS 6.0. You are likely to alter your AUTOEXEC.BAT file many times in the lifetime of the computer because the AUTOEXEC.BAT file reflects the way in which you use programs on the machine.

The most important line is likely to be a PATH line, determining where the machine will search for batch and program files after trying the current directory and the root directory of the hard disk. The form of the commands is PATH followed by a file path and using a semicolon to separate this from the next filepath. For example:

```
PATH C:\;C:\MSDOS;C:\BATS
```

ensures that the C:\root directory is searched first, then the C:\MSDOS directory and then the C:\BATS directory. You can extend this as much as you need, but remember that having a very long PATH line can slow down the action of the computer each time you type a program name without any specific path.

Keep the PATH statement for essential searches. Some programs add to the PATH statement in order to make it easier to start from any directory. It is better to write a batch file to start such programs, specifying the directory, than to allow the PATH line to become bloated in this way.

Another line that needs to be used in most AUTOEXEC.BAT files is:

```
KEYB uk,850,c:\msdos\keyboard.sys
```

which loads in a memory-resident program, KEYB, that configures the machine to use the UK keyboard (with its £ sign). Some computers make use of the US keyboard and do not need this line - if the line is used with a US keyboard you will find that some keys produce the wrong symbols.

This line assumes that the C:\MSDOS directory contains all of the necessary files, and since MS-DOS 6.0 creates this directory and fills it, the assumption is reasonable unless you are using an earlier version of MS-DOS. The KEYB command is a standard DOS command, and the UK portion specifies that the UK keyboard is to be used. The number 850 is a 'code page' number and, unless you are using equipment of IBM manufacture, the number is not of much significance. The last portion provides the name of the file, KEYBOARD.SYS and its path, and is essential unless KEYBOARD.SYS is placed in the root directory of the hard disk.

If this command is wrongly used you will get an error message 'Bad or missing keyboard file' while the machine is loading up. If you do not see the message, incorrect action is indicated by inability to make the Shift-3 key of a UK keyboard produce the £ sign.

MS-DOS 6.0 has a set of commands that were introduced with MS-DOS 5.0 which give much more control over the machine, and in particular, the DIR command is much improved. The older version of DOS would produce a directory listing which filled only half of the screen and which showed files in order of entry only. MS-DOS 6.0 allows the action of DIR to be modified by using an 'environment variable' called DIRCMD, a batch file parameter, whose values are allocated by using the SET command.

For details of DIRCMD and the other batch file commands that can be used within AUTOEXEC.BAT, see Chapter 6.

LOADHIGH, which can be abbreviated to LH, used before a command in AUTOEXEC.BAT allows a memory-resident program to be loaded into the reserved memory of a 386 or 486 machine - it has no application in 8088, 8086 or 80286 machines. The EMM386 driver must have been started in the CONFIG.SYS file, and DOS=UMB must have been used also to prepare the reserved memory (the upper part of the first 1 Mbyte of memory). If there is no space available in this memory region the program will be loaded into conventional memory.

A Device driver illustrated - ANSI.SYS

Using the line:

```
DEVICE=ANSI.SYS
```

in the CONFIG.SYS file will load in the ANSI screen handler. This does not mean any change to many of the programs that make use of DOS, because software such as word-processors, spreadsheets and databases use their own screen-control routines, but for use of DOS itself and for programs, such as some versions of BASIC, the facilities of ANSI.SYS can be very convenient.

Though ANSI.SYS is described as a screen handler, it also allows a considerable amount of manipulation of the keyboard, so that while using DOS you can assign keys (particularly the function keys) to various uses.

- ANSI.SYS is of limited applicability to modern computer users, but is of interest to anyone writing programs or modifying programs.

When the ANSI.SYS line has been used in the CONFIG.SYS file, the pattern of screen and keyboard can be changed by typing commands, all of which start with the ESC key. This means, for most users, that these commands cannot be entered directly, because MS-DOS uses the ESC key to terminate a command and move to the next line. Direct commands to ANSI therefore have to be made by way of the PROMPT command, which can make use of **$e** to mean the ESC code.
Example:

```
PROMPT $e[2J
```

- clears the screen, and leaves no prompt remaining. If you need to have the prompt restored, the necessary characters must be added in another prompt line.
Example:

```
PROMPT $e[2J
PROMPT $p $t
```

- clears the screen and gives a prompt that consists of directory and time. NOTE that if you use

```
PROMPT $e[2J $p $t
```

you will clear the screen and get a prompt, but each time you press ENTER the screen will be cleared, since the use of PROMPT makes screen-clearing part of the prompt that appears each time ENTER is pressed.

If ANSI commands have to be set up as a matter of routine, they can be read from a file. Such a file must, however, be written by an editor which will put the ESC character into place, and not all editors will do this because many interpret the ESC key to mean 'end of editing'. A few editors will allow codes, rather like the **$e** code of PROMPT, to place an ESC character (ASCII 27) into a file. You can, however, write a batch file in which the ANSI commands are placed in prompt form, using **$e** to mean the ESC character. The EDIT editor which is supplied with MS-DOS 6.0 will not place ESC characters into a file.

The ANSI command codes are listed below, with the ESC character shown as Esc. You will need to remember, then, that each sequence shown will start with **$e** if you are using a PROMPT line to put in the code. In the following list, **j** and **k** are used to mean numbers of up to 2 digits. Note that the case of letters is important, so that you cannot substitute **d** for **D**, for example.

Esc[j**A**	move cursor up j rows, unless already at top.
Esc[j**B**	move cursor down j rows, unless already at bottom.
Esc[j**C**	move cursor right j columns, unless at RHS.
Esc[j**D**	move cursor left j columns, unless already at LHS.
Esc[j;k**f**	move cursor to row j column k.
Esc[j;k**H**	move cursor to row j column k.
Esc[=j**h**	set screen width and parameters.
Esc[2J	clear screen, cursor to top left corner.
Esc[K	erase to end of line
Esc[=j**l**	reset screen width and parameters (note: letter ell)
Esc[j;m	set graphics.
Esc[6n	print cursor position.
Esc[j;k**p**	redefine key
Esc[j;k**R**	cursor to row j column k and print this position.
Esc[s	save cursor position.
Esc[u	restore cursor position.

Screen width and parameters for Esc[=jh command.

Value of j	Effect
0	40 column x 25 rows monochrome
1	40 x 25 colour
2	80 x 25 monochrome
3	80 x 25 colour
4	320 dots x 200 lines per screen, colour
5	320 x 200 monochrome
6	640 x 200 monochrome
7	wrap at end of each line

Graphics parameter numbers

Number	Effect
0	all graphics controls off
1	bold on
2	faint on
3	italic on
4	underscore on (not on colour type of display)
5	slow blink on
6	rapid blink on
7	inverse video on (foreground/background reversed)
8	concealed on (not displayed)
30	black foreground
31	red foreground
32	green foreground
33	yellow foreground
34	blue foreground
35	magenta foreground
36	cyan foreground
37	white foreground
40	black background
41	red background
42	green background
43	yellow background
44	blue background
45	magenta background
46	cyan background
47	white background
48	subscript
49	superscript

Note: some implementations of ANSI may not accept all of the codes shown in this table.

Example: The file shown below is a batch file that will clear the screen, and write a headline in bold flashing text, then return to normal.

```
prompt $e[2J
prompt $e[1;5m
prompt ECHO THIS IS THE HEADLINE
prompt $e[0m
prompt
```

The snag here is that it uses ECHO for placing text on the screen, and you cannot use ECHO OFF at the start of the file, otherwise the prompt commands have no effect. It is much better, if you need to place text on a screen, to use a word-processor or text-editor which can put in the ESC sequences, as described earlier, and use batch files only for making changes which are then used to affect TYPE commands, for example. However, another way round the problem is simply to use a PROMPT line to display the text, as long as this is cancelled when you need to have a prompt symbol used.

Keyboard reassignment is made using the Esc[**..p** command, and this requires both keycodes and a set of characters to be supplied. The keycode must be a number or pair of numbers, and the characters can be placed in the command as ASCII codes or in string form, such as "WORDSTAR". The function keys are referred to by using a two-number code with a zero as the first number, and numbers 59 - 68 as the second number.

Example:

Esc[109;77;83;45;68;79;83p

will redefine the **m** key (ASCII 109) to produce **MS-DOS**. You then have to avoid typing "prompt" and use "PROMPT" (or "proMpt") instead!

Example:

Esc[0;59;"This is F1";13p

will redefine the F1 key to give **This is F1** followed by a carriage return.

Example:

Esc[0,84;"This is SHIFT F1";13p

will redefine SHIFT-F1 to give the phrase **This is SHIFT F1**.

Function key codes

These are the numbers following 0; in the ANSI codes.

Key	Alone	Shift	Ctrl	Alt
F1	59	84	94	104
F2	60	85	95	105
F3	61	86	96	106
F4	62	87	97	107
F5	63	88	98	108
F6	64	89	99	109
F7	65	90	100	110
F8	66	91	101	111
F9	67	92	102	112
F10	68	93	103	113

Note that there are some later versions of ANSI.SYS in the public domain, such as NANSI.SYS.

ANSI.SYS allows the option /X which allows you to assign different uses to keys that are duplicated in 101/102 key keyboards, such as Home, End, PgUp, PgDn etc. The /L option forces the system to retain the setting of number of screen lines after leaving a program that may have changed this number.

DISPLAY.SYS and Code Pages See Chapter 11.

Redirection, pipes and Filters See Chapter 7.

Use in AUTOEXEC.BAT See Chapter 6.

3 Memory Management

PC memory

As noted earlier, the original PC machines could use a total of 1 Mbyte of memory, of which 640 Kbyte could be RAM used for programs, with the remainder used for ROM. In order to preserve compatibility of programs, later machines have had to accept the limitation of 640 Kbyte for program use despite the fact that the chips now being used provide for much more memory to be installed. The limitation was due to MS-DOS rather than to the design of the machines, and is carried over into MS-DOS 6.0.

The use of Windows as a Shell for MS-DOS (meaning a form of command controller for DOS) allows the extended memory of the 80386 and 80486 machines to be used, but since there is no provision built into MS-DOS for controlling memory an additional memory manager such as HIMEM.SYS must be installed. The use of memory managers is dealt with later in this Chapter, along with the MEMMAKER utility which allows the complex task of controlling the setting up of a memory manager to be automated.

Memory reports

Whether you have added extended memory to a 386/486 machine or are about to, a report on the current state of memory is useful and revealing, and there are several utilities which provide such reports. Of these, the most common, because it is supplied along with MS-DOS 6.0, is MEM. There is also a much more advanced diagnostic program, MSD, which is noted at the end of this Chapter.

Using MS-DOS MEM in its simplest form gives the information typically illustrated in Figure 3.1 for a 386 machine from Micro Surgeons Ltd. The report was taken after MS-DOS 6.0 was installed, but using the setup that had earlier been arranged (before the use of MEMMAKER, see later).

This is a report on the main (system) memory, showing that the conventional memory is 655360 bytes (640 Kbyte), of which some 586 Kbyte is available for programs, despite the use of some memory-resident programs (such as the PINCH program which was used to capture the screen display).

Figure 3.1
A typical MEM report from a 386 machine which has a total of 5 Mbyte installed.

```
Memory Type          Total =  Used  +  Free
----------------    ------   ------   ------
Conventional          640K      54K     586K
Upper                  28K       7K      22K
Adapter RAM/ROM       356K     356K       0K
Extended (XMS)       4096K     496K    3600K
----------------    ------   ------   ------
Total memory         5120K     912K    4208K

Total under 1 MB      668K      60K     608K

EMS is active.
Largest executable program size        586K  (600368 byt
Largest free upper memory block         22K   (22208 byt
MS-DOS is resident in the high memory area.

C:\>
```

In this example, there is a large amount of conventional memory available because much of MS-DOS 6.0 has been relocated to the first 64 Kbyte of extended memory, the region called "Upper" in this report.

The machine is fitted with a total of 5 Mbyte of RAM memory, and the report from MEM shows 4096 Kbyte (4 Mbyte) of extended memory of which only 496 Kbyte is reported as being in use. More will be used when the SMARTDRV memory cache is installed, see later. The figure shown as Total under 1 Mbyte consists of the normal 640 Kbyte of conventional memory plus the 28 Kbyte of upper memory. These are lumped together despite the 28 Kbyte being actually part of the extended memory because programs can be run in this small part of extended memory because of a quirk in the design of the first 80286 chips that has been continued into the later chips.

The report shows that "EMS is Active", meaning that expanded memory can be simulated if needed because the necessary memory manager is running.

Using MEM with switch commands

MEM can be used with several options (switches) that can be added following a slash sign. Each option can be used by specifying a letter, and the options /c, /d, /f and /m are exclusive - you can use only one of this set at a time. Any of the set, however, can be used along with the /p option which allows the output of MEM to be paged into one screen at a time.

By typing MEM /C /P as a command, information is made available on the amount of memory being used by programs. This is a much more extensive list, Figure 3.2, showing in detail how parts of the memory are used at the time when this analysis was carried out. The full command /CLASSIFY can also be used.

Figure 3.2
A MEM report on how memory is used by programs, showing the Upper memory still under-utilised.

ales using memory below 1 MB:

ame	Total		=	Conventional		+	Upper Memory	
SDOS	17773	(17K)		17773	(17K)		0	(0K)
ETVER	672	(1K)		672	(1K)		0	(0K)
IMEM	1088	(1K)		1088	(1K)		0	(0K)
MM386	3248	(3K)		3248	(3K)		0	(0K)
HSCAND	2480	(2K)		2480	(2K)		0	(0K)
OMMAND	2912	(3K)		2912	(3K)		0	(0K)
INCH	5520	(5K)		5520	(5K)		0	(0K)
OSKEY	4144	(4K)		4144	(4K)		0	(0K)
OUSE	17088	(17K)		17088	(17K)		0	(0K)
EYB	6224	(6K)		0	(0K)		6224	(6K)
EYCLICK	528	(1K)		0	(0K)		528	(1K)
ree	622848	(608K)		600480	(586K)		22368	(22K)

ory Summary:

ype of Memory	Total		=	Used		+	Free	
onventional	655360	(640K)		54880	(54K)		600480	(586K)
pper	29120	(28K)		6752	(7K)		22368	(22K)

ss any key to continue . . .

■ In this example, the only programs that exist in the memory, apart from MS-DOS itself, are the utilities loaded by AUTOEXEC.BAT. These are memory-resident and will remain in place until the machine is switched off (see later for details of how to remove memory-resident programs).

The listing shows MS-DOS taking up 17 Kbyte of conventional memory. This is not the full size of MS-DOS 6.0, only the portion that remains in conventional memory, and MEM does not show the part of MS-DOS 6.0 which is loaded into Upper memory. Upper memory consists of 64 Kbyte, and of this some 7 Kbyte is used and 22 Kbyte free, so that MS-DOS must be using the remainder. The message (not shown in this view) at the end of the report shows that MS-DOS is running in the Upper memory. It would be advantageous to relocate more programs to the upper memory.

Using MEM /D produces a similar display, but with more details of the use of memory blocks, Figure 3.3. This option is not intended for the average PC user, more for the programmer who needs to know about memory use.

```
Conventional Memory Detail:

Segment              Total            Name          Type
-------        ---------------     -----------     --------
00000              1039    (1K)                     Interrupt Vector
00040               271    (0K)                     ROM Communication A
00050               527    (1K)                     DOS Communication A
00070              2656    (3K)    IO               System Data
                                      CON           System Device Drive
                                      AUX           System Device Drive
                                      PRN           System Device Drive
                                      CLOCK$        System Device Drive
                                      A: - C:       System Device Drive
                                      COM1          System Device Drive
                                      LPT1          System Device Drive
                                      LPT2          System Device Drive
                                      LPT3          System Device Drive
                                      COM2          System Device Drive
                                      COM3          System Device Drive
                                      COM4          System Device Drive
00116              5072    (5K)    MSDOS            System Data
00253             15600   (15K)    IO               System Data
                    656    (1K)       SETVERXX      Installed Device=SE
Press any key to continue . . .
```

Figure 3.3

The memory block report from MEM/D

This also applies to MEM /M - which has to be followed by a program name before you press the ENTER key. This option will report on how a program is stored in the memory.

Memory managers

The use of one or more memory manager programs is essential if there is to be any use of memory above the 640 Kbyte barrier. The memory managers that you will need for 386 (and above) machines are supplied along with MS-DOS, and there are different memory managers supplied with expanded memory boards for XT machines which are not covered in this book.

A 386/486 machine is very likely to be used with Windows, so that the comments on Windows memory management with MEMMAKER should be read. The following deals with memory management for purposes other than Windows, using the HIMEM.SYS and EMM386.SYS of MS-DOS 5.0 or 6.0, since these are the memory managers that virtually every owner of a 386 machine is likely to have by now.

- If you use the MEMMAKER program to set up memory management, it will sense whether or not Windows is present, and set up accordingly, so that comments in this Chapter on differences between Windows and no-Windows setup apply only if you are setting up for yourself. Unless you have special requirements and specialised knowledge, it is always better to allow MEMMAKER to do the work for you.

MS-DOS 6.0 is provided with two memory managers. HIMEM.SYS is an extended memory manager which allows access to extended memory for DOS and for programs that use the XMS standard (at present, Windows and a very few others).

- Remember, however, that the heading of Windows includes any program that is designed to make use of Windows, and all of the leading software is either now available in this form or is being converted.

HIMEM.SYS also manages extended memory so as to avoid conflicts between programs, preventing programs from trying to make use of the same part of memory. HIMEM.SYS must be used **before** there is any attempt to make use of extended memory on any 80286, 80386 or 80486 machine.

This means that the first, or a very early, line of your CONFIG.SYS file should be:

```
DEVICE=C:\MSDOS\HIMEM.SYS
```

assuming that the HIMEM.SYS file exists in the C:\MSDOS directory of the hard disk.

- A lot of trouble can be saved simply by ensuring that this is the first line of the CONFIG.SYS file, and checking that it is still the first line after new programs have been installed, because SETUP programs often alter your CONFIG.SYS file.
- There are still some programs about that modify CONFIG.SYS without notifying you and though it is unlikely that they would delete your own CONFIG.SYS they might substitute another with the HIMEM.SYS omitted, or with your own CONFIG.SYS instructions tacked on at the end. It is always advisable to keep several backups of your CONFIG.SYS file on write-protected disks.

The following CONFIG.SYS file shows HIMEM.SYS placed further down the list, but still in an acceptable position:

```
DEVICE=C:\MSDOS\SETVER.EXE
country=044
files= 30
buffers = 30
drivparm=/d:1 /f:2
DEVICE=C:\MSDOS\HIMEM.SYS
SHELL=C:\MSDOS\COMMAND.COM C:\MSDOS\ /p
DOS=HIGH
```

- and in this case it is permissible because there is no command earlier than the HIMEM.SYS line that makes use of extended memory.

- The CONFIG.SYS file, like the AUTOEXEC.BAT file is one that varies from computer to computer, and you should not assume that commands shown in an example like this must necessarily appear on your own CONFIG.SYS file.
- If HIMEM.SYS is not placed first in the file it must certainly be placed ahead of any command that would make use of extended memory, such as, in this example, DOS=HIGH. The SMARTDRV.EXE disk cache program is normally run from the AUTOEXEC.BAT file.
- HIMEM.SYS cannot be used along with version 2 of Windows, but this is in any case unlikely now that Windows-3 is fully established.
- HIMEM.SYS takes up a small amount of conventional memory which must be balanced against the ability to release such memory by making use of extended memory.
- If you have used DOS=HIGH and get a message on booting up to the effect that DOS has been loaded in low memory, check to see if you have included HIMEM.SYS in the CONFIG.SYS file. If HIMEM.SYS is not present, DOS cannot be loaded into high (extended) memory. DOS will also load into low memory if there is any conflict caused by the first 64 Kbyte of extended memory being used for any other purposes.

HIMEM.SYS complications

The straightforward and simple HIMEM.SYS line illustrated above is as much as most users ever need. If problems arise that do not seem to arise from conflicts of memory-resident software (see later) it may be necessary to make use of some of the optional additions to the HIMEM command. Do not be discouraged by the long list of additions to the command, because these are designed for special circumstances such as:

1. Fine-tuning for faster use
2. Problems with older software
3. Problems with some hardware.

- and the use of MEMMAKER will create these additions for you, resolving more than 99% of the difficulties that are encountered.

■ The additions that follow can therefore be ignored unless complications arise, but before using any of these additions, check that HIMEM is correctly installed at or near the start of the CONFIG.SYS file, with the HIMEM.SYS program in the correct directory, and that problems are not caused by conflicts with other memory-resident programs. You might also find these notes useful for understanding the changes that MEMMAKER carries out.

■ Each addition or option to DEVICE=HIMEM.SYS is placed following a space and a slashmark, and more than one addition can be used (unless two would cancel each other).

1. Using DEVICE=HIMEM.SYS /HMAMIN=32 will reserve the extended memory for use by programs that, in this example, need 32 Kbyte or more. This reserves extended memory for programs that make more use of it. You can use figures from 0 to 63 in this option.

■ Without this addition, the first program requiring high memory will get exclusive use of all of it, even if it uses only a few bytes.

■ This is not as vital as it sounds because so few programs directly use extended memory. Ignore the addition unless a software manual specifically suggests that you use it.

2. Using DEVICE=HIMEM.SYS/NUMHANDLES=64 will allocate 64 handles, in this example, in place of the default 32. Numbers in the range 1 to 128 can be used.

■ A handle consists of 6 bytes of code in conventional memory that hold a description (for use by a program) of where part of the extended memory can be found. Handles are also used for locating expanded memory.

■ Programs that use extended memory will require at least one handle (for the program itself) and may need more (for data that the program uses).

The default setting of 32 is adequate for almost all likely eventualities, and this addition should be used only if a software manual (or a hint in a magazine) directs you to it.

3. Using DEVICE=HIMEM.SYS /int15=64 is needed only by some old programs which use extended memory in a way that conflicts with HIMEM. The number allocates Kbyte of extended memory, and using a value less than 64 results in no allocation for these programs being made. Values of 64 to 65535 can be used, subject to sufficient memory being available.

■ Use this addition only if advised - it would be much better to upgrade any programs that required this addition.

4. Using DEVICE=HIMEM.SYS /machine:1 specifies that the A20 handler is the correct one for the IBM PC/AT machine (or clone).

■ This ensures correct use of the A20 address line, unlocking the second megabyte of memory.

The A20 control is normally quite automatic, and this addition is needed only if A20 error messages are being delivered. An example is:

Unable to control A20 line

■ It may also be necessary if the keyboard locks up when HIMEM is in use.

There are 17 codes which can be used after /machine: so as to correct the use of the A20 line by specific machines. If you are experiencing problems, check for your machine in the following list, but remember that code 1 is the default.

Code	Machine
1	IBM PC/AT or clone
2	IBM PS/2
3	Machine using Phoenix Cascade BIOS
4	HP Vectra A or A+
5	AT&T 6300+
6	Acer 1100
7	Toshiba 1600 and 1200XE
8	Wyse 12.5 MHz 286
9	Tulip SX
10	Zenith ZBIOS
11	IBM PC/AT (alternative delay)
12	CSS Labs; IBM PC/AT (alternative delay)
13	Philips
14	H-P Vectra
15	IBM 7552 Industrial computer
16	Bull Micral 60
17	Dell XBIOS machines

A few machines use unexpected numbers, though most AT clones can use 1 as their A20 handler. The following additional list is known at the time of writing:

Machine	Number
COMPUADD 386 systems	1 or 8
Datamedia 386/486	2
Hitachi HL500C	8
Intel 301z or 302	8
JDR 386/33	1
Toshiba 5100	7
UNISYS PowerPort	2

5. Using DEVICE=HIMEM.SYS/A20CONTROL:ON will force HIMEM to take control of the A20 address line whether it was on or off at the time when HIMEM took effect. This is the default.

Using /A20CONTROL:OFF will allow HIMEM to take control of this line only if the line were OFF when HIMEM took effect.

■ In other words, using OFF allows other programs to take control of the A20 line even when HIMEM is to be used. This, once again, is rarely needed.

6. Using DEVICE=HIMEM.SYS/SHADOWRAM:OFF will switch off shadow ram on computers that can make use of this facility. Using /SHADOWRAM:ON will retain the shadow use. OFF is the default if the computer has 2 Mbyte or less of RAM.

■ Shadow RAM is extended RAM used by some chipsets, notably Chips & Technologies (C&T) and Headland. The ROM data is copied into this RAM and the machine is set to use this range of addresses rather than the ROM, because RAM is faster than ROM.

7. Using DEVICE=CONFIG.SYS/CPUCLOCK:OFF is a default setting, in which HIMEM is not allowed to change the clock speed (from Turbo to slow). Using ON in place of OFF allows HIMEM to control the clock speed.

■ Using the ON setting will slow down the action of HIMEM.

8. Using DEVICE=HIMEM.SYS /EISA directs HIMEM, used on an EISA machine with more than 16 Mbyte of extended memory to allocate all of the available extended memory.

■ EISA (Extended Industry Standard Architecture) computers are not commonplace, and not all will use more than 16 Mbyte of extended memory.

9. Using DEVICE=HIMEM.SYS /VERBOSE allows HIMEM to display status (and error) messages while it is loading - these are normally suppressed.

Problems with HIMEM.SYS

Problems with HIMEM.SYS are almost all concerned with conflicts, particularly if another memory manager (for an expanded-memory board) is present. No machine in the 386/486 class should require to use an expanded memory board.

One common source of difficulty is a conflict with some memory-resident program that is loaded either in the CONFIG.SYS or AUTOEXEC.BAT files, and a useful way of checking is to keep copies of bare-bones versions of these files, containing only the essential MS-DOS commands (such as KEYB, DOS=HIGH and so on). If the problem disappears when these copies are used in place of the original then by adding one program at a time, first to CONFIG.SYS and subsequently, if the problem does not reappear, to AUTOEXEC.BAT, you should be able to trace the cause.

- Remember that it is also possible to remove a line in CONFIG.SYS or AUTOEXEC.BAT from use temporarily by starting it with REM. This does not work on elderly versions of MS-DOS, but is a useful way of making temporary checks on MS-DOS 6.0 and above. An easier option is to reboot and hold down the F8 key when the Loading MSDOS message appears. This will allow you to determine which CONFIG.SYS lines you want to use.
- Remember also that you have to reboot to see any change in CONFIG.SYS take effect, and it is also desirable to reboot to see the new AUTOEXEC.BAT take effect, though you can type AUTOEXEC as a direct command.
- The Setup program for MS-DOS 6.0 will not even install HIMEM.SYS if another extended-memory manager program is active. If you have just upgraded to MS-DOS 6.0 and found that HIMEM.SYS is not present you will have to copy it by using EXPAND.EXE. Find the MS-DOS 6.0 disk which contains the file called HIMEM.SY_, and use EXPAND on this file to copy HIMEM.SYS to the hard disk.
- If you use the Intel Expanded-Memory Driver called EMM.SYS, you need to use the options /NE or /E when you install this driver with MS-DOS 6.0

- If your computer uses a Phoenix BIOS and MS-DOS 6.0 HIMEM.SYS does not work correctly, add

  /machine:1 or /machine:8

  to the DEVICE=HIMEM.SYS command in the CONFIG.SYS file.
- If you use the XMAEM.SYS and XMA2EMS.SYS drivers, these are disabled when you use MS-DOS 6.0 SETUP. If both drivers were used together, you can obtain the same results by replacing them with DEVICE=EMM386.EXE (see later) in the CONFIG.SYS file. If you use the XMA card, remove the REM command that MS-DOS 6.0 puts into the CONFIG.SYS file ahead of the DEVICE=XMA2EMS.SYS command.

Using EMM386

HIMEM should be used (and will be automatically installed by MS-DOS 6.0) on any AT machine whether 286, 386, 486 or higher. The other MS-DOS 6.0 memory manager utility, EMM386 is intended for use in 386 and 486 machines only; it cannot be run on 8088, 8086 or 80286 machines. Any attempt to run EMM386 on such machines will cause an error message.

The purpose of EMM386 is to allow the extended memory of a 386 or 486 machine to be used for two distinct purposes:

1. To make use of RAM along with addresses in the Upper Memory Block (UMB) using the address region of 640 Kbyte to 1 Mbyte and taking the RAM from part of the extended memory.

2. To make use of extended memory (if it is available) as expanded memory for the programs that can use expanded memory, such as DOS versions of AutoSketch, DeLuxe Paint-2, etc. Windows versions of programs can make use of extended memory managed by Windows itself.

The use of UMB memory is valuable, because several small programs can be loaded into that region and will run. Programs do not have to be specially written to be able to run in UMB memory, though there are a few which will not.

- By moving short memory-resident programs and utilities to UMB, conventional memory can be released, allowing large programs with no extended or expanded capabilities to make full use of the conventional memory.

EMM386 must not be used along with any other expanded memory managers. In other words, if your expanded memory is provided by a board in an expansion slot and needs to be managed by software provided with the board, do not install EMM386. Do not attempt to use EMM386 on a PC/XT machine or on an AT machine which uses the 80286 processor.

■ Remember that you cannot use the same memory for two different purposes. If you install EMM386 it will itself take around 80 Kbyte of extended memory which is not free to be used for anything else, and the extended memory that it converts to UMB or expanded cannot be used also as extended memory in its own right.

■ You can, however, use EMM386 for UMB uses only, leaving the rest of the extended memory free. This is well-suited to machines with only 2 Mbyte of RAM. If you have 3 Mbyte or more of RAM, full use of EMM386 along with HIMEM can provide very flexible options for the programs that you are likely to run, other than Windows.

■ Windows is always a special case, and EMM386 should not be used for expanded memory if you are intending to use only Windows programs. It can be installed if the programs you run under Windows are older programs which use expanded memory. For all other programs, Windows, aided by HIMEM.SYS, will manage memory for itself. EMM386 can, however, be used to provide UMB memory.

EMM386 is installed by a line in the CONFIG.SYS file that reads:

```
DEVICE=EMM386.EXE
```

This must follow the HIMEM line in the CONFIG.SYS file because EMM386 cannot take effect unless HIMEM is managing extended memory.

■ There is another step that you need to take if you want to use the Upper Memory Blocks, see the next section.

EMM386 Additions and Switches

There are two straightforward additions that can be made to the EMM386 line in the CONFIG.SYS file.

1. Using DEVICE=EMM386.EXE /NOEMS will start up the EMM386 manager for Upper Memory Block management only, with no expanded memory supplied.

■ This is useful if you have a small amount of extended RAM and you want to move short programs into UMB space to liberate the conventional memory, or if you have no need to use expanded memory (if you use Windows exclusively, for example).

2. Using DEVICE=EMM386.EXE /RAM will start up the EMM386 manager and allow it to control both UMB and expanded memory. This is the normal default, and can be used for machines with over 2 Mbyte of RAM. It must be used if you are running Lotus 1-2-3 V.3.1, since this requires some expanded memory.

■ If you want to use UMB memory for any purpose, you need to notify this in another part of the CONFIG.SYS file. You need either:

1. To add DOS=UMB to the CONFIG.SYS file OR
2 To change an existing DOS=HIGH to DOS=HIGH,UMB

This step connects the use of DOS in the conventional memory to its use in the UMB and is essential if you are to make any use of the UMB.

When this has been done, running MEM /C will give a readout such as has been illustrated earlier.

EMM386 complications

For most users, the default values that EMM386 uses are sufficient, and the only decision that needs to be made is whether or not to use the /NOEMS option. The options and additions that can be used with EMM386 are useful only if they are required and if you know how to use them. Note that several of these options require memory address number to be specified in hexadecimal code. In normal circumstances, using MEMMAKER will automatically set up any options that are needed, and the very few exceptions will be documented.

■ What this boils down to is that you should use such options only where there is a conflict of memory and you are advised to change the EMM386 command. Experimenting with these options and additions can cause your computer to lock up and you will be unable to restart it unless you have a floppy formatted as a system disk with a CONFIG.SYS and AUTOEXEC.BAT that contain no commands that might be problematic.

The following list of EMM386 options, therefore, is for information only and can be used to cross-check advice that you may have received, in the event of a lockup occurring. Remember that the use of high memory is always slightly problematic because of the interaction of different programs. Before you consider any alterations to the EMM386 command, try booting with memory-resident programs removed from the AUTOEXEC.BAT file. This can be done by placing the word REM ahead of each command line which is to be ignored.

1. Using DEVICE=EMM386 W=ON will enable the use of a Weitek maths co-processor. This is unusual, and most users of co-processors specify the simpler units made by INTEL, IIT or CYRIX. A Weitek processor is likely to cost more than the rest of a small computer. The ON can be changed to OFF if necessary, but this is the default if the /W option is not used.

2. Using DEVICE=EMM386 M1 specifies that the expanded memory page frame will start at the address C000 (hexadecimal). The page frame is the start of the address for a 64 Kbyte piece of expanded memory - the actual address corresponding to C000 is C0000 hexadecimal, 768 Kbyte.

- This is useful only if you need to force the start of the page frame to one of a preset range of addresses. This starting address is normally located automatically.

The address numbers that correspond to the code numbers, along with the equivalent number of kilobytes from the start of memory in this command are as follows:

Code	Address (hex)	Kilobytes equivalent
1	C0000	768
2	C4000	784
3	C8000	800
4	CC000	816
5	D0000	832
6	D4000	848
7	D8000	864
8	DC000	880
9	E0000	896
10	80000	512
11	84000	528
12	88000	544
13	8C000	560
14	90000	576

- Numbers 10 to 14 inclusive are used only for a machine in which the last 128 Kbyte has been disabled so that it has only 512 Kbyte of conventional RAM.

3. DEVICE=EMM386 FRAME=D400 would have the effect of forcing a page frame to start at the address D4000 (hex). Only the range of hex numbers shown

above can be used. You cannot use /M and /FRAME together.

4. DEVICE=EMM386 /PD000 would make the frame start at D0000; another way of specifying the starting address.

■ These alternatives are used so as to be compatible with other expanded memory drivers.

5. DEVICE=EMM386 P1=D400 makes page 1 of expanded memory use D4000 hex as its starting address.

■ The starting addresses for pages 0 to 3 inclusive must follow on from each other

6. DEVICE=EMM386 x=C000-D000 prevents EMM386 from using this specified range of addresses (taken from the list above).

■ This can be used if a range of addresses must not be used but for some reason it is not detected when EMM386 is started or by MEMMAKER. If you use an XGA display with EMM386.EXE, you may need to use this command to exclude some memory ranges. To decide which memory ranges to exclude you will need to look at the memory map when the XGA display is in use.

7. DEVICE=EMM386 i=D000-E000 specifies that this range of addresses corresponding to D0000 to E0000 can be used for expanded memory use.

8. DEVICE=EMM386 B=2000 specifies that the address 20000 (hexadecimal) is the lowest that will be used for swapping 16 Kbyte sets of data during the use of expanded memory. The default number is 4000 (address 40000).

■ It would be very unusual to need to change this.

9. DEVICE=EMM386 L=500 specifies that 500 Kbyte of extended memory should be left over after EMM386 has created expanded memory. The default is zero.

■ This could be useful if you need a mixture of expanded and extended memory and have enough RAM installed to cater for both.

10. DEVICE=EMM386 A=10 specifies that storage space for ten alternate registers will be used. This storage is used to preserve the state of a program that has been frozen while another program is running. The default is 7, allowing 7 programs to be running at one time.

■ Normally, you would carry out this multitasking type of action only by way of Windows, which attends to the memory management automatically.

11. DEVICE=EMM386 H=32 specifies that 32 handles will be allocated for controlling files. The default is 64.

■ This should not be altered unless you have a good reason for needing to change it.

12. DEVICE=EMM386 D=32 keeps 32 Kbyte free for a buffer to manage direct memory access (DMA) actions, other than those for floppy disks. The default is 16 and it is most unlikely that you would need to alter the amount.

13. DEVICE=EMM386 RAM= can be used to specify the range of addresses, following the equality sign, to be used for UMB. Normally, EMM386 will use whatever memory is available.

14. DEVICE=EMM386 NOVCPI disables support for VCPI applications if you have any.

15. DEVICE=EMM386 NOHIGHSCAN limits the extent to which EMM386 will search the upper memory area for available addresses. Use only if EMM386 presents problems when used without this option.

16. DEVICE=EMM386 VERBOSE will show a full report, including any errors, when EMM386 is being loaded.

17. DEVICE=EMM386 WIN A000-FFFF allows you to specify a range of addresses for Windows - the numbers shown are the minimum and maximum that can be used.

18. DEVICE=EMM386 NOHI prevents EMM386 from loading into an upper memory block. This will have the effect of releasing UMB memory space at the expense of conventional memory space.

19. DEVICE=EMM386 ROM=A000-FFFF can be used to specify a range of addresses which EMM386 can use for Shadow ROM if this not otherwise provided for -the numbers shown are the minimum and maximum that can be used.

The EMM386 direct command

In addition to the use of EMM386 as an installed memory manager, MS-DOS provides the EMM386 direct command as a way of checking and modifying the action of the manager. Typing EMM386 will produce a report such as that in Figure 3.4. The useful part of this shows that, in this example, 256 Kbyte of EMS expanded memory is now available.

The EMM386 command can be followed by options that enable it, disable it, or allow EMM386 to come into action when required.

Figure 3.4
A typical report obtained by using EMM386 as a direct command to show the amount of expanded memory available.

```
\>emm386

CROSOFT Expanded Memory Manager 386  Version 4.44
pyright Microsoft Corporation 1986, 1991

Available expanded memory . . . . . . . . .   256 KB

LIM/EMS version . . . . . . . . . . . . . .   4.0
Total expanded memory pages . . . . . . . .    40
Available expanded memory pages . . . . . .    16
Total handles . . . . . . . . . . . . . . .    64
Active handles  . . . . . . . . . . . . . .     1
Page frame segment  . . . . . . . . . . . .  D000 H

Total upper memory available  . . . . . . .     0 KB
Largest Upper Memory Block available  . . .     0 KB
Upper memory starting address . . . . . . .  C800 H

M386 Active.

\>
```

For example, using EMM386 /ON will force EMM386 on and EMM386 /OFF will force it off. Using EMM386 /AUTO will allow EMM386 to be used when required. This allows you to disable and re-enable EMM386 in the course of working with programs.

You can also use the /W=ON to enable the use of a Weitek co-processor, see earlier, or /W=OFF to disable the action.

DEVICEHIGH and LOADHIGH

These are optional forms of the DEVICE= command for the CONFIG.SYS file, and a way of loading memory resident (TSR) programs in the AUTOEXEC.BAT file, respectively. The simple forms are:

DEVICEHIGH=C:\MSDOS\SETVER.EXE
in CONFIG.SYS

LH KEYCLICK   in AUTOEXEC.BAT

- note that LOADHIGH can be abbreviated to LH. Taking these in order, DEVICEHIGH will place a driver into upper memory if such memory is available - if no memory is available the action is exactly the same as DEVICE, loading the driver into conventional memory.

DEVICEHIGH can be used with an optional L parameter which allows the regions of memory to be specified. These regions are numbered, and to find what numbers are available, use MEM /F. For example, using DEVICEHIGH /L:1=C:\MSDOS\SETVER.EXE will load the SETVER driver into memory in region 1. You can specify more than one region, for example by using L:1;2. A further number can be added to specify that the UMB size is enough to take the driver.

■ Many drivers require more space when first loaded than when they are running. You can specify this loading size as a number separated by a comma from the L:1 type of parameter. For example, using:

DEVICEHIGH /L:1,12048=C:\MSDOS\SETVER.EXE

will load SETVER into region 1 provided there is at least 12048 bytes free.

The /S option can be used in conjunctions with /L to specify that the UMB shrinks to the minimum size needed while the driver is loading. You are not advised to use this option yourself, and this information is provided only so that you can understand the effect of MEMMAKER on your CONFIG.SYS file.

The LOADHIGH (LH) command performs a similar action for AUTOEXEC.BAT files, and is used with the same options. The /L: option specifies the UMB region and this can be followed, separated by a comma, with a size number to specify the minimum size of UMB space that can be used. For example:

LH /L:0;1,42400 /S C:\MSDOS\SMARTDRV

will load SMARTDRV into regions 0 and 1 provided that a space of 42400 bytes is available, and shrinking the UMB to the minimum space when required.

A typical MEM/F report will produce information such as:

Region	Largest Free	Total Free	Total Size
1	9040 (9K)	9040 (9K)	27728 (27K)
2	139248 (136K)	139248 (136K)	139248 (136K)

- showing in this example that Region 0 is fully used (it is not reported on), but a small space exists in Region1 and ample space in Region 2.

■ Some care is needed here because if the machine setup CMOS Ram provides for the use of RAM as shadow ROM, this space is occupied, but will be counted as unused by MEM /F.

Using MEMMAKER

MEMMAKER is a program which automates the use of HIMEM.SYS and EMM386, and is useable only by 386/486, and higher, machines. Any attempt to use MEMMAKER on a 286 or lower machine will be met with a polite refusal. The use of MEMMAKER will always be advantageous unless you are sufficiently experienced in the use of HIMEM.SYS and EMM386 to be able to use the options and know which ones to use. Because these options present very great difficulties for most PC users, MEMMAKER has been devised to ensure that the less skilled user can set up a machine to its optimum capabilities.

Because MEMMAKER is concerned with organising the use of memory, it must be used with the memory as clear as possible. This means that the normal memory-resident programs should be installed but that you should not be using DOSSHELL or Windows. If you normally use a Network, it should be installed.

Once you have the machine running with the normal memory-resident programs, run MEMMAKER as follows:

1. With the C:\> prompt showing, type MEMMAKER and press ENTER.
2. You will see the opening screen, Figure 3.5. This summarises the MEMMAKER action. Note in particular that if you add any software that will become memory-resident (including DEVICE lines in the CONFIG.SYS file) you should run MEMMAKER again.
3. You are given the choice of Express Setup or Custom Setup. Custom Setup is used only if you are knowledgable about the way that you want memory to be used, and for the majority of PC owners Express Setup is preferable.
4. You will be asked if you use any programs that require expanded memory. The default answer is Yes, but change this to No if you normally use Windows programs, or if you make little use of programs that require expanded memory.

■ For example, AutoSketch 3.0 uses expanded memory, but only for large drawings that need the additional memory. If your drawings are small and/or simple, you can use AutoSketch without expanded memory.

5. MEMMAKER will then check for the presence of Windows, and make allowance for this.

Figure 3.5

The opening screen of MEMMAKER with its notes.

```
Microsoft MemMaker

Welcome to MemMaker.

MemMaker optimizes your system's memory by moving memory-resident
programs and device drivers into the upper memory area. This
frees conventional memory for use by applications.

After you run MemMaker, your computer's memory will remain
optimized until you add or remove memory-resident programs or
device drivers. For an optimum memory configuration, run MemMaker
again after making any such changes.

MemMaker displays options as highlighted text. (For example, you
can change the "Continue" option below.) To cycle through the
available options, press SPACEBAR. When MemMaker displays the
option you want, press ENTER.

For help while you are running MemMaker, press F1.

      Continue or Exit? Continue

ENTER=Accept Selection  SPACEBAR=Change Selection  F1=Help  F3=Exit
```

6. You are then notified that pressing ENTER will re-start the machine with the improvements implemented - there is a delay between pressing ENTER and seeing this happen.

Your computer should re-start normally, and you should see the MEMMAKER screen appear again to tell you that the settings will be used from then on. When you leave MEMMAKER your CONFIG.SYS and AUTOEXEC.BAT files will have been altered to place as many memory-resident programs as possible in the higher memory addresses (High memory and UMB memory). In addition, some options may have been added to the HIMEM.SYS and/or EMM386 lines.

If the computer does not restart normally, perhaps hanging up or giving unusual messages during booting up, reset again, and when the machine starts again you will see the MEMMAKER screen re-appear, asking you to opt for more conservative settings. NOTE that MEMMAKER will re-start even if the machine has been switched off and then on again.

■ The MEMMAKER screen will appear several times until all of the settings have been made and you confirm that the machine is running normally. Old CONFIG.SYS and AUTOEXEC.BAT files are preserved as CONFIG.UMB and AUTOEXEC.UMB file names in the MSDOS directory.

MEMMAKER will normally make a considerable number of changes to both the CONFIG.SYS and the AUTOEXEC.BAT files. Some of these may be to add options to the HIMEM.SYS or EMM386 lines, others are to place memory-resident programs in high memory or UMB space.

Using Custom Installation

When you opt for Custom Installation rather than Express Setup you will see the screen of Figure 3.6, which illustrates the uses of Custom setup. In particular you can opt to specify which drivers and memory-resident programs (TSRs) to include, whether or not you want to ensure that Windows has priority over upper memory areas, if you want to use some of the mono video memory for running programs, what inclusions and exclusions of memory areas you want to use with EMM386 and whether you want to move the Extended BIOS data area from conventional to upper memory.

The main problem is that you might not know how to answer these questions and what information to supply.

Figure 3.6
The Custom Setup screen of MEMMAKER,

```
Microsoft MemMaker

                        Advanced Options

Specify which drivers and TSRs to include in optimization?      No
Scan the upper memory area aggressively?                        Yes
Optimize upper memory for use with Windows?                     No
Use monochrome region (B000-B7FF) for running programs?         No
Keep current EMM386 memory exclusions and inclusions?           Yes
Move Extended BIOS Data Area from conventional to upper memory? Yes

To select a different option, press the UP ARROW or DOWN ARROW key.
To accept all the settings and continue, press ENTER.

ENTER=Accept All  SPACEBAR=Change Selection  F1=Help  F3=Exit
```

The other option, to scan upper memory aggressively, is also covered by Express Setup, and changing from Yes to No on this option is equivalent to opting for conservative settings in Express setup. Options are changed by pressing the Spacebar - some options allow more than a Yes or No pair of options and you can cycle through the options by using the Spacebar.

■ You have to make up your own mind on these points. If you have tried Express Setup and found that you needed to switch to conservative settings then it is likely that you could gain from using Custom settings provided you know what to look for. This type of information requires a book to itself (see the *Pocket Book of PC Memory*, for example) and the following is only a brief summary.

1. Assuming that using Express Setup with normal ("aggressive") settings causes a lockup, try to find what caused the lockup. The usual culprit is EMM386 being used on every piece of spare memory. If you press F8 at the "Loading MSDOS" message you can load in the drivers one by one into the CONFIG.SYS file. If the lockup occurs following a driver you have found the culprit. If it is EMM386 you can alter the options; if it is some other driver you can opt not to load it into high memory.

2. When you boot up the machine, opt to look at the CMOS RAM settings. You will need to find how to do this - on machines using the AMI BIOS, for example, you can press the DEL key when the screen message informs you. Other machines require you to hold another key down or to switch off the key lock on the main box. If your CMOS RAM settings include the use of SHADOW RAM, find out what addresses are used. You may find, for example that your settings are:

ROM Shadow at F000 for 64K
RAM Shadow at C000 for 32K

indicating that some 96 Kbyte of extended RAM is being used to hold the data from these addresses. EMM386 must not attempt to make any other use of this RAM, but MEMMAKER cannot necessarily find which parts of extended memory are being used in this way.

3. Another aspect of the problem is a line put in by MEMMAKER which is of the form:

DEVICE=C:\MSDOS\SIZER.EXE /25816 /8 C:\MSDOS\SETVER.exe

This line is a temporary one, and you will not see it if

MEMMAKER is successful, only if you have used the F8 key to feed in the lines of CONFIG.SYS one by one. In the example, attempting to place SETVER into upper memory has caused the problems, and you can use Custom Setup to exclude that driver from using Upper memory.

4. When you opt to select drivers and TSR programs, you are shown each in turn and asked to answer Y or N to the question about whether to include each driver or TSR in the optimisation process. If you know that, for example, SETVER causes trouble when loaded high you can opt not to use it.

5. As before, if you find the machine locking up when used with its new settings, you will find that MEMMAKER is automatically re-installed when you recover.

6. If you have excluded one driver which caused a lockup and you find that another driver later down the list now causes the lockup, the fault is almost certainly that EMM386 is trying to make use of a piece of memory that is already allocated, such as Shadow BIOS ROM or Shadow Video ROM

7. If EMM386 is incorrectly using memory that is used for Shadow ROM, you cannot alter this from within MEMMAKER, you need to place the exclusion options into the EMM386 line in CONFIG.SYS for yourself if you can - the only MEMMAKER option is to use conservative settings. You should opt for conservative settings, wait until you can use the machine with these settings, and then alter the EMM386 line, then try again using the aggressive settings.

- Every machine is individual in this respect of memory management, so that it is difficult to be more specific. Unless you really want to squeeze every last drop of memory out of the system and have enough information to allow you to do so, it is better to accept the MEMMAKER settings, conservative if need be, than to struggle with altering the EMM386 settings.
- Do not assume that all is well just because all of your drivers and TSR programs can be loaded into upper memory. You have to ensure that they will run correctly first - in my own machine, the hand-scanner driver would not run when located in UMB.

Using the SMARTDRIVE cache

For a machine with adequate memory, the most constricting influence on speed is disk access. The speed of the hard disk unit itself is measured in terms of average access time, and a figure of 20 milliseconds (20/1000 second) or less is very desirable. Older disk systems can be very slow; some early types had access times as high as 80 milliseconds and even fast modern drives seldom achieve access times of less than 15 milliseconds.

Given a reasonably fast disk system, the use of a disk cache is by far the best way of further increasing the speed of any AT machine. A disk cache uses some memory, usually extended memory, to hold information which is read from the disk or is to be written to the disk.

■ The best form of disk cache is memory located on the disk interface board, and any other form of disk cache is a second-best. Even second-best can be a very considerable improvement on working without a cache, however.

If data is being read frequently, a cache can hold enough data to ensure that the data can usually be supplied from the cache rather than directly from the disk. For frequent writes, the cache can hold data until there is too much to hold in memory and a disk write becomes essential. In either case, the cache is the main reservoir of data, and the computer reads from and writes to the cache if possible. Since the cache is memory, this reading and writing can be fast and efficient, very much faster than reading from or writing to a hard disk. In addition, a good cache system will make use of the disk drive at a time when nothing much else is being done, such as when the machine is waiting for you to press a key. In this way, disk speed has very much less effect on the overall speed of the system.

If the cache is being used for writing and the cache fills up, the content of the cache is saved to the disk. If the cache is being used for reading, the first request for data will cause the hard disk to be read and to read enough to fill the cache. Subsequent reads will be from the cache unless the data required is not in the cache, which will cause the disk to be read again. A small cache for reading is not efficient if small amounts of data are read from scattered parts of the disk, but if the cache is large it may hold almost all the contents of a directory.

If extended memory is used for a cache, a large amount of memory can be devoted to the cache, typically 1 Mbyte. A cache of this size will hold most of the contents of a 1.2 Mbyte or 1.4 Mbyte floppy disk and can greatly speed up hard disk actions. The use of extended memory as cache requires software to manage the use of the memory, and the cache software supplied with MS-DOS 6.0 is SMARTDRV.EXE.

This should not be confused with the older and much less efficient SMARTDRV.SYS. If you are using SMARTDRV.SYS you should upgrade to SMARTDRV.EXE as soon as possible and remove references to SMARTDRV.SYS from your CONFIG.SYS file. SMARTDRV.EXE is designed to work along with MS-DOS 6.0 and Windows 3.1, and you should be cautious about using any other cache software.

A disk cache can be read-only or read/write. Using a read-only cache is safe, because all the data that is being cached is duplicated on the disk, and if anything should happen to cause a reboot (a hiccup in the power line, for example) no data will be lost from the cache that cannot be replaced. A read/write cache, by contrast, carries the risk that there will be some data in the cache that has not been written to the disk, though as far as the program you are using is concerned, it has been saved. A reboot that is carried out for any reason will result in this data being lost. The greatest risk is that if the machine locks up with a program running, data that you think has been saved will not have been written on the disk.

Cache software which will cache writing as well as reading usually tries to get around this hazard by writing data to the hard disk within a 5-second deadline whenever there is a period in which the disk is not being used, and they also provide for a write command which can be used to force a write if you want to reboot and are not certain that the cache has written data.

No safeguards, however, will prevent data from being lost if you switch off abruptly, or suffer a power cut or a machine lockup, and if data is very precious it is probable better to disable write caching. SMARTDrive and other cache programs allow this to be done by using an option letter in the command that starts the cache running.

Unlike the older SMARTDRV.SYS, the new SMARTDRV.EXE is used in the AUTOEXEC.BAT file and is set up as follows:

1. Start an editor program and type as the filename C:\AUTOEXEC.BAT

2. At any place in the file, preferably near the start, add the line:

```
SMARTDRV
```

3. Save the file again.

-assuming that you are using a machine with adequate extended memory, and that the extended memory manager HIMEM.SYS is installed in the CONFIG.SYS file. Windows Setup will normally place the SMARTDrive line at the start of the AUTOEXEC.BAT file.

- A few memory-resident programs object to SMARTDRV being placed ahead of them, and you may need to move its position in the AUTOEXEC.BAT file if there are problems after installing SMARTDRV.
- If you encounter problems with SMARTDRV, such as slow action, odd reports (like 'Packed File Corrupt when using HELP') or problems with DBLSPACE on floppies (see Chapter 4) this is very often due to conflicts in high memory. Try first running without SMARTDRV - this should instantly cure the DBLSPACE problems and the odd messages. Then try running SMARTDRV in conventional memory. If all is still well, it points to a problem in the EMM386 line in CONFIG.SYS. This type of problem usually occurs after MEMMAKER has been used, and the culprit is usually a HIGHSCAN addition in this line.

By using only the command name, you allow SMARTDrive to select automatically the optimum operating conditions. These will depend on how much extended RAM is present and whether or not you use Windows. The defaults are:

Available Extended RAM	SMARTDrive uses:	Reduced by Windows to:
1 Mbyte or less	All	Nil
1 to 2 Mbyte	1 Mbyte	256 Kbyte
2 to 4 Mbyte	1 Mbyte	512 Kbyte
4 to 6 Mbyte	2 Mbyte	1 Mbyte
Over 6 Mbyte	2 Mbyte	2 Mbyte

Note that if your machine has only 1 Mbyte or less of extended RAM (a machine with 1 Mbyte total has only 384 Kbyte of extended RAM) then SMARTDrive will have no effect on Windows, since all of the available extended RAM will be used directly by Windows. For SMARTDrive to become really effective, the total extended RAM should be 4 to 6 Mbyte.

- A cache of more than 2 Mbyte is not really much more useful than one of 2 Mbyte, and any gain from using more memory than this is not commensurate to the cost of the memory. You should not consider using a RAMDrive unless SMARTDrive is able to make full use of memory and you have an application that needs RAMdrive.

Options for SMARTDrive

The new SMARTDrive version contains a wider range of options than the old SMARTDRV.SYS, and it should not be used along with any other form of disk cache software. If SMARTDRV.EXE is in a directory other than the root directory, its path must be shown in the command line. If, for example, the SMARTDRV.EXE files are in a directory called MSDOS, the command will be used in the form:

```
C:\MSDOS\SMARTDRV
```

The three main options are to show which drives will be included, the initial (main) cache size, and the Windows cache size.

By default, SMARTDrive will cache all of your drives other than CD-ROM and network drives. Floppy disks are by default cached for read only, and hard drives are cached for both read and write. You can exempt floppy drives from cache use by placing a minus sign following the drive letters, so that:

```
SMARTDRV A- B-
```

will ensure that drives A and B are not cached at all. The hard drive C will be fully cached for both reading and writing. The drive letter can be used alone, with the + sign or with the - sign. The drive letters are used as follows:

C used alone would cache this drive for reading only.
C+ would cache this drive for reading and writing.
C- would exempt this drive from cache use.

Remember that if you omit the drive letter C completely, the C drive will be fully cached - equivalent to using C+ in the SMARTDrive line.

The use of numbers for Initial cache size and Windows cache size is unnecessary if the default values shown in the table above are satisfactory, as they usually are. Note that the values of memory shown in the table are of available extended memory, which is not the same as total memory or the amount of extended memory that has been added. For example, if you have added 1 Mbyte of extended memory and have used only a small amount of the 384 Kbyte left over from the first Mbyte of RAM, the default values for SMARTDrive are 1 Mbyte of initial cache, with Windows able to take all but 256 Kbyte when it needs extended memory. The values of initial cache and the amount that is still available when

Windows needs extended memory can be stipulated by you if the default values are unsatisfactory. You can, for example, use values such as:

SMARTDRV A- B- 1500 512

to specify no caching of floppy disks, an initial read-write cache of 1500 Kbyte for the C drive, reducing to 512 Kbyte when Windows needs to use extended memory. Remember that these amounts are specified in Kbyte (not Mbyte) and they must be available - if you have not enough extended memory, or have tied up extended memory in other ways such as using some as expanded memory or for a RAMdisk (which may be pointless if SMARTDrive is being used), you cannot use such specified amounts.

If you are uncertain how much extended memory is tied up, for example by using UMB memory, it is easier and often preferable to allow the defaults to be used. The other options are used following the slashmark, and their defaults, where applicable, are sensible, so that you will not need to make use of the options except for special purposes.

/E:16 would specify that the cache moves 16 Kbyte of data at a time. The default is 8 Kbyte, and values used in this option must be powers of two such as 1, 2, 4, 8, 16, 32 etc.

/B:32 specifies a read-ahead buffer of 32 Kbyte. If a program needs to read 240 Kbyte from a file, SMARTDrive will read an extra 32 Kbyte in anticipation of the next read. The default is 16 Kbyte, and the number used must be a power of 2 (16, 32, 64, 128 etc). The other options do not concern values. They are present to enforce actions and will not necessarily be used in the SMARTDRV line of the AUTOEXEC.BAT file - some can be used in direct commands.

/C forces SMARTDrive to write all cached data to the hard disk. This option would be used in a direct command, so that if you suspected or feared that data had not been written to the disk you would type:

SMARTDRV /C

to enforce the writing of any such data.

This is seldom necessary, because writing takes place when there is no other disk activity. Use the /C option only if you are going to switch off or reboot abruptly and you are uncertain whether data has been written or not. You might also want to use this command at the end of a batch file that has started a program running, to ensure that all data is written before starting anything else.

/L can be used in the SMARTDRV line of AUTOEXEC.BAT to prevent SMARTDrive from loading into extended memory. Normally, if extended memory is available this is where you would want to store SMARTDrive now that the size of the SMARTDRV.EXE program is so much greater compared with the earlier SMARTDRV.SYS. Using the /L option might prevent some large programs for running because of lack of conventional memory.

/R will be used in the command SMARTDRV /R to clear the existing cache contents and re-start SMARTDrive from scratch. This is not an option that you should normally need.

/Q can be used in the SMARTDRV line in the AUTOEXEC.BAT file to suppress the information on SMARTDrive from appearing on the screen (and slowing down the boot process).

/S is used while SMARTDrive is in use, in the form of the command:

SMARTDRV /S

to obtain information on the success of SMARTDrive. A typical display of the /S option is shown in Figure 3.7, showing the number of hits (when SMARTDrive has supplied data without the need to read the disk) and misses (when the disk had to be read). The status of drives is also shown. This illustration has been taken on a small-memory system soon after booting, so that the proportion of misses is unusually high.

```
Microsoft SMARTDrive Disk Cache version 4.0.091 Copy-
right 1991,1992 Microsoft Corp.

Room for 120 elements of 8,192 bytes each
There have been 1,198 cache hits
and 1,051 cache misses
Cache size: 983,040 bytes
Cache size while running Windows: 0 bytes

Disk Cache Status drive read cache write cache buffer
                    C:    yes          no        no
For help, type "Smartdrv /?".
```

Figure 3.7
A typical display from the SMARTDRV /S command, with an unusually high proportion of misses.

/? is used in the command:

SMARTDRV /?

to display a summary of Help on SMARTDrive and its options.

- You can get a report on SMARTDRV from within Windows by using SMARTMON from Windows - see Chapter 10.

Double-buffering option and disk partitions

There is another SMARTDrive option for double-buffering which may need to be used on computers with the SCSI type of disk interface or which use an older type of BIOS chip. To find if you need this option, make sure that you are using the directory in which SMARTDRV.EXE is located and type the command:

SMARTDRV (press ENTER key)

This will bring up a report which, for a machine with no caching for floppy drives A and B, but with hard disk drives C and D might, for example, read:

Disk Cache Status

drive	read cache	write cache	buffer
C:	yes	yes	no
D:	yes	yes	no

- and the no answers in the buffer column indicate that all is well and no changes are needed. If you get yes answers in the buffer column, alter your SMARTDRV command line in the AUTOEXEC.BAT file to read:

SMARTDRV (any options) /double_buffer

This will be needed only for older machines and for machines using some types of SCSI interface, and if you are using a 386 machine it will almost certainly not need this line. Even older 286 machines may not need it - the crucial year for the BIOS is 1987.

Another problem tied up with hardware is the use of disk partitions. Versions of MS-DOS prior to 4.0 did not provide for a hard disk of more than 32 Mbyte to be controlled. If your main hard disk was of more than 32 Mbyte, it had to be partitioned, with one portion as drive C: (for example) and the other as Drive D:. Large hard disks might need to use three or more partitions.

MS-DOS 6.0 can cope with any practical size of hard disk without the need for partitions, so that if you format a disk under MS-DOS 6.0 you would normally opt to have a single partition. If your disk was originally formatted using an earlier version of MS-DOS that required multiple partitioning it is often worth-while to back up all of the hard disk and reformat it, using FDISK from MS-DOS 6.0 to create a single partition on a hard disk. You then have to restore all the software to your disk. This is not something that should be undertaken lightly, and only if you know what you are doing.

There are no problems with the use of SMARTDRV on partitioned disks when the MS-DOS FDISK utility has been used to create the partitions. In the past however, partitioning software has been available from other suppliers, and is often a source of conflicts. If you receive a message stating that you cannot load SMARTDRV, the problem may be due to such partitioning software. You can force SMARTDRV to load by specifying the /p option, but this may corrupt your hard disk if the hard disk contains more than 1024 cylinders or is not supported by the system's ROM BIOS.

You need to make certain, if you have used partitioning software other than the FDISK utility of Microsoft that you do not use SMARTDRV unless the hard disk corresponds to the restrictions above. Backup the disk and re-partition using FDISK if you want to make use of SMARTDRV with no restrictions. Better still, change to MS-DOS 6.0 at the same time and forget about partitions.

The MSD Utility

MSD (MicroSoft System Diagnostics) is an advanced package which will examine and report on the whole of your system. You can look at the report on screen, as illustrated here, or send the report to a disk file for printing out directly or by using a word-processor. There are three file report options depending on how you want the data organised.

The straightforward command MSD produces the screen illustrated in Figure 3.8. This consists of a summary, and you can gain additional information on each of the topics shown here by clicking the mouse with the cursor over the topic on which you want more information. The information for Computer will be information on the BIOS chip for any PC clone.

The Memory option has been clicked in Figure 3.9 showing a summary of the use of memory in the range from 640 Kbyte to 1024 Kbyte - this is shown in two screens, using the scroll bar at the side to move from one to another, and the illustration shows the upper part.

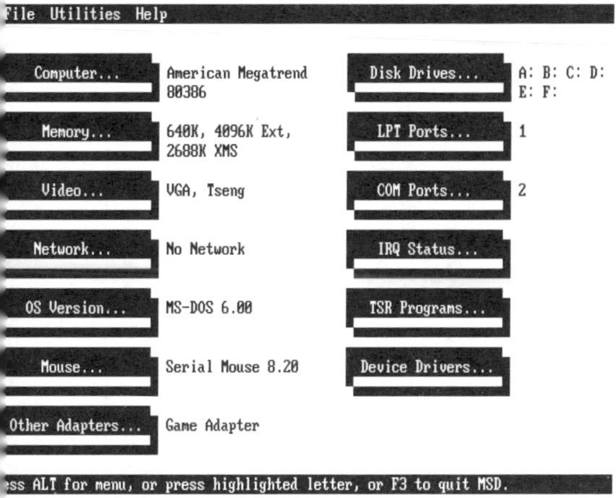

Figure 3.8

The opening screen of MSD showing the large range of reports this utility can generate.

Part of the TSR option is shown in Figure 3.10. This indicates how each TSR and driver uses conventional memory, showing what portions remain in conventional memory even though the main part of each TSR or Driver may have been loaded into high memory or UMB.

■ In general, MSD is more of a programmer's utility, and its most important use is to produce a disk file that can be sent (to MicroSoft, for example) for diagnostic purposes.

The MSD Options are:

B Produce output in black and white, if your display does not give a clear rendering in colour.

F Produce a report to a file, and include your name, Company and other details, for sending to MicroSoft. The filename (such as A:MSDREP.TXT) must follow the /F option.

I Do not detect machine data - use this only if you have problems in using the straightforward MSD command.

P Produce a report to a disk file, but with no name or other personal information. The filename must follow the option letter.

S Produce a summarised report to a specified disk file.

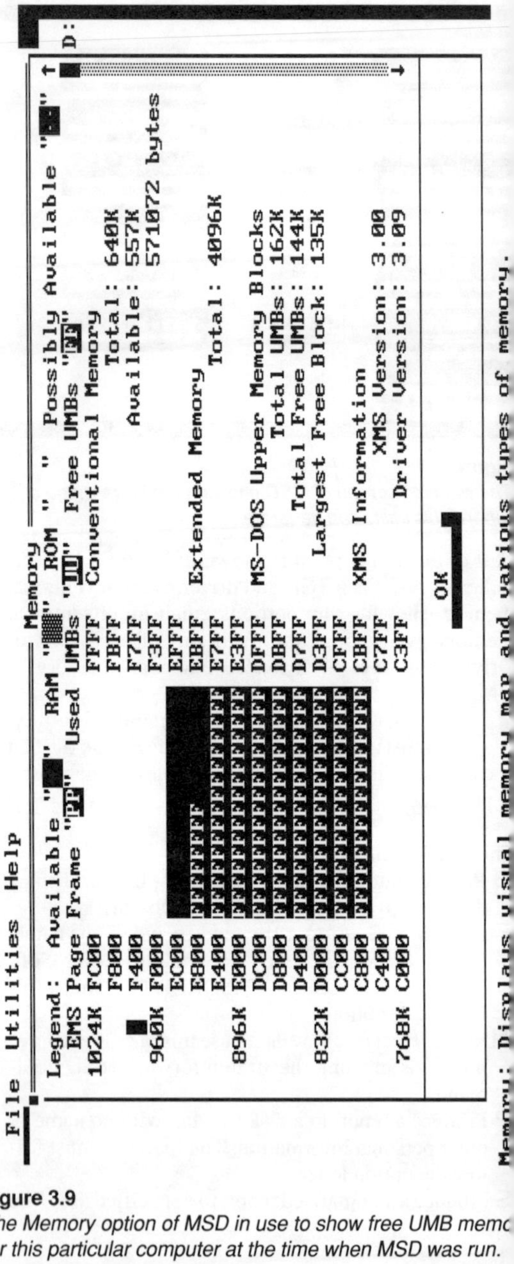

Figure 3.9
The Memory option of MSD in use to show free UMB memo for this particular computer at the time when MSD was run.

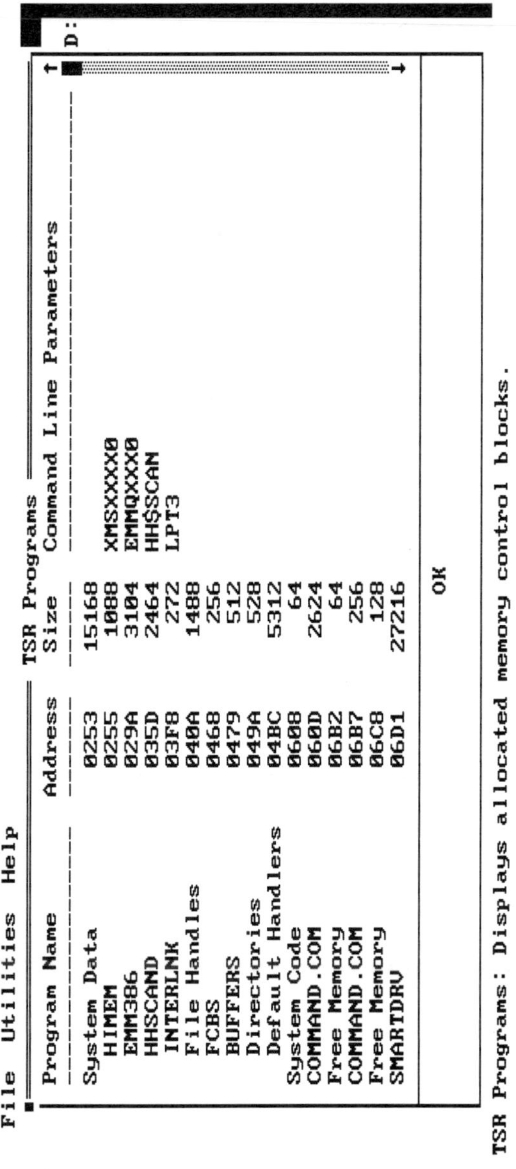

File Utilities Help
TSR Programs
Program Name Address Size Command Line Parameters
System Data 0253 15168
HIMEM 0255 1088 XMSXXXX0
EMM386 029A 3104 EMMQXXX0
HHSCAND 035D 2464 HH$SCAN
INTERLNK 03F8 272 LPT3
File Handles 040A 1488
FCBS 0468 256
BUFFERS 0479 512
Directories 049A 528
Default Handlers 04BC 5312
System Code 0608 64
COMMAND.COM 060D 2624
Free Memory 06B2 64
COMMAND.COM 06B7 256
Free Memory 06C8 128
SMARTDRV 06D1 27216
OK
D:
TSR Programs: Displays allocated memory control blocks.

Figure 3.10
The TSR options which will show how memory-resident programs are installed.

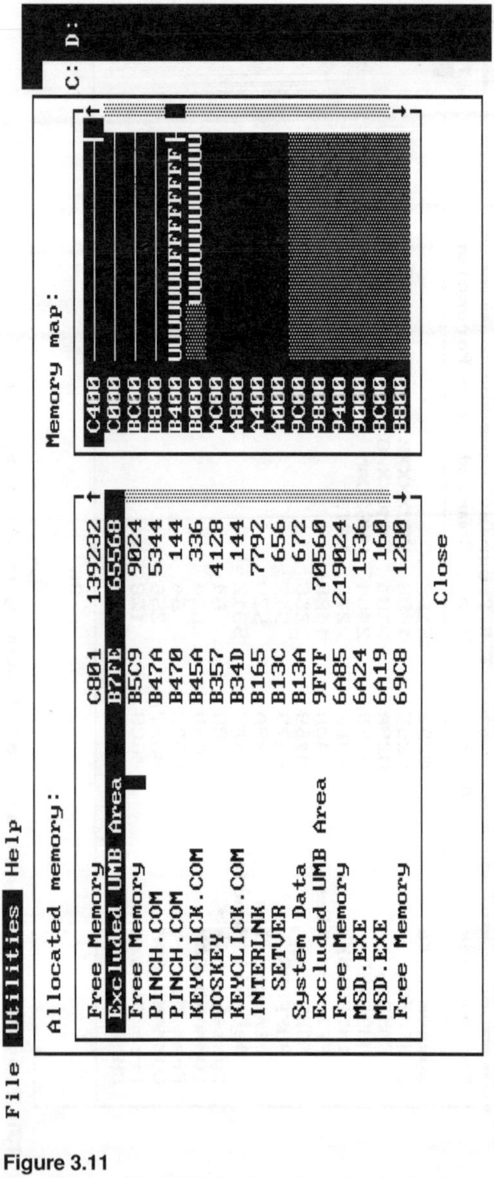

Figure 3.11

The Memory Block Display in action, showing both starting addresses for resident programs and a pictorial display.

The MSD menus consist of File and Utilities.

The File menu contains Find File, allowing you to search the hard disk for any named file. When you use this option you are asked to type the file name, and specify the starting directory, with options to include sub-directories, search the boot drive (usually C:\) or search all drives.

Another File option is to Print the report directly, not using a file, and the other main option is to view any of the CONFIG.SYS, AUTOEXEC.BAT or INI files that have been found on the disk.

The Utilities menu consists of Memory Block Display, Memory Browser, Insert Command, Test Printer and Black and White.

The memory block display is illustrated in Figure 3.11. It contains a list of resident programs on the left-hand side and a pictorial representation of memory use on the right. Moving the cursor to any program name will cause the memory display to alter so as to show the region of memory that is involved.

The Memory Browser allows you to search the ROM areas. This is a way of detecting messages and important information, as Figure 3.12 illustrates for a machine with an AMI BIOS chip. You can opt to search for a string of letters or codes if you know what you are looking for.

The Insert command allows you to alter some settings in CONFIG.SYS and AUTOEXEC.BAT.

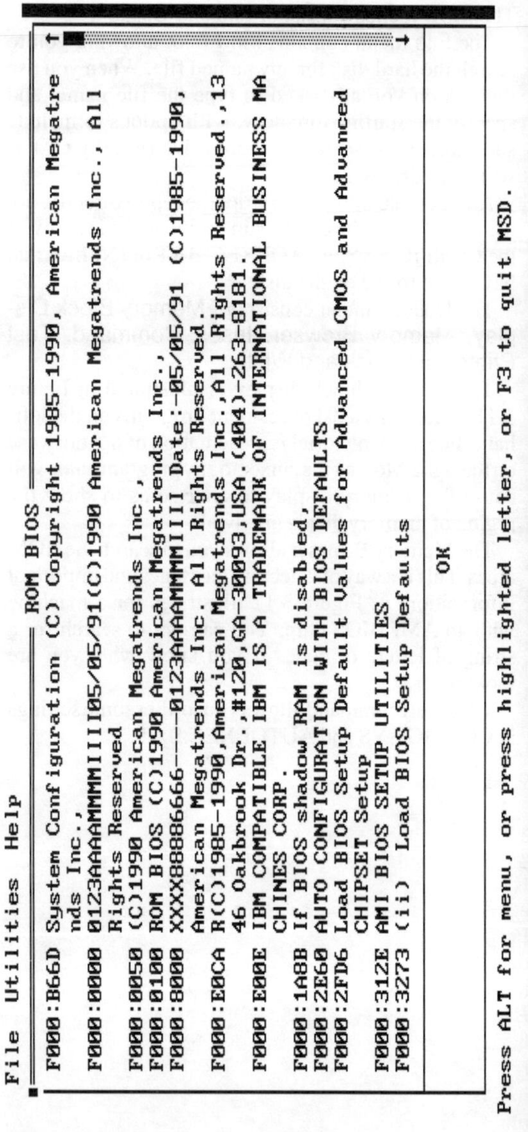

File Utilities Help
ROM BIOS
F000:B66D System Configuration (C) Copyright 1985-1990, American Megatre
nds Inc.,
F000:0000 0123AAAAMMMMIIII05/05/91(C)1990 American Megatrends Inc., All
Rights Reserved
F000:0050 (C)1990 American Megatrends Inc.,
F000:0100 ROM BIOS (C)1990 American Megatrends Inc.,
F000:8000 XXXX8886666——0123AAAAMMMMIIII Date:-05/05/91 (C)1985-1990,
American Megatrends Inc. All Rights Reserved.
F000:E0CA R(C)1985-1990,American Megatrends Inc.,All Rights Reserved.,13
46 Oakbrook Dr.,#120,GA-30093,USA.(404)-263-8181.
F000:E00E IBM COMPATIBLE IBM IS A TRADEMARK OF INTERNATIONAL BUSINESS MA
CHINES CORP.
F000:1A8B If BIOS shadow RAM is disabled,
F000:2E60 AUTO CONFIGURATION WITH BIOS DEFAULTS
F000:2FD6 Load BIOS Setup Default Values for Advanced CMOS and Advanced
CHIPSET Setup
F000:312E AMI BIOS SETUP UTILITIES
F000:3273 (ii) Load BIOS Setup Defaults
OK
Press ALT for menu, or press highlighted letter, or F3 to quit MSD.

Figure 3.12

The Memory Browser being used to look at messages in the ROM - keep a note of registration numbers in this section as they will identify your computer in case of recovery after theft.

4 Hard disk and Utilities

Hard disk installation

A new hard disk must be formatted, and on versions of MS-DOS that supported hard disk use, until the introduction of 4.0, partitioning into 32 Mb or smaller sections was necessary as well. MS-DOS 4.0 allowed larger partition sizes (but a program called SHARE.EXE needed to be run); MS-DOS 5.0 and 6.0 allow partition sizes up to 2 Gbyte in size so that splitting of disks into separate drive letters is not likely to be needed, and SHARE.EXE is not needed either.

At the time when hard disk drives used almost exclusively the MFM or RLL systems, it was normal to format hard disks in three stages. The low-level format, using FDISK, marked out the tracks on the disk, and was used to determine interleaving (reading and writing of non-consecutive sectors) and prepare for partitioning. The partitioning step, which is very rapid, divides a drive into one or more partitions, each of which can be used as if it were a separate drive, but with only one carrying the MS-DOS system tracks. Finally, the high-level format lays down the sectors, and prepares the File Allocation Table (FAT) ready for use. Unless the low-level format has been correctly done, neither FDISK nor FORMAT can be used.

Putting a new hard disk of the MFM or RLL type into service, therefore, required all of the formatting processes to be carried out. At the time of writing, MFM and RLL systems are obsolete and though such hard disks can still be bought, the IDE and SCSI types predominate. For that reason, no description of formatting MFM/RLL disk drives will be given here and the reader is referred to books specialising in Hard Disk systems, such as *Hard Disks Step by Step*, for this information. Modern hard disks of the IDE type are virtually always supplied ready-formatted and do **not** need FDISK even for forming their single partition. Their interleave is also set at unity, so that when, for example, 6 sectors are read or written they can be consecutive sectors. Older systems might use one sector and skip two or more so as to allow time for the memory that contained the data (the buffer) to clear before another read or write.

High-level format

Modern IDE disks require only a high-level formatting action, establishing file-allocation tables and directory, to be carried out. This makes use of the FORMAT utility on the system disk - make sure that it exists by typing DIR FORMAT.*. Make sure first that your new hard drive is not already fully-formatted - if you can obtain a DIR display then the drive is ready for use right away and the following description can be ignored. If the drive is supplied with MS-DOS installed it will be totally ready for use. If the drive needs to be high-level formatted you will almost certainly want to format Drive C as a system disk so that booting can be from this disk in future.

1. With a floppy system disk in A:, and logged to this drive, type:

FORMAT C: /S (press ENTER)

2. You will be asked to confirm - do so and wait until the formatting is complete which can take a considerable time on a large hard disk (150 Mbyte or more).

3. If your hard disk has already been partitioned into C: and D:, use FORMAT D: to format this latter partition, but do NOT use the /S part of the instruction which puts system tracks in place.

■ It would be very unusual to find a partitioned IDE disk nowadays, and if it were unformatted it would be well worth the effort to use FDISK to create one single partition.

4. Select C: again, and check using DIR that you can see COMMAND.COM listed on drive C. If it is not, copy this file by using:

COPY A:\COMMAND.COM C:\

5. Copy all SYS files, using:

COPY A:*.SYS C:\ .

6. From now on, it's a matter of taste, but my preference is to log on to C: drive and create a directory called MSDOS which contains all of the other MS-DOS utilities **except** FDISK and FORMAT. I also create a BATS directory which contains all batch files except AUTOEXEC.BAT (which is in the root C:\ directory). The AUTOEXEC.BAT file has to be created according to your own needs; mine contains the line:

PATH C:;C:\MSDOS;C:BATS

to ensure that the files in these directories can be run from any other part of the C: or D: disks.

Hard Drive maintenance

The installation of a hard disk is by no means a plug-and-go operation, so that by the time you have the disk running, it is already a considerable investment in time and effort. This is why the programs FDISK and FORMAT should not be allowed to remain on the hard disk, though you might need FORMAT for floppies, because if either is run inadvertently (usually after midnight) they can wipe all your efforts in a very short time. It seems odd that these programs appear to take so long when you are first formatting with them, but no time at all when you find you did not intend to use them.

Once the hard disk has been in use for some time, it will be well occupied, and the need for regular backups becomes important. One simple scheme is to back up only the data files that have been changed since the disk was last used. This is because program files should already exist in their original floppy disks, and if a program needs elaborate configuration before use, a backup of its configured form should also be held. Your data files are the most precious because only you can create them (and only you can delete them).

Another important point is that disk access times will steadily deteriorate as a disk is used, because of the creation and subsequent deletion of files, leaving spaces in the disk which are too small to be filled, and also causing large files to be scattered about the disk. The disk de-fragmenting software of MS-DOS 6.0 can be used to deal with this problem, see later, this Chapter.

Directories and directory structure

When hard disks first came into use, the amount of storage that they offered (10 - 20 Mbytes), though large compared to the capacity of a floppy disk at that time, was not enormous by modern standards, but it soon became obvious that new methods of maintaining a program directory were needed.

The extent of the problem becomes apparent if you look at the directory of a floppy disk that contains a large number of short programs. Typing DIR simply causes the titles to scroll up the screen, giving you no time to read each filename. You can make this easier by using DIR/P or DIR/W (or by using DOSSHELL in MS-DOS 6.0) but it is never easy to locate a program quickly and the display is always very cluttered.

In addition, there was no easy way of grouping programs in the early days so that, for example, a word processor and its text files, perhaps along with some printer utility programs and file viewing utilities, could be placed together separate from other programs. If programs can be held in separate directories there is also the possibility of allowing filenames to be duplicated within different directories, with no conflict. You might, for example, have a file called EXAMPLE in your word processing directory and a file called EXAMPLE in your spreadsheet directory, with no possibility of using the wrong file.

The method of organising programs and data on to the hard disk is built-in to all of the later versions of MS-DOS (3.0 onwards) and can, in fact, be used also on floppy disks, though there is seldom any need to do so (except for the 21 Mb floptical type of disks). By its nature, the hard disk will be used for all of your programs and current data (though data should be backed up on to floppy disks at intervals), and conflicts of filename are almost inevitable unless files can be kept in directories as if they had been stored on separate disks. The system must therefore provide for grouping, for locating files, and for allowing files to be located by programs if they are in different groups.

Directory trees

Directory trees are the MS-DOS method of making life tolerable for the user of the hard disk. The principle is to subdivide the directory system so that using the MS-DOS DIR command does not result in page after page of file listings and that saving a file does not cause problems of conflicting program names.

The system uses directory groups which are named like files (which is what they really are). Using DIR then shows the directory (group) names (but not the names of the files in them), along with the names of files in the main (root) directory. You can then call for a directory of one directory group only, greatly reducing the effort that you need to spend on finding anything useful.

■ One considerable advantage of keeping files in a directory structure is that the number of files that can be stored in a sub-directory is limited only by the disk capacity. When a large number of small files are placed in the root directory of a hard disk, there is a danger of exceeding the number of filenames that can be used long before the disk is full. By using a subdirectory this is avoided. In general, only a few essential files (such as CONFIG.SYS and AUTOEXEC.BAT) should be placed in the root directory.

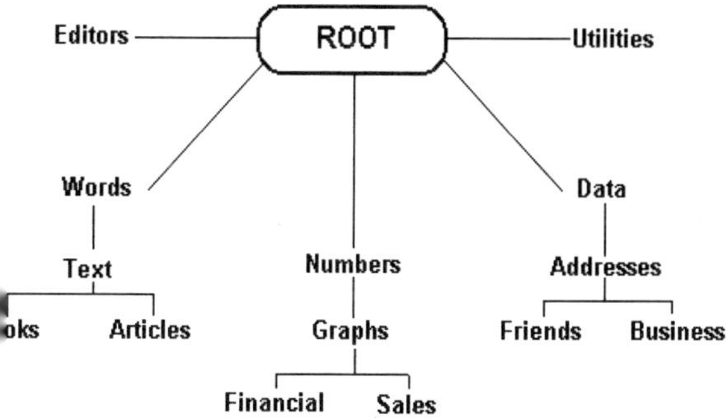

Main directories: Editors, Utilities, Words, Data
Sub-directories(1): Text, Numbers, Addresses
Sub-directories(2):Books,Articles,Financial,Sales,Friends,Business

Figure 4.1
A directory tree drawn in the conventional way. Think of it as a family tree with the Root as the ultimate ancester.

The name *tree* is slightly misleading, because it suggests a root in the ground and branches in the air. The directory tree should be thought of as a family tree, with the root directory as the ancestor of all the files, Figure 4.1. However you like to imagine it, the diagram indicates that when you call for a directory display, all that you will get initially is the set of names that appear in the **root directory**. Some of these names can be filenames of programs or data, and they will be indicated in the usual way. Other names can be of new directories, each containing its own files. These directory names are indicated either by the <DIR> following the name of the directory in place of the usual extension of a filename, or by enclosing the name itself in square brackets, as illustrated in Figure 4.3

In the example, three of these directory names are [Words], [Numbers] and [Data], names that are chosen to indicate what type of files will occupy the three subdirectories. Note that these names in square brackets are not names of files but names of other directories. The names are intended as illustrations only. Unlike older versions of MS-DOS, MS-DOS 6.0 treats these names as a variety of filename (which is what they are) and allows you to use the DEL command (and the Del key when you use DOSSHELL) on these names.

- There is also a DELTREE command which allows you to erase a directory along with all the files and sub-directories it contains. This has to used with great care.

Only a few directories need to branch from the root. One directory can branch from another, so that one is the parent directory and the other is the child, Figure 4.2. A child directory is often called a sub-directory -in this sense, every directory apart from the root is a sub-directory, and it is possible for a subdirectory to be a parent to some other sub-directory as well as being a child of its main directory.

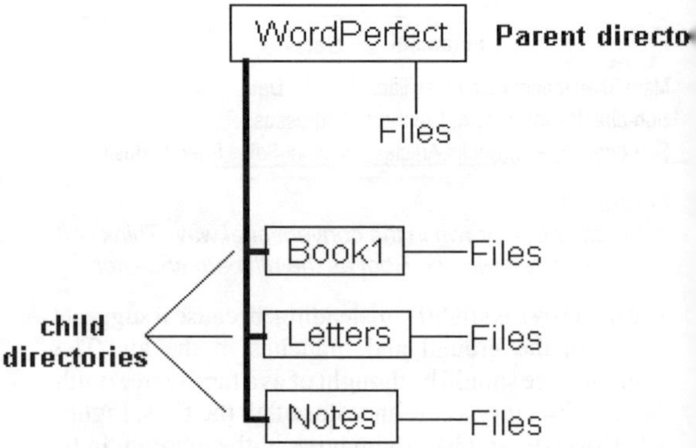

Figure 4.2
Parent and Child directories. These are relative terms - the Word Perfect directory in this example is a child of the Root directory as well as being the parent of the three shown here. This makes the family tree similarity even stronger.

The Root directory.

The root directory, C:\, is the one to which you have immediate and automatic access when you start to use the hard disk. Unless you have some pressing reason to place program or data files in the root directory, you should always reserve the root for storing mainly sub-directories. In other words, when you are using the hard disk as drive C:, typing DIR should give you a list like that of Figure 4.3, in which each item other than a few files appears between square brackets, signifying a directory.

```
C:\>dir

 Volume in drive C is HARDDISK
 Volume Serial Number is 1A36-730A
 Directory of C:\

[AFW]           [ARCHIVE]       [BATS]          [CONVERT]       [DTP]
[EDIT]          [MSDOS]         [NETBITS]       [OLD_DOS.1]     [PAINT]
[PCXFILES]      [SCAN]          [SCRNGRAB]      [SKETCH3]       [TEMP]
[TIFFS]         [UTILS]         [WINDOWS]       [WINWORD]       AUTOEXEC.BAT
BEFSETUP.MSD    CONFIG.BAK      CONFIG.SYS      DSVXD.386       HHSCAND.SYS
NCON.SYS        NET00000.SYS    NETSHARB.SYS    NETSHARE.SYS    NETUNITS.SYS
WINA20.386
       31 file(s)        56006 bytes
                      36714496 bytes free

C:\>
```

Figure 4.3
A typical directory printout for a C:\ root directory, showing that most of the entries are directory names rather than files.

Because the amount of storage is large - it is not unusual to have 200 -5000 files on a hard disk - you must use some planning, deciding on how you want to group your programs. You might, for example, group programs according to their uses, such as word processors, spreadsheets, databases, graphics and so on, with perhaps another directory for combined programs such as Symphony. You should certainly avoid placing data files in the root directory, and in many cases you would not want to place data files in the same directories as the programs, but in sub-directories, possibly grouped into different types of data like Letters and Articles, Home and Business etc.

The root directory is indicated in commands by using the backslash sign, \ which should not be confused with the forward slash /. The difference is important because many commands use both symbols, with the forward slash used to separate parts of the command. The root directory in the C: drive is therefore indicated by using C:\, and the root directory in the D: drive is indicated by D:\. The use of the backslash immediately following the drive letter (or immediately following a directory tree command) always means that the root directory is to be used. The backslash is also used as a separator to show the progression from a parent directory to a child, so that WORDS\TEXT shows that TEXT is a child of WORD. The 'prompt' that appears on the screen when MS-DOS 6.0 is running will show the current directory as C:\> or C:\WORDS> according to what is currently in use. The >part of the prompt means that MS-DOS is waiting for a command.

You have to be careful to distinguish these uses of symbols when you first start using a hard disk. The backslash symbol can be used by itself, so that DIR \ will produce a directory of the root directory. Take care over your use of the \ symbol, because careless use can lead to mistakes such as erasing the entire file contents of the root directory (you cannot erase directories unless they are empty). If you use the DOSSHELL of MS-DOS 6.0 such mistakes are less likely. Avoid the use of DELTREE (which can erase **everything**) until you are familiar with directory commands. Because of this, you should keep a system disk which contains copies of all the **files** that reside on your root directory. In particular, this should contain the CONFIG.SYS and AUTOEXEC.BAT files which set up the machine for use.

Creating directories

When you start work with a hard disk, you will probably start by creating a few entries into the root directory, and then probably into the first layer of sub-directories. Each directory has to be created and named - the names must follow the same rules as MS-DOS filenames, using a main name of up to eight characters and (if required) an extension of up to three letters. Using extensions for directory names makes these names more difficult to type and to remember, a point to note if you are not using DOSSHELL.

The computer must, however, create the subdirectory names in the correct form, not as filenames, and to do this requires the use of the MKDIR command, abbreviated to MD. The alternative, if you use DOSSHELL of MS-DOS 6.0, is to use the Create Directory option of the File menu.

Using MS-DOS by itself, if you are using (*logged to*) the root directory, and you want to create a sub-directory called WORDS, you do so by typing MD WORDS and pressing the ENTER key. This will cause some action in the disk drive, and when you use DIR from now on you will find the entry:

WORDS <DIR> or <WORDS>

depending on the type of directory display you are using, to indicate that WORDS is a subdirectory name, not a filename.

When you subsequently type DIR \WORDS you are now requesting the computer to 'follow a path' that starts with the root directory (symbolised by \) and proceeds to the WORDS subdirectory. This will give the display of the type shown in Figure 4.4, showing that there is just one file stored in this particular subdirectory, and the only other entries are the dot and double-dot. Note that MS-DOS always counts this set as being three files. Even in an empty sub-directory, the dot and double-dot are always counted as files.

```
C:\>md words

C:\>cd words

C:\WORDS>dir

 Volume in drive C is HARDDISK
 Volume Serial Number is 1A36-730A
 Directory of C:\WORDS

[.]             [..]
        2 file(s)              0 bytes
                        36708352 bytes free

C:\WORDS>
```

Figure 4.4
A DIR printout for a directory, showing the steps of creating and viewing the empty directory.

The dot is an abbreviation for the current subdirectory, [Words] in this example, the child directory, and the double dot indicates the previous directory in the path, the parent directory which in this example is the root directory. These dots can be used as if they were valid directory names in commands that require a directory name - you can, for example, use the command:

COPY ..\myfile.doc .

to copy a file from the parent directory to the current directory. This form of command requires very little typing, and is oddly neglected. One point to note is that any parent-child pair can use the same dot and double-dot form of command, so that the directory name is not needed.

You can create other subdirectory names such as ACCTS and DATA in the same way as before, starting at the root directory (type CD\ to return to the root) and using the name that you have chosen following the MD command. This method of creating a subdirectory applies also if you are starting from another subdirectory. If you switch to the WORDS subdirectory, for example, you can create the further subdirectories of BOOKS, ARTICLES and LETTERS. Each of these, Figure 4.5, will be a child directory of the WORDS directory.

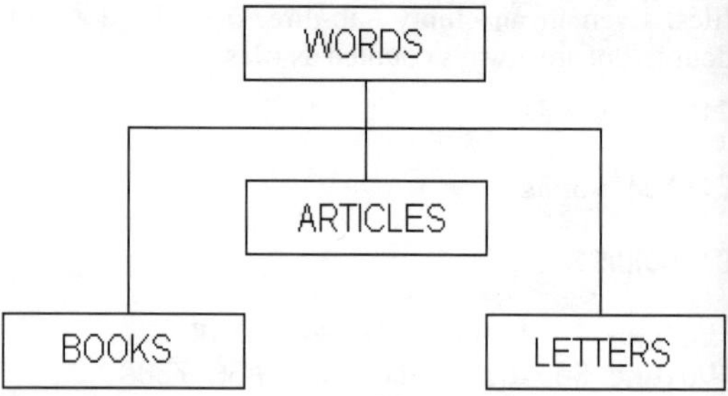

Figure 4.5
Other Child directories of WORDS created and shown in this diagram.

You have to be in the WORDS directory in order to create these subdirectories of WORDS. If you are in the root directory when you use MD BOOKS, for example, you will certainly have created a subdirectory called BOOKS but it will be a subdirectory of the root, at the same level as WORDS rather than as a subdirectory of WORDS, Figure 4.6. This implies that if you are setting up a hard disk from scratch by transferring a large number of files from floppy disks it is a considerable advantage to plan carefully first, using a tree diagram of the type that has been illustrated.

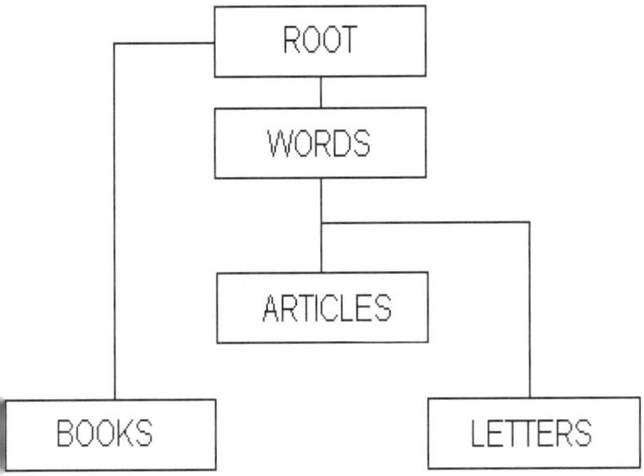

Figure 4.6
An incorrect sub-directory location caused by using the MD command from the wrong place (the root directory in this example.)

Without such a diagram, it is remarkably easy to create subdirectories that you don't need, and put files in places where you can't easily use them. A spoonful of common sense and organisation, in short, is worth a bucketful of technology at this point. The use of DOSSHELL (see Chapter 8) is **strongly recommended**, because it shows you the directory tree display as you are creating directories.

Moving between directories

The CHDIR (abbreviated to CD) command of MS-DOS is used to move from one directory to another. In the example above, you can return to the main root directory by typing the command:

CD \ or repeating CD..

There is an important difference between these commands, though they have the same effect in this example. The CD \ command will always return you to the root directory, irrespective of what directory was in use. The CD.. command will always return you to the parent directory of the directory you have been using. This is not necessarily the root directory, though it is one step closer to the root directory.

- If you use the DOSSHELL you can change directory by moving the cursor to the directory name (using the mouse or the cursor keys) and clicking the mouse button or pressing the ENTER key.

To move from any directory to a child of that directory, using MS-DOS directly, type:

CD dirname

- using the name of the child directory, with no backslash mark.

Moving from a directory to another directory that is neither a parent nor a child requires you to go back to a common parent; often as far as the root. The path is the set of directories that you visit on the way from one directory to another. Using DOSSHELL, you simply move the cursor to the directory you want and click the mouse button or press the ENTER key.

The most straightforward path to a set of files is from the root to any branch that stems from that root. You do not start with the backslash symbol if you are starting from a branch along a path, only when you start from the root, or if you need to go back to the root. For example, if you are in the subdirectory WORDS and you want to find BOOKS, a child directory of WORDS, you need only type:

CD BOOKS

- though you would need to use CD\WORDS\BOOKS if you had been in the root directory. You must start a path description with the backslash if you are going along any path that includes the root.

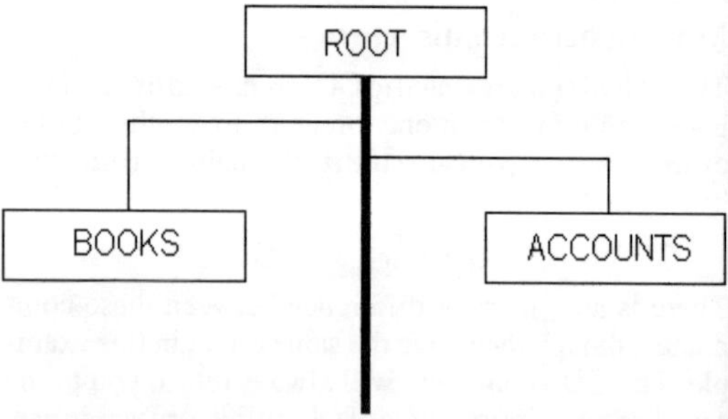

Figure 4.7
A path that involves moving back to the root. BOOKS is neither a parent nor a child of ACCOUNTS, so that the CD command must place the root symbol \ as the first step in the path.

As the illustration of Figure 4.7 shows, the path from BOOKS to ACCTS requires moving by way of the root directory, so that it needs CD\ACCTS. The search for a subdirectory covers only the one layer below the directory you are presently using, the children of that directory. It is always much easier to return to the root directory from any subdirectory, because this requires only the command CD \, using the backslash to mean the root directory.

Having seen that we can create new sub-directories and transfer to them, using MD and CD, the next step is how to make use of the files that are located in the various subdirectories. If this is your first experience of a hard disk then, before you start to transfer your own files from floppies, it's best to try out the principles using dummy files of text or files for which you have adequate backups.

You can create large numbers of directories, which can be in the layer immediately below the root directory, or in further layers, subdirectories of subdirectories. There is a practical limit to the number of layers you can use, determined by the number of characters in the path being limited to 63. This, however, can allow you to use up to eight layers and it would be unusual to need this number. For most purposes, two or three layers are quite sufficient.

The purpose of using the subdirectory structure is to make it easier to group your files, and the purpose is defeated if, to gain access to a file, you have to type something like:

```
\CD ROOT\layer2\layer3\layer4\layer5
```

Once again, this points out the importance of planning your use of the hard disk so that the groupings are logical and useful, and so that you do not feel the need for too many layers. The DOSSHELL allows you to create and find your way around the subdirectories very much more easily than by the use of the MD and CD commands.

How you organise these layers of subdirectories is very often up to you. Some programs that you buy will organise the directory structure for you, but others give you a completely free hand to arrange these things for yourself. It is quite likely that you will want to change the structure of your directories as you add programs and data to your hard disk, depending on how well you planned the operation in the first place.

For example, you might start by placing a word processor in a subdirectory called WORDS, and at the same time place a few utilities that you use along with your word processor in the same subdirectory. If you had only a few text files, you might very well place them in the same subdirectory.

As your use of the disk expands, however, you would soon find that your WORDS directory display was getting out of hand. Your text files might include internal memoranda, external letters and articles for some trade magazines. Your first reaction might be to place all of these in a subdirectory of WORDS called TEXT, creating the structure shown in Figure 4.8. This might suffice for a short time, but could not be a lasting solution, and a much better scheme would be to create three subdirectories from WORDS, called, perhaps, BOOKS, LETTERS and ARTICLES. This gives the structure which was shown in Figure 4.5.

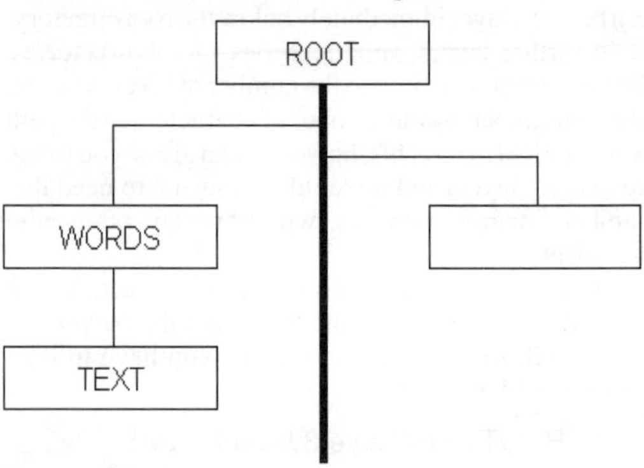

Figure 4.8
A first attempt at using a sub-directory, with TEXT being used to contain all of the word-processing documents that you create.

You could then, of course, create further subdirectories if you needed them. You might make a subdirectory called MEMO contain no text files, but only the further subdirectories MEMO91, MEMO92, MEMO93 and so on. Whether or not this is a good idea depends very much on how you work, and the fact that you can technically organise work in this way does not mean that it is an advantage to do so. Remember the old adage about putting too many eggs in one basket, because a hard disk, though less fragile than eggs or baskets, can be corrupted and can lose data.

Since all the programs that you have on your hard disk will have been transferred from the original floppy disks, which you will keep in a safe place, loss of programs is less important than loss of data, however remote the possibility of either event. Keeping backups is like insurance; you probably don't need it, but you'll be very grateful for it if you ever do need it. A good scheme is to keep backup copies of text, account or other data files on floppies, so that all the files from \WORDS\MEMO at the end of a year would be transferred to a floppy disk (or disks), and the MEMO subdirectory would be cleared ready for the next year's files.

In this way, the data on the hard disk is the current year's data only, and even this would be backed up on to floppy disk at regular intervals. Older data can be stored in archive form, or by using the DBLSPACE option on floppy disks (see later).

■ For large quantities of data such as test data the use of optical read/write disks is a perfect solution, allowing much faster access to data than tape streamers. The recent 150 - 500 Mbyte optical drives are well suited to industrial and business users; the smaller 21 Mbyte floptical drives to smaller business uses and for domestic use.

Continuing this example, you might want to treat your ARTICLES files differently because you might want to take material from an article typed in '91 to use in an article in '93. In this case it would be a considerable advantage to have subdirectories such as ART91, ART92, ART93 and so on to hold the article copy for each year. Such material is then easier and quicker to copy than it would be from floppy disks, though you would as a matter of course, always hold backup copies on floppy disks.

Book authors might want to keep everything that they had published on the same hard disk so as to make it easier to refer to a previous work. For office uses, it is certainly an advantage to keep external letters in year-by-year files for easy access.

Extended filenames

If a program file is placed in the root directory (which is not recommended), and you are using the root directory, the program can be run in the usual way simply by typing its name and pressing the ENTER key. Similarly, if you want to run a program that is in a sub-directory, you could move to that subdirectory by using CD followed by the path names, for example:

CD \UTILS

and then typing the name of the program and pressing the ENTER key. When you do this, the computer will be using the sub-directory when the program ends; it does not return to the root directory.

You can, however, remain in the root directory if you call the program by using an extended filename, meaning a filename that includes a path. For example, if you use:

\UTILS\WRDCOUNT

you can run a program called WRDCOUNT which is in the UTILS subdirectory, and then return to the root directory when this program is completed. The filename will show the full pathway to the program file, just as was required in the CD command. This enhancement of the filename to include the pathway through the directory is used also by other commands, such as DIR, COPY, DEL, RENAME and many others, allowing you to carry out actions on files that are not in the directory that you are currently using and allowing you to return to the current directory afterwards.

■ Note, however, that REN (or RENAME) allows the use of a path only to the old filename, and the new name will be placed in the same subdirectory as the old filename. See also the description of MOVE in Chapter 5.

Use COPY if you want to place a file from one subdirectory into another, remembering that COPY can also carry out renaming. For example, using:

COPY \WORDS\TEXT\art5.txt \OLDTXT\txt87.txt

will copy a file called 'art5.txt' from the TEXT subdirectory of WORDS into the OLDTXT subdirectory, using the changed filename of 'txt87.txt'. Figure 4.9 shows this move in diagrammatic form.

There is the same restriction on the extent of this full filename as there is on subdirectory layers. No path instruction from the root directory to the lowest subdirectory can use more than 63 characters, so that the number of levels is usually limited to eight. The name length for a subdirectory is limited to a maximum of 8 characters in the main name, and longer names will be chopped down to this limit.

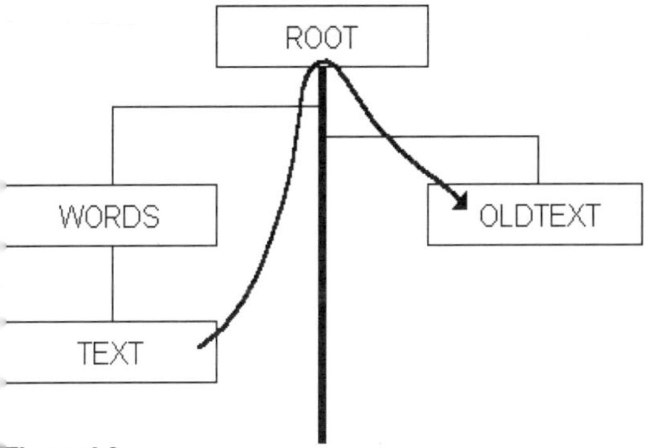

Figure 4.9
A diagrammatic view of a COPY action from one sub-directory to another, using a path through the Root.

Most users find the 8-character limit slightly restrictive. If you like, you can add a three-letter (or smaller) extension to the name of a sub-directory, using a dot to separate the 8-character main name from the extension of up to three characters. Remember that this full name will have to be typed when you use commands such as CD and when you use the directory path in a full filename.

The PATH command

We have seen that a program can be run from MS-DOS by:

1. Using the CD command to move to the directory that holds the program and then typing the program name, or
2. Typing the extended filename which includes a path.

There is a third method, which should be reserved for programs that you will want to run without needing to think where they are located, your most essential programs. This requires the use of a PATH command.

When a program name is typed and the ENTER key pressed, the machine tries to find the program in the directory that you are currently using. In the normal way of things, if the program cannot be found an error message is delivered and the machine waits for another command. The PATH command contains a list of other directories that should be searched if a program cannot be found in the current directory. You can, by using a PATH command, gain access to program files of the EXE, COM or BAT kind, which you would normally activate by typing the full path and name, or by going to the appropriate directory and typing the name alone.

Whatever you specify using PATH, the program that you are looking for will always be searched for in the current subdirectory first of all. It is always an advantage to start a PATH list with C:\. to ensure that the root directory of the hard disk will be searched (even if you have been using a floppy disk). The next most important directory to place in the list is C:\MSDOS, or wherever your MSDOS files are located, so that a typical PATH line would be:

PATH C:\;C:\MSDOS

separating the directory specifications by a semicolon.

Though the PATH command can be used at any time while you are working with MS-DOS, it is greatly preferable to place it in the AUTOEXEC.BAT file, so that the command will be run automatically each time the computer is booted. Using the PATH command will supersede all previous PATH commands.

To check by a listing on the screen what path you are currently using, type:

PATH (ENTER).

To close down all paths, type:

PATH;.

To specify several directories that are to be searched, remember that you must separate the paths by semicolons, for example:

PATH \WORDS;\ACCTS;\UTILS

which in this example will specify that when you need a program file the WORDS directory will be searched first, then the ACCTS directory, then the UTILS directory. The number of directories to be searched should be kept to a minimum, otherwise the search time will increase unduly, defeating the object of using PATH in the first place.

■ Many programs that are installed using a SETUP or INSTALL utility will alter the PATH line in your AUTOEXEC.BAT file, adding a path to the main files of the program. You need to watch for this action as it can make your PATH line unwieldy after a time.

Copying files to directories

When you are setting a hard disk for the first time, the most tedious action is the copying of files to the hard disk from floppies. Since it all has to be done, it make sense to make sure that the directories that you create are well-suited to your use of the disk.

Files can be copied using the COPY command of MS-DOS, but this can be slow and tedious because you need to check from the floppy disk directory what files need to be copied and issue separate commands unless all of the files are to be copied using COPY *.* C:

Remember that the command COPY A:*.* C:\ will copy all of the files from the disk in the A drive to the root directory of the hard disk. COPY A:*.* C:, with no backslash, will copy all of the files from the disk in the A drive to *whatever directory on the hard disk you are currently logged into*. If in doubt, always specify what hard drive directory you want to use as the destination of the files.

■ This type of action is much easier to carry out using the DOSSHELL, see Chapter 8. If you are working without DOSSHELL, remember that you can recall a previous DOS command, particularly if you use DOSKEY, see Chapter 7.

Not all programs can be made to run from a hard disk simply by copying their files from a floppy disk. In some cases, the programs will have to be re-installed, and backup copies of the original program distribution disks will have to be used, and a hard-disk setup or installation program run. Some of these installation programs will automatically create directories on the hard disk, other require you to have created directories before you run the programs. Check carefully from the program setup instructions.

Listing Files

The use of directory trees considerably alters the way in which you can make lists of your program and data files. When you have just switched on the machine, a DIR command will provide a list of whatever is in the root directory, and if you have organised things efficiently, this will consist of subdirectory names only, plus a few vital files.

Given a clean root display, you can then select a branch to look at, and by using a command such as:

DIR \WORDS\BOOKS

you can obtain a listing of all the files in this particular subdirectory. For most purposes, this will be all that you will need, and you can use the Ctrl-P sequence to make the listing appear on the printer as well as on the screen.

Every now and again, however, you need more than this, and you want to find how your disk is organised.

The problem is how you can tell what the structure of a directory is, assuming that you haven't drawn up a plan like that of the examples in this Chapter at the time when you started to put data on to the disk. In some cases, the structure may have been created in a rather haphazard way, and you will eventually start to wonder just what exists on the disk.

```
Directory PATH listing for Volume HARDDI
Volume Serial Number is 1A36-730A
C:.
├───MSDOS
├───OLD_DOS.1
├───BATS
├───WINDOWS
│   ├───SYSTEM
│   ├───TEMP
│   ├───MSAPPS
│   │   ├───MSGRAPH
│   │   ├───WORDART
│   │   ├───MSDRAW
│   │   ├───EQUATION
│   │   └───GRPHFLT
│   ├───WPWIN
│   ├───WPC
│   ├───TAP
│   │   ├───DOCS
│   │   └───TOOLS
│   ├───PUBLISHW
│   │   ├───STYLES
│   │   ├───DTP
-- More --
```

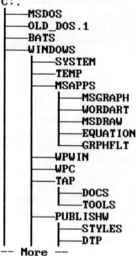

Figure 4.10

Part of a TREE command output as seen on screen. The root line is at the left-hand side of the screen with each successive layer of directories moved to the right.

MS-DOS 6.0 has a TREE command that will display the directory tree structure, and the form of output is illustrated in Figure 4.10. The TREE command can be used in two forms, one of which produces a list of subdirectories only, the other of which gives filenames as well. The default is to show subdirectory names only. If only subdirectories are shown this is useful as a summary of the directories that you have present, but if you want to have a complete list of all files on the disk, you need to add /F following the command. For example, the command:

\TREE C:/F

(assuming that TREE is available from the current directory, or is in a path that is searched) would produce a list with the filenames in each subdirectory shown as well as the subdirectory names. If the tree is a large one, as is almost inevitable, you can add |MORE to page the output. A simpler way of seeing the directory tree is to use the DOSSHELL, see Chapter 8.

You should also print, at intervals, lists of the files in each subdirectory. These can be obtained by using CD to get to the appropriate directory and then using DIR to list the files only. You will also see the parent and child entries, symbolised by the dots.

Deleting a directory

The most difficult part of using a directory tree consists of closing down a directory that you no longer need. This might be done because you have found a better way to organise your directories, or because the programs in the directory have been superseded by others.

A root directory cannot be deleted, and you cannot delete the subdirectory that you are currently using, so it's always desirable to start any deletion operations from the root directory. If, taking the conventional example, you wanted to close the BOOKS sub-directory, you would first have to DEL each file in this directory, using:

```
DEL WORDS\BOOKS\*.TXT
```

using the path to the files and using the wildcard so that each file is deleted, assuming that each file has the extension of TXT. You could, of course, use *.* to represent any file in this subdirectory, in which case you will be prompted to confirm that you really want to delete all of the files.

Only after all the files in a subdirectory have been erased can the subdirectory itself be deleted, using RD BOOKS, not DEL BOOKS. RD is short for RMDIR (remove directory), and it cannot, remember, be applied to the directory you are presently using. In other words, you cannot remove sub-directory BOOKS if you are working in this directory, you must work either from the root directory or from another sub-directory which is not a child (or any other descendent) of BOOKS, in this example.

The requirement to empty the directory of all files before deleting it can sometimes be a nuisance, though it does offer a considerable safeguard against deleting valuable files by making you consider all the files that have to be deleted. You can, however, short-circuit all this work by using the DELTREE command which will clear out a directory and delete it in one command. This utility should be used very carefully because it can be very destructive. My favourite nightmare is of using DELTREE when in the C:\ root directory.

A directory can also be renamed, an action which became available with MS-DOS 5.0. You can also alter directory attributes using the ATTRIB command (see Chapter 5), so that a directory can be made Read-only, Hidden, System or Archive. The MOVE command (see Chapter 5) will also rename a directory or move files from one directory to another.

Backing up a hard disk

MS-DOS 6.0 contains new MSBACKUP utility that is a very greatly improved version of the old BACKUP and RESTORE. There is still a RESTORE command that will read disks made by some older versions of BACKUP. If you have just installed MS-DOS 6.0 into your computer, you should as soon as possible configure the MSBACKUP command, even if you do not intend to use it right away. Configuration sets up and tests the command so that you can be certain that if a full backup is needed it will be successful.

■ Backup exists in two forms, the DOS form (MSBACKUP) and the Windows form (MWBACKUP). If your computer contains a copy of Windows, only the Windows Backup will probably be available for use, depending on your choices when you installed MS-DOS 6.0. If your computer does not contain a copy of Windows, only the DOS Backup will be available. See Chapter 10 for the Windows-specific versions. You can later install the 'wrong' version and use it if you want to.

The DOS form of BACKUP will be unconfigured when it is placed on the hard disk, and your first action is to configure it and test it, using the built-in compatibility test. If you have been using DOSSHELL, exit from it and continue as follows when the C:\> prompt appears:

1. Start by typing MSBACKUP and pressing ENTER. If this is the first time MSBACKUP has run you will be asked to Start Configuration - the only alternative is Quit. Click on Start (or press ENTER).

2. You are shown a display of machine configuration, Figure 4.11. This will almost always be correct, but if you are using a monochrome monitor make sure that this is listed, not the Colors1 or Colors2.

Figure 4.11
The Machine configuration display of MSBACKUP, which provides an analysis of the way your computer is set up.

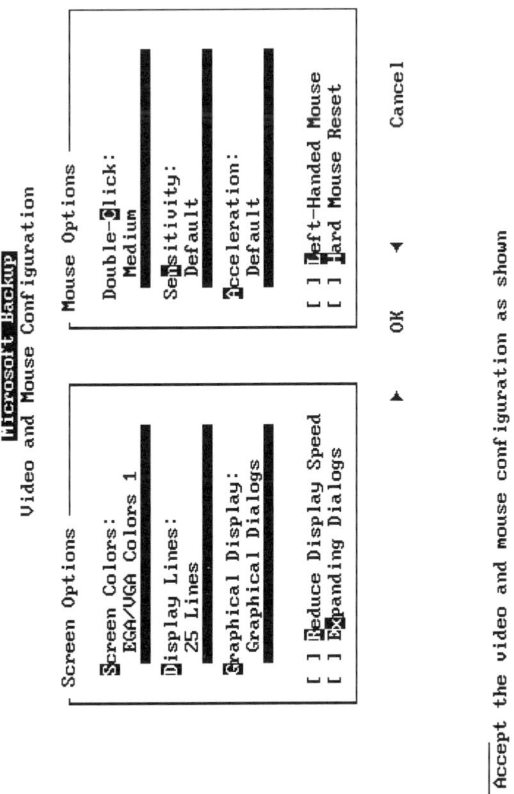

3. You are then asked to remove all floppy disks from the drive(s) so that Backup can determine how to detect when a disk has been changed. When this has been done you are asked to confirm the floppy disk configuration, Figure 4.12.

4. This is followed by a processor speed test which takes about half a minute. Following this you are asked to run the compatibility test. This test is automated, and when it runs you will see menus appear, selections made and confirmed and actions started without any need for you to do anything. Your only action is to feed in floppy disks. For the test, two 3.5" 1.4 Mbyte disks or their equivalent will be needed.

Figure 4.12
Confirming the floppy drive configuration - in this case the machine has both 5.25" and 3.5" drives, both high density.

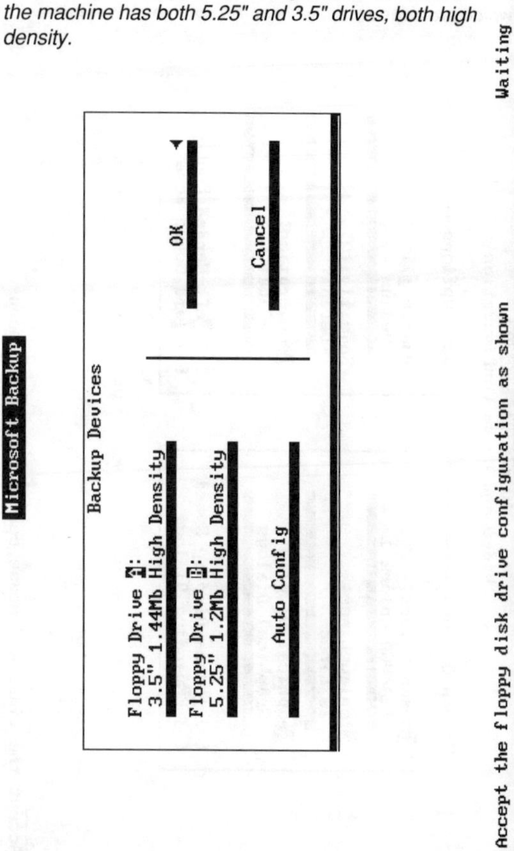

5. Click with the mouse cursor on Start Test (or press ENTER when this option is highlighted). When you are asked, select the floppy drive you want to use, and the disk density, Figure 4.13. After a short time you will be asked to insert a disk and the backup process will start. If there are files on the floppy disk, you are warned that they will be erased and you are given the chance to replace the disk. You can use an unformatted floppy as a backup disk if you want to, but this takes longer because the disk will be formatted as the backup is made.

6. The screen display will show the progress of the test backup. You will be asked to change disks when the first

'igure 4.13
;pecifying the drive and the disk density to be used for ıe Compatibility test.

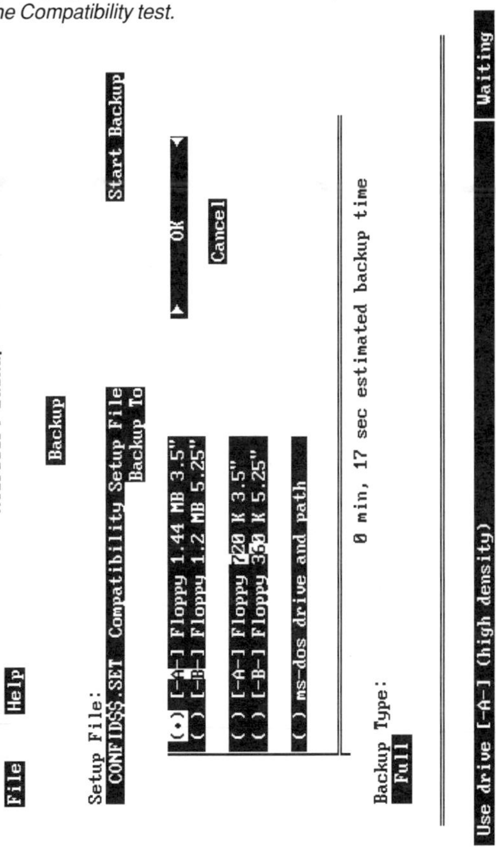

isk is full - the drive light remains on during this time nless you wait too long. When the backup is over you ave to click to confirm, and the recovery process then tarts.

. You will be asked to put the first disk in the drive gain and click on Continue. This starts the Restore ction and you will be asked to change disks at the ppropriate time. You are informed when the Compat- ɔility test is satisfactorily completed by an announce- ıent that pops up on top of the previous screen display, 'igure 4.14.

:. On the next screen that appears, click on Save, and n the last screen click on Quit. Backup can now be used

Figure 4.14
The end of the test announcement which pops over the main menu of MSBACKUP.

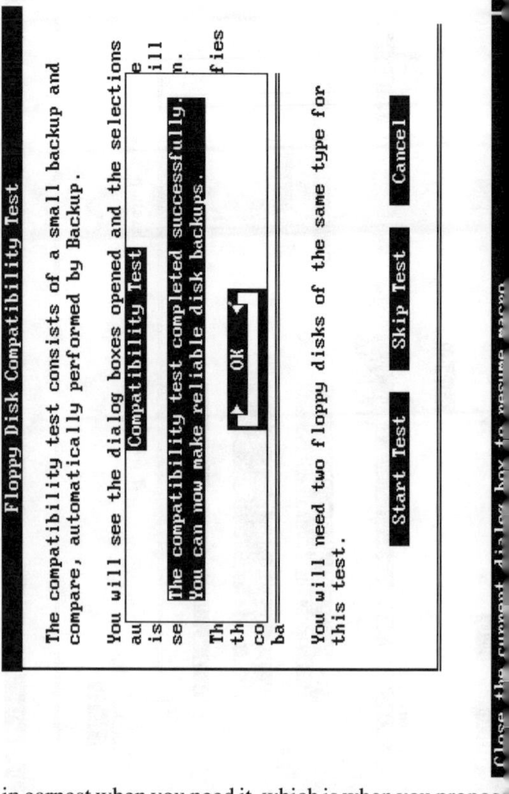

in earnest when you need it, which is when you propose to make any changes to your hard disk system such as defragmenting it or installing DBLSPACE.

The compatibility test uses no form of compression but when you make a backup in earnest the option to compress data is on by default, and this uses much the same compression as Doublespace - 1.9 Mbyte of files will fit easily on a 1.2 Mbyte floppy, for example.

- Note that you **cannot** use for MSBackup a floppy that has been compressed using DBLSPACE, see later. Such a floppy has DBLSPACE files on it and is seen by Backup as a used disk. If you opt to use such a disk the Doublespace files will be wiped and the disk will be treated as a normal disk.

Figure 4.15
The 'number of disks' figure in this display shows why so many users prefer a tape or floptical backup system.

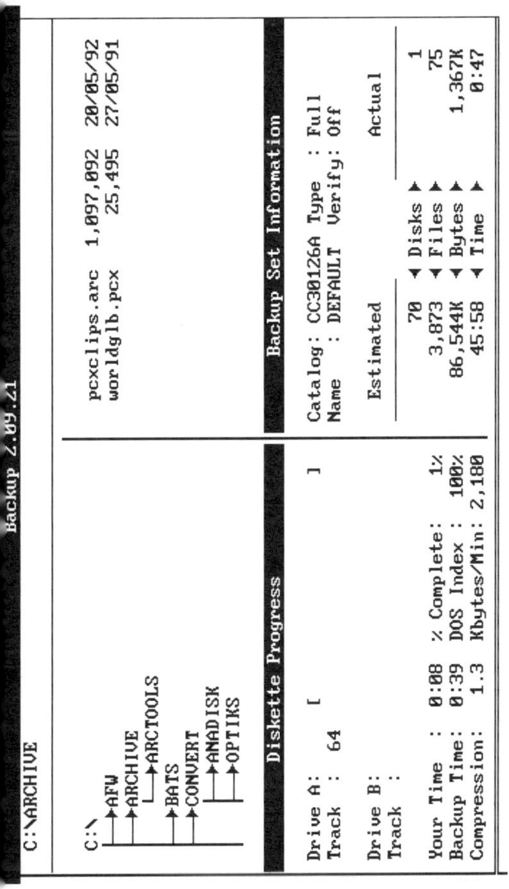

To use MSBackup for a total backup you start the program from MS-DOS, not from DOSSHELL or WINDOWS. Prepare a large number of disks, any label them with sequential numbers. The procedure is:

1. On the initial screen, select the drive you want to backup, usually the C: drive. Double-click to see the full file list. Select the floppy drive and disk type. The top right box which contain the phrase start backup will change to Start Backup when you are ready to start. Click on this.

2. You will be asked to insert the first floppy, and warned if it contains any data The display will show the estimated number of disks required - 70 in this example, Figure 4.15. If you do not have this number of floppies you can opt to cancel the backup.
3. Change disks as prompted until the last disk has been used. The estimated number may change as the backup progresses (often to a smaller number than was originally estimated).
4. Use the Quit option when the MSBACKUP screen returns, and place the backup disks in a safe place.

Partial Backup

A full backup is a time-consuming and floppy-consuming process unless you are working with 21 Mbyte (or larger) Floptical disks with the compression option of Backup in use. Backup, however, allows you a large range of choices:
1. You can opt for Full, Incremental or Differential backup. An Incremental backup backs up only the files that have changed since the last backup (full or incremental). The archive bit for each file is reset. A Differential backup backs up all files that have changed since the last full backup, plus any other files you select, but does not change the archive bits, so that the next differential backup will save the same set of files plus any others that have changed.
2. You can also opt to save all marked files, and when you take this option you are presented with a file list, Figure 4.16, on which you can tick files to be saved. The Special option allows you to backup files in a specified date range, or to exclude files such as Copy Protected files, Read-only files, System file or Hidden files. The Display option allows you to sort files by Name, Extension, Size, Date or Attribute, or to use wildcards to describe a set of files such as *.PCX.
3. The Options are illustrated in Figure 4.17 - avoid password protection unless you are certain that you can remember a meaningless password (if it means anything to you then it can be guessed by someone else).

Unformat and Undelete

Unformatting

One type of hard disk disaster which is rather more difficult to live with is reformatting the whole of the disk by accident. If you are in Drive C:, as you will be most of the time, then it's remarkably easy to type FORMAT

Figure 4.16
The File List which allows you to select files for selective backup.

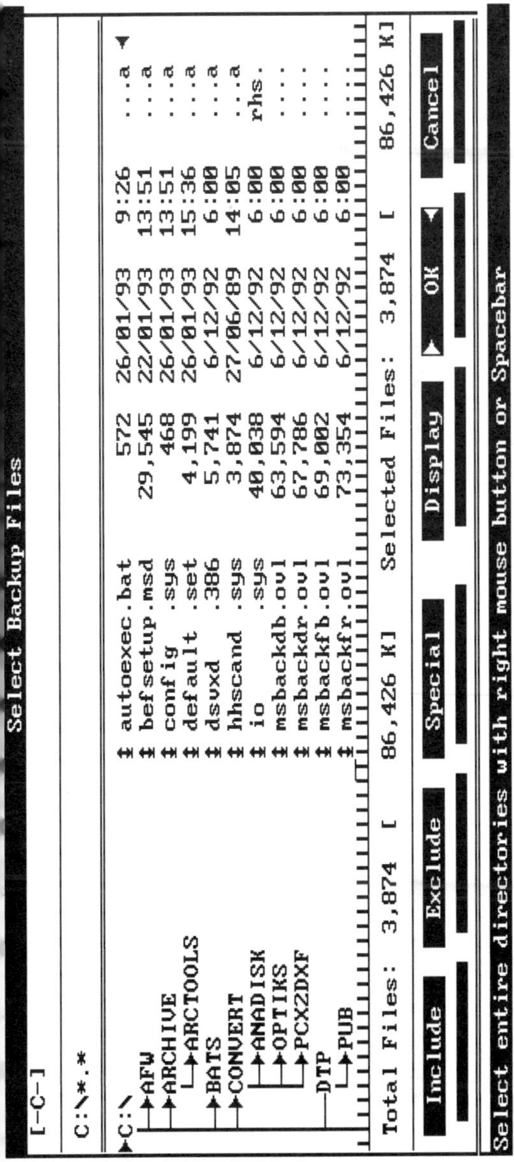

Figure 4.17
The Backup options - the defaults are sensible but your own needs might require you to alter some of these options.

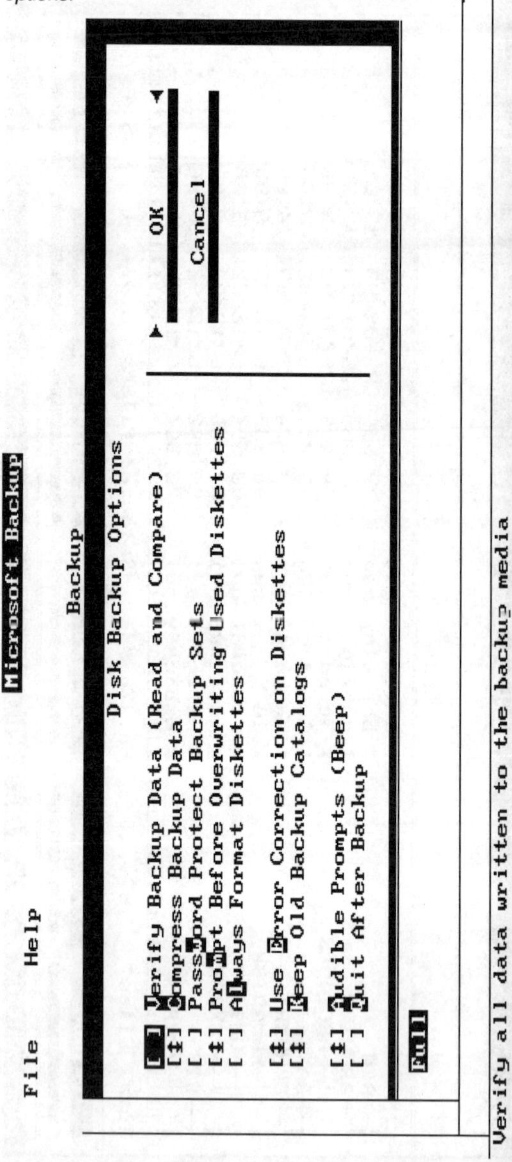

and press ENTER when you want to format a floppy in Drive A. One remedy is to make sure that the FORMAT.EXE program is not on your hard disk. Another safeguard is to carry out formatting using the Hard Disk Utilities Program Group of DOSSHELL. This will format a disk in drive A by default, and you would have to type C: in place of A: in order to format the hard disk. No matter how hard we try, though, mistakes can be made, particularly after midnight. The formatting of a hard disk makes all the files disappear from the directory, but unlike the unconditional formatting of a floppy the actual data is not replaced on the disk, only the root directory and FAT (File Allocation Table) data. You can therefore use an UNFORMAT utility that will give you some scope to recover files.

Unformatting in its simplest form does not restore the disk exactly as it was, though it can restore the directory structure and many of the files. What it cannot do is restore a file that was split up and stored in several different locations. For such a file all you can get is a set of 4 Kbyte files, each of which you have to work on. If these were program files, forget it, you must surely have a backup, but if they were data files then you can read them into your word processor one by one until you can assemble a complete file and record it. The work is tedious, but it will remind you to be careful about formatting. Never attempt to run a program file that has been made up from rescued fragments - its behaviour cannot be predicted and is most unlikely to be correct.

■ If you use the DEFRAG utility frequently there is less chance that important files will be fragmented - see later this Chapter.

As usual, MS-DOS 6.0 is better equipped than earlier versions to cope with the situation of an unintended format. There is an UNFORMAT command and if it is used correctly the disk, hard or floppy, can be restored, subject to one condition. The format must not have used FORMAT /U, which is the unconditional format command. Using FORMAT /U totally destroys any information that previously existed, and should be used only on a new disk, or a disk which has been reporting read and write errors and for which backups have been taken.

UNFORMAT can be used only under DOS, and if you have been using Windows or DOSSHELL you must be certain that you have closed these shell programs down before you attempt to use UNFORMAT.

1. Type UNFORMAT A: /TEST first, with a floppy in the drive. This will show what UNFORMAT will do, but does not actually carry out the actions. If you are working on a floppy drive you will be asked to insert a disk. The process can be a very lengthy one even for a floppy disk, so allow plenty of time (20 minutes or more for a 1.4 Mbyte floppy).

■ If you see a message referring to MIRROR you can ignore it - MIRROR was the name of the file undelete system used in MS-DOS 5.0; MS-DOS 6.0 uses two systems called delete-tracking and SENTRY. The delete-tracking system is the same as the MIRROR type of system.

2. When you have some idea of what UNFORMAT will do, you can use the command without the /TEST option. UNFORMAT must be followed by the drive letter of the drive you have accidentally formatted.

3. As UNFORMAT works it will show the directories of the disk. If you add the /L option you will see the filenames as well. You can also add /P to send all messages to the printer.

Undelete actions

MS-DOS 6.0 offers three layers of protection against the accidental loss of files because of unintended deletion. The lowest level depends on the fact that when a file is deleted its disk directory entry is changed (the first character of the name is replaced) but the data of the file is not deleted. Other levels depend on keeping a file of information about deletions. There are separate MS-DOS and Windows versions of UNDELETE, see Chapter 10 for the Windows version.

■ No form of undelete can be expected to be useful if a large number of new files have been saved since you deleted a file, because the space is likely to have been re-used. That said, you can sometimes be lucky and you might feel that you have nothing to lose.

The default system of protection is the lowest level, DOS, but when you use UNDELETE as a command the highest level, Sentry, will be tried first, followed by the second level, Tracking. The DOS method requires no preparation, no memory-resident program and no additional disk space. It is attractive if you maintain a good backup system and very seldom make an accidental deletion. It is also more suitable for un-delete actions on floppy disks. The higher levels of undelete are useful if your computer is shared with other users and unintended deletions are frequent. The Sentry system requires a memory-resident program (installed in AUTOEXEC.BAT) along with a disk file (limited to a maximum size of 7% of your hard disk) and the Tracker system needs only the memory-resident program, but no disk space.

- Do not expect UNDELETE for MS-DOS to deal with deleted sub-directories, or with files in deleted sub-directories. See Chapter 10 for the Windows version.

The use of UNDELETE with no parameters will start the Undelete action on the current drive and directory. For many purposes this is as much as you need. Figure 4.18 shows a typical screen output for UNDELETE A:. For each file that is found and reported as able to be recovered you are asked to press Y to confirm that you want to recover the file, and you also need to supply the first character of the filename.

Figure 4.18

A typical screen report on the Undelete action that will use MS-DOS directory un-deletion.

```
C:\>undelete a:

UNDELETE - A delete protection facility
Copyright (C) 1987-1993 Central Point Software, Inc.
All rights reserved.

Directory: A:\
File Specifications: *.*

Delete Sentry control file not found.

Deletion-tracking file not found.

MS-DOS directory contains    2 deleted files.
Of those,    2 files may be recovered.

Using the MS-DOS directory method.

   ?PRDTOC   DOC     17223 12/06/92 20:29  ...A  Undelete (Y/N)?y
   Please type the first character for ?PRDTOC  .DOC: A

File successfully undeleted.

   ?TPTOC    DOC     10525 13/06/92 10:01  ...A  Undelete (Y/N)?
```

You can specify by using a wildcard form of filename that UNDELETE is to restore only files of a particular specification. For example, you can use:

UNDELETE C:\PCXFILES*.PCX

to specify that only files in this directory and with the PCX extension letters should be restored.

The simplest options for UNDELETE are /DOS, /DT and /DS. If you add /DOS following the drive/path data you are requesting UNDELETE to use **only** the DOS system illustrated above, avoiding the messages about the other options. This option will be ignored if there is a Tracker file existing. The /DT options requests restoration of only the files that exist in the Tracker list (ignoring any others) and /DS requests restoration of only the files in the Sentry list, ignoring all others. You can use only one of these options in an UNDELETE command.

The more advanced protection options require you to add a line to the AUTOEXEC.BAT file, or to start the system by typing the line as a direct command.

The **Tracker** system will be installed by using a line such as:

UNDELETE /TC-200

which will keep track of deleted files up to a maximum of 200 on the C drive. If you omit the number, a default will be assigned. The default number depends on the disk size and is 303 for disks of 32 Mbyte and over, less for smaller hard and floppy disks. The range of numbers that can be used is 1 to 999. The drive letter must be specified.

■ Users of MS-DOS 5.0 will recognise this method as it was used by the MIRROR system.

When you try this out on a floppy disk you will see a screen output such as that of Figure 4.19. The first letter does not need to be supplied this time, and you only need to confirm whether or not you want each file restored.

The **Sentry** system is installed by using a line such as:

UNDELETE /SC

which in this example sets up Sentry for Drive C. When files have been deleted, using UNDELETE /DS will produce a screen output of the form shown in Figure 4.20 (for a floppy). Once again, you need to confirm whether or not you want to restore a named file.

Figure 4.19
A typical Tracker report on deleted files. You do not need to supply the first letter of the deleted file.

```
C:\>undelete a:

UNDELETE - A delete protection facility
Copyright (C) 1987-1993 Central Point Software, Inc.
All rights reserved.

Directory: A:\
File Specifications: *.*

   Delete Sentry control file not found.

   Deletion-tracking file contains    2 deleted files.
   Of those,      2 files have all clusters available,
                  0 files have some clusters available,
                  0 files have no clusters available.

   MS-DOS directory contains    2 deleted files.
   Of those,      2 files may be recovered.

Using the Deletion-tracking method.

      ATPTOC   DOC    10525 13/06/92 10:01  ...A  Deleted: 27/01/93 10:13
All of the clusters for this file are available.  Undelete (Y/N)?
```

Options

The UNDELETE direct command, particularly when either of its two higher levels have been installed, can be used with a number of options. You can use one of three options between UNDELETE and the drive letter:

/LIST will list the deleted files and indicate which can be recovered, but no recovery will be carried out. This can be used with all three levels of Undelete protection.

/ALL will recover all deleted files without the need to confirm. This is best used when you are working in a specified directory and with a named extension. If Sentry or Tracker is in use the files will be recovered with the correct names, but if only DOS recovery is used, the program will supply a first character of #. If this would result in two files bearing the same name, other characters will be substituted in order of:

#%&123456789ABCDEFGHIJKLMNOPQRSTUVWXYZ

Figure 4.20
A typical Sentry report on deleted files. Note that you get the other levels of reports unless you opt to use Sentry only.

```
C:\>undelete a: /ds

UNDELETE - A delete protection facility
Copyright (C) 1987-1993 Central Point Software, Inc.
All rights reserved.

Directory: A:\
File Specifications: *.*

    Delete Sentry control file contains    2 deleted files.

    Deletion-tracking file contains    0 deleted files.
    Of those,    0 files have all clusters available,
                 0 files have some clusters available,
                 0 files have no clusters available.

    MS-DOS directory contains    2 deleted files.
    Of those,    0 files may be recovered.

Using the Delete Sentry method.

      ATPTOC   DOC    10525 13/06/92 10:01  ...A  Deleted: 27/01/93 10:17
This file can be 100% undeleted. Undelete (Y/N)?
```

/PURGE is used only with Sentry, and will delete the contents of the Sentry file. If no drive is provided, UNDELETE will search for it, but you can speed the process by using, for example, /PURGE :C

The options that can be used following the drive/path information for UNDELETE consist of /STATUS, / LOAD, /U, /S, /T

/STATUS will display what form of protection is available for a nominated drive.

/LOAD will load the memory-resident part of the UNDELETE program, using information contained in a file called UNDELETE.INI.

/U will unload the memory-resident UNDELETE program. This is essential if you want to change from one system to another while the computer is switched on.

/S loads in the memory-resident part of the Sentry system and provides for creating a disk file. If the file UNDELETE.INI exists it will determine the extent of protection. The S letter can specify a drive or drives, using, for example, /S:C

/T loads in the memory-resident part of the Tracker system and provides for creating a disk file. If the file UNDELETE.INI exists it will determine the extent of protection. The T letter can specify a drive or drives, using,for example, /T:C and you can also specify a maximum number of files (in the range 1 to 999) to track. For example, /TC-200 will track up to 200 deleted files on drive C.

- Note that Sentry creates a subdirectory called SENTRY which contains a file called CONTROL.FIL. Tracker creates a file called PCTRACKR.DEL, not in a separate sub-directory. Both files and the SENTRY subdirectory are hidden, and become visible if you use DOSSHELL with the option to see hidden files switched on, see Chapter 9. The SENTRY subdirectory and its files are almost impossible to delete and will survive even an unconditional FORMAT.

The form of the UNDELETE.INI file is illustrated in Figure 4.21. This shows the UNDELETE file when SENTRY has been enabled, and the meanings of the lines are as follows:

[configuration]

archive=FALSE means that files with the archive bit set will not be recovered, because you have already backed them up.

days=7 means that a file can be purged when it is more than 7 days old.

percentage=20 specifies that no more than 20% of the available disk space can be used for deleted files.

[sentry.drives]

will specify the drives on which Sentry is keeping a track. The normal entry here is C=, specifying the hard disk drive.

[mirror.drives]

An entry such as A=5 here means that Tracker is used on Drive A with up to 5 deleted files tracked.

[sentry.files]

is used to define whatever need **not** be undeleted, and the list headed by s_files= contains a list of extensions for temporary files and others which are normally deleted by the system. It is unusual to need to alter this list unless to add other extensions which you, or a program you use, needs for temporary files

[defaults]

d.sentry=TRUE means that the Sentry method is in use

d.tracker=FALSE means that the Tracker method is not in use.

Figure 4.21
The UNDELETE.INI file.

```
Display  View  Help
To view file's content use PgUp or PgDn or ↑ or ↓.
[configuration]
archive=FALSE
days=7
percentage=20
[sentry.drives]
A=
[mirror.drives]
A=5
[sentry.files]
s_files=*.* -*.tmp -*.vm? -*.woa -*.swp -*.spl -*.rmg -*.img -*.thm -*.dov
[defaults]
d.sentry=TRUE
d.tracker=FALSE
<—┘=PageDown  Esc=Cancel  F9=Hex/ASCII                                  10:41
```

You can edit UNDELETE.INI to whatever you want, though it is normally maintained correctly by the line that you use to load Sentry or Tracker protection. If you want to alter the UNDELETE.INI file, use a text-editor, or a word-processor which will save files in ASCII form.

Disk and File defragmentation

The MS-DOS 6.0 DEFRAG utility will reorganise the disk, compacting the scattered file clusters caused by deletions into blocks of continuous file and totally reorganising all of the data on the disk. As it operates, DEFRAG will save file fragments in memory and then store them into new positions on the disk.

- You would expect that any power failure during this operation would cause loss of data and loss of the stored position numbers for the data fragments, but DEFRAG is claimed to be immune from this problem, as MEMMAKER is.
- There is absolutely no chance of recovering any deleted file after a disk has been defragmented, because the space that they occupied will have been re-used.
- If you have any doubts about disk defragmentation, make sure that your disk is fully backed up. In particular, keep a system floppy disk ready in case you get a message about the System files being unavailable (Non-System Disk or Disk Error). You may have to alter your CMOS RAM settings if you have set them to avoid booting from a floppy. If you cannot boot from the hard disk after carrying out a DEFRAG, re-install MS-DOS 6.0 from the original disks. Trouble is usually due to the use of memory-resident programs during the DEFRAG action.

DEFRAG should be used when you have deleted a large number of files, or when you become aware that disk actions are taking longer and requiring a lot of disk activity. The action should be used with caution, and with some preparation. The first essential action is to quit Windows or DOSSHELL, and try to ensure that no unnecessary memory-resident programs are running. You can reboot using the F5 key at the MS-DOS Loading prompt to ensure that no memory-resident software is installed. Remember that this will prevent any PATH from being established, so that you will have to find the directory that contains DEFRAG, usually by typing CD \MSDOS.

1. You should use CHKDSK /F first to ensure that there are no detached pieces of files on the disk. Wait until this action is complete and any file fragments either deleted or converted into complete files.

Figure 4.22
The fragmentation report showing that 95% of the files are not fragmented. The display, however, shows that there are gaps between files so that the disk space is inefficiently used.

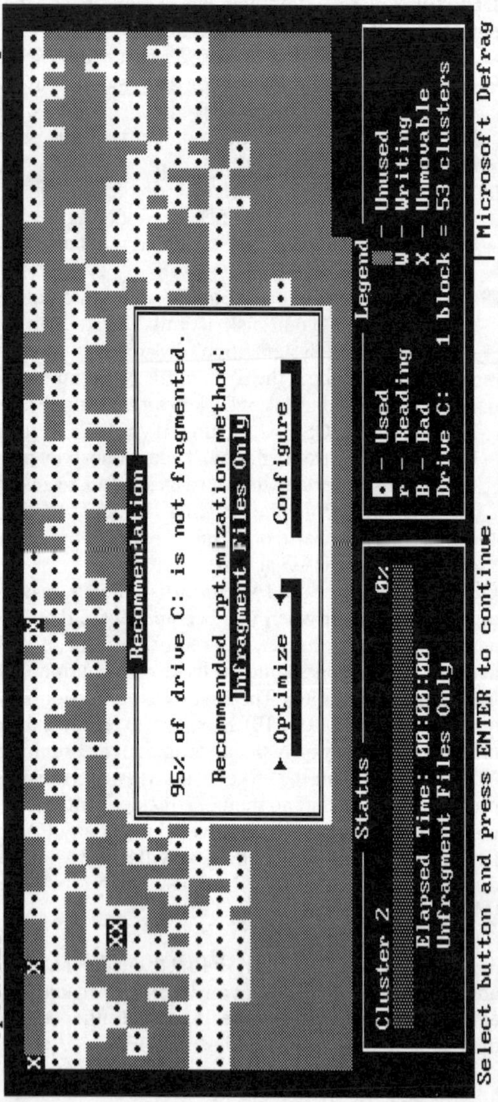

2. Type DEFRAG (ENTER). The system will (briefly) be checked, and you are asked to select which drive to defragment (optimize). You will normally select C: - there is little point in defragmenting a floppy disk.
3. The disk information is read and directories listed. You will then see the fragmentation report, Figure 4.22. Click to start the process. The process of shifting files will start, and the display illustrated what is being done.
4. If you do not want to use the recommended method, which in this example will defragment files but leave spaces between files you can click on Configure to select a method for yourself. This provides the options of Begin Optimization, Drive selection, Optimization method, File Sort, Map Legend. Full Optimization, the usual preference, takes considerably longer than the Unfragment Files only option.

■ Note that you can leave DEFRAG by pressing Alt-X. Options such as File sort can also be obtained by using the command line, see later.

5. When you opt to change the Optimization method, the process does not start until you use Begin Optimization.
6. It is often advisable, if you have had any memory-resident programs running, to re-boot the computer after using a DEFRAG. Figure 4.23 shows the results of a completed full defragmentation.

The DEFRAG program is normally loaded into Upper memory if this is available, and the recommended de-fragmentation process will depend on the result of checking the drive - the illustration shows a drive on which a large number of files have been deleted but with only a small percentage of the disk fragmented.

■ DEFRAG cannot be used over a network or over INTERLNK. The DEFRAG reports are not identical to those from CHKDSK because of differences in the way that files are counted.

DEFRAG can be used with a number of options in the command. The simplest option is to follow DEFRAG with a drive letter and colon (such as DEFRAG C:) so that the specified drive is defragmented with no need to specify in a menu. The other options follow any drive letter and are each preceded by the slash (/). Note that some options cannot be used together because they produce opposite effects.

/F Defragments files and arranges files so that there are no spaces between files.

/U Defragments files, but leaves any empty spaces that occur between files.

Figure 4.23
The results of a full compression as they are shown on the screen.

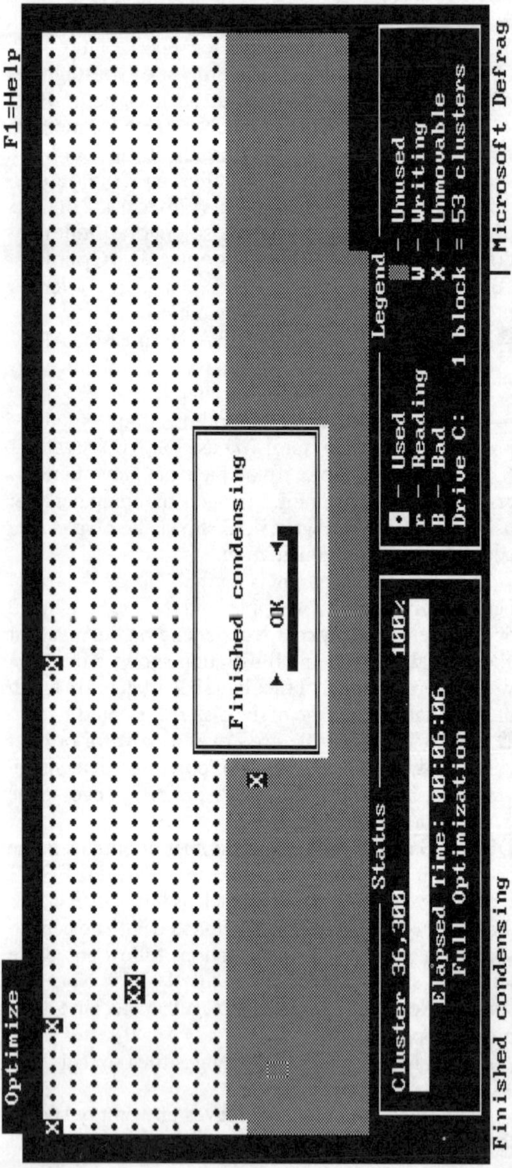

/S Defragments files and uses a sorting order determined by the following letter which must be separated by a colon or a space. In the following list the use of the colon is illustrated.

:N Alphabetical order of name
:N- Reverse alphabetical name order
:E Alphabetical order of extension
:E- Reverse alphabetical order of extension
:D Order of date and time, earliest first
:D- Order of date and time, most recent first
:S Order of size, smallest first
:S- Order of size, largest first

/B Causes the machine to re-boot after defragmentation is compete.

/V Verifies that files have been written. This slows down the DEFRAG action and does not confer any particular protection on the writing process.

/SKIPHIGH Runs DEFRAG from conventional memory, taking up space that otherwise is used for storing files, and so slowing down the action.

/LCD Uses DEFRAG in a form more visible on an LCD display.

/BW Uses DEFRAG in a form more visible on a monochrome screen display.

/G0 Disables the mouse and graphics character set for the DEFRAG display - use only if you have no mouse.

Using DBLSPACE

DBLSPACE is a form of archiving program that is permanently in use and which allows your disk space to be used more efficiently by compressing data as it is saved. The program is loaded in as the machine boots up (a line in the CONFIG.SYS file determines the position of DBLSPACE.BIN in memory) and it remains in memory, intercepting each save and load to or from the hard disk.

The use of DBLSPACE can, on average, double the amount of data that can be stored on a hard disk, at the cost of slightly slower disk access, since the compressing and decompressing actions have to be done each time. The time penalty is negligible if a good disk cache program, such as SMARTDRV.EXE, is in use. The doubling is an average - some files can be only slightly compressed, others by a greater factor. On a machine which I use for text, the factor was around 1.8. On a machine used mainly for graphics, the factor was 2.0.

There have been various space-releasing programs available before DBLSPACE, but these cannot be guaranteed to be perfectly compatible with MS-DOS. If the STACKER utility is in use, its files can be converted into DBLSPACE format when DBLSPACE is installed.

- When a drive has been established with DBLSPACE, it must be used with DBLSPACE utilities for undeleting and defragmenting. You should not attempt to use the normal UNDELETE or DEFRAG on a DBLSPACE drive, and special DBLSPACE versions of these utilities are supplied as part of the DBLSPACE program.
- Floppy drives can be double-spaced, but this requires you to use a MOUNT and UNMOUNT procedure, rather like a format, on each doubled disk each time you use it, as well as an initialisation for each doubled disk. If you do not exchange disks with other people, you can place these necessary commands in the AUTOEXEC.BAT file and gain the advantage of using floppies with a much greater file capacity. Even if you sometimes need to prepare a disk for other users, you can always turn off the Doublespace action easily and use the drive with a normal disk.
- When you use DOSSHELL, placing a normal disk into a drive and using the F5 refresh key will unmount the double-space disk; and using the drive on another disk from DOS will have the same effect. You can mount a floppy either through a direct command or by way of a batch file. If you use DOSSHELL, you will get an warning message unless you have turned off multi-tasking. If you want to run DBLSPACE actions from DOSSHELL you can write a Program Item (see Chapter 8) to do this.

As always when a major change is about to be made on a hard disk, you should ensure that the drive is fully backed up. See the entry for MSBACKUP in this Chapter, and remember that you may need a very large number of floppy disks. If you have a tape streamer or Floptical system, use it rather than backing up on floppies.

To install DBLSPACE, make sure first of all that you have fully escaped from any form of Shell program such as Windows or DOSSHELL. Ideally, you should not have any memory-resident programs running. No screenshots have been used in the following description because the PINCH program was not running.

1. You are offered the choice of Express Setup, the

default, or Custom Setup. Custom Setup is useful only for unusual circumstances, and you need to be more knowledgable about your hard disk system in order to use it. To proceed with Express Setup, press ENTER. This will create the doublespaced disk and convert all of your existing files. The procedure can be lengthy for a large hard disk.

- Note that if the disk has become almost full it will be impossible to use DBLSPACE. Back up some large files and then delete them and defragment the disk before trying again.

2. You will see a time estimate - it was 50 minutes for my 130 Mbyte hard disk. You are warned that the machine will be re-started in the course of the conversion. You are asked to press the C key to start the doublespace conversion. The time estimate which is shown on the screen may alter in the course of conversion - don't be surprised if it promises completion in 33 minutes and then alters this to 40 minutes, because the time needed depends on the structure of the files and this is unknown until compression is started.

3. CHKDSK is run automatically before the work starts. The computer re-starts and the system is checked. What is happening is that files on the disk are being compressed into one large file called DBLSPACE.000 which is held on the hard disk, but with a different drive reference letter (H in my example). The C drive can still be used as it was before and shows the normal directory. Loading a file from the C drive now causes the file to be extracted from its packed form, and saving a file to the C: drive packs the file in again.

- The C: drive is referred to as the compressed drive, and the other (imaginary) drive as the Host drive.
- A few files are left unaltered, notably the MSDOS.SYS, IO.SYS and COMMAND.COM files, and any permanent swap file used by Windows. These are placed on the Host drive, the part of the hard disk which is used also to store the compressed file.
- DBLSPACE creates hidden files which, if you work with MS-DOS or Windows will normally remain hidden. If you use DOSSHELL, however, you can opt to make hidden files visible, and if you do this it is possible to delete these files. You risk losing virtually all of your data if you delete these hidden files, so it is advisable never to work with the DOSSHELL option to make hidden files visible unless it is essential to do so.

Custom Setup

Custom Setup is not required unless you have special needs. You might want, for example, to keep half of a hard disk uncompressed, to compress a different hard disk (not the C: drive), or to decide for yourself what drive letter to allocate to the Host, or what estimate of compression ratio to use. You also have a choice of compression methods.

1. When you start Custom Setup you are asked whether you want to compress an existing drive (usually the C: drive) or a new drive. One of the main reasons for using Custom Setup is that you have added another hard drive to the machine and want to compress it.

2. You can also choose the compression methods for yourself - but until you have some experience of using compressed files you cannot really make an informed choice.

3. You can then select the drive and change the default compression settings if you want to.

4. The compression process will start when you press the C key.

Working with a compressed drive

Working with a compressed hard drive is, as far as you are concerned, just the same as working with the drive as it existed before compression, showing the same structure of directories. If you use DOSSHELL or WINDOWS you will see more drive letters appearing on the File Management screens, and you may be able to see hidden files with DOSSHELL, in which case you should use the Options menu to turn off this facility (see Chapter 8 for details of using DOSSHELL). The main differences are in the actions of undeleting and defragmenting.

Because your data now exists in the form of a huge single file, the normal CHKDSK and DEFRAG utilities are meaningless, and you should not attempt to use them. These actions are now available from DBLSPACE, either from the main menu of DBLSPACE or by way of commands.

To use these actions from the menu:

1. Leave DOSSHELL or Windows completely if you have been running either of these Shell programs and you find that you cannot use DBLSPACE from them. If you have found that DBLSPACE works from DOSSHELL or Windows, then you can use the Run

Figure 4.24
The DBLSPACE menu as it first appears, showing the main menu and the Tools menu which contains the DEFRAG and CHKDSK utilities for compressed drives.

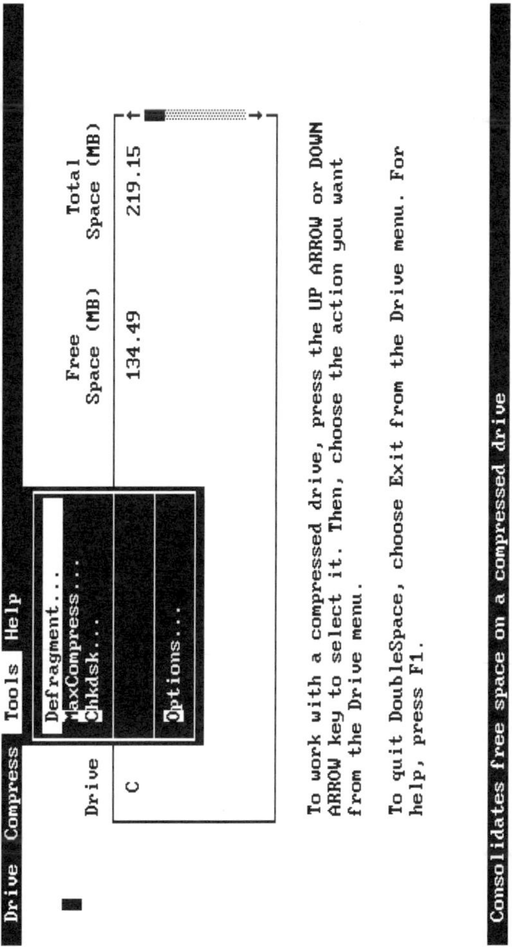

command. Type :

DBLSPACE (press ENTER).

You will see the DBLSPACE menu screen. Click on Tools to see the menu, Figure 4.24.

2. Select the action that you want, usually Defragment or Chkdsk, either by double-clicking with the mouse or moving the cursor and pressing ENTER.

The alternative is to carry out these actions by using commands from DOS directly by using option words following a DBLSPACE command. To defragment type:

DBLSPACE /DEFRAGMENT

and to check the compressed file use

DBLSPACE /CHKDSK

The full range of command line options following DBLSPACE is:

/CHKDSK to check the integrity of the compressed file. The /F option can be attached to ensure that errors are fixed.

/COMPRESS to compress the files on an existing drive, hard or floppy. A hard drive must have at least 1 Mbyte of free space, a floppy at least 200 Kbyte. The drive letter is used following the Compress (or COM) option word. For example, using:

DBLSPACE /COMPRESS A:

will compress the disk in the A: drive. You can specify a letter to use for the host drive by following COMPRESS with /NEWDRIVE=L: (for example).

You can reserve uncompressed space on a drive by using /RESERVE=1 to leave in this example 1 Mbyte of space (if possible). The default for a hard disk is 2 Mbyte uncompressed space.

/CREATE will create a new compressed file on an uncompressed drive.

The drive letter follows the /CREATE options and additional options are:

/NEWDRIVE=H to make the compressed drive use this letter

/SIZE=2 to make the compressed file fill 2 Mbytes of disk space, or

/RESERVE=2 to make the compressed file of a size that will leave 2 Mbyte free. You can specify a reserve of zero if you want to allow the compressed file to fill the drive.

■ You cannot use both /SIZE and /RESERVE in the same command.

/DEFRAGMENT will defragment the compressed file on the current Host drive. You can specify another drive letter if you want to work on another file (such as a floppy disk).

/DELETE will delete the whole compressed file contents. This will result in loss of the entire contents (which might have been the contents of your entire hard disk). You may be able to UNDELETE this file from the MS-DOS UNDELETE command. If so, you will still need to use the DBLSPACE /MOUNT command to re-mount the file so that it can be used again.

/FORMAT will format the entire compressed file as if it were a real drive.

This process destroys data, and cannot be reversed with any kind of UNFORMAT. Be warned.

/INFO displays details about the current compressed file, the space used and space free, file name, actual and estimated compression ratios.

/LIST lists and describes all the local drives. Network drives are not listed.

/MOUNT prepares to use a compressed file as a drive. A compressed file on a hard disk is normally mounted automatically, and mount needs to be used only for floppy disks and the rare case of an undeleted compressed file on a hard disk. You can use the command in the form:

/MOUNT=001

if you want to select a particular file by its number. The /NEWDRIVE=J: form of option can be used to assign a drive letter to the file when it is mounted - normally a default letter will be assigned.

/UNMOUNT disassociates a compressed file from a drive letter. The C: drive cannot be unmounted, except by deleting the file and undeleting it. The UNMOUNT option is used normally with a floppy drive when a disk is to be removed. It is not always necessary to use UNMOUNT - see earlier on the use of DOSSHELL with compressed floppies.

/RATIO allows the **estimated** compression ratio to be changed. For example, using /RATIO=1.7 will change the estimated value to 1.7. In general, you should change the estimated ratio so that it matches the known compression ration for your existing files. You can specify the drive, or use /ALL for all drives, using lines such as:

DBLSPACE /RATIO=1.7 C: or

DBLSPACE /RATIO /ALL

/SIZE allows you to alter the size of a compressed file (if it is not full). If there is free space on the disk, you can enlarge the file; or you can create more free disk space by reducing the size of the compressed file. You can specify the size you want (and the drive letter) or the reserved (uncompressed) space you want; not both together. Examples are:

DBLSPACE /SIZE=100 C:

to make the C: compressed file hold 100 Mbyte

DBLSPACE /SIZE /RESERVE=10 C:

to leave 20 Mbyte of free space.

Using DBLSPACE with floppies

The use of DBLSPACE with floppies can be a very practical way of gaining extra space for backing up file in the ordinary way (using COPY or XCOPY rather than BACKUP). Each disk that you want to use must first be converted to a DBLSPACE disk, and it has subsequently to be mounted before use and unmounted after use.

1. Place a formatted floppy in the drive you want to use for doublespace floppies. Type DBLSPACE, and from the COMPRESS menu, select Existing Drive.

2. The drives will be checked, and the drive with the floppy will appear on the list, Figure 4.25. Press ENTER to carry out the compression, and then the C key to confirm

■ As an alternative, you can use the command:

DBLSPACE /COMPRESS A:

3. The disk is now a double-space disk, and it contains a large hidden file which can be packed with data. This disk must be mounted if you want to use it as you would use an ordinary disk, and it should be unmounted after use. Note that the floppy drive is not affected. Immediately you take out the compressed floppy and use the drive for this or any other floppy the disk will be treated like any ordinary disk.

Figure 4.25
The DBLSPACE list showing a floppy drive. Note that a floppy ***drive*** *is not doublespaced, only the disk it is using at the time.*

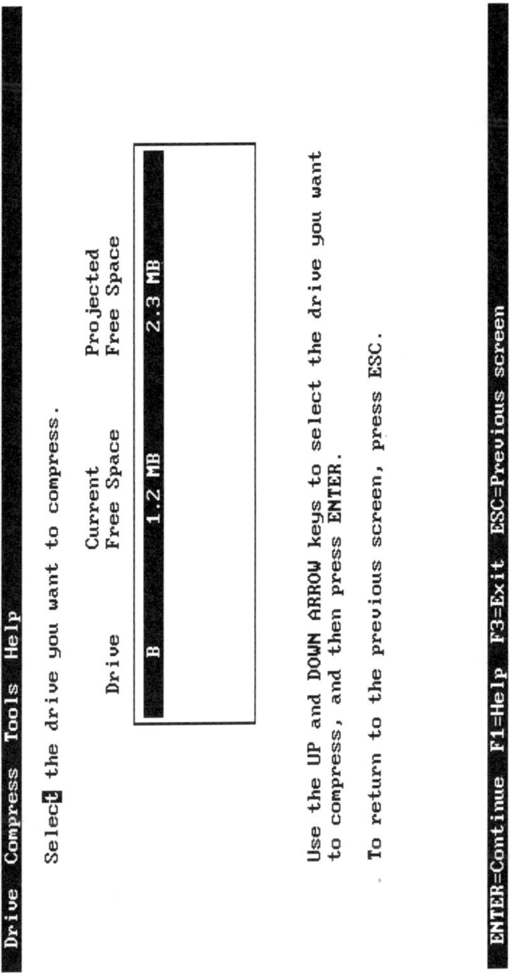

4. If you always want to work with compressed floppies, put into your AUTOEXEC.BAT file a line such as:

DBLSPACE /MOUNT A:

- or whatever drive letter you are using.

You should use:

DBLSPACE /UNMOUNT A:

before you remove the disk.

You might place these lines into batch files for programs that used the double-space disks. Good candidates are graphics programs that produce large files.

When a floppy is double-spaced, the effect is to place a file called DBLSPACE.000, size 1,457,152 bytes for a 1.4 Mbyte disk, on the disk (along with a small text file). The DBLSPACE.000 file has its System, Read-only and Hidden attributes set and is most easily dealt with using DOSSHELL with the Display Hidden/System Files option ticked. If you copy this file to any other floppy, using both floppies as if they were not doublespaced, the second floppy can be used as a doublespaced floppy.

■ This suggest a shorter way of making double-space floppies. Use CHKDISK on a newly-formatted floppy, followed by DBLSPACE /COMPRESS A: and DBLSPACE /FORMAT A: to ensure a perfect DBLSPACE.000 file. Un-mount the floppy and use DOSSHELL to copy the DBLSPACE.000 file to a directory on the hard disk. To create double-spaced floppies, just copy this file to other formatted floppies of the same type, treating them as normal floppies.

You can encounter some odd problems with compressed floppies. If you get a message to the effect that a compressed floppy cannot be mounted because of an unrecognised error #105 there are two known causes:

(a) When the floppy contains data and you have write-protected the floppy. Remove the write-protection and try again.

(b) When you have just completed another action with the drive, using a compressed floppy, and have not un-mounted the other compressed floppy. Try a DIR action on an ordinary floppy then insert the compressed floppy and use DBLSPACE /mount A: again.

■ Another point to note when working with compressed floppies is that you must not remove the floppy from the drive until all actions are completed, and the rules are not the same as for ordinary floppies. If, for example, you use DOSSHELL to mark a set of file on the hard disk and then copy these files to a compressed floppy you would consider the action over when the last file was copied. If, however, you now press the DEL key to delete the marked files on the hard disk, you will see the floppy drive light come on before the deletion takes place. If the floppy is not in the drive the delete action cannot be done without marking again.

- You can copy all the files of a compressed floppy without mounting the floppy, using the method described earlier. Using normal methods, simply copy the file DBLSPACE.000 from the compressed floppy to an ordinary formatted floppy of the same (or larger) capacity. The second floppy will now behave as a compressed floppy (which it is - the file is the compressed data).

- In some circumstances, a compressed 1.4 Mbyte floppy can hold **less** data than an uncompressed 1.4 Mbyte floppy. If, you example, you have a large number of small text files in directories on an ordinary floppy you may find that copying them to a compressed floppy with the same directory structure leads to a Disk Full message before all the files are copied. The overhead required to compress a file becomes uneconomic for small files of a few hundred bytes.

- If when you mount a floppy the drive light stays on with nothing else happening, or the machine suddenly reboots, the fault may not be in DBLSPACE. Try removing SMARTDRV (place a REM at the start of the SMARTDRV line in AUTOEXEC.BAT) and then mounting the floppy. If this now works it points to a problem with SMARTDRV.EXE. Try replacing the SMARTDRV.EXE file or, if this does not work, altering its position in AUTOEXEC.BAT. If you have recently used MEMMAKER it may have altered the EMM386 line to use HIGHSCAN, and this is causing a conflict of use of high memory. Sometimes this is indicated by locking up when you use DBLSPACE / UNMOUNT rather than with /MOUNT.

If you get a 'CRC Error' message from a double-spaced floppy it can be very difficult to recover data. This form of error is not a DBLSPACE problem but a disk-corruption problem, which is why the DBLSPACE / COMPRESS routine starts with using CHKDSK on the disk. A CRC error on an ordinary floppy can often be a minor problem if it affects only one file, but on a double-spaced floppy there is only one file. The only answer to a corrupted disk is to use a low-level disk reader program to copy the file - a text file can be copied in bits if necessary because the bits can be put together again. This can be time-consuming and should not be attempted on a program file, only on text files or other data files for which small errors will not be important.

- If you have a second hard disk, normally D:, and you double-space it, its data will be found on the host (K:, for example), with only DBLSPACE.000 on the D: drive. This is the opposite of the action on the C: drive.

5 The MS-DOS 6.0 commands

At one time, MS-DOS commands were listed in two classes, internal and external. The difference was important in the days when machines used only floppy drives, because an external command resided on the MS-DOS disk and needed this disk to be inserted before the command could be used. The internal commands are already resident in memory, as part of COMMAND.COM, when the MS-DOS system is booted up. For hard-disk users the difference is academic, because the external commands are as easily available as the external commands provided:

1. The external command files are kept in a directory, usually named as MSDOS,
2. The PATH statement in the AUTOEXEC.BAT file names the MSDOS directory.

In the following list, all commands are dealt with in alphabetical order. Commands which are dealt with in detail in other Chapters (such as those pertaining to the hard disk or to batch files, AUTOEXEC.BAT and CONFIG.SYS) have been noted but without lengthy explanations in this Chapter. Commands which are seldom used nowadays (some of which should in any case be avoided on modern systems), or which (like DEBUG, EDLIN and EXE2BIN) are intended to be used by programmers only, are not described in detail, and the internal/external classification is noted for the benefit of anyone using MS-DOS 6.0 on a floppy-only machine, such as a small lap-top, or a networked machine with a local floppy drive.

- See Chapter 2 for details of the CONFIG.SYS and notes on the AUTOEXEC.BAT instructions, and Chapter 6 for details of batch file commands, including AUTOEXEC.BAT, and their uses.
- Commands which are not intended to be used by the owner-driver are not included. An example is CHKSTATE.SYS which is used by MEMMAKER (to restore MEMMAKER after a re-boot) and is removed when MEMMAKER completes its work

APPEND External

NOTE: Must not be used with Windows or while Windows Setup is in use.

The MS-DOS command APPEND does for data files what PATH does for program files, allowing the machine to search through different drives or directories for the data file that you want. Suppose, for example, that you have created three subdirectories called TEXT, SPSHEET and DBASE for keeping word processed text, spreadsheet data and database data respectively. You will have to specify the full path and name for data that you want to save, such as NEWBOOK\chap1.txt, but with APPEND operating, you need not do so when you want to read data, since you can then specify a file name such as sheet1 and have all three subdirectories automatically searched for this file. The APPEND command uses the same syntax as the PATH command, with semicolons used to separate the different directories or drives.

Example: APPEND \TEXT;\SPSHEET;\DBASE

This example shows the three subdirectories as if they were one branch from root level, but of course you could specify items like \WP\TEXT\LETTER or \ABILITY\TEXT if you wanted to be more specific.

Like the PATH items, APPEND would normally be placed in a batch file that would be run before starting up a program that required the files to be searched. Another option to consider is that since the use of APPEND makes files available to any program that does not specifically request a path, these files are available to all programs. For example, if you specify that you want a file called B:\needed or one called \DATA\LET\jones.let then these specific files will be obtained with no reference to the APPEND list, but if you simply ask for jones.let then the current drive/directory will be searched, followed by the list specified in the APPEND command.

APPEND, used alone, will produce a listing of the current APPEND paths in the order in which they were originally typed, which is the order in which files are searched.

APPEND, like PATH, can be revoked by using the form:

APPEND;

This means that you can have an overall set of PATH and APPEND commands in an AUTOEXEC.BAT file, but still alter the search path completely in the batch file for any program that requires something different.

There are three options for APPEND, /X , /PATH, and /E. Using /X in the form /X:ON or /X:OFF allows directory searching to be switched on or off when programs are being executed. The default is /X:OFF.

The APPEND /X:ON must be placed before the main APPEND path in a batch file, and should be used only once in a session.

Example: APPEND/X:ON APPEND \TEXT

- will allow a command such as DIR *.TXT to provide a directory of all files with that extension that exist in the TEXT directory.

The /PATH option uses /PATH:ON or /PATH:OFF to allow searching an appended directory for a file whose path has already been specified.

The default is /PATH:ON.

The /E option allows the APPEND path to be put in as an environment variable called APPEND, using the form:

SET APPEND = C:\text

- which will have the same effect as the more usual syntax. Using APPEND in this form allows you to see a list of appended directories by using the SET command with no parameters.

The use of the /X and /E options can cause problems when files are both read and written, as you may find that you can read from the correct directory but not write to it without specifying the directory explicitly -and not all programs permit this. In addition, any APPEND path should be cancelled before using MSBACKUP or RESTORE, and the APPEND path should appear in a batch file after any ASSIGN command (see later this Section). Some books on MS-DOS make no mention of the options for APPEND because its use can in some cases cause more problems than it solves.

ASSIGN External

This command should be treated as obsolete and used only if absolutely unavoidable. It is not part of MS-DOS 6.0 and if it appears on your disk (from an earlier version) it should be deleted.

ATTRIB External

is a command that acts on a file or a set of files to alter the read-only, archive, system or hidden settings. When a file is saved, there is one byte allocated in the directory, following the filename and extension bytes, for attributes, meaning special features of the file. Six of the eight bits of this byte are currently used by MS-DOS as follows:

Bit 0 Read-only
Bit 1 Hidden file
Bit 2 System file
Bit 3 Label used
Bit 4 Sub-directory file
Bit 5 Archive bit

These attributes are **on** if the bit is **1**, **off** if the bit is **0**. The significance of **on** bits is:

Read-only: the file cannot be written to or appended to, and it cannot be deleted.

Hidden: the file is not seen in a normal directory listing.

System: the file is used by MS-DOS, and does not appear in a normal directory listing. This will usually be a SYS file.

Label used: applies to a disk root directory to show that a label name is present and should appear in the directory.

Sub-directory: shows that the file is part of a sub-directory and should not be listed in a normal directory search (APPEND can cancel this).

Archive: the file has been altered since it was last backed up (used by MSBACKUP, and other backup systems).

The ATTRIB command allows the read-only, archive, system and hidden attribute bits to be altered, using code letters R, A, S and H (uppercase or lowercase) with + meaning on and - meaning off. These letter codes are placed between the command word and the filename, but if the command word is used without a letter code, it will show if either of these two attributes is on for a specified file. The filename can include wildcards and you can switch both S and H attributes off by using a single command containing -S -H.

■ Attributes for a directory can also be changed. The directory name must be used in full - you cannot specify a wildcard in a directory name.

There is one option, /S which is useful when ATTRIB is used with a wildcard filename. When the /S follows the filename, any matching files in subdirectories will be listed.

Example: ATTRIB BOOKTXT.TXT
produces on screen:

R A:\BOOKTXT.TXT

- meaning that this file is read-only, it cannot be deleted or edited.

Example: ATTRIB +R C:\LURK\KEEPIT.DOC

- will make the file KEEPIT.DOC in this sub-directory a read-only file.

Example: ATTRIB +R VAL*.*/S

- will make any file whose name starts with VAL, placed in any sub-directory, into a read-only file.

Example: ATTRIB -R *.*/S

-will make any file on the disk which is read-only into read-write, so that it can be deleted or edited.

Example: ATTRIB -A JUSBAK.OLD

- will remove the archive attribute from the file JUSBAK.OLD so that commands (such as MSBACKUP or XCOPY) will not make another backup copy of it.

BREAK Internal

Used mainly as a CONFIG.SYS command, see Chapter 2. BREAK can also be used as a direct command using BREAK ON or BREAK OFF.

BUFFERS CONFIG.SYS command.

The command can be used only in the CONFIG.SYS file. See Chapter 2

CALL Internal

Batch file internal command, see Chapter 6.

CHCP Internal

Can be used alone or followed by a code page number. For an IBM system that uses code pages to accommodate printers and screen displays for different alphabets, CHCP will choose the code page for each device. For more details of code pages, see Chapter 11. Few users use, or need to use, code pages.

CHCP cannot be used unless NLSFUNC (an external command) has been used once (possibly in the AUTOEXEC.BAT file).

Example: NLSFUNC
CHCP

produces on screen the message:

Active code page: 850

- reporting that the active code page is 850, the multilingual page.

Example: CHCP 437

-sets the code page to 437, the (default) older US English page.

CHDIR or CD Internal

Displays or changes the current directory. Used alone (or followed by drive letter only) will display the current directory path that is being used in that drive. CD followed by a drive letter can be used to show the current path in a drive that is not being used at present (there must be a disk in the drive).

CHKDSK External

is a disk utility whose purpose is to check how a hard disk is used for storing files, and also to report and correct errors. When a disk, particularly a hard disk, has been used for some time, several files will have been deleted and others saved. It would be too much to expect a new file to fit in exactly the same space as a deleted one, so that the later files are likely to be spread over several parts of the disk, each part being a space that has been released by deleting an old file.

CHKDSK is used to report on how the storage space is allocated among directories, hidden files, normal files and free space, and it will also show, when it is applied to a file, how that file is split up for storage purposes, and if any files are damaged. Optionally, CHKDSK will also attempt to mend disk faults that it finds, and will issue one or more of a large set of error messages if faults are found.

IMPORTANT NOTES:

1. Because of the way that CHKDSK uses memory, it **must not** be used while the machine is running MicroSoft Windows or DOSSHELL, and it also affects other forms of 'front-end' windowing programs.

2. CHKDSK must never be used on drives created by the SUBST command, nor on network drives.

3. CHKDSK does not report physical damage to a disk. Sectors reported by CHKDSK as BAD are not used by MS-DOS and can be disregarded unless the number increases each time you use CHKDSK (a sign of either a virus or impending end of life for the disk).

4. CHKDSK will not fix a cross-linked file - you should make copies of both affected files and delete the originals.

5. A CHKDSK report can be redirected to a file, but not if the CHKDSK /F form has been used.

Example: CHKDSK C:

-produced the display for an elderly hard-disk -

```
Volume FILECARD created 5 Feb 1988 14:14
32610304  bytes total disk space
  110592  bytes in 6 hidden files
  165888  bytes in 71 directories
20834304  bytes in 1492 user files
11499520  bytes available on disk
  655360  bytes total memory
  179680  bytes free
```

This shows the analysis of files and directories, and also the memory analysis, something that can be useful. The comparatively small amount of memory shown as free reflects the use of the machine - the CHKDSK program was run while a word-processing program was also being run. Using this in the form CHKDSK C: > A:REPORT would have sent the output to a text file in drive A.

Example:

CHKDSK C:\WSTAR\BOOKS\POCKTDOS\PDS1.TXT

- produced the display for this file:

```
Volume FILECARD created 5 Feb 1988 14:14
32610304  bytes total disk space
  110592  bytes in 6 hidden files
  165888  bytes in 71 directories
20873216  bytes in 1497 user files
11460608  bytes available on disk
  655360  bytes total memory
  179824  bytes free
C:\WSTAR\BOOKS\POCKTDOS\PDS1.TXT
Contains 5 non-contiguous blocks.
```

In this example, a filename has been specified as well as a disk drive and path, and the report ends with a note on the file, which contains 5 non-contiguous (not touching) blocks. This is an indication that the file has become very scattered in the course of editing, and that access to it will be slower.

For the actions of re-organising a hard disk using DEFRAG so that files can be brought together, see Chapter 4. CHKDSK should be used before any disk defragmenting utilities are used.

CHKDSK has two command line options:

/V will report on progress as the disk is being checked.

/F will repair damaged files as far as is possible. Using the /F option means that the CHKDSK process can be slow, as any damaged files will be repaired. Sections of files which cannot be allocated anywhere are placed into files with names such as FILE1.CHK, FILE2.CHK and so on. These are useful only if they are text files, because program files cannot be put together again and run. You can use /F/V to make both the mending and the reporting actions run together. Note that the /F option does not make a scattered file into a unified file, it closes open files and tries to reallocate fragments and has no action on correctly closed files, no matter how scattered they are. An indication that CHKDSK/F is needed is nonsensical DIR reports, like files of many Mbytes or names that consist of non-alphabetical characters.

Note: messages of CHKDSK make reference to disk organisation, such as referring to clusters (groups of sectors). You do not need to know in detail what these names refer to, but any numbers that appear should be noted in case you need to use them in conjunction with another program for file recovery.

■ If you use DBLSPACE then there is a separate CHKDSK within the DBLSPACE menu which should be used. There is no point in using the ordinary CHKDSK on a double-spaced disk.

The report messages of CHKDSK are:

Contains n non-contiguous blocks - indicates that the file is scattered. If most of your files return this message, the disk needs to be re-organised.

Convert directory to file (Y/N)? - means that the directory whose name is shown is no longer usable, and you have the option of converting it to an ordinary file format, which would allow you to use file-recovery utilities to extract data from the file.

Convert lost chains to files (Y/N) - a file fragment has been found. Answer Y if this is a text (ASCII) file, N otherwise.

n bytes disk space freed - a file has been shortened releasing space on the disk.

n lost clusters found in m chains - you have the option of converting these unattached fragments into a file, or delete them.

The standard error messages are:

Allocation error, size adjusted - error in allocation of disk sectors, which the /F option can repair.

Corrections will not be written to disk - errors found, not repaired. Try again with the /F option.

Entry has a bad attribute/link/size - directory fault found.

Errors found, F parameter not specified - Errors can be corrected by using CHKDSK again with the /F option.

Has invalid cluster, file truncated - Damaged file found and closed. Can be used only if a text file. If this was a program file, delete it immediately, do not attempt to use it.

Probable non-DOS disk. Continue (Y/N)? - Disk unformatted or formatted by a different type of machine.

Tree cannot be processed beyond this point - error in subdirectory branching from the named directory.

Disk error writing FAT1 or FAT2 - File allocation table on disk can be corrected. Two tables exist, and the number is shown. You will have to use a disk utility (PC-Tools Plus, Ultra, Nortons) to correct the FAT.

Crosslinked on cluster n - a cluster is allocated to two files. Copy each file to another disk, and then salvage.

Insufficient room in root directory - you are converting fragments into files, and have run out of disk space. Copy complete files to another disk, delete from the faulty disk, and use CHKDSK again.

Invalid subdirectory - incorrect entry in a subdirectory, which might be repairable if the /F option is used.

Example: CHKDSK C:\WP\TEXT*.TXT/F/V

-checks the disk and all files with the TXT extension, looking for errors, reporting them and attempting to mend damaged files.

CHOICE Internal

This is a (new) batch-file command, dealt with in Chapter 6.

CLS Internal

Clears the screen and restores normal video (bright on dark) display. A few elderly PC machines require the line:

DEVICE=ANSI.SYS

to be placed in the CONFIG.SYS file (see Chapter 2) before CLS can be used.

COMMAND External

starts up another processor program for implementing internal commands, normally another copy of COMMAND.COM. This is used in order to allow a program, the parent program to be left temporarily, but retained in memory while another program, the child program is run. Since this second program is run using a second copy of COMMAND.COM in its own memory space, there should be no conflicts with the parent program. The second copy of COMMAND.COM is released by typing EXIT (press ENTER). The drive and path for the second processor can be specified following COMMAND.

■ The primary command processor is specified by the SHELL= line in the CONFIG.SYS file, and all the options noted for COMMAND can be used in that format.

Example: COMMAND

- loads in the second copy of COMMAND.COM, which will be released when EXIT is typed.

There are four option letters, /C, /E, /K and /P, and also /MSG.

The /C option allows a command to be executed by the second COMMAND.COM as soon as it is loaded.

Example:

COMMAND C:|MSDOS /C TYPE NOTE.TXT

- will load the second copy of COMMAND.COM from the C:\MSDOS directory and perform a TYPE action on the specified file. Use EXIT to return to the original task.

The /E option allows the allocation of memory for environment variables (see SET) to be changed, using a number 160 to 32768 bytes, which should be a multiple of 16.

Example: COMMAND /E:1024

- will load in the second copy of COMMAND.COM and make a space of 1024 bytes (1K) for environment variables. The environment variables from the parent program can still be used.

■ This is the only way of changing the environment space.

The /K option is followed by a colon and a filename (with path) to specify a batch file (other than AUTOEXEC.BAT) or program to be run immediately after the command processor is loaded. Its use should be confined to the MS-DOS Prompt in Windows (type /K into the Optional Parameters box in the DOSPRMPT.PIF file of Windows).

The /P option is used when copy of COMMAND.COM is to be made permanent and used even after EXIT is typed. This is necessary for the initial copy of COMMAND.COM and is therefore used in the SHELL= lines of the CONFIG.SYS file. It may also be necessary if the /E option is used to change the size of the environment. The /P option will be ignored if the /C option has been used.

/MSG specifies that all messages are to be stored in memory rather than on disk. This is a specialised option for floppy-only machines and must be used along with the /P option. Use these options if you see messages such as Parse Error or Extended Error appearing on a floppy-only machine when the MS-DOS system disk is not in the drive.

COMP External

Is not supplied with MS-DOS 6.0, and if it is present on your disk (from an old version) it should be deleted. The modern equivalent is FC.

COPY Internal

A multi-purpose command which can copy files to disk, to screen or printer, alter date and time of files, or can combine files into one single copy.

1. Copying one disk file to another

This can be done either retaining the name, or with renaming. The basic form of the command is:

COPY SOURCE DESTINATION

with the files SOURCE and DESTINATION specified. The words must be separated by at least one space.

If no destination filename is used, the current directory and drive is assumed; but this must not be where the source file is located - you cannot copy a file to its own drive and directory.

If only a drive letter or path is shown as the destination, the file is copied to this drive or directory using the same name.

A wildcard can be used in the name and the first file to fit the description will be copied.

Example: COPY A:oldata.txt

- if the current drive is B:, this will copy the file OLDATA.TXT from the A: drive to the B: drive, using the same filename.

Example:COPY A:OLDWORK.DTA C:\OLDSTUFF

- will copy the file called OLDWORK.DTA into the OLDSTUFF subdirectory on drive C:, using the same name.

Example: COPY B:*.TXT C:\TEXTFILE

will copy the first file with extension TXT on the disk in

drive B to the directory TEXTFILE in drive C.

If both a destination drive or path and filename are typed, the file will be copied and renamed.
Example:

COPY A:OLDTEXT.DOC C:\REWORK\NEWONE.DOC

- will copy the file called OLDTEXT.DOC from drive A to the subdirectory REWORK on the C: drive, and rename this file as NEWONE.DOC.

Wildcards can be used in order to copy and change the names of a number of similar files.

Example: COPY A:OLD?.* C:\NEWSET\NEW?.*

- will copy files such as OLD1.TXT, OLD2.BAT, OLD3.DOC and so on to the files NEW1.TXT, NEW2.BAT, NEW3.DOC, in which the new files take the same value for the wildcard characters as applied to each of the old files.

When these copies are made, the directory entry for the copied file shows the original date and time of creation. The date and time can be altered as part of the copying process by adding +,, to the source filename in the COPY command, except when the copy is being made to the current drive, when only the + is needed. This form of the COPY command cannot usefully employ wildcards, because only the date and time of the first file that is copied will be changed.

Example: COPY A:OLDFILE.DOC+,, C:\NEWSTUFF

- will copy OLDFILE.DOC into the subdirectory NEWSTUFF, and change the date and time information to the date and time of copying.

Example: COPY A:DATAFIL.TXT+

- will copy DATAFIL.TXT from the A: drive to the current drive and change the date and time to the date and time of copying.

2. Copying to/from devices

A device, in this context, means screen, serial port, or printer, and MS-DOS allows another device called NUL which will simply do nothing with a file. NUL is a way of preventing a message from being seen in some circumstances, or for testing that a COPY command will work, without the need to wait for anything to be copied. The Device abbreviations are:

CON for the monitor screen and keyboard.

PRN or LPT1 for the main printer

NUL for the Null device.

Note: The letters AUX or COM1 are used for the serial

port, but COPY will not necessarily receive from this device, although it can send ASCII text (no Crtl characters) to the serial port. The printer can use LPT1 or LPT2 if two parallel ports are fitted.

COPY is used with device names usually to send a file to the screen or printer, but it can also be used to cause text to be copied from the keyboard to a disk file or direct to the printer. When a disk file is created in this way, the copy action runs until the key combinations Ctrl-C or Ctrl-Break are pressed. When copying is used from keyboard to printer, the end of each line must be signalled with Ctrl-N before the ENTER key is pressed on the line, and the printing is done when Ctrl-Z is pressed, and then the ENTER key.

Example: COPY A:LETTER1.DOC PRN

- will copy the file LETTER1.DOC to the printer. A wildcard can be used in the filename if you are not sure of the precise name. The file must be in ASCII code, and this means that files made by many well-known word-processors will produce strange effects, depending on the type of printer, because of the use of codes in the range 128 to 255, or in the range 1 to 31. Most word-processors have an option that allows files to be recorded in ASCII form (or permit a print to a disk file), and another solution is to pipe the file through a filter program which will correct the characters into ASCII codes. See Chapter 7 for details of using pipes and filters.

Example: COPY C:\OLDTEXT\LET5.DOC CON

-will copy the file LET5.DOC, in the OLDTEXT subdirectory, to the screen. A wildcard can be used in the filename.

Example: COPY CON C:\BOLDPRNT.BAT

-will copy whatever you type on the keyboard into a file called BOLDPRNT.BAT until you press the Ctrl-C (or Ctrl-Break) keys.

Example: COPY CON PRN

-will copy what you type on the keyboard to the printer when you finally press Ctrl-Z and then ENTER. The end of a printed line must be marked with Ctrl-N.

3. To combine files

The source files are shown following the COPY command word in order, using the + sign between each pair. The destination file is shown in the usual way. Source files can be taken from any disk or directory provided

that no disk changing is needed during the copy action (though it is possible to swap the disk in one drive while a file is being copied from another drive).
Example:
COPY A:FILE1.DOC+C:\OLDBITS\FILE2.TXT C:\NEWBITS\NEWONE.TXT
-will copy FILE1.DOC from the A: drive, and then append the file FILE2.TXT from the OLDBITS directory, naming the new file NEWONE.TXT and placing it in the NEWONE directory. Note that there must be no space on either side of the + sign.

This form of COPY will also take a wildcard description, so that it can be used to join a number of files with a very compact command.
Example: COPY A: NOTE?.* B:TOTAL.TXT
-can be used to join files in the A: drive, called NOTE1.TXT, NOTE2.DOC, NOTE3.WRD and NOTE4.ADD into one file called TOTAL.TXT on the B: drive.

COPY options

The COPY command allows three option letters A, B and V to be used. Of these, V is the most useful, as it checks that the copy has been made, with an error report if it has not, or if the copy is not of the same size as the original. This is equivalent in action to the VERIFY command, and its use will slow down COPY actions. Using the /V option does not check that the copy is identical to the original; you need to use FC for that purpose.
Example: COPY A:PRECIOUS.TXT C:\VALUE/V
- will copy the file called PRECIOUS from the A drive to the subdirectory called VALUE on the C drive, and verify that the copy has been made.

The A and B options are intended to specify ASCII and Binary files respectively. The difference is that an ASCII file of text has its end marked with the Ctrl-Z character, code 26, but a binary file must always be copied until the last byte, as indicated by the length of the file number, has been dealt with. If these options are not used, COPY assumes a binary action for any straightforward copying of files, and an ASCII action when files are being combined. Trouble can be expected if you are trying to make an ASCII copy of a word-processor file which uses the Ctrl-Z characters for purposes other than marking the end of the file. For this reason, COPY with no options will use binary copying as a default so that it is normally un-necessary to specify /B unless you previously specified /A.

- Use /A for a COPY to a device (such as a printer) which might carry out specialised actions (like changing print size) if it received a non-ASCII character.

Example: COPY A:TXTFIL.DOC/A B:

- will copy TXTFIL.DOC from drive A to drive B, copying everything in TXTFIL up to the end-of-file byte, code 26. This byte is not copied to the B drive, so that the file copy will not be identical. Subsequent uses of COPY will be ASCII copies unless the /B option is specified.

Example: COPY A:TXTFIL.DOC/A B:/A

- will copy TXTFIL.DOC from drive A to drive B, and will copy the end-of-file byte also. Subsequent copies will be ASCII copies unless the /B option is specified.

Example: COPY A:PROGRAM.COM/B B:

- will copy the binary (program) file PROGRAM.COM from drive A to drive B, treating this as a binary file. The /B option is needed only if a previous use of COPY employed the /A option. There will be an end-of-file byte added to the copy, so that the copy is not identical to the original.

Example: COPY A:PROG.EXE/B B:/B

-will copy the binary file PROG.EXE from drive A to drive B, with no end of file marker on the copy. This is required only if a previous COPY command used ASCII options on both files. This is a better form of option for copying files that are liable to contain Ctrl-Z characters inside the text.

COUNTRY CONFIG.SYS command, see Chapter 2.

CTTY Internal

This is a command that is used to pass control of the computer from the keyboard, usually to something that is connected to the serial input. The 'something' can be an auxiliary keyboard or another computer, and when CTTY has been used, this other device has **complete** control, allowing MS-DOS commands to be entered and executed. Once CTTY has been used to pass command, only the remote device can return command by issuing another CTTY command, other than by re-booting the PC machine. To disconnect, assuming a remote computer has control, CTTY CON must be typed on the remote machine.

Example: CTTY AUX1

- will hand over command to the serial input, which must be connected to a serial keyboard or to the serial port of another computer which can send signals to your machine. Your machine will lock up if there is nothing suitable connected.

Example: CTTY CON

- will restore the normal use of the keyboard on the main machine.

In general CTTY is little-used, because it's generally more useful to run specialised communications or networking software when you communicate with other computers. See Chapter 11 for the use of MS-DOS INTERLNK. Many programs which do not use MS-DOS as an intermediate for input and output will not be affected by using CTTY.

DATE Internal

This allows the date to be set in the internal clock of the computer. Normally you would set the correct date, but there is nothing wrong in setting another date if you feel this might be useful. One application of setting an incorrect date is to avoid Friday 13th being used, since some viruses are activated on this date, see Chapter 9.

The older type of PC machine required the date (and time) to be set each time the computer was switched on, but all modern machines use a battery-backed clock circuit that requires no re-setting except for the change to and from Summer time. When batteries need to be changed on such machines, they can be changed while the machine is switched on, so that the date and time information is not lost.

The form of the DATE command is DATE alone, which prints the date and asks for you to alter this if you want (press ENTER to leave it alone, or type a date and then press ENTER; or DATE followed by a date, which will enter that date. Date format is determined by the country file of MS-DOS, and for the UK is DD-MM-YY. If you keep finding dates like 6-23-89 then you are using the US country setting in which dates are written in MM-DD-YY order. If the entered date is not valid (wrong format or an impossible date) you will be prompted to enter a corrected version.

Example: DATE

-prints the date on screen, and asks if any update is needed.

Example: DATE 05-02-89

-makes the date 5th February 1989 for a computer that uses UK date conventions. This is 2nd. May in the default US date convention.

DBLSPACE External

Starts the doublespace utility for managing compressed-data disks, see Chapter 4 for details.

DEBUG External

This is a program, written many years ago, for the use of programmers, allowing short pieces of machine code to be written, tested and analysed, or an existing machine-code program to be checked. DEBUG is of the same generation of programming as ED, and there are better options for machine-code users. See the book "*Starting MS-DOS Assembler*" (Sigma Press) for details of using DEBUG and more convenient methods. Notes on the use of DEBUG are included in Appendix C.

DEFRAG External

De-fragments files and can re-organise the allocation of space on the hard disk. See Chapter 4 for details. Note that a separate defragmenting utility is used for compressed files created using DBLSPACE. You must never use DEFRAG from within Windows or DOSSHELL.

DEL (or ERASE) Internal

Either DEL or ERASE can be used to delete files, either single files or, using a wildcard, in groups. If the use of DEL or ERASE would result in deleting all the files on a disk or in a directory, you will be asked to confirm the command by typing Y or N. DEL (ERASE) cannot be used to delete a directory, for which the RD or DELTREE commands can be used.

Example: DEL arcturus.008

-will delete the single file on the current drive/directory with this name

Example: DEL A:*.TXT

-will delete all files with the extension letters TXT on the A: drive.

Example: DEL B:*.*

-will delete all files on the disk in the B: drive. You will be asked to confirm that you really intend this to be done with the message:

Are you sure (Y/N)

and the files will be deleted only if you answer Y. Using N or any other letter will leave the files as they are.

DEL has one option only, DEL /P, which will provide a prompt for each deletion.

■ The RMDIR command is used to delete an empty directory, and DELTREE to delete a filled directory.

Note that the file(s) that are deleted using DEL or ERASE in this way are not in fact removed or replaced in the disk unless other files are recorded over them. If a file or set of files is deleted by mistake, then follow the following procedure:

1. If the files were on a floppy disk, make a backup copy of the disk on to a new formatted disk using the DISKCOPY utility (which will copy the deleted files as well). The computer can then be used with other disks. If the files were on the hard disk, then do not save any other files on to the hard disk. Continue work on floppy disks if possible.

2. Use the UNDELETE utility of MS-DOS to recover the file. For full details of using UNDELETE, see Chapter 4.

The important point is not to record any more data on the disk which would replace the files that have been deleted in error. For some file types, such as text files, it is possible to recover some of the remaining data if another file has been recorded over the deleted file, but only the portion that has not been over-written can be recovered.

Note that if you have more serious problems with file loss, particularly from a hard disk, which cannot be treated by the use of file recovery programs, then there are specialists, such as Alan Solomon, of S & S Enterprises Ltd. (see advertisements in magazines) who can recover data under remarkably adverse conditions. These services are expensive, but if a set of files represents a year's work, the price is reasonable.

DELTREE External

Will delete a directory along with all of its files and its sub-directories (and files in the sub-directories). The directory to be deleted must be specified, and cannot be the current directory. You will be prompted to confirm the deletion. There is one option /Y, which will run the DELTREE action without prompting for confirmation.

■ DELTREE pays no attention to attributes such as Read-only, System or Hidden. It can be used with a wildcard specification but this should never be done unless you are absolutely confident that it will not destroy valuable data. If you are going to use DELTREE at all you should ensure that the SENTRY system of undeletion is in use.

Example: DELTREE C:\TEMPFILE

- will delete all files and subdirectories in TEMPFILE and the TEMPFILE directory itself. You will be asked to confirm the deletion.

DELTREE can be used with wildcards, but this use is very risky and should not be attempted unless Sentry Undeletion can be used.

DEVICE CONFIG.SYS command, see Chapter 2.

The standard device drivers are ANSI.SYS, DISPLAY.SYS, DRIVER.SYS, DBLSPACE.SYS, EGA.SYS, EMM386.EXE, HIMEM.SYS, INTERLNK.EXE, POWER.EXE, RAMDRIVE.SYS, SETVER.EXE and SMARTDRV.EXE.

DEVICEHIGH CONFIG.SYS command, see Chapter 2.

DIR Internal

DIR is the directory command, the method of finding what files are contained on a disk or a directory. It can be used to display all files, details of one file or a group answering to a wildcard description, or to test if a file or set of files is present. The command word can be used alone, followed by a drive or path or by a complete file specification, and can be modified by various option letters. The most general use is to list all files in the current directory, so that the command applies to the current drive, and consists only of DIR.

Example: DIR

- this produces a display such as:

```
 Volume in drive A has no label
 Directory of A:\
PCSCAP TXT     384   29-01-89   18:56
PDS1 TXT     18944   31-01-89    9:33
PDS2 TXT     23424   31-01-89   15:02
PDS3 TXT      8448   31-01-89   15:03
PDS4 TXT       896   29-01-89   18:54
PDS5 TXT       768   29-01-89   18:55
PDS6 TXT       640   29-01-89   18:55
PDS7 TXT       640   29-01-89   18:55
PDS8 TXT       640   29-01-89   18:56
PDSAPP TXT     384   29-01-89   18:56
PDSPRF TXT    2048   30-01-89   11:30
 11 File(s) 301056 bytes free
```

which shows the files that are present on this drive, along with the label name, if any, and the amount of disk space that is free for use. The files are shown one on each line as a default mainly because the original PC machine used a 40-character per line screen display. The modern MS-DOS versions 5.0 onwards allowed a much more flexible use of DIR with option letters and the use of the auxiliary DIRCMD file. The full options list is as follows (upper or lower case letters can be used):

/a - display only files with stated attributes
/b - show only file-name (no dates, sizes)
/c - display the compression ratio of Double-space files
/l - display directory in lowercase
/o - specify a sorted directory (name, extension, date, size order)
/p - page the output to one screen at a time
/s - search all subdirectories of current directory
/w - display directory in wide form

Of these, the /o and /a switches allow specification letters to be added, using the -sign to mean NOT. For the /o switch, the syntax is typically:

DIR /o:n

to mean alphabetical sort by name and the full list is:

n alphabetical by name
-n as above, but reverse order
e alphabetical by extension
-e as above, but reverse order
d by date and time, earliest first
-d by date and time, last first
s by size, smallest first
-s as above, largest first
g with directories grouped before files
-g with directories grouped after files
c by compression ratio (Doublespace files), lowest first
-c by compression ratio (Doublespace files), highest first

Note that g and -g can be used with other options, but the g or -g options should be placed first, so that DIR /o:gn will show alphabetical order of name with directories first, and DIR /o:-gn will show alphabetical order of name with directories placed last.

The main /C option assumes that the Host drive for DBLSPACE files uses 8 Kbyte clusters. By using /C[H] the actual cluster size of the host drive will be taken into account. The /C[H] form cannot be used with /B or /W. It is also possible to determine the format of each DIR command in advance by using a SET DIRCMD line in the AUTOEXEC.BAT file, see Chapter 7. If such a default has been installed in this way, an ordinary directory can be specified by using the options such as -w which reverse the effects.

For the attributes /a switch, the additional letters are:

h	only hidden files displayed
-h	no hidden files displayed
s	only system files displayed
-s	no system files displayed
d	only directory names displayed
-d	no directory names displayed
a	only archive files (ready for backup) displayed
-a	only files that are already backed up are displayed
r	only read-only files displayed
-r	only read-write files displayed

DIR is very often used with wildcards, but it does not need to have a wildcard character typed if either the main name or the extension is to be substituted.

Example: DIR A:FILE

- is equivalent to DIR A:FILE.* and it will display all files on the A: drive with the filename FILE, but with different extensions.

Example: DIR B:.BAT

- is equivalent to DIR B:*.BAT and will display any file that has the extension letters of BAT on the B: drive.

DIR will also display a directory if one exists on a disk, or inside another directory. When a name in a listing is a directory, the DIR listing shows the name but with <DIR> inside angled brackets following it rather than the usual size, date and time details (another option is to show the name inside angled brackets). This allows you to use the CD command to move to that directory if required, or to use a DIR command that includes the directory in order to find what files are contained in the directory. A directory listing can also be redirected to a disk file or to the printer, see Chapter 7.

Example: DIR/W

will display files in the wide format shown below:

```
Volume in drive C is IDEDISK
Volume Serial Number is 16CD-1219
Directory of C:\
[123R23]      [ARCHIVE]     [ASSEMBLY]    [BATS]        [EDITOR]
[MONEY]       [MSDOS]       [NETUTIL]     [SENTRY]      [STD]
[TEMP]        [UTILS]       [WP51]        AFTCOMP.CHK
AFTCOMP.DIR   AFTSETUP.MSD  AUTOEXEC.BAK  AUTOEXEC.BAT
BEFCOMP.CHK
BEFCOMP.DIR   BEFSETUP.MSD  CAMERA.COM    CATCH.COM     CHKLIST.MS
COMMAND.COM   CONFigure BAK CONFIG.SYS    DISKMAP.DAT   DRIVER.SYS
DSVXD.386     EMSCOMP.EXE   MMREAD.ME     MONEY.BAT     MOUSE.INI
NCON.SYS      NET$25.COM    NET0000.SYS   NETSHAR8.SYS
NETSHARE.SYS
NETUNITS.SYS  OPT3.BAT      VMODE.EXE     WINA20.386
     43 file(s)      247043 bytes
```

Figure 5.1
Note the directories shown first in this portion of a DIR listing.

DISKCOMP External

is intended for floppy disk users only, and should not be applied to a hard disk, nor to RAMdisk nor to networks. It allows two floppy disks to be compared, noting any differences. The command is by now obsolescent. The options, seldom used, are:

/1 - compare Side 1 of each disk only

/8 - compare only first 8 sectors of each track

DISKCOMP must not be used if ASSIGN, JOIN or SUBST have been previously used and not cancelled.

DISKCOPY External

used for floppy disks to make a complete copy of one disk to another disk of **identical** type. The destination disk should preferably be formatted and unused, but if it contains files, these will be over-written. If it has not been formatted, then formatting will be carried out before copying - but this takes longer. The source disk from which files are to be copied should **always** be write-protected before starting to use DISKCOPY, particularly if a single floppy drive is being used. DISKCOPY has no application to a hard disk.

The important point about DISKCOPY is that it copies byte-by-byte with no regard for files, so that system tracks, hidden files, deleted files, corrupted files etc. will all be copied across to the destination disk. The disks must be **fully compatible** in layout - you cannot use DISKCOPY when one disk is a 3.5" 720 Kbyte type and the other is a 5.25" 1.2 Mb type, for example. Always use DISKCOPY if you want to make an exact copy of a disk which contains files you want to work on with a disk utility program (if,for example, you want to 'undelete' files, or try to fix a CRC error fault).

The options /1 and /V can be used.

/1 will copy only one side of the source disk

/V will verify that the copy exists - it does not verify that each byte has been correctly copied.

NOTES:

1. DISKCOPY cannot be used on hard drives nor on networked drives.

2. The volume serial number of a floppy disk is not copied.

3. Any file fragmentation that exists on the source disk will be copied to the destination disk.

4. Using DISKCOPY on a MS-DOS System disk will create another System disk. COPY and XCOPY will not do this.

5. If DISKCOPY is used on a machine with a single floppy drive, you will be prompted to change disks when necessary.

Example: DISKCOPY A: B:

- copies the entire contents of the disk in drive A to the disk in drive B. If this is used with a single drive you will be prompted to change disks.

Example: DISKCOPY A:

- uses single drive only, and prompts you to change between source and destination disks as required.

Messages:

Formatting while copying - destination disk was unformatted.

Copy another diskette (Y/N)? - another copy.

Copy not complete - source disk probably copy-protected or corrupted.

Disks must be the same size - destination disk has incorrect format.

Target diskette is write protected - remove write-protect tab.

DISPLAY .SYS CONFIG.SYS command, see Chapter 2.

DOS CONFIG.SYS command, see Chapter 2.

DOSHELP External

Displays a summary of Help for DOS commands. The command word should follow DOSHELP, with a space between. The other way of producing DOSHELP is to type the command word followed by /?.

Example: DOSHELP DIR

will display help on the DIR command, with syntax, notes and examples.

DOSKEY External, see Chapter 7.

DOSSHELL External, see Chapter 8.

DRIVER.SYS CONFIG.SYS command, see Chapter 2.

DRIVPARM CONFIG.SYS command, see Chapter 2.

ECHO Internal, see Batch files, Chapter 6.

EDIT External

EDIT starts the editor program from the command line. The old EDLIN program can be deleted from the disk and forgotten forever. EDIT is available only if the QBASIC.EXE program remains on the disk - if this program has been deleted to save space you cannot use

EDIT. You might prefer to use an editor which required less disk and memory space, such as the Amstrad RPED.

You can start EDIT with or without a filename. If you start without a filename you will see a reminder screen that you have to remove by pressing the Esc key and you then have to select File - Open to load a file. Starting in the form:

EDIT C:\AUTOEXEC.BAT

will short-circuit all these preliminaries for editing a file that already exists or which you want to create.

EDIT allows you to use the options /B, /G, /H, and /NOHI.

/B will use monochrome for the Editor, making it easier to use with a monochrome monitor. If you do not use /B you can change the colours from within EDIT by using the Options menu.

/G should be used only if you have a CGA monitor (very rare nowadays).

/H uses the highest possible resolution that is possible with your monitor.

/NOHI allows you to use 8-colour monitors (incapable of using high-intensity colour) in place of the default 16-colour type.

EGA.SYS CONFIG.SYS file, see Chapter 2.

EMM386.EXE CONFIG.SYS file

for creating UMB or Expanded memory - see Chapter 3 for details.

EXIT Internal

This is used when a program has allowed a return to MS-DOS (using COMMAND) so as to allow you to make use of one or more MS-DOS commands. In order to avoid removing the program from memory, a new copy of COMMAND.COM is started up and the MS-DOS command(s) run from the new copy. When the commands are finished, typing EXIT (then press ENTER key) will return you to the original copy of COMMAND.COM which is running the program that you temporarily left. EXIT has no effect if COMMAND used the /P option.

EXPAND External

This is used to convert files in compressed form on the MS-DOS distribution disks into their normal useable format. No wildcards are permitted, so that if you need to expand a large set of files it is better to set up the EXPAND command inside a batch file using the FOR command (see Chapter 6).

The normal syntax is EXPAND source-file destination-file, in which the full filename must be used. The compressed MS-DOS files have an extension that ends with the underscore character _ so that they can easily be recognised. The full name of the expanded file must be supplied. You can specify more than one file in the command, but without specifying the expanded names. Example:

EXPAND A:\DBLSPC.EX_ C:\MSDOS\DBLSPC.EX

will expand and copy the file from the disk in the A drive to C:\MSDOS.

Example:

EXPAND A:\DBLSPC.EX_ A:DBLSPC.HL_ C:\INH

will expand the two files and place them in the C:\INHERE directory. The names will be unchanged.

FASTOPEN External

allows fast access to any file that has been used during a session, by temporarily storing the location that the file occupies on the disk into the memory of the computer. This can be used only with a hard disk system, and does not apply to networks, floppies nor RAMdisk. It is particularly advantageous if you do not use a cache memory for this purpose and if large directories are used. The number of files can be specified, each needing 35 bytes of memory. If no number (10 to 999) is specified, 34 files will have their details stored. FASTOPEN is intended to be used when the programs that you run are, in the main, compilers or databases. There is no particular advantage in using FASTOPEN along with other types of programs.

For practically all purposes, the use of cache memory, see Chapter 3, is preferable.

FASTOPEN, if required, can be included in the AUTOEXEC.BAT file, since it ought to be used only once in a session, and should be used before any work is done. It can alternatively be used with INSTALL in the CONFIG.SYS file. You must not use FASTOPEN if you also use ASSIGN, JOIN or SUBST. You must not start FASTOPEN from inside WINDOWS or DOSSHELL and you must not use DEFRAG while FASTOPEN is in use.

The only option is /X which allows the FASTOPEN file to be held in expanded memory (not extended memory).

Example: FASTOPEN C:50

- will start the use of FASTOPEN, with up to 50 files having their details held in memory.

FC External

File Compare is used to compare two files and display differences, and is an upgraded replacement for the old COMP. FC can be used for ASCII (text data) files or binary files, but the main applications are to text files. The options list for FC is as follows:

/a Abbreviates the output when a difference is found so that only the first line of a set is displayed.

/b Makes a binary (bit by bit) comparison

/c Ignores the case of letters when comparing files

/L Compares ASCII characters. This is a default for text files, but would have to be specified if you were comparing files with extensions EXE, COM, SYS, OBJ, LIB or BIN

/Lbn Allows up to n differing lines to be noted - the default is 100, and if there are more than this number of differences the excess is ignored.

/n Displays the numbers of the differing lines (text file comparisons only)

/t Does not treat TAB characters as spaces (they are usually treated as a set of eight spaces)

/w Ignore number of spaces, so that a file which uses, for example, two spaces between words is not treated as differing from one which uses one space.

/nnnn Synchronisation distance. The number of up to four digits is the number of file lines that have to match after a difference is found. If there is a difference within this range, all of the lines will be shown as mismatches.

FCBS CONFIG.SYS command, see Chapter 2.

This command is obsolete, and only a few old programs will require FCBS to be in use.

FDISK External

is used to prepare an old-style MFM or RLL hard disk for formatting. See Chapter 4 for details. The modern version of FDISK will allow disk partitions of up to 2 Gbyte to be used. Modern IDE drives are pre-formatted and do not normally require the use of FDISK

FILES CONFIG.SYS command, see Chapter 2.

FIND External

is a text file utility that allows each place where a set of characters (a string) has been used to be found in a file, a keyboard input, or when used as a filter the output of a program. These last two options are valuable features which are seldom used. For filter use of FIND see Chapter 7.

Option letters, used between FIND and filename:

/C display line number(s) where the string was found
/I specify that the search ignores the case of letters.
/N number the lines to show position in file
/V display all lines except these containing the string

The string to be found must be enclosed in quotes ("), and if the string contains quotes, double quotes must be used. Care is needed about small words or letter groups - if you specify "a" you will get each line that contains the letter in a word, but if you specify " a ", with spaces, then only the letter used by itself will count.

■ FIND, used without a filename, can be used as a filter.

Example:

FIND "computer" C:\text\oldbook\chap1.txt

-will find each place where the word "computer" occurs in the selected file.

Example: FIND " the "

-will find when you type the word "the" , and note this by repeating the line on screen. Type Ctrl-C or Ctrl-Break to end the search.

Example: FIND/N "third" C:\CHK1.DOC

produces on screen (on my system)

---------- C:\chk1.doc

[4]This is the third in CHK1

FOR Batch file internal command, see Chapter 6.

FORMAT External

prepares a floppy disk for use, or wipes a previously used disk clean. This is one of the few commands that (in its /U Unconditional option) can totally delete data beyond hope of recovery unless there is a Sentry file on the disk. It can be used for a hard disk, and though it will not necessarily destroy all of the data beyond recovery (depending on the disk partitioning), hard disk users should ensure that FORMAT is not present on the hard disk.

- The UNFORMAT command can deal with recovery of files from any disk that has been unintentionally re-formatted, but not if the /U option was used. Use /U only for new disks and for re-formatting disks which have been troublesome and whose data is safely backed up.

After a disk is formatted, you will be prompted for a label name (see LABEL). If you type nothing and press ENTER the disk will contain no label name. A unique volume number is allocated to each disk by the system. There are many options, several of which are of little interest except to users of odd disk formats. When FORMAT is used from a floppy disk, the disk containing FORMAT should be write-protected.

Example: FORMAT B:

- with the disk containing the FORMAT program in the A: drive, this will format another disk whether you have a single drive or a twin drive. For a twin floppy drive you will be prompted to put the disk to be formatted into drive B:, for a single drive you will be prompted to change disks.

- You should not attempt to format a 5.25" 360 Kbyte disk to 1.2 Mbyte capacity. You can, however, format a 3.5" 720 Kbyte disk to 1.4 Mbyte if a second hole is drilled in the casing -but you need to ensure that the hole is of the correct diameter, in the correct position, and is cleaned of all drilling-swarf. This could invalidate your floppy-drive guarantee. In my experience, some 99% of all 720 Kbyte disks will format to 1.4 Mbyte without problems - the exceptions are usually 3.5" 720 Kbyte disks given away with magazines (some of which only just re-format as 720 Kbyte)

The options, in order of usefulness are:

/S - put system tracks on to the disk while formatting. This must be **the last option** if several options are specified.

/V:name - Place an 11-character label name on the disk after formatting -if you omit this you will be prompted for a name.

/B - Format with 8 sectors per track and leave space for system tracks to be added later. See SYS command.

/F:size - Format to the specified size, using a number of kilobytes or megabytes specified as follows (showing acceptable forms for each size) for various sizes of disks. Note that these sizes include several that are obsolete.

5.25"	160	160k	160kb			
5.25"	180	180k	180kb			
5.25"	320	320k	320km			
5.25"	360	360k	360kb			
3.5"	720	720k	720kb			
5.25"	1200	1200k	1200kb	1.2	1.2m	1.2mb
3.5"	1440	1440k	1440kb	1.44	1.44m	1.44mb
3.5"	2880	2880k	2880kb	2.88	2.88m	2.88mb

■ It is sometimes necessary to specify /F:720 when formatting a 720 Kbyte disk in a 1.4 Mbyte drive. Note that the 1.4 Mbyte disk is referred to as 1.44 Mbyte - this results from taking 1Mbyte as 1000 Kbyte instead of 1024 Kbyte as is done for memory.

/T:80 - Format with 80 tracks (if disk drive permits). This can be used to format a 3.5" 720K disk on a 1.44Mb drive. Do not use along with /F.

/N:8 - Format with 8 sectors per track (instead of 9). N is usually used along with T for an unusual format.

/8 - Format with 8 sectors per track.

/1 - Format as a single-sided disk.

Restriction: FORMAT must not be used on any drive that has been the subject of ASSIGN, JOIN or SUBST commands.

Example: FORMAT B:/S

- formats a disk with system tracks to use as a self-starting disk.

Example: FORMAT A:/V

- will carry out the formatting as usual, and then prompt for a label of up to 11 characters.

Example: FORMAT B:/B

- will format a disk with 8 sectors per track and with system tracks left vacant so that they can be added later using the SYS command.

Example: FORMAT C:

- will format a hard disk which has been partitioned by using FDISK previously.

FORMAT returns ERRORLEVEL codes which can be used in batch files, see Chapter 6.

GOTO Internal batch file command, see Chapter 6.

GRAPHICS External

can be used along with for CGA, EGA or VGA screen systems to allow a screen-dump (printing on paper the screen appearance) for specified types of printers. This command would normally be put into the AUTOEXEC.BAT file if you frequently used screen-dumps, it would otherwise be preferable to run it from a batch file to avoid the need to look up the parameters.

When GRAPHICS has been used, pressing the Print Screen key (alone) will print the screen display. The usual VGA 640 x 480 type of screen display will be printed sideways on the paper. You cannot print a Super-VGA (800 x 600 or higher) using GRAPHICS. Do not press the SHIFT key along with the Print Screen key. The GRAPHICS command is followed by the printer type, the file specification for the printer and a set of options. The printer type must be taken from this set:

COLOR1 - IBM PC Color Printer with black ribbon
COLOR4 - IBM PC Color Printer with red/green/blue ribbon
COLOR8 - IBM PC Color Printer with cyan/magenta/yellow/black ribbon
HPDEFAULT - any Hewlett-Packard PCL printer
DESKJET - a Hewlett-Packard Deskjet printer
GRAPHICS - an IBM Personal Graphics Printer, ProPrinter or Quietwriter
GRAPHICSWIDE - an IBM Personal Graphics Printer with 11" carriage
LASERJET - a Hewlett-Packard Laserjet printer
LASERJETII - a Hewlett-Packard Laserjet II printer
PAINTJET - a Hewlett-Packard Paintjet printer
QUIETJET - a Hewlett-Packard Quietjet printer
QUIETJETPLUS - a Hewlett-Packard Quietjet Plus printer
RUGGEDWRITER - a Hewlett-Packard Rugged Writer printer
RUGGEDWRITERWIDE - a Hewlett-Packard wide-carriage Rugged Writer printer
THERMAL - an IBM PC-convertible thermal printer
THINKJET - an IBM Thinkjet printer.

If the printer name is not followed by a filename and path for a printer information file, the GRAPHICS command will look for a file called GRAPHICS.PRO (the printer PROfile) on any of the directories specified in the PATH line in AUTOEXEC.BAT.

Options: The options are /R, /B, /LCD, and /PRINTBOX

/R Prints the image as seen on a monochrome screen - white characters on a black background. The default is to use the normal black characters on a white background.

/B Prints the background in colour for COLOR4 and COLOR8 printers only

/LCD Prints using the screen shape of an LCD screen rather than of a CGA screen

/PRINTBOX can be used as either /PRINTBOX:STD or /PRINTBOX:LCD. Whatever is used here must match the setting in the GRAPHICS.PRO file.

Using /PRINTBOX:LCD makes the use of the /LCD option unnecessary.

GRAPHTABL External

is an obsolete command and if present on your hard disk (from an old MS-DOS version) should be deleted.

HELP External

Starts the MS-DOS Help system and, used alone, provides a list of Help topics. Clicking with the mouse on any topic will produce more detailed Help, with sections for Syntax, Notes and Examples. In most Help pages there are cross-referred topics that can be clicked on to produce more Help, and the following keys an be used:

Alt-C - go to the Help index page
Alt-B - go back to previous page
Alt-N - go forward to next page.

The File menu allows the choice of Print or Exit, and the Search menu allows you to search for a key word for which Help may be available.

The other method is to specify a topic following Help. The options are /B, /G, /H and /NOHI.

/B allows the use of a monochrome monitor along with a CGA video card.

/G should be used with a CGA screen to permit fast screen updating

/H displays using the highest resolution the screen can achieve

/NOHI Allows the use of an 8-colour monitor which cannot show high-intensity colours

Example: HELP DBLSPACE

will show the Help pages on this command, along with cross-references that you can click on.

HIMEM.SYS CONFIG.SYS command

used to manage extended memory, see Chapter 3.

IF Internal batch file command, see Chapter 6.

INCLUDE CONFIG.SYS command

used when multiple options exist in CONFIG.SYS, see Chapter 2.

INSTALL CONFIG.SYS command

used to load some types of memory-resident programs from CONFIG.SYS rather than from AUTOEXEC.BAT, see Chapter 2.

INTERLNK External

Connects two computers together by way of a serial or parallel link. The hardware connection must exist, and the device driver INTERLNK.EXE must be run in the CONFIG.SYS file. The computers can then share drives and printers. See Chapter 11 for details.

INTERSVR External

Used to operate an INTERLNK connection on the server machine, see Chapter 11. It can also be used, along with CTTY, to transfer the INTERLNK files to a diskless machine.

JOIN

is now obsolete and if it exists on your disk (left over from an older version of MS-DOS) it should be deleted.

KEYB External

is the keyboard driver program which can use a pair of letters to denote country, and can in addition be followed by a code page for the particular character set for the few users who need code pages. Another option allows the path to a keyboard file to be typed.

Example: KEYB UK

- will select the UK version of the key layout, assuming that this is in the current directory.

Example: KEYB CF,863

- will select the Canadian French keyboard layout, using Code page 863 for its characters.

Example: KEYB GR,437,C:\MSDOS\keyboard.sys

- selects the Greek keyboard layout, using Code page 437 and specifying that the keyboard driver file is on the \MSDOS\ path.

KEYB is generally used in the AUTOEXEC.BAT file, but can be placed in the CONFIG.SYS file by using the form:

INSTALL=C:\MSDOS\KEYB.COM UK,850, C:\MSDOS \KEYBOARD.SYS

Note that the use of Code Page numbers is usually unnecessary - unless the steps outlined in Chapter 11 have been used, such numbers will be ignored. If the code page number is omitted the commas on each side must not be omitted, making the example above read:

INSTALL=C:\MSDOS\KEYB.COM UK,,C:\MSDOS\KEYBOARD.SYS

LABEL External

allows a name of up to 11 characters to be put into the disk directory as a volume name or label. The LABEL name will appear each time the directory for the disk is printed, as the VOLUME name.

- It is an advantage to use a label name for a hard disk, as this will prompt for approval if an attempt is made to delete all files.

The name can include spaces, though the characters

* ? / \ | . , " ; : + =< > ( ) [ ]

are not allowed. If you have a labelled floppy disk in a drive that has been affected by ASSIGN or JOIN then the label will not appear on a directory listing.

LABEL, used alone or with only a drive specified, allows a label name to be entered, or an existing name to be deleted. If the ENTER key is pressed when the label name is called for, any existing name can be deleted with the following option. The alternative method is to type the new label name following the LABEL command.

LABEL should not be used when ASSIGN or SUBST have been used.

Example: LABEL B:

- will produce a prompt for a new label name. This can be typed, then ENTER pressed, or ENTER can be pressed by itself. You are then asked:

Delete current volume label (Y/N)?

- which allows you to delete an existing label, or even the one you have just entered.

Example: LABEL A: ACCOUNTS

- will label this disk as ACCOUNTS when the directory is displayed

LASTDRIVE External CONFIG.SYS command, see Chapter 2.

LOADFIX External

This is a command which is designed to overcome a problem that has arisen only because of the relocation of device drivers to upper memory. If practically all of the drivers have been relocated, it is possible to release part of the first 64 Kbyte of memory, and programs can then be loaded and run starting in this part of memory.

Some (elderly) programs are designed to detect this as an error and will issue messages such as:

Packed file corrupt

when this happens. By prefacing the program name with LOADFIX, this message is suppressed and the program will run normally.

Example: LOADFIX C:\TRIAL\probprog.EXE

will correctly load and run a program that has presented problems.

- Note that the Packed file corrupt message can also be obtained because of problems with SMARTDRV - see Chapter 3.

LOADHIGH Internal

an AUTOEXEC.BAT file command to load memory-resident programs into high memory, see Chapter 2.

MEM External

memory diagnosis, see Chapter 3.

MEMMAKER External

Starts the memory diagnostic and optimisation program, see Chapter 4.

MENUCOLOR External CONFIG.SYS

allows the choice of colour for background and foreground (text), and can be run from CONFIG.SYS but only from a menu block, see Chapter 2.

MENUDEFAULT External CONFIG.SYS

used in a menu system to define a default set of commands, see Chapter 2.

MENUITEM External CONFIG.SYS

Used in a menu system to define a menu item, see Chapter 2.

MKDIR or **MD** Internal,

creates a new directory, see Chapter 4.

MODE External

is a complex multi-purpose command for altering settings relating to screen, printer, serial port and keyboard use. It can set the screen output to 40 or 80 characters per line, and to colour or monochrome (assuming that the screen **can** be switched). A parallel printer can be set to print 80 or 132 characters per line and 6 or 8 lines per inch, assuming that the printer is capable of such settings. A serial output can have its serial protocols of baud rate, parity, number of data bits and number of stop bits set so as to suit a serial printer or modem. Output to the parallel port can be re-directed to the serial port as a way of printer-switching. The letters that follow the MODE command decide which peripheral will be affected, and the codes which are used are listed below.

■ **MODE** is very seldom directly required, because there are usually other ways of carrying out these actions - programs which require changes will, for example, provide a menu-operated choice. If you need a **MODE** command frequently it can be put into a batch file (see Chapter 6), possibly into AUTOEXEC.BAT.

LPT1: Parallel printer, port 1
COM1: Serial output, port 1
40, 80, CO40 or CO80: Screen character/colour options

MODE can also be used for preparing, activating, displaying and restoring code pages for the few cases where these can be used.

Parallel-printer control

MODE will use the port name, usually LPT1, followed by the number of columns per line and the number of lines per inch, with the P option used to prevent time-out messages being printed if the printer is slow. This applies also if the printer incorporates a buffer of its own which means that there will be a comparatively long interval between successive calls for characters for the printer. A laser printer with a large buffer memory will almost always require the use of the P option, though if the printer is driven by a word-processor, the action may be built in to the word-processor.

Example: MODE LPT1: 132,8

-sets the parallel printer to 132 characters per line, 8 lines per inch. The default is 80 character per line, 6 lines per inch. To set only the number of lines per inch, omit the first figure but keep the comma.

Example: MODE LPT1:,8

-sets 8 lines per inch, leaving characters per inch setting unchanged.

Example: MODE LPT1:,,P

- will make it easier to send text continuously to a slow printer such as a daisywheel type. This can be done in the AUTOEXEC.BAT file.

Serial port control

This is specified by using COM1 or COM2 (one of these may already be used by an internal modem); COM3 and COM4 if they are fitted can also be specified if they are correctly set up. The COM specifier will be followed by figures for:

Baud rate, using 110, 150, 300, 600, 1200, 2400, 4800, 9600 and 19200.
Parity, which is N (none), O (odd) or E (even).
Databits, the number of bits per word, 7 or 8.
Stopbits, the number of stop bits, 1 or 2
- and also the P specifier to prevent time-out signals

The default settings are even parity, 7 data bits and 1 stop bit (2 stop bits if 100 baud is selected).

The existing setting will be used as a default if in a MODE command there is nothing placed between the commas - there must always be at least three commas present.

Example: MODE COM1:1200,N,8,1

- sets up to use the serial port with 1200 baud, no parity, 8 data bits, 1 stop bit. This is a very common combination of settings for modem use.

Example: MODE LPT1:600,,,1,P

- changes baud rate to 600, makes no change to parity or number of data bits, uses one stop bit and will send to a slow printer (as for parallel printer).

■ Note that these settings are not normally required because you would use a communications program to carry out all of the settings and the transfers.

Screen settings

- note that not all computers will accept some of these settings, since their usefulness depends on the type of graphics card that is fitted.

MODE 40 - 40 character per line, which is useful for large-print displays on screen.
MODE 80 - the default 80 character per line.
MODE BW40 - 40 characters per line monochrome
MODE BW80 - 80 characters per line monochrome
MODE CO40 - 40 characters per line colour
MODE CO80 - 80 characters per line colour

MODE as applied to the screen can also be used to test and adjust the centring of text. Used in the form MODE, with L or R, the screen text can be moved left or right. This is seldom useful without the added option T which will allow a test of the screen centring to be made at the same time.

Example: MODE,R,T

produces on screen:

01234567890123456789012345678901234567890123456789012345678901234567890

Do you see the leftmost 0? (Y/N)

- and you can press Y if this character is visible, N if not. This can be followed by using MODE,L,T to test for the right-most character.

Note that these alterations made by MODE apply to MS-DOS only - any program that you run is likely to make its own settings.

Redirection of a printer

This works in one direction only - the redirection of a print output from the default parallel port to the serial port, or the cancellation of this redirection.

Example: MODE LPT1:=COM1:

-makes all output that is normally sent to the parallel printer go to the serial port instead. Note that there must be no spaces either side of the = sign.

Example: MODE LPT1:

-restores the parallel port. Use MODE LPT1:,,P if the output is to a slow printer.

MODE used with Code pages

See Chapter 11 for an outline of the use of code pages. The files DISPLAY.SYS and PRINTER.SYS must have been used in the CONFIG.SYS file if MODE is to be used for this purpose.

MODE can be used to prepare code pages for use from the CPI files that are present on the MS-DOS distribution disk. The MODE command should specify CON or PRN, and the information files will also be specific to the devices. The files normally supplied:

4201.CPI for IBM Proprinter 4201 (several other printers, such as the Canon bubblejet, emulate this printer.)

5202.CPI for IBM Quietwriter III and emulations

EGA.CPI for EGA video board

LCD.CPI for LCD screens on portable computers.

Example:

MODE CON CODEPAGE PREPARE=((850,860) C:\MSDOS\EGA.CPI)

- will prepare codepage files for the EGA screen and pages 850 and 860.

Example: MODE PRN CODEPAGE SELECT=850

- selects the use of codepage 850 for the printer, assuming that a suitable CODEPAGE PREPARE line has been used.

Example: MODE CON CODEPAGE /STATUS

- will print out the currently used codepage for the screen, along with the numbers of other codepages that have been prepared.

Example: MODE PRN CODEPAGE REFRESH

- will renew the use of codepages on a printer that has been turned off at some time and which is no longer responding to code page information after being turned on again.

MODE used for typematic rate

The keyboard repeat rate (typematic rate) can be controlled using the MODE command so that, for example,

MODE CON: rate=10 delay=2

will arrange the keyboard so that the rate of repeating a character when a key is held down will be around 10 repetitions per second, and the delay before the repeat action starts will be 0.5 seconds. The unit of rate is computer clock ticks, range 1 to 32, and the delay can be 1, 2, 3, or 4 in units of 0.25 second.

MORE External

is used only as a filter in conjunction with the output of other programs. See Chapter 2.

MOVE External

Moves files from one drive or directory to another - this is a copy action followed by deletion of the original files. When a single file is moved, it can also be renamed in the process. If the destination directory contains a file with the same name, this file will be over-written by the moved file.
MOVE can also be used to rename a directory, using the old name as the FROM part and the new name as the TO part of the command. The restriction is that both the old and the new names must themselves be within the same directory - for instance, you could **not** use:

```
MOVE C:\oldname  C:\TEMP\NEWNAME
```

Example:

```
MOVE  CHAP1.TXT  CHAP2.TXT  C:\BOOKS\BOOK1
```

MSAV External

Scans the computer disks and memory for known viruses. See Chapter 9 for details of the DOS version, and Chapter 10 for the MWAV Windows version.

MSBACKUP External

Controls the backup and restore actions, allowing a backup to be made of all or part of a hard disk. See Chapter 4 for details. The Windows equivalent is MWBACKUP (in the MS Tools Group) and if your computer contains a copy of Windows, the Windows Backup will have been installed in preference to the DOS variety.

MSD External

A diagnostic utility that provided a detailed technical report of your computer, see Chapter 3.

NLSFUNC External

is another of the code-page utilities which is seldom, if ever, required. Normally, the information that is specific to a country such as currency sign and whether it is placed before or following a number, the time format and the date form, are all contained in the file that appears in the COUNTRY command (see earlier, this section). If a different file is to be used, then NLSFUNC can be followed by a path and filename. If the COUNTRY file is to be used, NLSFUNC must be run first.

Both NLSFUNC and COUNTRY should be used in the AUTOEXEC.BAT file, or in a separate batch file if these changes have to be made for the use of one particular program (the word-processor that you use to write to customers in Greece, for example).

Example: NLSFUNC

- sets up ready for the use of COUNTRY.

Example: NLSFUNC C:\MSDOS\FOREIGN.SYS

NLSFUNC can be installed in the CONFIG.SYS file, using INSTALL, see Chapter 2.

NUMLOCK CONFIG.SYS

determines whether the Num Lock key is on or off when the computer is booted up. See Chapter 2 for details.

PATH Internal

determines the directories that should be searched when a program name is typed. For more details, see under AUTOEXEC.BAT, Chapter 2 and Chapter 6.

PAUSE Internal batch file command

see Chapter 6.

POWER External

reduces power consumption on a portable or laptop machine when programs or devices are idle. This is useful only if the hardware conforms to the Advanced Power Management (APM) specification (as is normal nowadays). The CONFIG.SYS file must contain a line such as:

DEVICE=C:\MSDOS\POWER.EXE ADV:MAX

POWER, used with no parameters, will display the current settings. The main parameters that can be used are ADV, STD and OFF, and ADV can use options of MAX, REG and MIN. These same options can be used in the CONFIG.SYS installation.

POWER ADV allows you to use :MAX, :REG or :MIN. Using :MAX enforces the maximum possible conservation of power; the default setting is :REG. If problems are encountered, :MIN can be used to give device and program performance precedence over battery life.

POWER STD allows only the hardware power management that is built into the computer to be used. If the computer has no built-in power management system, this option turns off all power conservation measures.

POWER OFF turns off all power management actions.

PRINT External

is a command whose effect is to print an ASCII file of text on the printer. When you use PRINT, followed by the name of a file, the file will be printed on paper, but the computer can still be used for other tasks. PRINT is a time-sharing action, one that is done by loading in text in batches from the disk, storing the text in memory, and sending the text to the printer in any spare time that the computer happens to have.

You cannot, of course, remove a floppy disk from which the computer is reading the text, or alter the directory if you are working from a hard disk but you can load in a program from another drive or run such a program while the printing is being carried out. A hard disk user would normally use CD to get to the directory where the files for printing were stored, and have a suitable PATH set up to the PRINT command. Once printing has started, other programs can be run provided that this does not involve another CD command to leave the current directory.

You cannot carry out any other printing action until the printer is free for use again. The action of PRINT can set up a queue of files to be printed, and unless you terminate the action in some way, you cannot use the printer for any other printing actions.

When you make use of the PRINT command for the first time in a computing session, you might want to change some of the settings. These settings can be changed by issuing command letters in the first PRINT command, but at the first use of PRINT, you can also make one alteration without any special effort. This option is of the name of the device to which print characters will be sent, and the option takes the form of the question:

Name of list device [PRN]

You then press ENTER unless you are using a serial printer, in which case you can type COM1: and then press ENTER. Obviously, the printer must be connected and switched on, with continuous paper ready.

When printing starts, the normal prompt, such as C>, will return to show that printing is being done in the background, and that you can use the machine for other purposes.

There are several other options that can also be made at the time of the first use of PRINT. This can be done at the same time as you specify a list of files to be printed, or you can type PRINT by itself followed by these selections, as follows:

/B:1024 sets the print buffer store to 1024 characters. The larger the number here, the easier it is to interleave the printing action with any other computing. Use numbers that are multiples of 512 preferably. The default is 512.

/D:LPT2 specifies that the printer is connected to port LPT2 (which might be a network port). The default is to use LPT1.

/Q:12 allows you to use a queue of up to 12 files waiting to be printed. The default is 10.

/S:5 means that the computer will spend one sixth of its time in printing, using a ratio of computing to printing of 5:1 . The default is 8. It is not always possible to predict what effect this will have on the rate of printing, because if the printer has itself a large buffer memory, the effect may be negligible.

/U:1 and /M:2 are default values that are best left alone unless you want to experiment. The numbers that can be used can range from 1 to 255, and they control the timing of switching over from computing to printing and from printing to computing.

At the end of a PRINT document, the printer takes a new page so as to separate the documents that are being printed. In addition, PRINT allows the use of a queue of files.

Example: PRINT TXT1 TXT2 TXT3 TXT4

- would cause all four of these files to be printed, with a blank sheet of paper separating each pair of documents. You can add more files to the queue while PRINT is operating by using /P.

Example: PRINT TXT5/P

-adds the file TXT5 to the existing queue if there is space for it. With the default value of 10 files in the queue, this is seldom a problem. Strictly speaking, the use of /P is necessary only if /C has previously been used.

You can remove files from the queue by using /C or /T. The use of /C removes a file, so that if you type:

PRINT TXT4 /C

-before this file has been printed, it will be removed from the queue. Using PRINT /T removes all files from the queue. You can use wildcards in the filename if you want to place a number of files in the queue with a short command. You can also use paths in the filenames. Be careful about queue lengths, because this and the other settings that are made when PRINT is first used, cannot be changed until the machine is reset and restarted with MS-DOS.

- PRINT is not used as much as you might expect, because most text files that are used are generated by and printed by word-processors and are not simple ASCII files of the kind that PRINT requires. You should always use a word-processor's own Print command in preference to PRINT.
- Note that the options /D, /B, /U, /M, /S, /Q can be used only when the PRINT command is used for the first time after booting the computer. If you want to use one of these commands again on a subsequent PRINT, you must re-start the computer.

PROMPT Internal

is used to change the normal prompt from the form:

C:\>

or C:\MSDOS>

to some other form, which can include date and time if needed. The PROMPT word can be followed by ordinary text, which will make this text into the new prompt. If PROMPT is used alone, it restores the default message. Changing the prompt message would normally be used in the AUTOEXEC.BAT file, see Chapter 2.

Example: PROMPT Type command:

will make the prompt appear as:

Type command:

rather than as simply C>

Example: PROMPT

- will restore the normal C> type of prompt.

PROMPT can also be used with a set of special characters, all preceded with the dollar sign, to place other quantities into a prompt. One of these character pairs $e can be used to alter screen conditions if the

ANSI.SYS file has been used in the CONFIG.SYS file, see Chapter 2. The special characters are:

`$b`	the	character
`$d`	the current date
`$e`	the ESC character (ASCII 27)
`$g`	the > character
`$h`	backspace and erase previous character
`$l`	the < character (note letter ell, not number 1)
`$n`	the current default drive
`$p`	the current drive/directory path
`$q`	the = character
`$t`	the current time
`$v`	the MS-DOS version number
`$$`	the $ sign
`$_`	the new-line character
`$¯`	the carriage-return and new-line characters

Any other characters following the dollar sign are ignored by the PROMPT command.

Example: `PROMPT $p$g`

produces on screen:

```
C:\DIR1\DIR2>
```

Example: `PROMPT $d $t $n $g`

produces on screen:

```
Tue 06-10-1992 13:36:18.54 C >
```

at the time when this command was issued.

■ The prompt can be changed from within Windows 3.1 by editing the WINPMT environment variable.

QBASIC External

starts the QBASIC interpreter running so that you can write or run programs in this language. For details, refer to specialised books, such as *The QBASIC Book* (Ian Sinclair) from Bruce Smith Books Ltd.

■ Note that if you delete the QBASIC.EXE file from your disk you cannot use EDIT.

RAMDRIVE.SYS CONFIG.SYS

see Chapter 2. RAMDRIVE should be used only if SMARTDRIVE cannot be used.

RECOVER External

is not supplied with MS-DOS 6.0. If it exists on your disk from an old DOS version, delete it.

REM Internal

Used in AUTOEXEC.BAT and CONFIG.SYS commands as a way of making a comment or preventing a command from being executed. See Chapters 2 and 6 for details.

REN (or RENAME) Internal

is used to change the name of a file, or a group of files if a suitable wildcard is used. A directory does not count as a file in this respect, and cannot be renamed by using the REN command. MS-DOS can rename a directory by using the MOVE command, and DOSSHELL (see Chapter 8) will also carry out this action. The normal use of REN allows for a wildcard character in both oldname and newname.

Example: REN A:OLDFILE.TXT OLDFILE.BAK

-renames the extension of OLDFILE, retaining the main name.

Example: REN A:*.TXT *.BAK

- will change all TXT extensions to BAK extensions

Example: REN C:\FIRST\FILEA.DOC FILEB.DOC

-renames FILEA.DOC to FILEB.DOC, and there is no need to repeat the path information for the new name, since REN does not copy data. If the same path is included, the renaming will be carried out normally. If you attempt to use a different path in the new name, REN will stop with an error message of Invalid parameter.

Example: REN TEXT?.TXT CHAP?.TXT

-will convert TEXT1.TXT to CHAP1.TXT, TEXT2.TXT to CHAP2.TXT and so on

REPLACE External

is a command that allows for another method of making selective backups and updates by replacing or adding files from one drive/directory to another. The command requires you to specify one path and filename, followed by a path that ends with a directory. The filename that is specified in the source drive or directory will then be used to replace a file of the same name in the second drive or directory, the destination. If no such file exists in the destination directory, the command stops with a message to this effect (No files replaced).

A wildcard file specification can be used for the source file, so that several files can be replaced in a backup action.

The options of the command allow for the addition of the specified file to the destination directory, replacement over a range of sub-directories, for prompts (Y/N for each replacement), for replacement of files that have the Read-only attribute set (see ATTRIB, this section), and for waiting for a disk to be inserted so that single drive users are catered for.

Example: REPLACE C:\WORDS\CHAP1.TXT BOOK
- will look for the file CHAP1.TXT in the BOOK directory, and replace this with the file copy in the WORDS directory.

Example: REPLACE C:\TEXT*.TXT A:
- will replace any files with the TXT extension on the A drive with the TXT files from the TEXT directory.

The option letters are /A, /P, /R, /S, /W and /U. All are placed after the destination drive or directory name.

The /A option allows the file from the source drive or directory to be added to the destination if no such file exists to be replaced. If a matching file exists, then nothing is done.

Example: REPLACE A:MYDATA.DAT B:/A
- will add the file MYDATA.DAT to the disk in the B drive unless the file is already present on that disk.

The /P option will cause a prompt:

Replace mydata.dat (Y/N)?

to be issued for each file.

The /R option will allow files to be replaced even if they are marked as read-only files by using the ATTRIB command.

The /S option will make the destination directory include all subdirectories, and if a drive is specified, all directories on the drive.

Example: REPLACE A:/CHAP?.TXT B:\ /S
will use the specified files (with a wildcard) to replace any files of matching name stored at any part of the disk in the B drive.

The /U option will replace only the files that are older than the replacing files.

The /W option allows the process to be interrupted and a message issued so that you can change from the source disk to the destination disk on a single- floppy system.

REPLACE returns ERRORLEVEL codes that can be used in a batch file, see Chapter 6.

RESTORE External

replaces files to the hard disk that were backed up to floppy disks by using the old BACKUP command. This can also be done from another hard disk if the files were backed up on to the other hard disk by BACKUP. You can opt to restore a single file, a directory, or the entire contents of the floppies or other hard disk.

■ Files that have been backed up by using MSBACKUP or MWBACKUP must be replaced using the same program, you cannot use the old RESTORE command which is provided for compatibility only. The MS-DOS 6.0 RESTORE command can restore backups made by versions 2.0 to 5.0 of MS-DOS.

RESTORE must not be used when the commands APPEND, ASSIGN, JOIN or SUBST have been in use.

The options of RESTORE are:

/A:dd-mm-yy restore files carrying this or later date.
/B:dd-mm-yy restore files carrying this or earlier date.
/D displays the files that are available for restoring, without carrying out the restoration. The destination drive/directory must be shown even though it is not used.
/N restore files that were deleted.
/M restore files that have been altered or deleted.
/P do not restore a file that has been changed since backing-up. This avoids replacing a new version of a file with an old one, and should always be used unless the new file is known to be corrupted.
/S restore a complete directory structure, including files and subdirectories.

■ Note that RESTORE does not restore the System files IO.SYS and MSDOS.SYS.

You can also use the /L and /E options which are followed by the time, allowing you to restore files made on or later than the specified time or on or earlier than the specified time, using the same syntax as /A and /B.

Example: RESTORE C:\WP\TEXT\chap1.doc

- asks for first floppy disk to be inserted, then press any key. The screen will show the date of the backup, then a message about successful backup. You will be prompted to change floppy disks if this is needed (remember that the disks should have been numbered in order of use when BACKUP was used).

Example: RESTORE C:\WP/P

- restores files that belong to this directory and have not been changed since backing up.

■ You should use the modern MSBACKUP of MS-DOS 6.0 or MWBACKUP in Windows in preference to the older commands.

RMDIR (or RD) Internal

hard disk directory removal, see Chapter 4.

SET Internal

is used to set 'environment variables'. These are assignments that can be made in advance of running a program that uses them, and the assignments are stored in a piece of memory (normally 160 bytes) that is set aside for this use. If you attempt to store too much in this space, you will get the ominous error message Out of environment space. The amount of environment space can be increased by using a SHELL line in the CONFIG.SYS file, see Chapter 2. The use of SET depends on the programs that you run, and may not be necessary for many of your programs. The form of the command is SET name=text, where the name is one that will be used to pass the text to a program. There must not be any space on either side of the = sign.

The environment settings are stored as ASCII codes in the portion of memory that is set aside for them, with each string terminated by a zero. The end of the last string is marked with two zeros.

SET, used alone, will print on screen all of the existing environmental settings. Usually these will include COMSPEC, the file that has to be used for commands (usually COMMAND.COM) and PATH, showing the PATH set in the AUTOEXEC.BAT file. Using a line such as:

```
SET THISNAME=
```

with nothing following the equality sign will reset the use of THISNAME, so that this no longer appears in the SET list. For using environment parameters in batch files, see Chapter 6.

Example: SET COMSPEC=C:\COMMAND.COM

- will ensure that MSDOS will search drive C root directory for COMMAND.COM when this has to be reloaded after being overlaid with a program.

Example: SET TMP=D:\
-means that a program which uses TMP to represent temporary storage space can make use of a RAMdisk that has been set up as drive D:

Example: SET PATH=C:\COMPILE
-means that a program which uses PATH to define where it will look for programs will use C:\COMPILE rather than follow the paths that have been set up in a PATH command.

Example: SET
-will print on screen all the present settings of environment variables.

Example: SET ENVVAR=
-will cancel any assignment to the variable ENVVAR.

SETVER External

Allows MS-DOS 5.0 or 6.0 to pass an earlier version number to another program. Several programs read the version number of MS-DOS and will not run correctly if the 'wrong' version number is read - many such programs did not allow for version numbers beyond 3 in the belief that this was the ultimate in MS-DOS. SETVER will also allow such a program to be recorded in a list, so that the correct number can be reported when the program is used.

To allow the SETVER table to operate, the CONFIG.SYS file must contain a line that loads SETVER.EXE, see Chapter 2.

The SETVER for MS-DOS 6.0 comes with a list already constructed of the following programs, showing the version numbers that they look for:

WIN200.BIN	3.40	WIN100.BIN	3.40
WINWORD.EXE	4.10	EXCEL.EXE	4.10
HITACHI.SYS	4.00	MSCDEX.EXE	4.00
REDIR4.EXE	4.00	NET.EXE	4.00
NETWKSTA.EXE	4.00	DXMA0MOD.SYS	3.30
BAN.EXE	4.00	BAN.COM	4.00
MSREDIR.EXE	4.00	METRO.EXE	3.31
IBMCACHE.SYS	5.00	REDIR40.EXE	4.00
DD.EXE	4.01	DD.BIN	4.01
LL3.EXE	4.01	REDIR.EXE	4.00
SYQ55.SYS	4.00	SSTDRIVE.SYS	4.00
ZDRV.SYS	4.01	ZFMT.SYS	4.01
TOPSRDR.EXE	4.00	NETX.COM	5.00
EDLIN.EXE	5.00	BACKUP.EXE	5.00

ASSIGN.COM	5.00	EXE2BIN.EXE	5.00
JOIN.EXE	5.00	RECOVER.EXE	5.00
GRAFTABL.COM	5.00	NET5.COM	5.00
NETBEUI.DOS	5.00	LMSETUP.EXE	5.00
STACKER.COM	5.00	NCACHE.EXE	5.00
KERNEL.EXE	5.00	REDIR50.EXE	5.00
REDIR5.EXE	5.00	REDIRALL.EXE	5.00
IBMCACHE.SYS	5.00	DOSOAD.SYS	5.00
NET.COM	3.30		

SETVER must, for example, be used when an older Amstrad machine, such as the PC1512, is updated to MS-DOS 5.0 or 6.0, to avoid the Amstrad-specific programs such as MOUSE.COM from stopping with error messages.

The standard format is:

SETVER OLDPROG.EXE 3.2

to make the program which was designed to detect version 3.2 run under MS-DOS 6.0. This will also enter the program and its version number into the version table so that it will run without problems subsequently. You should ask yourself if you really need such old programs.

You can also use SETVER in the following form:

SETVER oldprog /delete

to remove this name and version from the version table. You can also use the /QUIET options to suppress messages during this process.

SHARE External

is used for networked systems so that files can be shared by each computer on the network. For each file, MS-DOS will allocate a sharing code which is used to decide which users can make use of the file. SHARE allows memory to be set aside for the sharing codes. When a program that is running on one machine in a network is using a file, it may use SHARE to put a lock on that file so that no other user has access in that time. The other function of SHARE is to allocate memory for locking codes.

Example: SHARE

- prepare for file sharing using default values of 2 Kbyte for sharing codes and enough memory for 20 locks.

The options /F and /L can be used to specify the filespace (in bytes) and the number of locks respectively.

Example: SHARE/F:4096/L:30

-provides for 4096 bytes = 4 Kbyte of memory for sharing, and 30 locks.

■ This command is seldom required as such because networking software will attend to all such tasks.

SHELL CONFIG.SYS command

Loads the COMMAND.COM interpreter, see Chapter 2 and COMMAND (this Chapter).

SHIFT Internal batch file command

see Chapter 6.

SMARTDRV External

Loads and runs the Smartdrive disk cache program, see Chapter 4.

SORT External

is used mainly as a filter, requiring input and output to be specified. See Chapter 7 for details which apply also to SORT used other than for filtering.

STACKS CONFIG.SYS command, see Chapter 2.

SUBMENU CONFIG.SYS

used in a menu system within CONFIG.SYS to run a sub-menu. See Chapter 2.

SUBST External

is an obsolete command that allows you to substitute a letter for a valid but unused drive in the place of a path. It should not be used on any modern system because it can cause conflicts with the commands:

ASSIGN	CHKDSK	DATAMON	DEFRAG
DISKCOMP	DISKCOPY	FDISK	FORMAT
LABEL	SYS		

as well as with the older commands BACKUP, MIRROR, RESTORE and RECOVER.

SWITCHES CONFIG.SYS command

See Chapter 2.

SYS External

transfers the hidden MSDOS.SYS and IO.SYS files and COMMAND.COM to a formatted disk provided that room has been made for them during formatting. This is done either by using SYS on a formatted but unwritten disk, or one that has been formatted with /S or /B options to make space for the system files. SYS cannot be used on a disk that has been formatted in the ordinary way and then has files recorded on to it.

Example: SYS B:

-transfers system files to disk in drive B, which should have been formatted using /B or /S.

TIME Internal

is used to set the computer clock, or to report the current time. When TIME is used, the current time will be printed, and you can then type in a correction, in the form that is specified for your country. For the UK set, this is usually HH:MM. Time is not set using seconds, but when the ENTER key is pressed the seconds figure is assumed to be zero.

Example: TIME

-gives the current time, and asks you to enter a new time. Press ENTER if you do not want to change the time.

Example: TIME 15:15

-changes the current time to 3.15 p.m. The setting is made when the ENTER key is pressed on the typed time number, so that it is possible to synchronise the setting to the seconds hand of a watch or to telephone or TV time signals.

You can use the options A or P following the time to signify a.m. or p.m. If you type a time of 12.00 or less, TIME will take this as being a.m. unless you typed 12.00P. A time such as 13.00 is taken as being in 24-hour clock (military time). Note that the timekeeping of a PC is very poor because the count of the (quartz) crystal is done using software that can be interrupted by such actions as mouse movements.

TREE External

Displays directories and subdirectories. To print the output your printer should be able to cope with the IBM graphics character set - most dot-matrix printers can be arranged to emulate the IBM ProPrinter, and H-P Laserjet or compatibles can be set for the PC-8 characters.

If TREE is used alone it will display the tree diagram for the current drive and directory. The alternative is to follow TREE by the drive and directory you want to use. Note that using TREE C:\ will result in a diagram that is usually too large to print on one screen or one sheet ofpaper. You can use | MORE following the TREE command to force the output into screen pages.

The two options are /F and /A.

/F will cause the names of files in each directory to be displayed.

/A will use normal characters to be used in place of graphics characters if your printer cannot display the IBM graphics characters.

TYPE Internal

is the command that allows a file to be copied to the screen, so that its action is equivalent to that of COPY filename PRN. TYPE must be followed by a valid filename, which can include a drive, a path, main filename and extension. Wildcards are completely ignored, and if you attempt to use a wildcard you will get an error message File not found.

- To force TYPE to accept wildcards, make use of the FOR..IN..DO construction, see under Batch files, Chapter 6.

Only ASCII files are suitable for use with TYPE, because TYPE filters out characters in the range 0 to 31 that cannot be displayed. In addition, because TYPE is intended for ASCII files, the presence of the ASCII end-of-file character (code 26) will end the use of TYPE on a file. The extended character set (codes 129 to 255) is shown, however, so that output from WordStar, or any other source of text in which some ASCII characters have 128 added to the code number (the 7th bit set) will show as characters in various European alphabets, or as mathematical symbols.

TYPE does not page its text, so that the screen scrolls continuously. The scrolling can be halted by pressing Ctrl-S or Ctrl-NumLock, and restarted by pressing Ctrl-Q, though on some computers, any single key will restart scrolling, and some keys have the unfortunate effect of inhibiting the Ctrl-S effect, so that scrolling cannot be stopped again. Using Ctrl-C or Ctrl-Break will end the display.

The lack of paging can be overcome by using the MORE filter (more useful for hard-disk users), see Chapter 7. As an alternative, there are several screen-display utilities available that allow paging and also the ability to browse through a document, scrolling backwards as well as forwards. Many such utilities are available as public domain programs, but several are fairly old and do not necessarily accept filenames with directory paths. All of these versions of TYPE are external programs.

If each page shown by TYPE is to be printed, press Ctrl-P or Ctrl-PrtSc before pressing ENTER on the type command, and again after the TYPE session has finished. In general, it is more satisfactory to use COPY filename PRN than to use TYPE for printing files in this way.

Example: TYPE C:\WORDS\FILE1.DOC

-will display the file FILE1.DOC on the screen, showing all of the ASCII codes present in the file and scrolling the screen as it fills up. Ctrl-S stops the scrolling, Ctrl-Q restarts it, and Ctrl-C (or Ctrl-Break) ends the action.

Example: TYPE A:READ.ME (Ctrl-P then ENTER)

-will print the file and also show it on screen. The printer must be ready to use before this command is issued. After typing the file, Ctrl-P must be pressed again, otherwise everything that is typed will be echoed to the printer and if the printer is switched off, the computer will appear to lock up. To release such a lock, switch the printer on, press Ctrl-P, and then switch the printer off again.

UNDELETE External

used for restoring deleted files. See Chapter 4, Hard Disk commands, for details.

UNFORMAT External

used to restore a hard disk to the state it had before a FORMAT (but not a FORMAT /U) command was executed. See Chapter 4 for details.

VER Internal

is used to print on the screen the version of MS-DOS that is currently being used.

Example: VER

on my computer produces

MS-DOS Version 6.00

VERIFY Internal

has to be followed by ON or OFF. When VERIFY ON has been used, any file that is saved on a disk will be checked to ensure that the copy has been made. The checking is not character-by-character, but the sum of ASCII codes of characters (a checksum) so that it is possible that the copy might be incorrect due to two errors cancelling each other out, but this is most unlikely.

Using VERIFY ON will certainly detect the effect of trying to record over a faulty sector on a hard or floppy disk. Using VERIFY OFF turns off the checking, and VERIFY, typed alone, will indicate whether VERIFY is on or off. VERIFY is normally OFF, and can be switched on by using VERIFY ON in the AUTOEXEC.BAT file (see Section 4).

- Note that no messages are delivered unless a disk save is faulty, so that you do not normally know whether VERIFY is on or off. The VERIFY action is the same as that used for the /V option of the COPY command.

Example: VERIFY
shows on screen:

VERIFY is off

Example: VERIFY ON
- will switch on verification for file copying.

VOL Internal

is used to print on screen the label of a disk (see LABEL), which is the name of up to 11 characters that you give to the disk. This applies mainly to floppy disks, and allows you to recognise your disks even if any paper labels have dropped off from the outside. It has little applicability to hard disk use except to require confirmation of erasing all files. The label name is also displayed when the DIR command is used.

Example: VOL
-displays label of disk in current drive.

Example: VOL B:
-displays label of disk in another drive.

VSAFE External

monitors the computer for virus infection and displays a warning if it detects the type of action that is used by a virus. See Chapter 9 for details.

XCOPY External

is an enhanced file copier which allows for selective copying of files that have archive bits set, or according to date. The main advantage of XCOPY, however, is that it can create a copy which has the same directory structure as the original disk. Unlike BACKUP, XCOPY produces files that can be used in the normal way, with no compression, but this means, of course, that a much larger number of floppies would be needed to achieve backup of a hard disk as compared to the use of BACKUP. In addition,because XCOPY tests the archive attribute of a file (see ATTRIB), it can be used in a batch file to ensure that files that have just been created are backed up without backing up files that have not been altered.

The XCOPY command is followed by the source and the destination drives and paths (if applicable), along with up to 8 option letters if these are needed. Wildcards are permitted for the source files.

Example: XCOPY C:\WORDS*.* A:

- will copy all the files from the WORDS directory and any of its sub-directories on to the disk in the A: drive, preserving the sub-directory structure of the original.

The option letters are /A, /D, /E, /M, /P, /S, /V, and /W, all of which are used following the destination drive and path.

The /A option ensures that only files that have their archive bit set (see ATTRIB, this Section) will be copied. Using /A does not reset the archive bit, so that when archive bit copying is used it is nearly always in conjunction with /M.

The /D option is followed by a colon and a date, so that only files which have been created or changed on or following this date will be copied.

The /E option must accompany the /S option, and it allows empty sub-directories to be copied as well as those which contain files.

The /M option copies only files which have the archive bit set, and will reset the archive bit after copying so that the same file will not be copied again unless it has been altered.

The /P option causes the system to ask for confirmation of each copy in the form:

C:\WORDS\CHAP1.TXT (Y/N)?

so that you can check each copy and determine for yourself whether or not to proceed.

The /S option allows files to be copied from a directory and also from all of the sub-directories of that directory. This can be very useful when a wildcard is being used in the file name.

The /V option will verify each copy after it is written to check that it is identical to the original.

The /W option will prompt you to swap disks during copying, so that XCOPY can be used with a single-floppy machine.

Example: XCOPY C:\BOOKS*.TXT A:/M/S
- will make copies of all files with the TXT extension from directory BOOKs and any of its sub-directories, copying only the files whose archive bits are set, and resetting the bits after copying so that no further backup will take place unless the files are subsequently changed.

6 Batch files

Introducing Batch Files

Many users of the PC have only ever used the computer MS-DOS commands directly, typing a command and then pressing the ENTER key so that the command is carried out at once. This type of use is called interactive, and the alternative is called batch use, in which you issue a set of commands and then let the computer get on with the job of carrying out each one in sequence. Obviously, the commands have to be typed in rather a different way so that you can achieve this, because what you are doing is to write a miniature program of commands that are intended to be executed later and in a particular order. This is done in MS-DOS, much as it is done in other operating systems, by writing a file that is recorded on to a disk. The set of commands is sometimes referred to as a 'job control language'.

This type of file as used in the PC is called a batch file, and by typing the name of such a batch file, just as you type the name of a program, you can make the computer carry out, in sequence, the commands that are contained in the file. Each batch file has the extension letters of BAT, and you should not use these extension letters for any other type of file. Suppose, for example, you created a batch file which contained instructions for copying all files from the C:\WRITEM directory that had been modified since 1/1/1993 to a floppy in drive A. This batch file might be called BAKEMUP.BAT. The important point about such a batch file is that to carry out this action all you need to do is to place the disk in the drive and type BAKEMUP, the name of the batch file. This assumes that your batch files are placed in a directory which is notified in the PATH command in AUTOEXEC.BAT, so that a batch file can be called from any directory.

■ Batch files work particularly well in conjunction with DOSSHELL, allowing you a degree of control over your computer that is hard to achieve in other ways, even by using Windows. The combination of DOS with batch files also allows you to use the machine faster than can be achieved by manual commands or the use of Shell programs.

Creating a batch file

A batch file is simply a set of commands, normal MS-DOS commands, recorded in ASCII file codes like any other text. You can create batch files with the EDIT editing program that is part of the MS-DOS 6.0 system when it has been correctly installed. You **cannot** prepare batch files with a word-processor unless the word-processor has been set to produce ASCII files -any other setting is likely to place unrecognisable codes into the text.

- The EDIT program is, in fact, part of the recent BASIC language, QBASIC, that is supplied along with MS-DOS 6.0. If you delete the files of QBASIC in order to save disk space, you will be unable to use EDIT.

You can make use of any other program that is described as a text editor, and there are many of these available as public domain or shareware, as well as commercially-sold products. Owners of the older Amstrad machines can use the RPED editor program, which is compact, simple and ideally suited to typing batch files. Another method is to prepare the text of a batch file with a word-processor which allows you to create files of the ASCII type, meaning files which contain only one code for each character on the keyboard, with no hidden codes for controlling printers.

A batch file, whatever its purpose, consists of the usual commands of MS-DOS, plus a few very useful (internal) commands that are peculiar to batch files, and which make the batch file much more like a programming language in its own right. Each batch file must have the extension letters BAT, since this identifies it as a batch file when you look at the disk directory. The fact that the file has this extension also allows the machine to locate the file when you type the main filename. If you do not use the extension BAT, then the file will simply be treated like any other file of text, not as a batch file. There is a very special reserved name for a batch file, AUTOEXEC.BAT. If you have a file of that name on any disk which contains the DOS tracks (normally the C:\ hard disk), then whatever is contained in this batch file will be carried out automatically after the machine has read the DOS and before it is ready for use by you, see also Chapter 2.

Since this book is written primarily for users of MS-DOS 6.0, the main emphasis will be on the facilities that this DOS provides, one of which is the EDIT program. When MS-DOS 6.0 is installed on a hard disk, the EDIT program is placed into a directory called MSDOS and can be put into action at any time by typing the name EDIT and pressing the ENTER key. If you are working from floppy disks, the fact that EDIT depends on the presence of the QBASIC files makes it rather bulky and you might want to seek a shorter editor that leaves plenty of room on a disk.

Figure 6.1
The screen for the EDIT program when it starts. This provides a blank space for typing, and a set of menus on the top line.

- If you use Windows you can create batch files with the Notepad editor. These batch files can be used to run DOS programs efficiently from Windows. For details, see *Newnes Windows 3/3.1 Pocket Book* (Butterworth-Heinemann).

Assuming that you are using a hard disk and that MS-DOS 6.0 has been installed as directed, complete with QBASIC, you start up (invoke) EDIT simply by typing EDIT, and when you see the screen notice about clearing the Welcome notice, pressing Esc. The screen appearance is then as shown in Figure 6.1, and you can start typing text at once. Pressing the Alt key activates the menus on the top line so that pressing the F key will then bring down the File menu, pressing the E key will bring down the Edit menu and so on. If, as is general now, you are using a mouse, you can select these menus using the mouse in the usual way and avoid the need to use keys for this purpose.

The EDIT program is capable of quite extensive work, but the only commands you need to know for writing batch files are the OPEN, SAVE and SAVE AS commands, all of which are in the File menu.

OPEN is used to alter an existing batch file, and when you use OPEN you will be asked to supply the filename of the file you want to alter. EDIT assumes this will use the TXT extension, but all batch files use the BAT extension.

SAVE is used to save an altered file, one that you started by using OPEN, so that the altered file is saved under the same name and to the same directory.

SAVE AS is used when you have created a new file and you need to specify a directory and name for it. Another use is to change the name of a file that was loaded using OPEN.

As an example of using EDIT, you can start EDIT and OPEN your existing AUTOEXEC.BAT file. With EDIT running, select the File menu and OPEN, using either the mouse or the Alt-F and O keys in succession. The screen appearance for the OPEN menu is then as shown in Figure 6.2.

When this filename is changed by re-typing *.BAT (you can place the cursor just following TXT and backspace to erase TXT, then type BAT), the appearance will change to that of Figure 6.3. The file name of AUTOEXEC.BAT now appears in the Files list because in this example this is the only BAT file in the C:\root directory.

Figure 6.2
*The Open item clicked to display the menu. The filename, whose default is *.TXT has been changed to *.BAT so that clicking on <OK> will show the AUTOEXEC.BAT file in the FIles list. Note that you can move to any directory by clicking on the name in the Dirs/Drives list.*

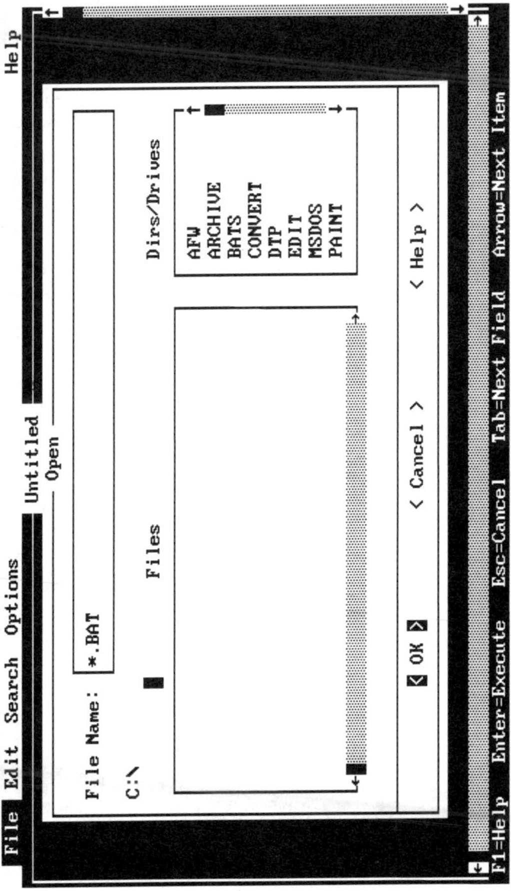

The Dirs/Drives list at the right hand side can be used to change to a floppy drive or to a different hard-disk directory. Place the mouse cursor over the black rectangle at the side of this box (the scroll-bar), click the mouse button and hold it down.

Figure 6.3
Specifying BAT files in the OPEN commands - there is only one BAT file in the root of C:

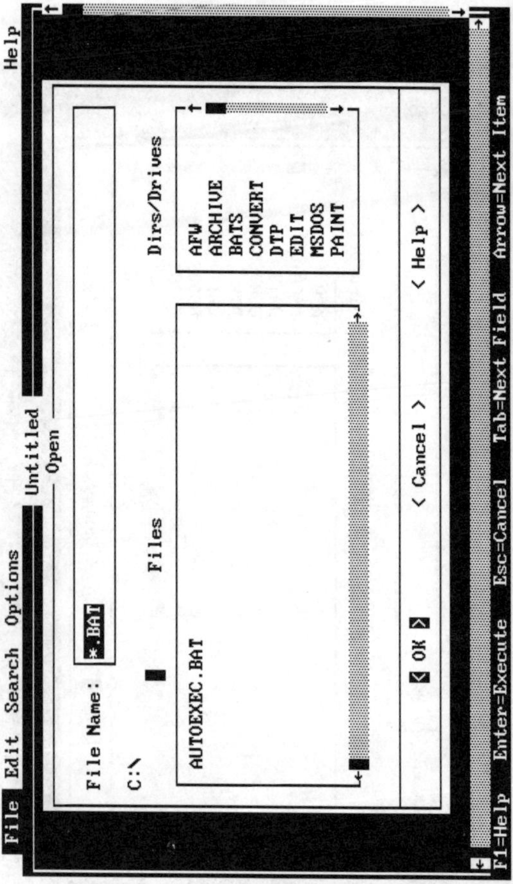

Moving the mouse will now drag the box down to see other directory or drive names. Release the mouse button when the name you want to see (which can include [A] or [B]) appears. Put the cursor on the name and click to make this the current drive or directory.

Using keys, press the Tab key to get to the box containing the file name, press the down-arrow cursor key to highlight the name AUTOEXEC.BAT.

Figure 6.4
The AUTOEXEC.BAT file for a 386 machine as seen on the EDIT screen. Note how MEMMAKER has shifted some programs into high memory.

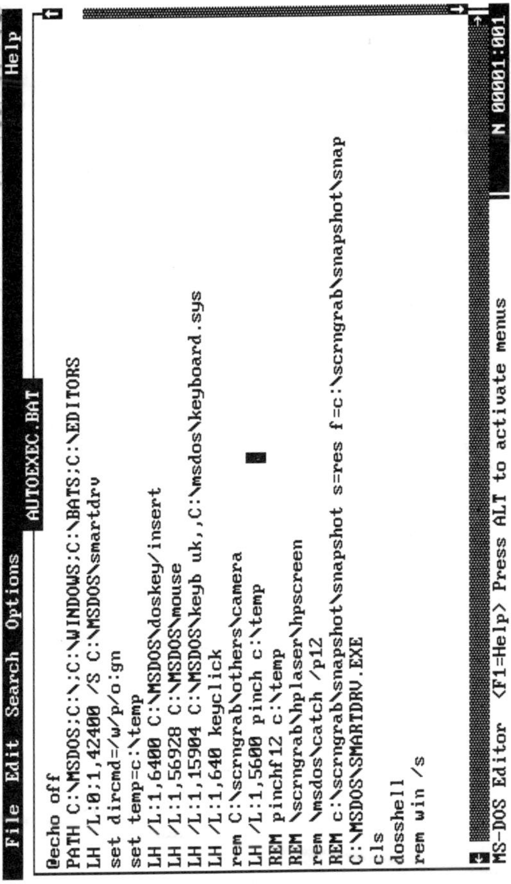

When you have the AUTOEXEC.BAT filename in the Files box, double-click with the mouse when the cursor is on the name. If you are using keys and have highlighted the name, press the ENTER key. You should now see your AUTOEXEC.BAT file - Figure 6.4 shows an example for an 386 machine.

Do **not** attempt at this stage to make any changes to this file - the example is intended only to show how

OPEN can be used to work on an existing file. If you have made absolutely no changes, you can select File and SAVE to save it back to the disk. If you are in any doubt, simply select File and EXIT. The AUTOEXEC.BAT file on the disk is not altered when the file is opened, only when a file is saved using the name of AUTOEXEC.BAT.

If you are using an editor other than EDIT you will have to find for yourself how the OPEN, SAVE and SAVE AS commands are used.

A simple batch file

We can look now at how a simple batch file can be constructed and used. The batch file used as an example will make all the files in a directory called C:\TEXT into read-only form and will be called, logically enough, RO.BAT. We start, then by running EDIT.

With EDIT running, you should be looking at a screen such as was illustrated in Figure 6.1. Do **not** use the OPEN command, because you are going to create a new file, not edit an old one. If you have already opened a file, use New from the File menu to clear this out.

Each command the batch file needs to use a line of its own, and is typed as it would be if you were typing direct commands - in this case there is only one line to type:

ATTRIB C:\text +R

and press the ENTER key so as to take a new line. You can then quit EDIT.

The file now has to be named and saved. Select the File menu, and from this use SAVE AS. This will bring up a File Name and Directory box, Figure 6.5, which allows you to select a filename and directory. Double-click on the directory you want to use (in this case, BATS), type the name of the file (in this case RO.BAT) and click on OK. You might want to use the C:\ root directory to contain your RO.BAT file.

Once the file has been saved, it can be invoked by typing RO (press ENTER key), assuming that you are using the directory in which the batch file is recorded, or a suitable path, see later.

You can stop a batch file in the middle of its action by pressing the Ctrl-C keys (hold down both Ctrl and C). This brings up a message asking you to confirm that you want to stop the batch file by typing Y or N. Typing Y will stop the batch file and return you to MS-DOS. You can also use Ctrl-C to stop temporarily (perhaps to get

Figure 6.5
The short batch file typed and SAVE AS selected to save this to disk - a file name will have to be provided and a directory selected.

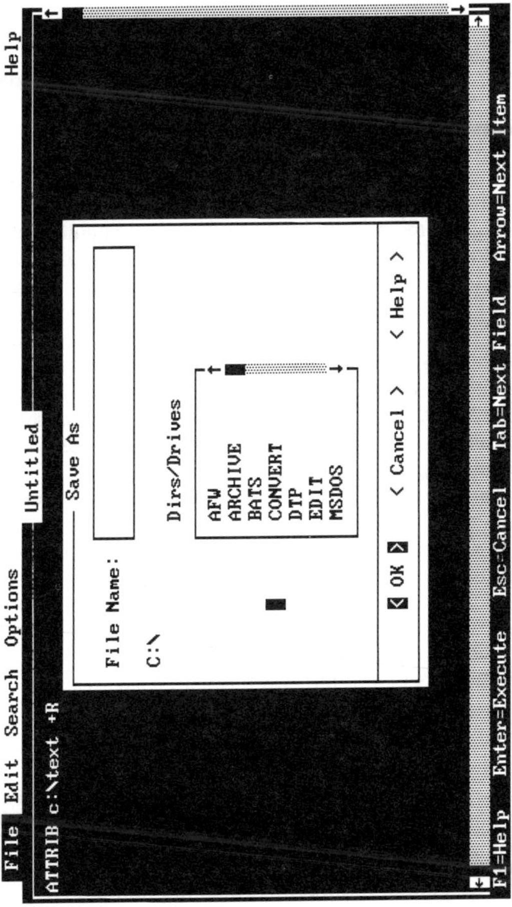

a printer ready, for example). When you press the N key, the batch file will resume.

The Pause key or Ctrl-S can also be used to halt a batch file temporarily until you press any other key. There is no option to end the batch file in this case, however.

Using a batch file directory

Batch files are short and take up very little space on a disk, particularly on a hard disk. It is tempting to keep such files on the root directory (called C:\) of the hard disk, but this is undesirable for several reasons.

1. The batch files will be mixed up with other files and with directory names.

2. If you use the DEL *.* command in error on your hard disk you will delete all of the batch files

3. A disk can carry only a limited number of files in its root directory, but an unlimited number (apart from disk space restrictions) in a subdirectory. A sub-directory is therefore the best resting place for a large number of short files.

4. A batch file will run only if there is no COM or EXE files of the same main name in the same directory.

The root directory of a hard disk should be used mainly for other directories, with the absolute bare minimum of files, only the files placed there by MS-DOS need to be in the root directory. By far the best position for batch files is a separate directory called (for example) BATS. By creating such a directory and using it for all batch files you make it easier to work on your batch files and to obtain a list of all batch files easily.

To create such a directory, type C:\ (press ENTER) to ensure that you are using the root directory of the hard disk. Now type MD BATS (press ENTER). This will create the BATS directory. To go to this directory, type CD BATS (press ENTER). Any batch file you create while you are using this directory will be placed into this directory. To return to the root directory, type CD\ (press ENTER).

In addition, you need to alter the PATH line in the AUTOEXEC.BAT file so that the BATS directory is in the search list. A line such as:

```
PATH C:\MSDOS;C:\WINDOWS;C:\BATS
```

ensures that directories called MSDOS, WINDOWS and BATS will be searched in that order when a program of batch file name is typed and the ENTER key pressed. The PATH line, if you did not have one earlier, will have been created when MS-DOS 6.0 was installed so as to ensure that files in the MSDOS directory could be used. If you are not using WINDOWS, the line:

```
PATH C:\MSDOS;C:\BATS
```

would suffice to ensure that the MSDOS and BATS directories were searched. By adding C:\BATS to your existing PATH line, you can ensure that when you type the name of a batch file, the batch file will run no matter what drive or directory you happen to be using at the time.

Uses of batch files

The simplest use of batch files is in running programs. On a hard disk you will have a large number of programs grouped into different directories, and to run a program you need to type the full filename, including the path to the directory, meaning the set of directories from the root directory. This can require some agility in typing and a good enough memory to recall the directory route for each program - no mean feat if you have several hundred programs on the disk.

Batch files simplify this by allowing you to type the details just once and use them when you want by typing the name of the batch file. Suppose, for example, that you use a directory for a program called PAINTIT which is C:\GRAPHICS\ART\PAINT\PAINTIT, in which the PAINTIT program is in a directory called PAINT which is in a directory called ART which in turn is in a directory called GRAPHICS. There would normally be other programs and directories in each of the directories as well, but we need only know the path to the program we want.

In this example, typing the full name each time you wanted to use the program would be painfully tedious, and liable to error if you mistyped any letter. By using a batch file called PAINT.BAT and containing this full command line, you ensure that all you ever need to type is PAINT, and you could even use the shorter name P.BAT and type P to run it if you used nothing else with this letter and could remember this use. This batch file, PAINT.BAT or P.BAT, can be placed in the BATS directory, so that typing PAINT (or P) will always run this batch file (but see below for conflicts of names) no matter what directory you start from.

The batch file method of starting a program becomes even more useful if any fixed 'parameters' have to be supplied with the filename. Suppose that when you use the PAINTIT program you need to type the filename and follow it with commands that will indicate the use of a monochrome screen and the use of a directory for files that the program will create (drawing files in this example). A line such as:

C:\GRAPHICS\PAINT\PAINTIT -m C:\DWGS

would mean that the display was monochrome and the files were to be placed in the directory called C:\DWGS. Instead of typing all of this out each time, creating a batch file with this line reduces your effort to typing PAINT - and if you named your batch file as P.BAT, you would only have to type P and press ENTER in order to run it. Using a batch file for each of your main programs makes it far easier to run these programs that any amount of pointing and clicking with a mouse - and you can determine for yourself what you put into your batch file.

Simply running a program is in itself a useful application of a batch file, and the reduction in effort that it can achieve is very well worth while, as is the reduction of the number of errors caused by mistyping a long name, forgetting a long path and so on. Another useful point is that the batch file can deal with the case of requiring a subsidiary program to be loaded.

Suppose, for example, that each time you use a graphics program called DRAWIT you need to run a program which sets up your printer; we'll imagine that the program is called DOTTIT. Starting the DRAWIT program without DOTTIT allows you to make drawings and save files, but does not allow you to print the drawings so that in order to print you need to leave DRAWIT, run DOTTIT, start DRAWIT again and print the files.

All this is tedious and a strain on the memory, so by creating a batch file called DRAW.BAT you can incorporate these actions automatically, using lines such as:

C:\PRINTER\DOTTIT

C:\GRAPHICS\DRAWIT

to run the program called DOTTIT which is in the PRINTER directory and then run the program called DRAWIT which is in the GRAPHICS directory.

From now on, you can ensure that these actions are carried out in correct order by simply typing DRAW and pressing the ENTER key. This will run the batch file which will execute the two programs in order, and you will never again find yourself having to leave one program, run the other and then start again. The only problem that this system can generate is that if the first program is one that remains in memory, running the batch file for a second time in a session may cause problems (lack of memory, because the memory is filled with identical copies of a program). This can be avoided (see Chapter 3), but for many purposes the problems do not arise because a program is used only once in a session.

Conflict of names

It is quite possible for a batch file to have the same name as a program file, and for two program files to have the same name but with different extensions. There is no conflict if the files are in different directories - the file that is in the directory that is searched earliest will be run, the others ignored. If the files are in the same directory, the MS-DOS priority system is that the COM file will run, the others will be ignored. If only EXE and BAT files of the same main name are present, the EXE file will be run. The BAT file is at the end of the chain, hence the usefulness of a separate BATS directory which is searched early in the PATH statement.

Batch file Parameters

A parameter, as far as running programs is concerned, is a piece of information that is added to the program name. The (imaginary) example that was used previously of PAINTIT -m C:\DWGS makes use of the two parameters -m and C:\DWGS to configure the program for a monochrome screen display and for placing data files in the C:\DWGS directory. This sort of use of parameters is quite common, and for this type of example, the parameters are fixed - you would normally retain the same display and always want to put the files into the same directory.

Some programs, however, require parameters that might not remain unchanged. A word-processor might require you to specify the directory for its data files, and you would probably need to keep more than one directory, such as one for letters, one for financial documents, one for addresses, one for short articles and so on. There would be little point in entering a fixed name into the batch file line that started such a program; what you need is a method of specifying the parameter as you type the batch file name, just as you would specify it when you typed the program name.

This is catered for in batch file use by the *parameter names* %1 to %9 (%0 is used to mean the name of the batch file itself). Suppose, for example, that you have a word processor called SHRDLU and it can be started by typing its name followed by a space and then the name of the directory that contains the files you want to use with it. With just one parameter to use, the main line of this batch file will be something like:

C:\WORDS\SHRDLU %1

in which %1 is a placeholder for the name that you will type when you start the batch file running. If you call this batch file PEN and you start it by typing PEN LETTERS, then the name LETTERS is the first parameter name, and it is assigned in place of %1, so that the effect is as if you had typed:

C:\WORDS\SHRDLU LETTERS

starting the word processor and making use of the correct data directory.

This provides very much more flexibility than the use of a fixed name within the batch file, and the parameter %1 can be used more than once in the batch file if this is required. You might, for example, want to copy all of the files in whatever directory was selected to a floppy after ending use of the word-processor, in which case the lines in the batch file:

C:\WORDS\SHRDLU %1

COPY %1*.TXT A:

would see to it that the directory was chosen and later used to copy all files with the extension of TXT (in that directory) to a floppy in the A: drive. An extension of this method uses XCOPY to copy only the files that have been altered since the previous time the backup was performed.

You need to remember what the parameters stand for. In the example, %1 will be a directory name such as LETTERS, and in a filename it will be followed by the backslash (\) and then by the name of the file itself. When the batch file substitutes LETTERS for %1, the complete filename must be in its correct form. Note that when you use a batch file along with DOSSHELL (see Chapter 8) you can ensure that you are prompted for each parameter, with a reminder of what is needed.

Whether omitting a parameter will cause an error message or not depends on the command that uses the parameter. For example, if the command is DIR %1, then omitting a parameter when you call the batch file will provide a directory listing for whatever directory you happen to be in, rather than an error message. You will get an error message only if the absence of a parameter makes the command impossible to execute. This is not necessarily obvious. For example, if you used DEL B:\%1, then omitting a parameter will be taken as meaning *.*, all files to be deleted, and you will get the usual message about whether you want to do this or not. This could lead to unwanted and unwitting deletion of all files in a directory - and you might be using the root directory of the hard disk at the time. To get around this, the absence of parameters can be detected, see later, and can be used to cause the batch file to be abandoned with a warning message.

The number of parameters that you can use in a straightforward way is 9, %1 to %9 inclusive. You can, in fact, use more parameters by recycling numbers with the SHIFT command. This is most unusual because very few programs require so many parameters that would need to be changed each time you used the batch file - it is more usual for all but one or two parameters to remain fixed.

■ Note that a name which you supply for a parameter must not contain any spaces. A space is always taken as a separator between parameters. This can cause problems if you want to write a batch file which uses parameters other than filenames.

Using ECHO

Batch files can make use of a set of commands of their own, many of which can be used only in batch files. One useful command is ECHO which exists in several forms.

@ECHO OFF will suppress the appearance of the batch file commands on the screen. Whether you use this or not is a matter of choice. Some batch file users like to see the commands appear, others do not. It is an advantage to leave the command out when you first try out a batch file, because the appearance of the commands on the screen indicate the progress of the file.Once you have tested the batch file thoroughly you can use @ECHO OFF to suppress the printing of these command lines.

ECHO has another use, to make text appear on the screen even when @ECHO OFF has been used. The text in this case is not the command lines, which remain suppressed, but any text you like to put in. For example, if your batch file contains the line:

ECHO Do you want to copy this file to A:\ ? (Y/N)

then the words of the message (but not the word ECHO) will appear when this line is run. You can use this to deliver reminders (a simple HELP system), warnings (about deleting files, for example) or error messages (about absence of parameters, for example) or any other use you can think of. You can make a batch file which consists only of ECHO lines in order to provide outline documentation for a program; such a batch file can be called from another batch file if required, using CALL (see later).

Pipes, filters and redirection in Batch-files

The use of piping, filters and redirection is particularly valuable in batch files, because once you have constructed the batch file with all of its commands, you can use it for any files that you need to exercise these actions on. One example is an indexing program. This is intended for indexing words in a book, so that each entry consists of a word or phrase, then a comma, and then a page number.

■ This example uses several batch-file commands that have not yet been explained in this Chapter.

The file provides for calling up a simple editor (the RPED editor which comes with the Amstrad machines) to create the list of words and page numbers, and then recording this. The file is then sorted into order, and recorded again so that it can finally be processed by a word-processor. The form of the batch file allows you to use it in the form:

```
INDX TXTFIL.TXT
```

for a new index, or in the form:

```
INDX OLDTXT.FIL NEWTXT.FIL
```

when an old index has to be extended.

```
echo off
cd\textutil
echo Is this a new index?
choice
if errorlevel 2 goto oldie
del tmpind
rped tmpind
sort < tmpind > %1
goto endit
:oldie
rped %1 tmpind
sort < tmpind > %2
 :endit
cd\wstar
ws
cd\
```

This asks if the index is new so that if a very long index had been recorded half-way through, it could be resumed. If the index is a new one the temporary file *tmpind* is deleted (it might not exist on the disk, but this does not matter), and the RPED editor program is then called to create a file called *tmpind*. Once this has been created, and after leaving RPED, the SORT line arranges the index into alphabetical order and files this under the filename that was supplied for use with a new index. The GOTO ENDIT line then moves to the set of lines which call up the word processor (WordStar in this case) so that the index can be put easily into printable form.

For an old index, both old and new names have been provided, and jumping to label :oldie will cause RPED to be called with instructions to read the first file and, when finished, to save under the filename *tmpind*. The usual sort then follows, and the file is recorded under the second name that was supplied in the command line for the batch file. The word processor is then called up as before.

Another use of piping is to overcome the inability of some commands to accept wildcards. One well-known example is FIND, so that FIND is not particularly useful for directory lists, but if a listing of a complete directory is obtained from CHKDSK (so that all files can be read), then FIND can be used as a filter to locate specific parts of a filename, such as the extension (but without using the wildcard characters). As an example:

```
CHKDSK/B | FIND ".TXT" | SORT | MORE
```

will obtain all the file and sub-directory names, pass them to FIND so that the extension TXT can be located, and then SORT to put into order. Since this is likely to be used on a hard disk, MORE is added to page the output.

The extension name could be passed to this in a batch file by using %1 in the usual way, but whatever is typed in the command line must be in capitals.

Suppressing messages from commands

@ECHO OFF will suppress the appearance of the lines of the batch file itself, but it will not suppress the messages from MS-DOS commands. For example, if you include in a batch file the command:

```
COPY C:\SHRDLU\TEXT\*.TXT B:
```

then as each file copies you will get a message of the form

C:\SHRDLU\TEXT\CHAP1.TXT
C:\SHRDLU\TEXT\CHAP2.TXT
C:\SHRDLU\TEXT\CHAP3.TXT

- and so on for each file. This can be suppressed by using the normal MS-DOS facility of redirecting the messages away from the screen. The destination can be a file if you wanted to keep a record, but if you simply want to remove the messages, they can be sent to NUL to make them vanish.

The format of the command needs to be altered to:

COPY C:\SHRDLU\TEXT*.TXT B: > NUL

with a space on each side of the > (redirection) sign. When the command has been modified in this way, there will be no indication other than the activity of the disk drive that anything is happening. This is not always wise, and it is better, if you want to avoid these messages, to remind yourself what is happening and when it is completed.

This can be done by using messages of your own before and after the command, and a further refinement can be added with the PAUSE command (a batch-file command). For example, if the piece of batch file above is altered so as to read:

ECHO Copying to B: - please place disk in drive
PAUSE
COPY C:\SHRDLU\TEXT*.TXT b: > NUL
ECHO Copying completed.

then when the first message is printed on the screen it will be followed by a message that reads:

Press any key to continue...

and the rest of the batch file will not run until you have pressed a key.

■ Get into the habit of using the spacebar as 'any key' when this message appears, because 'any key' is misleading - some key combinations could cause problems. Using the spacebar is always safe.

Going back to the example, pressing a key will then allow the copy action to take place, but with no on-screen reminders of what files are being copied. The message about copying being complete appears after all of the files have been copied, so that you know when this action is ended (allowing you to remove the floppy disk, for example).

Remember that a lot of messages can make the screen look cluttered. You can use the MS-DOS command CLS in a batch file to clear the screen, and this command can be placed at any point in a batch file. This allows any subsequent message to appear on an otherwise blank screen. If you want a line of text to appear on a clear screen, but not at the top of the screen, you can use ECHO. (a full-stop following ECHO) to move one line down. If you want to space text out from the left hand side you must add the spaces yourself.

Using REM

REM is another word that can be used inside a batch file (and also in CONFIG.SYS, see Chapter 2). Its effect is to cause any following text on the same line to be ignored, and it is used to allow a batch file to carry reminders about how it works. The semicolon **;** can be used in the same way as REM.

This is important if you have written an elaborate batch file and may need to alter it at some time in the future. By placing reminders about the actions, you save yourself the effort of working out what was intended. This can be a considerable time-saver because it is quite surprising how easily the purpose of actions can be forgotten. Another use is to 'REM-out' any line in a batch file that you want to be ignored during testing (for example).

Note, for example, how REM lines added to the earlier example make it clear what has been intended, and save effort when the batch file is edited.

```
@ECHO OFF
ECHO Copying to B: - please place disk in drive
PAUSE
REM Press any key to continue
REM allows time for inserting disk.
COPY C:\SHRDLU\TEXT\*.TXT b: > NUL
REM copies files to B and suppresses file name
messages
ECHO Copying completed.
REM Disk can now be removed.
```

These REM lines are not displayed because of the use of @ECHO OFF. You should not use the symbols >, < or | in a comment line that starts with ; or REM.

Running sub-files with CALL

One batch program can run another, simply by placing the name of the batch program as a line in the other batch program. For example, if your batch program needs to end by making use of another batch program called ENDIT the lines:

```
REM Copy files
COPY C:\TEXT\*.DOC B: > NUL
ECHO Files copied.
ENDIT
```

will carry out the copying of files, notify you when the action is complete, and then set the other batch file ENDIT into motion. This is particularly easy if you place all of your batch files into the same directory, but if the files are scattered you might need to specify a directory for the ENDIT batch file in this example.

Suppose, however, that the first batch file were of the form:

```
REM Copy files
COPY C:\TEXT\*.DOC B: > NUL
ECHO Files copied
ENDIT
ECHO Now put another disk in drive B:
PAUSE
COPY C:\123\ACCTS\*.wk1 B: > NUL
ECHO Copy complete.
```

in which another set of copy actions is needed following the use of ENDIT. This in its present form will **not** work. When a batch file is used within another in this same way, its termination ends the first batch file. In other words, when ENDIT runs in the above bad example, its end is the end of all batch file activity (unless ENDIT uses the name of yet another batch file), and the second set of copy actions will not run.

To make the ENDIT batch file run and then return to the original file, the command word CALL must be used.

```
REM Copy files
COPY C:\TEXT\*.DOC B: > NUL
ECHO Files copied
CALL ENDIT
ECHO Now put another disk in drive B:
PAUSE
COPY C:\123\ACCTS\*.wk1 B: > NUL
ECHO Copy complete.
```

- so that in this example, after ENDIT has run, control returns to the first batch file and ensures that the second COPY action takes place.

This is important if, for example, you use one batch file to call up a file of Help notes (using a command such as TYPE NOTES.DOC), because you would certainly want to return to the first file from this one. In other batch files, however, you might not need to return - if, for example, the second batch file were run because of an error in the first one.

Advanced batch commands

Batch files, even at their simplest, are an extremely useful way of automatically carrying out a sequence of steps, an extended program pathname, or simply abbreviating a command, but their real strength comes when you can make use of the full set of batch commands in your files. For the more advanced user, a batch file can be a miniature program in its own right, dealing with a complex set of commands on files that can, of course, include such points as redirection, pipes and filters.

The most useful of the more advanced batch techniques make full use of the % parameters. In addition, there are several commands which allow batch files to select, to test and to work on lists of files. These advanced batch commands can be used, for example, to compensate for deficiencies in the action of some MS-DOS utilities. For example, some utilities will not accept a filename that contains a wildcard character (such as *.TXT), but by making use of a batch file that feeds filenames in correct form to the utility, wildcard use can be obtained. If you use programs that do not create backup versions of files, a batch file can be written which will to some extent make up for this deficiency.

An XCOPY example

As an example of how a batch file can be used to supplement the use of a program, the use of XCOPY in a batch file will be illustrated here. XCOPY is a standard utility of MS-DOS which, unlike COPY, can be used with some extra parameters that extend its usefulness by making the copy action more selective. The simple use of XCOPY is the same as that for COPY, with the format of **XCOPY source destination**. What makes XCOPY so useful is the list of optional command letters, see the XCOPY entry in Chapter 5.

As an example, consider the problems of backing up files created by a word-processor on a hard-disk machine. You would not want to make a backup copy of every file the word-processor has ever produced each time you left the program, but it would be decidedly useful to be able to backup the files that had been modified in a session. Working in this way, you have a backup of all your recently-edited files on a floppy disk or set of floppies and you can decide for yourself when to erase the copy on the hard disk or when to erase the backup for the older files. This can save a lot of tedious back-up work. In addition, the backup files can be in an accessible form, unlike those of MSBACKUP.

- You can use a double-spaced floppy, providing a reasonable amount of backup space. This floppy can be mounted by using a line in the AUTOEXEC.BAT file or in the file that calls the program which produces the data files.

In the example, we can assume that the word-processor is being started from a batch file and that the directory for the text files has been set within the batch program, such as by using:

```
CD \WORD\TEXT
\WORD\SHRDLU
```

so setting the current directory as that of the text files and then calling the word-processor into action by providing its full pathname and its filename. When the word-processor ends its action, normally when you select QUIT or some similar option, the next item on the batch file should carry out the copying. A useful choice is:

```
XCOPY C: A: /m
```

which will copy files selectively from the current directory in C: (which has been set as \WORD\TEXT) to the floppy in the A: drive, and copying only the files with the archive attribute set. You would normally precede this by a message warning you to place a disk in the A: drive, and a PAUSE step to allow time. As each file is copied, the archive bit in the original (on the hard disk) has its archive bit reset so that it will not be copied by this command again unless it has been altered by using the word-processor or other program on it.

- The archive attribute (see entry for ATTRIB, Chapter 5) is a small part of each file. It can take a value of 0 (reset) or 1 (set), and is always set to 1 when the file is used by a program. XCOPY is one of the few MS-DOS utilities which makes use of this attribute.

XCOPY will not copy files that are classed as hidden or system (which do not appear in a directory listing). This suggested use of XCOPY can be extended. Suppose that the \WORD\TEXT sub-directory contained other sub-directories use for other files (one for letters, one for notes, one for ideas, one for articles for magazines and so on). You might in the course of an editing session work with files from more than one of the sub-directories, so that it would be useful to backup all of the files that had been altered. This requires only one small alteration to the XCOPY line, making it read:

```
XCOPY C: A: /m/s
```

and with this version of XCOPY in use you could alter the start of the batch program to set the directory to that for SHRDLU rather than to a text-file directory.

Other batch actions

These examples illustrate the use of a batch file before a program, to prepare directories, and after a program, to copy files selectively. These principles can be greatly extended. Suppose, for example, that your computer uses the later 286, 386 or 486 chip and is fitted with extended memory. Some of this extended memory (if it is not all taken up by using Windows) can be used as RAMdisk, meaning that the memory can be allocated a disk file letter and used as if it were a disk. The difference is speed - memory is much faster than any disk, both for reading and for writing.

One use for such a RAMdisk is in holding the spell-checker for a word-processor. Spell-checking involves selecting each word in a document and checking it against all the words in the spell-checker dictionary that start with the same letter. This requires a lot of disk fetching if the dictionary is on the hard disk, but if the dictionary is on RAMdisk the action is very fast, and a long document can be checked very rapidly.

Since RAMdisk is memory and will be deleted when the machine is switched off, it must have the dictionary copied to it each time the word-processor is selected. This means that the copying action should be made part of the batch file that runs the word-processor - the setting up of the RAMdisk itself will be done using a line in the AUTOEXEC.BAT file.

A typical line for copying a dictionary to RAMDISK would be:

```
COPY C:\WORD\MAIN.DCT D:
```

where the RAMdisk is using the letter D: as its drive name in this example. The computer will allocate this letter when the RAMdrive is created, and it will remain the same unless you add some other drive, so that you can type this letter into the batch file as shown. See the entry for LASTDRIVE in Chapter 5 for details of making more drive letters available if needed.

Where a spell-checking system is used, there is usually a personal dictionary as well, containing words that are not in the main dictionary (such as personal and placenames, or specialised words). This dictionary can also be copied over for faster use, though it is not so essential, using an additional line such as:

COPY C:\WORD\PERSONAL.DCT D:

following the copying of MAIN.DCT.

Remember that these are examples - you will have to use the names that your own word-processor uses.

Copying a dictionary to D: does not mean that it is usable. Many word-processors will allow you to specify once and for all where the dictionary files are kept (your answer would be D:\), but some will always report absent dictionary files until you specify D: or whatever drive you are using. A few older word-processors insist in the directory files being in the same path on the new drives as they were on the C: drive, so that if the files were in C:\WORD they have to be placed in D:\WORD. This requires the batch file to be of the form:

```
D: MD WORD
C:\WORD
COPY *.DCT
D:\WORD
```

before the word-processor program is started. This also creates a new problem - if you leave the word-processor and then start it again you will get an error message to the effect that D:\WORD cannot be created because it already exists. You can deal with this by adding the command DEL D:*.* as the last line in the batch file, clearing the RAMdisk, or by testing for the existence of files in D: before copying (see later for the IF EXIST type of command).

RAMdisk can also be used to hold batch files - these will run much faster from RAMdisk than from a hard disk. You might need, depending on how you use the computer, to place the RAMdisk drive letter in the PATH statement. For most purposes, however, it is preferable to use SMARTDRV to speed up all disk actions rather than use precious memory on a RAMDRIVE.

The ability to use sets of commands before and after running a main program is one of the supreme advantages of using batch files, saving you the effort of needing to remember all the steps that have to be carried out at these stages. The DOSSHELL also allows these actions to be programmed in, either by running a batch file, by calling up batch files, or by incorporating commands into the DOSSHELL program commands - more of this in Chapter 8.

Batch sub-commands

The use of parameter numbers such as %1, %2 and so on, can greatly increase the control that you can achieve along with a set of batch file commands, but this is only a taste of what can be achieved. There are several command words, batch sub-commands, that are used in batch files, and can be used only in batch files. If you don't know any programming languages, it is less easy to learn the use of some of these commands, but on the other hand, if you do know a programming language such as BASIC, you have to remember that though the batch subcommands are similar to some BASIC commands, they are by no means identical.

The most important of these commands are used to provide two of the main actions of any computer programming language, test-and-branch and looping. The test-and-branch command uses the words IF and GOTO, and the looping commands use FOR, IN and DO. As for any programming language, these words are reserved for use in batch files and must be used in the correct form (their *syntax*).

A test action is one that compares two quantities (numbers or words) to find if they are identical or not. The result of the test will be either TRUE (they are identical) or FALSE (they are not identical); there is no provision for any other possible result. A branch action is one that forces the lines of a program to be carried out in a different sequence. Normally, the commands of a batch file are written with one command per line, and the program starts at the first line and works through the lines in order to the last line. A branch will alter this sequence, allowing a number of lines to be skipped. If several lines are skipped, but still moving to the last line, the branch is a forward branch; if the lines are skipped so as to return to an earlier line, the branch is a backward one. The word GOTO is used to specify where a branch must lead in the event of a TRUE reply from the IF test.

A test need not necessarily be followed by a branch using GOTO, because the test allows for automatic progress to the next line in the event of a FALSE answer. In many examples, however, this would lead to incorrect action of the batch program as we shall see.

The form of a typical test is :

```
IF item==specified
```

in which *item* can be any letter, digit or name, and *specified* is some other letter, digit or name. Either of these can be a parameter such as %1, %2 and so on, allowing tests to be carried out on parameters that are entered when the batch file is started. Neither *item* nor *specified* should contain any spaces, because a space is taken as being a separator between entries.

For example:

```
@ECHO OFF
IF %1==D DEL \WORD\TEXT\OLDFILE.TXT
\WORD\SHRDLU
```

assumes that a word processor called SHRDLU is held in the WORD directory. If this batch file is recorded and named PEN, then it can be started in two different ways. If you start the batch file by typing PEN D then a file called OLDFILE in the \WORD\TEXT directory will be deleted and following the deletion the word processor will run. If you start the batch file by typing PEN with no parameter, or by using PEN A or any letter other than D, the deletion will not be carried out, and the word processor will run as if the second line did not exist.

The rules for test-and-branch are strict.

1. There must be **no space** on either side of the double equality signs, nor between the signs.
2. There must be spaces used to separate the command word IF from the conditions and between the parts of the command as shown.
3. If you start the file without supplying a parameter you will get an error message (Syntax error) when the test line runs, but the batch file will not stop, it continues to the next line.

The letter D or d, in this example, can be used - but the batch file will discriminate between upper and lower case letters used in this way, so that if you specify D you cannot use d and if you specify d you cannot use D. In all other respects a batch file treats upper and lower case letters as identical.

■ The MS-DOS manual shows the condition in the form:

IF "%1"=="D"

but the quotemarks are not essential to the working of the test, as the preceding example has shown.

One of the important ways of using a test is to check that a batch file has been entered with the correct number of parameters - as we have seen, failure to provide a parameter will cause a Syntax error message to appear with MS-DOS 5.0 and 6.0 batch files, and since any sort of error message is likely to strike terror into the heart of the user who does not expect it, we should arrange our batch files to avoid that kind of thing.

You might think that the line could be written as:

```
IF %1==D DEL \WORD\TEXT\OLDFILE.TXT > NUL
```

but redirection of messages to NUL does not permit the redirection of the message Syntax error from the batch file, though it would lose any message from the DEL command. In other words, the > NUL step is taken as belonging to the DEL command and since the DEL command is not carried out unless a D has been entered, the error message will still appear.

The requirement to detect that nothing has been entered as a parameter requires a rather peculiar form of test, using a line such as:

```
IF *%1==*
```

The important point here is to avoid a space, and the test does so by using the * as a dummy character - any character other than a percentage sign would do in its place. By testing for *%1 being equal to *, we are testing whether the parameter %1 exists - many programming languages would simply test to see if %1 were equal to a space, but this type of test cannot be used in a batch file.

Another option is a test of the form:

```
IF "%1"==""
```

To demonstrate this action, try this short example, calling it PARAM.BAT -

```
@echo off
if *%1==*
echo No Params
Echo Parameter is %1
```

and try calling it using first PARAM and then PARAM A. You will find that if you use no parameter the 'No Params' message is delivered, but if you enter a letter, number or word, then whatever you entered will be repeated in the last ECHO line of the file. Note that the last line is always carried out even if no parameter has been entered. Lines are executed in sequence unless a GOTO instruction is used.

The GOTO command.

The command GOTO is used to make the execution of a batch file move from one line to another which is not the normal next line in order. Like all instruction words, GOTO has to be used in exactly the right way, and that way involves the use of a label. A label in this sense is a word (meaning some collection of letters or digits) which is used to pinpoint the position of a line, the line that follows the label.

Each label name must be in a line of its own, and to make sure that a label can be distinguished from a command, it is prefixed by a colon. The label must be a single word with no spaces, and only the first eight characters of a label are used - though you can type as long a name as you like. For example, if your label name is :THISISTHEPLACE, the program will take this is being :THISISTH . Note that if you tried to use a label called :THISISTHEWRONGPLACE it would be treated as the same label, since its first eight characters are identical.

The command GOTO is used followed by the label word, excluding the colon and using a space between GOTO and the word. For example, if the label word is :GOHERE then a suitable direction to this would be GOTO GOHERE. The line that will be executed following GOTO GOHERE will be the line immediately after the label word :GOHERE.

For example, look at this use of a test for use of a batch file name with no parameter. The batch file is called PARMTEST.

```
@echo off
if *%1==* goto NOPARAMS
REM Rest of file in here
GOTO ENDIT
:NOPARAMS
ECHO You must enter a filename after  the batch
ECHO name, such as PARMTEST A:TEXTFILE
:ENDIT
```

In this example, we can trace what will happen in either possible case. If no parameter name is provided the test in the second line will give a TRUE answer and the program moves to the NOPARAMS label. This runs the two ECHO lines so that the reminder is issued, allowing the user to re-run the batch file with the correct parameter entered next time. If the parameter is supplied, the second line gives a FALSE result so that the GOTO part is ignored and the instructions of the batch file are obeyed. To save space this part is represented as a REM line. The GOTO ENDIT line then ensures that the two ECHO lines are not used, because the message would be inappropriate - the automatic progression of a batch file from one line to the next would otherwise automatically run the two ECHO lines.

There is an alternative method which can be used to deliver the message, and it becomes particularly useful if more than one message might need to be delivered in different circumstances. This is to use a CALL to another batch file to attend to the message. This can be a better solution if the message is elaborate or if more than one message needs to be delivered.

For example, if the main program is called NEWPARM.BAT and it needs to test for a parameter being used, it can now be written in a form such as:

```
@echo off
if *%1==* noparms
rem rest of file here
echo Parameter is %1
```

and this will in turn need another batch file to be written and named NOPARMS.BAT. This latter file can take a form such as:

```
@echo off
echo No filename supplied.
echo Please use in the form NEWPARM filename
echo END
```

and by using NOPARMS in the first batch file you will ensure that there is no possibility of returning from the message batch file to the first batch file. Since the first file cannot be used without its parameter, there would be no point in returning to it in any case. If a different type of test were being made, and you might need to return to the first batch file, a line such as CALL NOPARMS would be used.

The principle of testing can be extended to the example shown below, using a main batch file and a subsidiary. In this example, however, the subsidiary file alters the parameter to provide a default. The main file can be saved using a name such as ACHECK.BAT

```
@echo off
if %1==A: NOAH
 if %1==a: NOAH
rem Other parts of file
echo Parameter is %1
```

This file will accept a drive letter or hard disk path as a parameter, and will test for the A: drive being specified. If any other drive has been used, the batch file proceeds to do whatever it has to do (only a REM line is shown for the sake of illustration), but if the A: drive has been specified, the subsidiary batch file NOAH is run (not called - there must be no return to the main file in this way).

- Note that there are two separate tests, one for A: and one for a: because the batch file distinguishes between upper and lower case in a test.
- You can also use a NOT test such as

  ```
  IF NOT %1==A:NOAH
  ```

  to test for a name not being equal to another

The NOAH.BAT file for this example is:

```
@echo off
Echo Cannot use drive A:
Echo C: drive will be set as default
ACHECK c:
```

in which the reminder is delivered, and the original batch file is called again, using the default value of C:. It would be greatly preferable if you could type a corrected drive letter, but a batch file can accept a parameter only in the command line; there is no provision for entering anything at any other point (such as a PAUSE) in a batch file. The DOSSHELL is more flexible in this respect.

Testing for presence of files on a disk

Another important IF test in this set is to find if a file exists in a selected directory (or drive). The test:

```
IF EXIST filename
```

- in which *filename* can include a full path, will be TRUE if the file *filename* is in the stated directory or on the selected drive, and whatever follows the IF test will be carried out. To test for a file not being on the drive or directory, you can use IF NOT EXIST filename, which will allow the following action to be carried out if the file is not present. Use of this type of test avoids the error messages that appear when you try to delete or rename a file that is not on the disk.

As an example, try the following:

```
@echo off
IF EXIST %1\*.TXT echo Text files(s) existing in %1
```

- saving this file as TXTEST.BAT. If you then type the name followed by the usual space and then a drive or directory, you will find from the message whether any files with the extension of TXT exist in that drive or directory. Note that if you omit any drive or directory, the message will print out but with a blank in place of the drive or path. To be more effective, this batch file needs a line that will check for absence of a parameter, as detailed earlier.

Note the form of the filename as %1*.TXT, so that the parameter %1 can be a drive name such as A: or a directory path such as C:\WORDS\TEXT. This simple file can be elaborated to test for other types of file. Though tests for extension letters are shown, the tests could be made for specific file names.

```
@ECHO OFF IF *%1==* GOTO NOPARM
IF EXIST %1\*.TXT ECHO Text file(s) in %1
IF EXIST %1\*.BAT ECHO Batch file(s) in %1
IF EXIST %1\*.DOC ECHO DOC files(s) in %1
GOTO ENDIT
:NOPARM
ECHO Must specify drive letter (such as A:)
ECHO or path such as C:\WORD\TEXT
:ENDIT
```

You can use the result of the IF test to deliver a message, and wait for you to insert the correct (floppy) disk. This is a very common action in batch files that install programs, and the file that is tested for can be one that is specific to a disk and placed on that disk - you could make a file consisting of a single letter, for example, and call it simply A. This would lead to a batch file such as:

```
@ECHO OFF
:START
ECHO Please place disk A in drive A:
PAUSE
IF NOT EXIST A:\A GOTO NOTHISDISK
REM OTHER COMMANDS HERE
GOTO ENDIT
:NOTHISDISK
ECHO This is not the correct disk -
GOTO START
:ENDIT
```

In this example, the PAUSE provides time to select the correct disk and place it in the drive. When a key (the spacebar preferably) is pressed, the disk will be tested. The test this time is IF NOT EXIST, a variation on IF EXIST which can be very useful for applications like this. The other commands would usually be concerned with loading files from the disk, and by selecting the correct disk error messages can be avoided. Note that the GOTO START command forms a loop which will end only if the correct disk is inserted or the Ctrl-C keys pressed.

You can make files, using a text editor, which have a name but no contents, so that you can have the filenames of DISK1, DISK2 etc. placed on their respective disks, but with no actual file recorded - the EXIST test is concerned only with the name of the file. Files with no contents are not copied by the COPY command of MS-DOS, so that this creates some copy-protection.

The IF EXIST or IF NOT EXIST type of test can be applied to a filename only, not directly to a directory name, but the presence of a directory can be checked by testing for a directory which contains the file NUL - every directory contains this! A test such as:

```
IF EXIST C:\TEMPS\NUL CALL ITSTHERE
```

will make the call to the subroutine if the C:\TEMPS directory exists, regardless of its contents.

Loop actions

A batch file may be required to repeat a set of commands until some condition is satisfied. The most common requirement is to carry out an action with each one of a set of different files. This could, of course, be done on an individual basis, using commands, or on a batch basis by putting the name of each file into the batch command. All of this is a waste of valuable human time, however, and it's much better done by the machine. The batch command that uses the words FOR, IN and DO is arranged to carry out just this type of repetition action on a group of files. The snag is that the form of the command is by no means simple if you have never programmed, or if you haven't encountered this type of command in programs such as dBASE-2.

The command consists of the words FOR..IN..DO, and the FOR is followed by a *variable name*. This consists of two percent signs followed by a letter, so that %%a, %%b, %%c and so on are all valid variable names. The point of this is that during the execution of the command, this quantity, the variable name, will take the name of each file in turn from a list or set of files that you provide as parameters in the batch file. By using a variable name such as %%a, you can command actions on that file, such as DEL %%a, TYPE %%a, PRINT %%a and so on. This means that whatever action you have specified for %%a will be carried out on each file in the set in turn.

Note carefully the difference between this and the use of %0, %1, %2 and so on in the command to start a batch file. These are parameters which are **passed into the batch file** command by you when you type the name of the batch file and want to specify the file names that it will work on. The %%a, %%b, %%c are **internal** parameters that are used to specify a filename from a list that is contained inside the batch file. To avoid confusion, the digits 0 to 9 cannot be used with the %% sign. Following FOR %%a, you need to specify the set of files that will be used, and whose names will be represented in sequence by %%a (or whatever letter you have used). This is done by typing IN, and then the set of filenames in brackets. The set can be specified by using a wildcard, so that you can type IN (*.TXT) for all files using the .TXT extension, or you can specify a list of files, with the names separated by a space, such as:

IN(CHAP1.TXT, CHAP5.TXT, CHAP10.TXT).

If you have used a wildcard, each file that corresponds will be represented in turn by %%a and whatever actions you have specified carried out. When the list is more selective, as in the second example, only these specified files will be used. Finally, you need to specify what has to be done with each file, and this is whatever follows the word DO. If, for example, you used DO DEL %%a, then each file from the list would be deleted in turn, whereas if you used DO TYPE %%a, then each file would be displayed on the screen, and you would probably wish to use the MORE filter, see below, to ensure that the display was arranged in screen pages.

For example, try this batch file with the name LISTBAT.BAT:

```
ECHO OFF
FOR %%a in (%1\*.BAT) DO TYPE %%a
```

- which will show all of your BAT files on screen when you type LISTBAT and follow it with the path to the directory in which your batch files are placed - for example: LISTBAT C:\BATS.

The problem with this type of file is that it scrolls if there are a lot of files and you will need to use CTRL-S to stop the list at intervals. This is because the filters such as MORE cannot be used in this type of command. This is unfortunate, but acceptable, because the use of CTRL-S to stop the listing, and any other key to restart it, is quite easy.

Note that the FOR..IN..DO commands can also be used directly (not in a batch file) as an MSDOS command, with %a in place of %%a (etc.). In this form, redirection and pipes can be used so that the command:

FOR %a IN (*.BAT) DO TYPE %a > COLLECT.TXT

will work; the batch equivalent does also. The pipe commands using | with a filter like MORE or SORT do not work with FOR..IN..DO in either format.

Another restriction is that the command that follows DO has to be a single command. You cannot list a set of commands to be carried out in sequence here, only a single command and any variable names that go with it. You cannot evade the single-command restriction by using something of the form DO GOTO LIST, with a set of commands starting at label point :LIST. The GOTO will be executed, but the commands that follow will not accept the variable name of %%A or whatever has been used.

The most useful aspect of FOR..IN..DO is that it allows the use of commands with wildcards. There are several MS-DOS commands which do not accept wildcard filenames in their normal form, and by incorporating such commands into a FOR..IN..DO line, you can make use of any wildcard file description you like to use. The file commands which do not accept wildcards are:

DEBUG

EDIT

EXPAND

FIND

PRINT

TYPE

and the earlier example has illustrated the use of FOR..IN..DO with TYPE to allow a wildcard to be used with this command.

Of this list, it is most unlikely that you would want to use DEBUG or EDIT, with wildcards, and the uses of some of the other commands with wildcards are limited.

As an example, however, look at this use of FIND:

```
@ECHO OFF
FOR %%A IN (%1\*.BAT) DO FIND %2 %%A
```

The FIND command needs to be followed by a 'string' meaning some text to find, enclosed in quotes; and by a filename (with path if necessary). In this example, saved as FINDIT.BAT, the batch file would be executed using a command such as:

```
FINDIT C:\BATS "FILTER"
```

to allow the word FILTER to be found in any of the batch files. This allows the FIND action to be used on a set of files in a directory or on a floppy disk, and it can make searching for words much easier. The output from FIND consists of a list of the files searched. If the word is found, the line in which it appears is printed under the filename.

The batch file can be made more useful by allowing upper and lower case to be treated as identical, and also by redirecting the results into a file. This allows the file to be inspected at leisure, using a word-processor or text editor (or the file-content reader of DOSSHELL). If this is not done, the results of FIND may scroll past too quickly to read.

The modified version is

```
ECHO OFF
R %%A IN (%1\*.TXT) DO FIND /i %2%%A >> FINDFILE.TXT
CHO ALL DONE
```

-which needs some explanation. The /i part is a modifier (switch) for FIND which allows FIND to accept either lower or upper case letters interchangeably. The >> FINDFILE.TXT places the results of the FIND action into a file called FINDFILE.TXT, and since no specific directory has been provided, this file will be located on the same directory as the FINDIT batch file. By using the >> for of redirection, each FIND is added to the existing results, so that the FINDFILE contains the result of all the FIND actions on different files. This batch file can be a very useful way of searching a set of files for a word. Note that only a single word can be found, because a batch file will not accept a space in a parameter.

■ If you want to search for a phrase containing spaces, use the command in its DOS form directly (not in a batch file) as, for example:

```
FOR %A IN (C:\WORDS|TEXT|*.TXT) FIND "as it happens" %
```

- note the use of **%A** in this form rather than **%%A**.

Using SET variables

The command word SET is used in MS-DOS to assign a value to a 'variable' name, a process which is familiar to anyone who has ever carried out any programming, even at the simplest level. A variable name is, like a batch file parameter, a convenient abbreviation for a name, phrase or number which can be assigned with any value, hence the term 'variable'. The parameters %1 to %9 are variables in the sense that they will be assigned with values that you type when the batch file is invoked; these values are not set for all time in advance. SET provides another way of using variables.

The syntax is simple:

SET varname=data (note the single equality sign) will carry out the action. The names are stored in a short piece of memory called the environment space, and remain there until the computer is switched off. You can, of course include a SET command in your AUTOEXEC.BAT file to ensure that a setting is always made, and one that is always advised is:

```
SET TEMP=C:\TEMP
```

assuming that you have a directory called C:\TEMP. This setting ensures that any program that creates temporary files (as many do) will make use of an existing directory rather than creating some arrangement for itself.

If you have created too many SET assignments, the memory space is likely to be exhausted, and you will get the ominous warning message:

```
Out of Environment
```

You can arrange, in the AUTOEXEC.BAT file, to lay aside more environment space by altering the SHELL line in your CONFIG.SYS file (assuming the use of MS-DOS 5.0 or higher). For example, if your existing SHELL line in CONFIG.SYS reads:

```
SHELL=C:\MSDOS\COMMAND.COM C:\MSDOS\ /p
```

this will make the environment space 256 characters by default. To increase this to 512, alter the line to:

```
SHELL=C:\MSDOS\COMMAND.COM C:\MSDOS\ /e:512 /
```

- you can use larger numbers if you need, but it would be unusual to require much more than 512 characters for SET commands.

Many programs can make use of SET variables, and some programs require you to place such commands into a batch file for starting the program, or into your AUTOEXEC.BAT file. For example, AUTOSKETCH requires the lines:

```
set asketch=C:\SKETCH\SUPPORT
set asketchcfg=C:\SKETCH
```

to be placed in the batch file that is used to start the SKETCH program, and these lines also illustrate well the format of a SET command.

You can include a SET line in or outside of a batch file, but when a SET variable is used in a batch file it must be enclosed by percent signs. For example, if you have, inside or outside the batch file:

```
SET source=C:\WORD\TEXT
```

then if you want to use this variable in a batch file it must be referred to as %source%, such as in COPY %source%*.TXT B:

The important differences between this use of %source% and using a parameter such as %1 are that %source% can be assigned outside the batch file, or in another batch file, and will remain assigned, stored in the environment space memory, to be used by any batch file or program, until the computer is switched off or until the SET action is reversed. See later for the use of %config% in AUTOEXEC.BAT.

The SET action can be cleared, using the same example, by using:

```
SET source=
```

with nothing entered following the equality sign. Until this is done, the variable can be used in any batch file. This allows you, for example, to create variables for various directory paths in your AUTOEXEC.BAT file so that these paths can be used in any other batch file without the need to specify them fully or to enter them as parameters. If you want to be sure what is going on, write down the effect of substituting for %sketch% the name that has been assigned.

Using the SET command by itself before you add any SET lines will produce a display such as:

```
COMSPEC=C:\MSDOS\COMMAND.COM
PATH=C:\MSDOS;C:\WINDOWS;C:\BATS
DIRCMD=/w/p/o:gn
```

which shows the SET actions that are built into your system. The first variable name, COMSPEC, shows the directory path and name of the command file for the operating system, normally COMMAND.COM. This allows programs to locate this file automatically. The PATH line has been mentioned earlier; it defines the directories that will be searched for programs (including batch files) after the current directory and the root directory have been searched. The DIRCMD entry in this list configures the use of DIR so that the listing is wide, one screen at a time, and sorted in order of name, directories first. See Chapter 7 for details of the DIRCMD environment variable.

One useful batch file action is to add to the PATH temporarily for the convenience of a program. Suppose that you want to make use of a program called PINXIT which needs to find files in your C:\GRAPHX\PAINT directory. You could, of course, add this permanently into your PATH line in AUTOEXEC.BAT, but the longer the PATH line the slower the find actions will be, and it makes sense to use this addition temporarily, adding it in the batch file and removing it after the file ends. This can be done using lines such as:

```
@echo off
SET oldpath=%path%
SET PATH=%path%;C:\GRAPHX\PAINT
PATH
REM PINXIT
REM Put in program here
PAUSE
SET PATH=%oldpath%
PATH
```

- in which the PAUSE line has been placed to give time to show the action. The line: SET oldpath=%path% is essential in order to preserve a record of the original PATH line in the AUTOEXEC.BAT file. Without this, it will be more difficult to restore the original path; you would have to type the full PATH line again, and alter it each time you altered the PATH line inthe AUTOEXEC.BAT file. By assigning the PATH to the variable oldpath, you keep a note of it for use later.

The SET PATH=%path%;C:\GRAPHX\PAINT line will then add this directory path to the existing path. When the batch file reaches the PATH line, this will print out (in this example):

```
C:\MSDOS;C:\BATS;C:\GRAPHX\PAINT
```

to show that the new path has been added. This line is not necessary - it has been added simply so show that the new path has been added.

The PAUSE is used to give you time to read this change, and would not normally be necessary because the usual next step would be to run the PINXIT program of the example. After the program has ended, the line:

```
PATH=%oldpath%
```

will restore the original PATH as it existed before the change. In this example, the line PATH has been added once again to show that the original PATH line has been restored.

Shifting Parameters

It is unusual to need more than one or two parameters in starting a program, and if you want to work on groups of filenames with an MS-DOS command, this is the type of action for which the DOSSHELL is eminently well suited. There are, however, some applications in which you might not be sure how many parameters you might need, and for such examples, the SHIFT command can be useful.

SHIFT, as its name suggests, will re-cycle all the parameters. Suppose that you have used parameters %1 and %2, with C:\WORD assigned to %1 and *.TXT to %2. When you use SHIFT, C:\WORD will be assigned to %0 and *.TXT to %1, with %2 now unused. The value that was assigned to %0, the name of the batch file, will no longer be assigned to any parameter.

The manual uses the word ‘copy’ of this action, but ‘move’ is a better description - the %2 parameter in the example above is assigned to %1 but nothing is assigned to %2; it is cleared.

A simple example is:

```
@echo off
:loop
if *%1==* goto endit
del %1
shift
goto loop
:endit
Echo All done
```

which will delete a set of files specified as parameters following the name of the batch file. The important point about this example, is that the number of files is unlimited - you are not restricted to any particular value as you would be if you used parameters %1 to %9. Each time the SHIFT line is run, the %1 parameter will refer to the next file in the list, and the action will continue until the list is empty, as gauged by the IF test in the third line.

The MD-DOS manual example shows how a directory name can be used as a first parameter and stored as an environment variable in a SET line. This allows a drive or directory to be assigned for the duration of the command, using %1 for the name of each file in turn.

ERRORLEVEL tests

When a program ends, it can leave a stored number called an exit code, and a batch file can test this number using an IF (or IF NOT) form of test. Few programs leave an error number, and of the MS-DOS utilities, only the following use this system - the list shows the program name and the meaning of each number. The number 0 always means that the program action was successful, so that this number is not included in the lists. The MOVE command returns only the errorlevel number 0.

DEFRAG
1 An internal error occurred
2 The disk contained no free clusters, no space for DEFRAG to work in
3 Ctrl-C was pressed
4 General error stopped action
5 Error in reading a cluster
6 Error in writing a cluster
7 File allocation error - use CHKDSK /F before trying again
8 A memory error occurred
9 Insufficient memory for DEFRAG to work

DISKCOMP
1 Differences were found
2 Ctrl-C used to stop process
3 Critical error occurred
4 Initialisation error

DISKCOPY
1 Nonfatal read/write error
2 Ctrl-C used to stop process
3 Critical error occurred
4 Initialisation error

FIND
- 1 Search completed, no match found
- 2 Error in search, not completed

FORMAT
- 3 Ctrl-C used to stop process
- 4 Fatal error
- 5 Format stopped by user

KEYB
- 1 Invalid code, page or syntax
- 2 KEYBOARD.SYS file bad or missing
- 4 Error writing to screen or reading keyboard
- 5 Code page not prepared

REPLACE
- 1 Incompatible MS-DOS version
- 2 Could not find source files
- 3 Could not find source or destination path
- 5 No access to files
- 8 Insufficient memory available
- 11 Wrong syntax for command

RESTORE
- 1 Could not find files to restore
- 3 Ctrl-C pressed to stop process
- 4 Error occurred, RESTORE stopped.

SETVER
- 1 Invalid switch parameter used
- 2 Invalid filename specified
- 3 Insufficient memory available
- 4 Invalid version number format
- 5 SETVER could not find version number
- 6 SETVER.EXE file not found
- 7 Invalid drive specified
- 8 Too many parameters in command
- 9 Missing parameters in command
- 10 Error in reading SETVER.EXE file
- 11 SETVER.EXE file corrupted
- 12 SETVER.EXE does not support version table
- 13 No space in version table for new entry
- 14 Error writing to SETVER.EXE file

XCOPY
- 1 No files found to copy
- 2 Ctrl-C pressed to stop process
- 4 Initialisation error
- 5 Disk write error

NOTE: Initialisation errors are errors detected before a program starts, while the system is being checked. These can include insufficient memory, insufficient disk space, invalid drive\directory names or bad syntax. The usefulness of these exit codes depends on the extent to which you are likely to use the commands with which they are associated. Bearing that in mind, the best example to use is one based on XCOPY, whose action has already been demonstrated. The following shows use being made of the XCOPY exit codes in a skeleton batch file.

```
@echo off
if *%1==* goto noparm
XCOPY %1 b: > NUL
if errorlevel 5 goto disk
if errorlevel 4 goto init
if errorlevel 2 goto ctrl
if errorlevel 1 goto nofile
echo Copy action complete
goto endit
:disk
echo Disk write error occurred
goto endit
:init
echo Cannot start action - please check
command
goto endit
:ctrl
echo You pressed Ctrl-C; action aborted
goto endit
:nofile
echo No files found to copy
goto endit
:noparm
echo No source file(s) specified.
:endit
```

in which each errorlevel number is tested in turn and an appropriate GOTO used to direct the use of a suitable message. In order to avoid confusion from the built-in error messages of XCOPY, these have been lost by using the > NUL redirection in the XCOPY line, so that the only error messages that appear are the ones you provide in this batch file. You can try this out with the only conditions that are easy to simulate -the choice of a source with no files, such as \WORD*.DOC in a directory which contains no DOC files; or the use of Ctrl-C to terminate the action when a number of files are being copied. Initialisation errors are unlikely unless the floppy in drive B is full, and if a disk write error occurs you really have problems or have used an unformatted floppy (in which case the General failure type of error message will be issued from MS-DOS - this one cannot be redirected).

The example above shows the codes being dealt with in descending order, and this order is very important. The ERRORLEVEL test detects the presence of a number which is equal to or greater than the number in the test. In other words, using ERRORLEVEL 3 will provide a TRUE result if the exit code is 3, 4, 5 or any higher number. By arranging the tests in descending order, we ensure that the higher numbers will be detected first if they exist, and will not interfere with the detection of the lower numbers.

The ERRORLEVEL tests are important, despite the limited list of programs above, because they are the way by which small utilities can be written to enhance batch file action. For example, a menu program can be written to permit a range of number keys to return the same numbers as exit codes, allowing ERRORLEVEL to be used to deal with the codes. This forms the basis for a much superior menu system. The test for ERRORLEVEL can make use of a GOTO, or it can call up another batch file, or move to a batch file from which there is no return.

The CHOICE command

The addition of CHOICE in MS-DOS 6.0 marked the first change to batch file commands for some time, and it fills a noticeable gap, the previous lack of any form of menu choice. CHOICE used alone will simply pause and show the choice of [Y,N] (you can use upper or lower case keys), but by adding parameters and options a message can be delivered, a different choice of keys shown and a time-limit set (with a default key returned following the pause). The menu actions that follow CHOICE are made using the Errorlevel number that is returned. The text of any message is placed following any options and, like ECHO, is placed following a space. If the / character is used in the text the whole text must be put between quotes.

The errorlevel number is derived from the order of items that are displayed. For the default of Y,N the number 1 is returned for Y and 2 for N; if you had specified A,B,C then A would give 1, B gives 2 and C gives 3 and so on.

The CHOICE options are:

/C Specifies keys in the form /C:ynp. In this example, the permitted keys are Y, N or P, returning Errorlevel codes 1, 2, and 3 in that order. In this example, the screen message will show the prompt [Y,N,P]

/N The prompt is not displayed, but text and keys are still valid. This allows you to display a more meaningful message in an ECHO line just prior to the CHOICE line.

/S Make CHOICE case sensitive - it is normally not case-sensitive

/T Use a timeout in the form /T:Y,25. In this example, if there has been no response in 25 seconds, the Y key will be taken as having been pressed.

The normal errorlevel codes start at 1 for the first key and ascend for each key listed. An errorlevel of 255 indicates an error. If an incorrect key is pressed, the computer will beep and CHOICE will await a correct response (unless a timeout has been specified).

■ Remember that the errorlevel number must be tested in descending order.

SUMMARY OF BATCH KEYWORDS

CALL Runs another batch program and then returns to the calling batch program.

CHOICE Prints a message, pauses and waits for the user to press one of a set of keys (default is Y,N). An Errorlevel number is returned corresponding to the key pressed.

ECHO Allows text to be printed on screen during the running of a batch file. @ECHO OFF suppresses the lines of the batch file itself.

FOR The loop command consisting of FOR..IN..DO which allows a parameter such as %%A to take values from the IN set and to DO the described actions.

GOTO The command which allows a jump to the line following a label name (preceded by a colon). The form is GOTO NEWPLACE, where the label :NEWPLACE has been used on the desired line. GOTO is normally used following a condition, or to allow some unwanted lines to be skipped.

IF The test keyword, taking the form IF %1==name, to test for a variable value.

PAUSE The 'Press any key' step that gives the user time to change a floppy or other action before pressing a key to continue the batch file.
REM The reminder keyword used to place notes in a batch file, or to temporarily prevent a line from being used.
SHIFT The command which shifts the assignment of the parameters %0 to %9 so as to release %9 (or whatever is the highest number used) for new uses.

The AUTOEXEC.BAT file

AUTOEXEC.BAT is the only batch file that is run automatically (though you can force the system to run another file name by using the /K:name option in the COMMAND line of CONFIG.SYS). The commands used in AUTOEXEC.BAT are normal batch file commands, and most of them are concerned with loading memory-resident programs.

Many of the lines in your AUTOEXEC.BAT file are very much up to you, reflecting your needs and the various utility programs you have available. You will almost certainly want to use MOUSE if you have a Microsoft mouse, or some other mouse-activating program if you are using another make of mouse. If you use another type of mouse, try it with the Microsoft MOUSE.COM program because most mice will work with this driver. To use it, make sure that MOUSE.COM is in the \MSDOS directory, no other mouse program is in a searched directory, and use the line:

```
C\MSDOS\MOUSE
```

in your AUTOEXEC.BAT file.

Another important line is:

```
SET TEMP=C:\TEMP
```

which provides a location for temporary files that many programs produce. By specifying a hard-disk directory (which must exist - you should create it before you add this line to AUTOEXEC.BAT) you direct all temporary file to this directory. This avoids problems such as will occur when you are logged on to a floppy and in the absence of the TEMP line a program tries to create a temporary file on the floppy, which might be full or write-protected.

You may also need to use a line to control your display adapter (such as SETVID VGA), or to operate the MS-DOS 6.0 UNDELETE Sentry facility which makes it possible easily to recover a deleted file. You will probably want to use a SET DIRCMD line to ensure that the DIR command is set up the way that you want is, and other utilities such as the keyclick etc. from PDSL can be started if required.

If you want to alter the prompt line you can use PROMPT in the AUTOEXEC.BAT file, and you may possibly also want to use MODE. If you have sufficient extended memory you can add SMARTDRV, and if you are worried about virus infection (of the computer anyway) you can use VSAFE, see Chapter 9.

You can end your AUTOEXEC.BAT file with the line:

```
DOSSHELL
```

in order to run the DOSSHELL, see Chapter 8. As an alternative you can use WIN in order to run Windows.

A new development in the AUTOEXEC.BAT of MS-DOS 6 is the ability to select alternative versions. This is possible only if a menu system (see Chapter 2) is being used in the CONFIG.SYS file and it makes use of the %config% environment variable.

Suppose, for example, that your CONFIG.SYS file is set up with choices as detailed in Chapter 2, in which the choices are windows or dos. Whichever choice you make when CONFIG.SYS runs will be assigned to the environment variable %config% and this can be picked up in AUTOEXEC.BAT by using lines such as:

```
GOTO %config%

:dos
;do DOS stuff here
GOTO endit

:windows
; do Windows stuff here

:endit
```

The first GOTO line will use the word assigned to %config% to go to one or other of these label names, and it is up to you to place whatever commands you want in these spaces. You need to remember to place a GOTO following the first option so that the second option is not carried out immediately following the first.

■ All of the AUTOEXEC.BAT commands that are common to these different requirements should be run ahead of these choice lines.

7 Using DOSKEY and Macros

Using DOSKEY

Older versions of MS-DOS could make limited use of the function keys for commands, notably the use of F3 to repeat the whole of the most recent command, and F1 to repeat the most recent command character by character (allowing a character to be changed). Versions 5.0 and 6.0 expand this facility into a much more useful key macro system which, at its simplest, allows any command line (not just the most recent) to be recalled and edited or re-used. The older F-key uses for F1 to F5 are still available. DOSKEY is memory-resident, can be loaded into upper memory, and takes up about 3 Kbyte of memory when installed.

The simplest use of DOSKEY requires only that DOSKEY should run, and most users will want to place this command line into the AUTOEXEC.BAT file. Once DOSKEY has been run, all commands are stored (up to a default limit of 1024 characters - more can be obtained) and can henceforth be recalled in order by using the cursor up/down keys and the Page Up and Page Down keys.

Suppose, for example that after starting the machine you used DIR, then CD\MSDOS and D!R/W, followed by COPY *.SYS B:. After using this set, the Page Down key will recall the most recent command (the COPY command) and Page Up will recall the oldest, the DIR command. The Up arrow will recall an earlier command than the current one, and the Down arrow key will move to a later command. Any recalled command can be run, as normal, by using the ENTER key.

In addition to allowing old commands to be recalled, DOSKEY allows for the easy editing of commands. The cursor keys can be used to move the position for editing (used alone to move by one character, with Ctrl to move by one word) or the HOME and END keys can be used to move to the start or end of the line respectively. The default editing mode is overtype, meaning that a new character will replace the character under the cursor. If you want to use Insert, so that a new character will be inserted at the cursor position, install DOSKEY by using:

```
DOSKEY /INSERT
```

- this can be useful if you have just worked on a file called VERS9.txt and want to work on VERS10.TXT.

You can use the normal delete keys on any line, and pressing Esc will delete the whole command. The other options are /reinstall, /bufsize, /M (or /MACROS), and /H (or /HISTORY).

1. The /reinstall switch will load another copy of DOSKEY into memory, allowing a new version to be used. This also clears the existing memory buffer of stored commands.

2. The /bufsize switch can be used to alter the default 512 bytes allowed for storing DOSKEY characters, so that /bufsize=2048 will allocate 2048 characters for this purpose. The smallest buffer size you can allocate is 256 characters.

3.The /M switch will display a list of all the macros stored in the memory, and this can be copied to a file by using a command such as:

```
DOSKEY /M >MACFILE.DOC
```

or redirected to the printer.

Key	**Action**
F1	Copies characters from the stored line to the screen, one by one each time the key is pressed.
F2	Searches for the next key character (so that F2 X will find an X in the stored line) and insert all of the stored line up to that point.
F3	Copies the whole of the stored line to the screen, or the remainder of the line if some has already been copied with F1.
F4	Searches for the next key you press (as for F2) and deletes up to that point in the stored line.
F5	Copies the visible command into store, and deletes the visible command (use F3 to restore).
F6	Places the Ctrl-Z character, shown as ^Z, at the end of the visible command line.
F7	Display all stored command lines, numbered.
F8	Search for a matching line in store - type the first part of the command you want to recall and press F8 to get the full command.
F9	Recall stored line using its number - you are asked to type that number when you press F9.
F10	Display all macros

The following Alt F-key combinations are used:

Alt-F7	Erase all stored command lines.
Alt-F10	Clear all macros

Figure 7.1
The Function key actions when DOSKEY is in use.

4. The /H switch similarly displays all of the stored command lines, and this also can be redirected into a file or to the printer.

The function keys F1 to F5 retain their former uses, and new uses are assigned to keys F6 to F10 - Figure 7.1 shows a list of all these F-key uses. Note that the MS-DOS manual refers to a stored command line as the 'template'. All of the stored lines can be cleared by using Alt-F7.

Macro action

A **Macro** is a stored set of commands that will run when some key combination is pressed - there is a strong similarity with a batch file, but the macro is stored in memory and is executed by pressing keys, whereas the batch file is stored on disk and is executed by typing its name and pressing ENTER. The Macro action of DOSKEY is invoked by using the format macroname=text following the DOSKEY command.

- Many programs, including word-processors, spreadsheets and databases, also possess their own Macro language, allowing you to assign various stored commands to key combinations.

Each macro uses a name, and though the MS-DOS manual illustrates two-letter names, you can use single letters or longer names; the case of letters is ignored. Obviously, the system is most useful when one or two-letter combinations are used, since this makes for the minimum amount of typing. Though it is possible to have macros with the same name as a DOS command (the macro will run if there is no space between the prompt and the macro name; the command will run if one or more spaces exists) this is not really advisable (would you ever remember?).

- Note that there is no provision for using F-keys in macros, because these keys are widely used by programs and frequently re-assigned.
- The keys which have been assigned to macro use will not retain these uses when a program is running - if you have assigned A for giving a directory, you cannot get this effect while you are running, for example, a word-processor. The macro assignments will be returned after the program has ended and the Dos command line symbol (such as C:/>) reappears.

A separate DOSKEY line is needed for each macro, so that to assign DIR to A and COPY *.* B: to B you would need to use:

DOSKEY A=DIR

DOSKEY B=COPY *.* B:

- remember that pressing Alt-F10 will clear all macros from the memory. The macros are lost when the machine is reset or switched off, so that it can be useful to make a Macros batch file, by using:

DOSKEY /M > KEYMAC.BAT

which can be called from AUTOEXEC.BAT to reinstall the macros for use on another occasion. Such a file will consist of lines such as: A=dir, and you need to use a text editor to add the DOSKEY command at the start of each line.

The use of key macros can be easier and faster than the use of batch files, particularly when a set of actions is needed frequently. However, the key macros are stored in memory and will be deleted when the computer is switched off unless the commands have been placed into a batch file that has then been edited as noted above. In addition, a macro cannot exceed 127 characters, whereas a batch file can be of any practicable length.

1. To stop a macro running, Ctrl-C must be pressed **as many times as there are commands** in the macro.

2. The use of GOTO in a macro is not allowed, and a macro cannot be run (though it can be created) from inside a batch file (though a batch file can be run as part of a macro command).

3. There is nothing in a macro that corresponds to the use of @ECHO OFF in the batch file.

In other ways, however, the macro language follows the methods used for batch files, and Figure 7.2 lists some of the special characters that are used in the two types of files - note that the macro special characters all use the $ sign as their first character. Like batch files, macros can be typed with parameters following them, such as DX BOOK1.TXT, where DX is a macro command and the parameter is the filename BOOK.TXT.

- Any macro can be deleted by typing the line that created it without the text, so that typing DOSKEY A= will delete the macro for the letter A.
- You cannot run a macro from a batch file, so there is no point in placing macro commands in batch files.

Use	Batch	Macro
Parameters	%0 - %9	$0 - $9
Redirect output	>	$G
Append output	>>	SGSG
Redirect input	<	$L
Pipe data	|	$B
Separate commands	$T	
Print dollar sign	$$	
Accept-all parameter	$*	

NOTE: A macro which uses parameters does so in the same form as a batch file, so that you could type:

XY A:file1 B:file2

for a macro that required two parameters $1 and $2.

Figure 7.2
Macro and batch file parameters compared.

Using DIRCMD

MS-DOS 6.0 has produced a set of new commands which give much more control over the machine, and in particular, the DIR command is much improved. The older versions of DOS would produce a directory listing which filled only half of the width of the screen (because it had been designed for a 40-character screen width) and which showed files in order of entry only. MS-DOS 6.0 allows the action of DIR to be modified by using an 'environment variable' rather like a batch file parameter, whose values are allocated by using the SET command.

To alter the action of DIR, the variable DIRCMD needs to be set, and the settings that can be used are:

/a list only files with specified attributes -
- :a files ready to backup
- :-a files unaltered since previous backup
- :d directories included
- :-d files only, no directories
- :h hidden files
- :-h excluding hidden files
- :r read-only files
- :-r excluding read-only files
- :s system files
- :-s excluding system files

/o control order of sorting displayed files:

- :c sorted by compression ratio, lowest first
- :-c sorted by compression ratio, highest first
- :d sorted by date and time, earliest first
- :-d sorted by date and time, most recent first
- :e alphabetical order of extension letters
- :-e reverse alphabetical order of extension letters
- :g directories arranged before files
- :-g directories arranged following files
- :n alphabetical order of name
- :-n reverse alphabetical order of name
- :s order if file size, smallest first
- :-s order of file size, largest first

/p one screen of listing at a time

/w list over the full width of the screen
/-w use only half the screen width for list

The main commands are always preceded by the slash sign and where a command such as /a or /o can take other parameters (more than one if required) these can be grouped together, with no spaces, following one single colon.
For example, the line:

```
set dircmd=/w/p/o:gn
```

sets the directory listing as wide (/w), one screen at a time with no scrolling (/p) and with sorting in use with directories ahead of files and all in alphabetical order of name(/o:gn).

Note that using SET DIRCMD like this only sets the default format, and you can still obtain DIR listings in any form you want out of the possible set listed above. For example, if the DIRCMD uses /w for a wide listing, which provides less detail about files, you can obtain an ordinary width listing by typing DIR /-w, turning off the DIRCMD setting temporarily for this command only.

Redirection

Redirection means the transfer of data from one output or input device to an alternative. The data will normally be the output from a program which would normally be directed to the screen, or the input to a program which would normally be taken from the keyboard (assuming that all such inputs can be put into a file - this could mean finding a file editor that could work with Ctrl characters)

Redirection in MS-DOS makes use of the signs > and < to indicate the direction of the flow of data, with > meaning a redirection of output and < meaning a redirection of input. Looking at output redirection first, the form of the command is :

command > output device

- which makes use of the usual abbreviations for the output devices. The most common requirement is redirection of screen output to a file or redirection to a printer. For a file redirection, the filename will have to be specified, for a parallel printer, use PRN. There must be a space on the pointed side of the > sign.

Example: DIR C:\wp\text> dirfil.doc

- will put the directory of C:\wp\text into a file called dirfil.doc. This file can then be used like any ASCII file, so that it can be read into a word processor etc.

Example: TYPE B:blurb.txt> prn

- will print the file blurb.txt on the parallel printer (the printer must be wired up and switched on).

Example: TYPE A:other.doc> aux

-will send the file other.doc to the serial port, to a serial printer or another computer. The serial port must have been correctly set up using MODE. The use of AUX and COM1 is interchangeable (you might have to specify COM2 if this is the serial port you use). This redirection works satisfactorily both with serial printers and with direct-links to other computers, rather like using COPY filename AUX.

Using the redirection sign >> has the effect of appending data to an existing text file.

Example: DIR B:>> prnfil.doc

- will add the directory of the disk in the B: drive to the file prnfil.doc (in the current drive) without deleting the present contents of the file. If no such file exists it will be created.

Another 'device' that can be used for redirection is NUL. When this is used, the output of the program 'disappears', it is not displayed on screen nor printed. This can be used as a way of testing that something will be read correctly, and also as a way of making sure that an output from an action that is carried out in a batch file does not cause any screen output (as it would even with ECHO OFF used).

Example: DIR A:> NUL

- will read the directory of the disk in drive A and consign it to oblivion. The disk drive motor is the only indication that something has happened. This redirection is a useful way of preventing your screen from filling with unwanted messages while a program is working- it is particularly useful for the AUTOEXEC.BAT file because many of the program that are installed memory-resident will provide messages which you will want to see only if you are making changes or in the event of problems.

The input redirection is less often used in such straightforward ways, because it is seldom necessary to redirect an input and few programs take input in a way that permits redirection. If an input is needed from the serial port it is always better to use a communications program, because the use of AUX or COM as sources of *input* is not necessarily supported, and there is the problem of transferring the end-of-file character.

One possible exception to the use of redirection in inputs is taking inputs from a file. If a program requires a number of commands that are delivered from the keyboard as you start it up, these can *possibly* be taken instead from a file in which each command has been put on a separate line. The problem is to find a program that will accept such redirection, and many popular programs do not, or if they do, can hang up at the end of the file. It is often necessary to use an editor that can place Ctrl and Esc characters into the file, and in this respect the word-processor PC-Write (obtainable at one time as shareware) is very useful. In general, it is better to avoid input redirection except into Filter programs, see later.The MS-DOS commands that accept keyboard inputs will all accept redirection. This redirection ceases when the file ends.

Example: `TIME <CONFIL.DOC`

-will alter the time setting, reading a time that has been stored in the file CONFIL.DOC on the current drive. This is not exactly a normal requirement.

Redirections generally should be confined to directing outputs to the parallel printer or to a file, and for redirecting an input to a filter, because other actions do not necessarily work well or reliably.

Pipes and Filters

A pipe is another method of transferring data from one program to another, and is the preferred way of getting the output of a command to affect the input of another. The syntax is to use the | sign between the programs which are to be connected in this way. Once again, however, the programs that accept input data from a pipe are usually the MS-DOS commands or other programs written for the purpose. These latter programs are the filters, and their purpose is to alter the output from or the input to a program.

Piping is achieved by creating a temporary disk file, so that you cannot operate piping unless this file can be written. This is not possible if your disks are all write-protected or if they are full. For example, if you type:

TYPE A:README.DOC | MORE

this can work only if a temporary file can be created on Drive A:, and this may not be possible if the disk is write-protected or full. MS-DOS 6.0 allows you to use a TEMP variable in the AUTOEXEC.BAT file which provides a space on the hard disk (or another disk) for such files. This is done using:

SET TEMP=C:\temp

assuming that the directory called temp exists on Drive C in this example. You may have such a line in your AUTOEXEC.BAT file already for the purposes of another program, in which case MS-DOS 6.0 allows the same space to be used when a pipe command is running. The temporary file that is created will be deleted after the pipe action has been completed.

The file that is created is called %PIPEX.$$$, which is, intentionally, not the sort of snazzy title that you would want for your own files. This ensures that there is little or no chance that the file of that name will already exist on the disk when a pipe is created, because the pipe file is deleted immediately following the pipe action, leaving no trace on the disk.

Filters

The filter programs that are usually supplied with MS-DOS are FIND, MORE and SORT, of which FIND can be used for purposes that are separate from piping. All three are external, meaning that they are programs which have to be on a disk in the current drive or on a path, such as C:\MSDOS, which can be searched. The effect of the filter is to select or rearrange data which has been piped to it by a program, and then pass that modified data to the screen, or on to another program by way of a pipe, or to a printer by way of a re-direction. Most filter programs are used in conjunction with TYPE or DIR, the two MS-DOS commands which provide an output of text.

FIND

FIND is a good example to take in order to demonstrate the difference between program use and filter use for the same purpose.

1. FIND "Spotless" textfil1.txt
2. TYPE textfil1.txt | FIND "Spotless"

The first example uses FIND as a program which searches the specified file for the word "Spotless" and whose output will appear on the screen. The second example uses TYPE to pass text to FIND used as a filter, with the result again appearing on the screen. Used as a program, FIND is followed by the phrase to be found and also the filename.

Used as a filter, FIND appears following the pipe sign (|), and is itself followed only by the phrase that is to be found. The text that is to be searched by the FIND filter has to be passed along the pipe from another program, and in this case TYPE has been used as a way of selecting the text. Normally, TYPE would display the text on the screen, but with FIND interposed between the TYPE command and the screen output, only the selected output is shown. Remember that FIND, like the other filter program, is external, so that the program must be present on the current drive or on a directory which will be searched, using a PATH line in the AUTOEXEC.BAT file.

The use of FIND as a filter makes it of considerably wider use than FIND used only as a program. For example, suppose that the root directory of your hard disk contains several hundred files (which is bad organisation, but that's another matter). To find files created in 1991 we can use:

DIR C:|FIND "91"

because each date is stored in the form DD-MM-YY (unless you have forgotten to use the COUNTRY file to adapt to UK date conventions).

FIND allows four option letters /C, /I, /N, and /V which are placed between FIND and the item to be found.

The /C option alters the output of FIND to provide a count of the number of lines in which the item is found.

The /I option makes the action case-insensitive, so that a search for **Smith** will also produce **smith**.

The /N option prints out a line number as well as the line that contains the item.

The /V option displays the lines that do not contain the search item.

MORE

The MORE filter simply cuts text into pages which can be displayed on the screen. If data is sent to the screen through the MORE filter, then one screen full of data will be displayed at a time, with the message

—More—

appearing at the bottom of the screen. The next page can then be displayed by pressing any key. To send a text file through this filter, you have to specify that the contents of the file will be piped to the filter, and if the command that is used to provide the text would normally send it to the screen, then so also is the output of MORE sent to the screen.

Example: TYPE READ.ME | MORE

-will place the contents of the file READ.ME on the screen, one page at a time, assuming that the MORE program is on the same disk as READ.ME.

You could, of course, further redirect the output to the printer by using the command in the form:

TYPE READ.ME | MORE > PRN

and an alternative is:

MORE < READ.ME > PRN

which uses redirection rather than piping. Note the different order, also that the TYPE command is not needed because the < sign implies that the file READ.ME is used as an input to MORE.

SORT

SORT is the other standard filter, and its effect is to arrange text data in alphabetical order of the letter in the first column (and when two words have the same first letter, then the second letter will be taken into account and so on).

Example: DIR | SORT

-will place on to the screen a directory of the current disk or directory which is sorted in alphabetical order. The output of DIR has in this example been piped through SORT, and so to the screen.

Example: TYPE INXIT | SORT
- when INXIT consists of a list of names in any order, will produce a sorted list on the screen.

The SORT command and filter allow options which can be a number or the letter R, placed immediately following SORT and separated by the usual stroke mark.

The /+5 option will sort the file by the order of the character in the 5th column, in this example. Any valid column number can be used. This can be useful if the list consists of four places for numbers, a comma, and then a word. The default is to use the first column.

The /R option sorts the items in reverse order, highest value first and then to lowest.

If you use both options, the /R option must be placed first.

Combined pipe, filter and redirection

The actions of piping, filtering and redirection can be combined, as long as the correct order of writing filenames and symbols is observed. A few examples have already been illustrated.

Example: DIR | SORT > ALPHADIR.TXT
- will sort a directory into order and send the results to a file called ALPHADIR.TXT so that when you TYPE or PRINT the file ALPHADIR.TXT, you will find that the directory is in alphabetical order. You could equally easily have directed the alphabetical listing to the printer by using PRN in place of the filename in the example above.

Another common requirement is to take data from one file, sort it, and then file it under another filename. This has already been illustrated, but it can bear mentioning again.

Example: SORT < OLDFIL > NEWFIL
- will take the output from the file OLDFIL, filter it through SORT and then send the sorted result to the file called NEWFIL. SORT is in this example being used as a program along with redirection.

8 The DOSSHELL

Introduction

The DOSSHELL is a mouse-and-menu controller for MS-DOS which was first introduced with MS-DOS 4.0. It was revised considerably for MS-DOS 5.0 and has been slightly revised for Version 6.0. DOSSHELL allows users of MS-DOS 6.0 to dispense with any other utilities of this type, making a considerable saving of memory. In the normal course of installing MS-DOS, the commands that would make DOSSHELL run at switch-on may not be installed (the AUTOEXEC.BAT files would have a last line consisting of DOSSHELL), so that you need to call up DOSSHELL from the familiar DOS command line C:\>. This is done by using the command dosshell (press ENTER), assuming that the DOSSHELL files have been placed in the C:\MSDOS directory and that this directory is named in the PATH line of AUTOEXEC.BAT.

The first appearance of DOSSHELL is illustrated in Figure 8.1. It consists of three sections with a set of option and drive selections at the top of the screen and reminders on key actions at the foot. The Directory Tree window shows the layout of directories on the disk, with a + sign used to indicate a directory that contains subdirectories. The window on the right hand side of the upper part of the screen shows the files in the marked directory - the default starting point, as shown here, is the root directory. When you place the mouse pointer on to a directory and click the mouse button the files list of DOSSHELL will show the files of that directory.

- The window display format depends on the View options that you select, see later, so that the display illustrated here may not appear on your own version. The display can also be controlled by options in the DOSSHELL command line. For VGA screens it is better to change the display to the graphics type.

Display options

The display options can be used to determine whether you use the text or the graphics screen, and the number of lines of information that can be placed on the screen. When this option is selected, the menu that appears offers the choice, for VGA screens, of:

Text 25 lines 43 lines 50 lines

Graphics 25 lines 30 lines 34 lines 43 lines 60 lines

Figure 8.1
The initial appearance of DOSSHELL when it is first used on a text screen - this appearance will change when you tailor DOSSHELL for your own use.

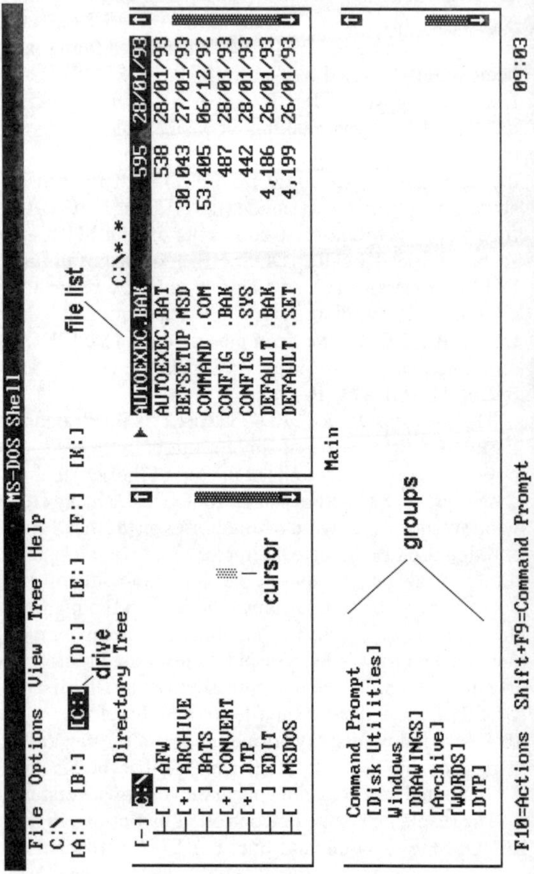

- and the graphics displays look rather different, as Figure 8.2 shows. There is a Preview option to show what a display will look like before you commit yourself to using that option. These options assume that you are using a modern type of display, and since most machines now use VGA, the assumption is justified. Using the higher-resolution displays (more lines per screen) allows you to see much more information on the screen at

Figure 8.2
The typical Graphics screen appearance of DOSSHELL, with the Display mode panel superimposed. The Preview option allows you to see what a display mode looks like.

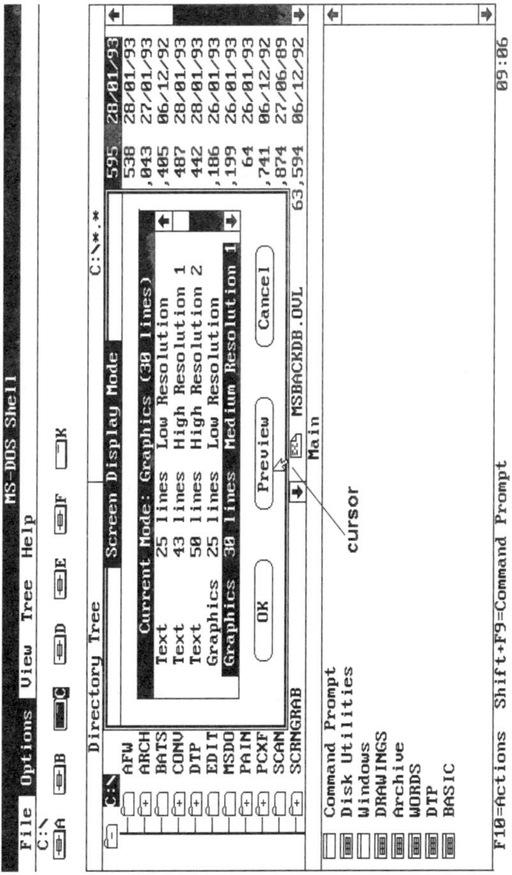

a time. This is useful if you want to see all of the files in a directory, or if you want to select a large block of files. The disadvantage is that the display is less clear, and you have to move the mouse very carefully if you want to select one file out of the list.

The colour options are not particularly relevant if you are using a monochrome display, but they allow a considerable choice for users of VGA colour screens.

The range of options is:

- Basic Blue
- Ocean
- Monochrome-2
- Monochrome-4
- Reverse
- Hot Pink
- Emerald City
- Turquoise

and if you are using a monochrome VGA display (which is much sharper and clearer than a colour display) the Monochrome-4 option is a very good one, allowing for two shades of grey along with black and white. If you have a monochrome monitor you will find only the Monochrome options available - the colour options used on a mono monitor look the same as the Monochrome-4 option.

As far as the colour displays are concerned, if you are using a colour monitor you can please yourself - some combinations are easier to read than others but all are usable. Remember that if you want to print screens the printing will usually be in black and white and in some cases it is better to use the Monochrome-4 option even with a colour VGA screen in order to see what will be printed.

Working with DOSSHELL

The mouse cursor which appears on the screen when DOSSHELL is in use with a text-screen display is shaped like a shaded (or coloured) box. The mouse cursor for the graphics screen (shown in the remaining illustrations in this Chapter) uses the familiar arrow shape, and whatever cursor is used provides the main control actions. Three actions in particular are important, clicking, double-clicking and dragging.

Clicking is used to select an item that you want by placing the cursor over the item name or icon and depressing the left-hand mouse button and releasing it, fairly quickly. If the mouse arrow is over an filename at the time, the name will change colour (or shading) to show that it has been selected for one of the actions of DOSSHELL. If the cursor is over the name of a menu (top line of screen) the menu will be displayed.

Double-clicking means pressing and releasing the left-hand mouse button twice in quick succession. If the mouse arrow is over an program name at this time, the program will run. If the cursor is over an item on a menu,

Figure 8.3
The scroll-bar on a DOSSHELL screen which can be used along with the mouse to display different parts of the directory tree.

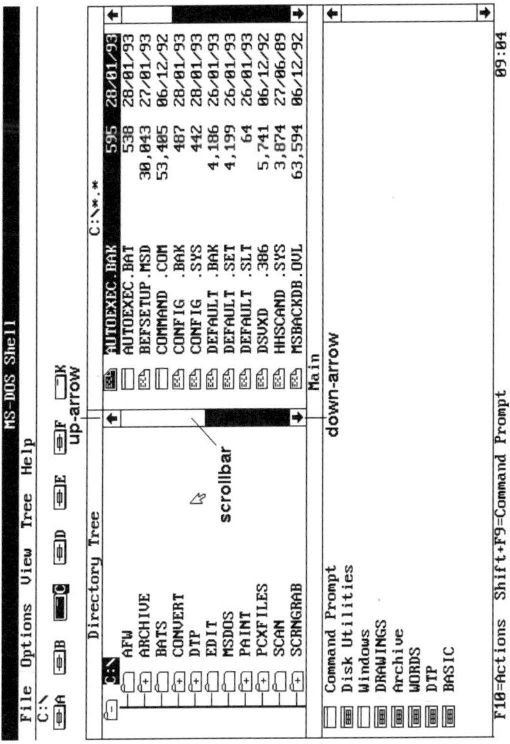

that item will be chosen and used by any action that you select from the Files menu.

Dragging means moving the mouse while an item is selected and the left-hand button is being held down. This is a way of making the scroll-bars on the directory or files boxes move on the screen when the mouse is moved along your desk. The scroll-bars are released when the mouse button is released. Dragging is also used on file moving and copying actions.

- The scroll bars, Figure 8.3, are the sets of lines at the right-hand side or bottom of a display window. Dragging the button of a scroll-bar will shift the text or the picture in a window. Drag the scroll-bar up to move the image down, and drag the scroll-bar down to move the image up.

■ DOSSHELL, like Windows, can use mouse dragging with some enhancements. These involve holding the Shift key down while clicking the mouse button or holding the Ctrl key down while dragging the mouse - see later for details.

Task switching introduction

DOSSHELL, like Windows, allows you to switch from one program to another without the need to shut down a program first. The convenience of this is immense if you have never experienced it before. You could, for example, be working on a letter, using a word processor. At some stage, you need to look at a worksheet to find a figure from an accounts statement. The conventional method would be to save the word processor letter file, shut down the word processor, open up the spreadsheet, load in the correct worksheet, read the figures, jot them down, save the worksheet, quit the spreadsheet, open the word processor, find the letter file and load it in, and then find the correct position in the document.

Using DOSSHELL this can be reduced to pressing a key combination to save the word processor on disk, pressing another key combination to start the spreadsheet, finding the figures, and pressing another key combination to get the word processor back, still at the same place in the document. The very considerable advantage in this is that it allows you to *suspend*, rather than quit, a program, with the document of data file still in place and ready to resume. This avoids the most infuriating part of shutting down a program - the difficulty in finding the data file, loading it in again and finding the correct place to resume.

■ The switch from one program to another is far from instantaneous. It involves a considerable amount of disk effort (which you can hear), and the faster your hard disk drive the quicker program swapping can be. Using SMARTDRIVE with write cahcingseems to slow the action down, if anything. You can speed up the use of DOSSHELL program swapping considerable by working entirely from RAMDISK, but this option is useful only if you are using a machine with at least 2 Mbyte of RAM memory, and it allows a more limited number of programs over which swapping can be used. The methods used for task switching will be noted later in this Chapter.

The file and program option

The file and program option which is the default when you first make use of DOSSHELL, shows directory and file information in the upper part of the screen. The program information shown on the lower half of the screen is not of the program files that exist on the disk, but program groups (see later) that you arrange to display in this portion. Some groups already exist when you first run DOSSHELL.

■ The idea of groups is a comparatively new one in MS-DOS, introduced with MS-DOS 5.0 (though it has been used in MS Windows-3 and other shell programs). The principle is that programs that belong together can be grouped so as to make it easier to run them and to switch from one to another.

When you start DOSSHELL with a file and program display, the directory window will show the files in order, starting with the root directory at the top of the display. The files in this directory are listed, in alphabetical order, in the Files window at the right hand side of the top part of the screen. You can scroll either window independently of the other.

To scroll the directory window, select any name in the window by placing the mouse cursor over a name and clicking the mouse button. Then scroll in any of the following ways:

1. Place the mouse cursor on one of the arrows in the scroll bar, and click the mouse button to scroll the display up or down by one window height.
2. Place the mouse cursor in any space in the scroll bar not occupied by the slider box, and click to move the slider box to that position.
3. Place the mouse cursor over the slider box in the scroll bar and drag the box to a new position. Release the mouse button when you have dragged the box to its new place.

If you want to scroll down the filenames in a single directory, you must first shift to the appropriate window by moving the mouse cursor to that window and clicking. The same scroll-bar actions can then be used as described for the directory window.

■ You must make certain that you are in the correct window before you attempt any scrolling actions. The files display will not alter when you scroll the directory, and the directory display does not alter when you scroll the files window. If you select a directory name by placing the mouse cursor on the name and clicking, the Files window will alter to show the files in that directory.

The drive letter selection

Whatever the opening display of DOSSHELL, the available drive letters will be displayed near the top of the screen (and again, if the dual-files option is selected, see later). DOSSHELL will list each drive, including RAMdisk, as a letter enclosed in square brackets, such as [A] [B] [C]. The default will be [C] when you are using a hard disk. A machine which runs on a network, or uses INTERLNK (see Chapter 11) and DBLSPACE (See Chapter 4) will show a large number of drive letters.

You can change to another drive simply by placing the mouse cursor on another drive letter and clicking the mouse button. If you change to a floppy drive in this way, make sure that there is a disk in the drive. You will see a warning message if a drive is not available, but this can take some time to deliver and you cannot use DOSSHELL during this time. When you use INTERLNK and DBLSPACE there may be some drive letters listed which do not correspond to any actual devices.

- If you often make use of floppy disks along with the hard disk (for backup purposes, for example, you can save time by keeping a disk in the A: drive for as long as you are using DOSSHELL. This avoids any error messages when you are frequently swapping drives. It can be particularly useful if you are using DBLSPACE in the batch file that starts DOSSHELL so that the floppy drive is double-spaced - this requires you to have a disk in the drive at Boot time, so that you might need to place a PAUSE in the batch file, or use the option that exists on some BIOS versions (like AMI) to boot only from the hard disk, ignoring the floppies.

File Display Options

The file display options are obtained from the View menu - place the cursor on this menu name (at the top of the screen) and click the mouse button to bee the list. The option which is currently in use will not be listed, so that of the following you will see only three:

Single file list
Dual file list
All files
Program/File list

Figure 8.4

A single file list as it appears on the screen. This shows directories on the left and the files for the selected directory on the right. The C:\ files are displayed because this is the selected directory.

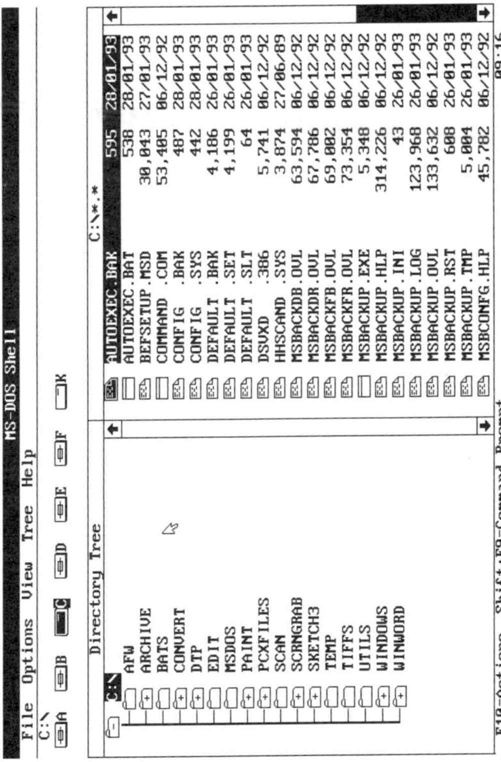

- since the Program/File list is the default when you first use the DOSSHEll, the first three items are the most likely to be visible. Another option, Program List will be dealt with later.

These options allow you to use the mouse for file actions and to work with blocks of filenames in a way that is not possible using MS-DOS commands directly. A block is a set of filenames that have been marked out (by a colour change or change of shading). A file-handling command that is used when a marked block exists is applied to all of the marked files in the block. These files may be selected either from a single directory or from various directories on the disk see later.

Figure 8.5
The presence of sub-directories is indicated by the [+] sign and they can be revealed by clicking on this sign. The [-] sign indicates that the tree has been expanded.

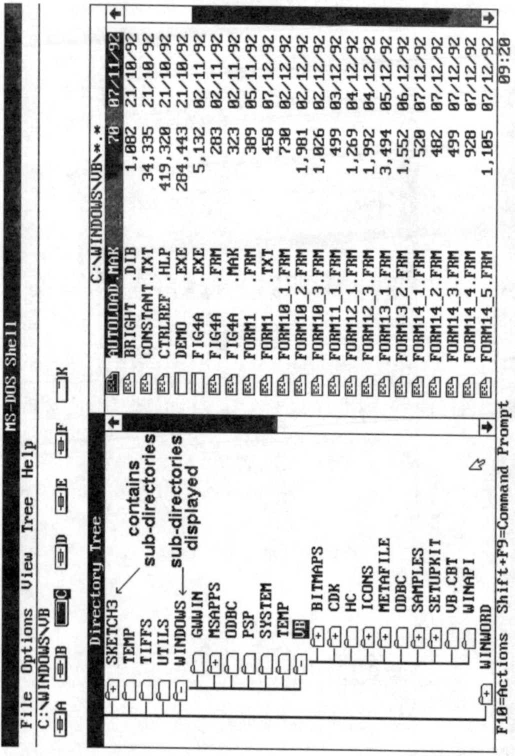

The form of a single file list is shown in Figure 8.4. The Directory Tree occupies most of the left-hand side of the screen, and the files list starts in the right hand side. Each list can be scrolled independently by using its scroll bar as described earlier. In this example, the whole of the root directory can be seen in one view, a very considerable advantage. Even if this is not possible, very little scrolling of the Directory window is needed to look at all the directories on a hard disk, and it is correspondingly easy to look at all of the files in a directory by selecting that directory.

Each directory will appear beside a status box, a box on the graphics screen or square brackets on the text screen. This can be empty, or contain a [+] or [-] sign.

Figure 8.6
The Dual File list. Each list now contains the directory and file structure that should be familiar by now, and using this form of list makes it very easy to copy or move files from one drive/directory to another.

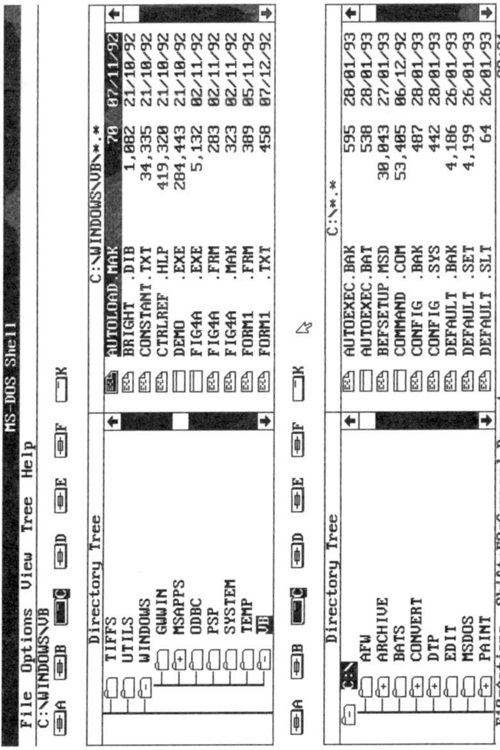

1. The [ ] box indicates that the directory contains files, but no sub-directories. Clicking on the box or on the directory name will cause the files of that directory to appear in the Files list on the right hand side.

2. The [+] box indicates that the directory contains other sub-directories. Clicking on the box will reveal the sub-directories, listed under the main directory name (Figure 8.5). Each of these sub-directory names will be next to a box, and some may be marked with a [+] to indicate that there are further sub-directories (click on the [+] box to reveal them, so **expanding** the tree).

To select files in any of these directories, click on the box or on the name of the directory.

3. The [-] box indicates that the sub-directories are already displayed, and clicking on the box will make these names disappear again, leaving the main directory name marked by its [+] box (this is **collapsing** the tree).

- Remember that the file list and the directory list can be scrolled independently. To change to a new file list, click on the box or the name of the directory whose listing you want to see.

The Dual-file list is selected from the View menu by clicking on its title when the View menu appears. The immediate effect is to split the screen into two main windows, both identical, showing the directory and file list that the single file display had been showing, Figure 8.6. The directories and files will, as usual, be in alphabetical order unless you have opted for a different order (see later).

The windows are completely independent, and you can alter the drive, directory and file display of one without affecting the other. You could, for example, show the directory of the hard dive and its files in the top window, and a directory of a floppy disk in the A: drive, with its files, on the lower window. You could equally easily display one hard disk directory and its file in one window and a different directory on the same hard disk in the other window. This type of display is particularly useful if you want to copy, move or compare files on different drives or directories.

- Remember that if your computer is set up to use a RAMdisk, this also can be used in such a display. This makes it much easier to transfer files between RAMdisk and hard disk or between RAMdisk and floppy. You can also use INTERLNK to transfer files easily to another machine.

When you select All Files from the View menu, you will see a list such as that illustrated in Figure 8.7. The files list is on the right hand side, and it consists of all the files on the disk, arranged in alphabetical order (unless you have opted for some other order). If files bear number titles, such as 123.CNF, the numbers are arranged in order of size ahead of the alphabetical entries.

This listing is of all disk files, in order and irrespective of directory. On a hard disk, this listing may be of several thousand files, so that the files window needs to be scrolled if you want to see more than a small selection of files. Since the files are in order, it is fairly easy to find one that you want. This type of display is particularly useful to find files by name if you do not know which

Figure 8.7
The All Files list of DOSSHELL. This contains all the files of the hard disk (over 3000 in this case) arranged in alphabetical order.

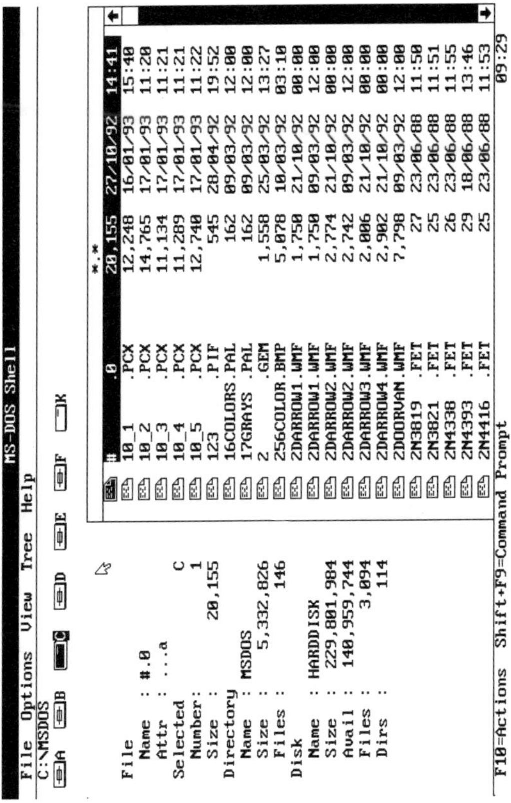

directory to look at. It is also useful to find if files are duplicated, with more than one copy in different directories.

- The All-Files display also allows you to select a block of files taken from various different parts of the hard disk. This is one method by which a block of files can be assembled irrespective of directory.

The left hand side of the screen, when the All-Files option has been used, displays data on one file, on any block selection that has been made, on the directory containing the currently marked file, and on the disk as a whole. The File display will appear, by default, for the first file in the list, and this filename will be marked in the file window by a shaded band or a change of colour. The File display will show the name of the file, and will list its attributes as **a** (archive), **h** (hidden), **s** (system) or **r** (read-only).

- When you first use the All-Files list, no hidden/ system files will appear on the listing. These files appear only when the Options menu has been used to show File Display Options, and the option to show hidden files has been selected, see later.

The Selected portion of the display shows the disk letter, normally C when you are working with the hard disk. Since at least one file will always be selected (the one marked by the shading or colour) there will always be an entry for number of files (default 1) and Size. When a block of files has been marked, the number of such files and the total size will be displayed.

- The total size will be important if you intend to copy the files to a floppy disk. If you attempt to copy more files than a floppy will hold, the action will be attempted, but some files will not be copied. This contrasts with Windows which will simply prompt you to change disks when one floppy is full.

The Directory entry shows the name of the directory for the currently selected file - this is particularly useful if you find two files of the same name and want to find which directories they use. The Size entry shows the total number of bytes used for the whole directory, and the Files entry is the number of files in that directory.

- If a block has been marked, the Directory entry will apply to the last-marked item in the block.

The Disk part of the display does not change as you select or mark files, because it concerns the disk itself, and will not alter unless you are adding or deleting files. The Disk name is shown, and if you have not given a name (or Volume Label) to your hard disk you ought to do so, using the ordinary MS-DOS LABEL command. This is a partial safeguard against re-formatting your hard disk inadvertently. You may intend to format a floppy disk, but have typed or selected C instead of A, for example. If a hard disk has a Name (Volume Label) you will not be allowed to format the disk unless you type the label name. MS-DOS 6.0 allows recovery from an accidental reformat of a hard disk, but a lot of time and emotion can be saved by simply not doing it in the first place.

The total size of the hard disk is shown, along with the amount of space that is available. The Files entry shows the number of separate files on the disk, all of which, apart from hidden files, will be listed in the Files window, and the Directories entry shows how many directories have been created (some may be empty).

- The obvious use of the All-Files list for locating duplicated files and files that are no longer needed makes this a good way of clearing and re-organising a hard disk. You would normally follow up such an action by compressing the disk with DEFRAG, see Chapter 4. You must quit DOSSHELL (and any other memory-resident program that you can enter and leave) before you run DEFRAG or any other disk compressing software.

The Repaint and Refresh options on the View menu are for use in special circumstances, and each is selected by clicking on the title. This will run the action and return you to the DOSSHELL menu. They start to become useful when you are running programs from DOSSHELL and swapping to and from various programs.

Refresh is used to update the file display. When file copying or creating actions are carried out by programs other than DOSSHELL itself, the details of the new or altered files are not notified to DOSSHELL. When you obtain a DOSSHELL listing (whatever you have opted for) of a disk, the disk is read, and the directory stored in memory. All subsequent displays are based on that stored list, and the list is altered if files are deleted, moved or erased using DOSSHELL. Windows, by contrast, does update its display.

If other programs are being run and are altering files this has the effect that when you switch back to DOSSHELL the directory display is out of date - it does not show any changes that were carried out by the programs that have just been running. This applies only when you are running all of your programs from within DOSSHELL, as you normally would. If you exit DOSSHELL, run a program that alters files and start DOSSHELL again, the directory displays of DOSSHELL will be correct.

The Refresh option allows the files of a disk to be read again, creating a new stored list which will find the altered files. This takes a little time, particularly for the hard disk, and it also returns you to the default display, so that if you had the cursor placed over a directory of the hard disk before refreshing the display, it will be on the root directory after the refresh process is completed - this acts to indicate that the refresh is finished, but makes the action more time-consuming.

- Always check what directory you are using before and after using Refresh. It would be considerably better if Refresh acted only on the current directory, or gave the option of current directory or whole drive.

The Repaint option is rather more exotic. If you run from within DOSSHELL a memory-resident program (like MSDOS PRINT), the way that DOSSHELL works requires the memory-resident program to end before DOSSHELL can be used again. When this happens, the screen may still show some of the display ofthe memory-resident program, and selecting Repaint will remove this. It is quite possible that you may never need to use Repaint if you do not run memory-resident programs that alter the screen display.

The Options menu

The Options menu allows you a considerable choice, some of which concern display options (which could just as well have been placed in the View menu) and system options. The list presented in the Options set is:

Confirmation
File Display Options
Select across directories
Show information
Enable Task Swapper
Display Colours

of which the Select across Directories and the Show Information do not lead to any other menu. The Display and Colors options have already been dealt with and Task Swapping options are noted later.

Select across Directories is a 'switch' option. Selecting it will mark the line with a dot to indicate that the action is on. In this state, a block of files can be selected using files from different directories. This allows DOSSHELL to move and copy files in ways that are very time-consuming when used with other systems. You can, for example copy a different file from each of thirty different hard-disk directories on to a floppy.

The Show Information option applies to the currently selected file (or to the last files in a block to be selected). The information is the same as appears on the left-hand side of the screen in the All-Files list. The Selected part of the information is useful as a way of showing if a block of selected files will fit on to a floppy disk, since it shows the total size of the block.

Confirmation options provide a safeguard against carrying out actions hastily, such as marking a set of files for deletion and then realising that some files ought to have been retained. This is particularly likely if you have selected a set of files by extension letters, without looking at the file names individually. When confirmation is switched on, you will be asked to confirm each action individually, so that whether you are working with one file or a large block, each name will be shown and you will have to reply by clicking on the appropriate box, OK, Cancel or Help.

There are three classes of confirmation actions, and by default all three are marked on. They are:

Confirm on Delete
Confirm on Replace
Confirm on Mouse Operation

and each has beside it a box which is either empty or marked with a cross, Figure 8.8. Clicking with the mouse cursor on the cross will remove the cross, also removing the confirmation action. Clicking on an empty box will place a cross in the box, re-establishing the confirmation action.

Confirm on delete is useful to retain if you are worried about accidentally deleting files. Once you are experienced with the use of DOSSHELL, it can be useful to remove this safeguard, because it can make a long task of deleting a large bunch of files. With this confirmation switched off, you can mark a block of files, press the Delete key, confirm once and delete all of the files with no additional confirmation for each individual filename.

Confirm on Replace affects the copying of files. If a file of the same name exists in the destination disk or directory, this option will require you to confirm that the new file is to replace the old file, and to assist you, the details of each file are shown. This also is a useful safeguard when you start to use DOSSHELL at first, but you may want to dispense with it later, particularly if you make a lot of backups of files.

Confirm on Mouse Operation is used when you carry out block actions on files using the mouse rather than by use of the keyboard or menu commands. It is remarkably easy, when copying a set of files to a directory using the mouse, to make the copy to the wrong

Figure 8.8
The Confirmations options list. To turn a confirmation on, click on the box so that a cross appears.

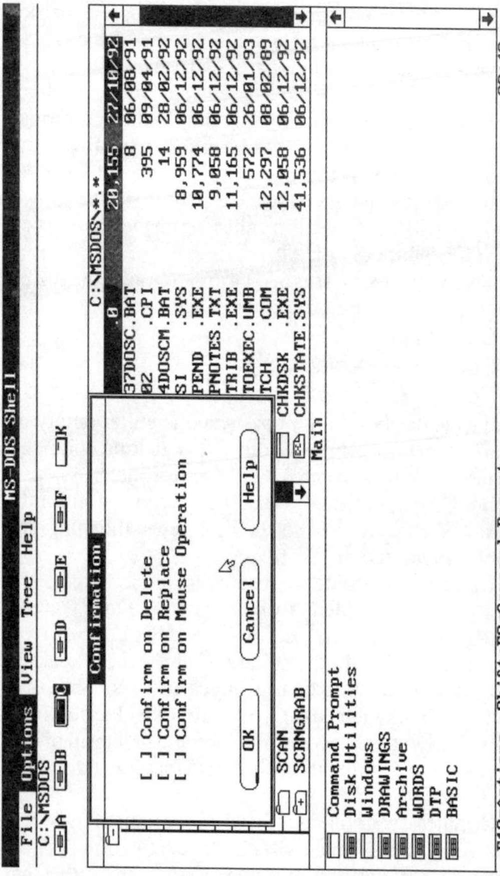

directory, and by retaining the cross in this option box, you will be reminded by a message of what you are trying to do and be given an opportunity to escape or confirm.

- In general, you should keep the Confirm options switched on unless you find them restrictive. You can always switch a Confirm option off while you carry out a block action, and then switch it on again afterwards. Once you are experienced in using DOSSHELL you may want to turn off one or more of the Confirmation actions.

Figure 8.9

The File Display options that offer the options of showing Hidden or System files, sorting into descending order, and all the sort options.

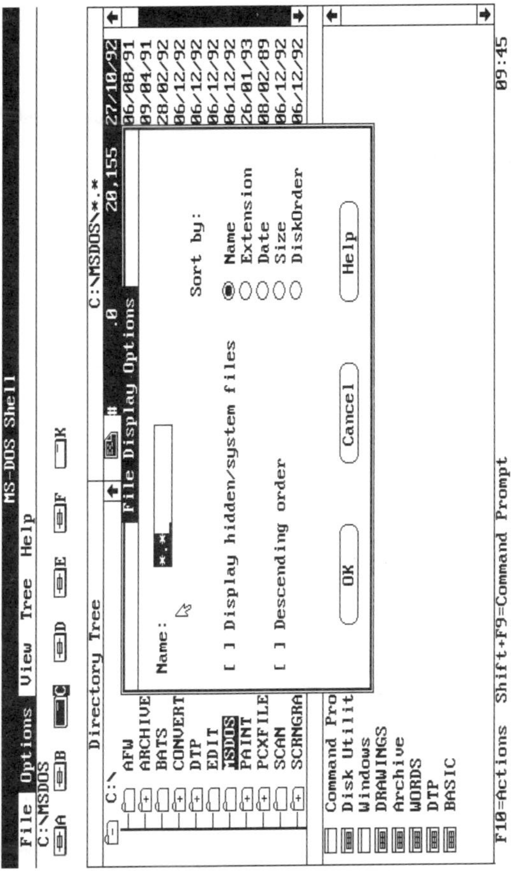

The File Display Options, Figure 8.9, offer you the choice of how you display files in the File window, and how you can select files. The cursor appears on the File Name line of the window that appears, and the default name is *.*, meaning all file names are acceptable. You can type a name of a single file, such as CHAP1.TXT, of a set of files with a common extension set, such as *.TXT, a name that might be used with various extensions, like 123.*, or leave the entry as *.*

- If you use anything other than *.*, the display of files from that point on will be restricted to files that fit your specifications. If, for example, you typed *.DOC, then only files with the DOC extension will appear in any of the file window lists. This can lead you into thinking that some directories are empty when, in fact, they contain a large number of files but none that fits the description. Check the File Display Options when you find an empty directory and make sure that the name is *.*.

You should use a restricted file specification only when you intend to select files in this way, and replace the *.* description afterwards. In general, a specification such as *.DOC will be used in conjunction with the Select All option in the Files menu, see later.

The right-hand side of the File Display Options window is concerned with the ways that the files will appear on screen sorted into order. The options are:

Name
Extension
Date
Size
Disk Order

and the normal sort order, whatever the basis of the sorting, is ascending, from low to high, from A to Z.

You can opt for descending order by clicking on the box marked with this option. A dot will appear in the box when you have selected descending order, and can be removed by clicking on this box again.

Sort by Name is the default, so that files are always displayed in a list that is in alphabetical order of the main name, and with names that consist of digits (like 123.CNF) placed ahead of names that start with a letter of the alphabet. This sort by name is used even when other specifications are used, such as opting for only DOC files to be displayed.

Sort by Extension allows files to be shown in order of extension letters, so that files with the same extension will be shown together. In this sort order, files with no extension will appear in the list ahead of the files with extensions, and extensions that consist of punctuation marks and dollar signs will appear ahead of numerals which are then followed by the alphabetical extensions. This type of sort order can be useful when combined with an All-Files display, in order to see all the files with the same extensions. Another possibility is to nominate the extension in the Name line (such as *.$$$) and to use All-Files to see all the files with that extension, and no other files. This allows temporary files (created by programs for temporary use) to be checked.

Sort by Date is particularly useful when you suspect that you have several files of similar names but with different dates, indicating different versions. This option will produce a list in which the oldest files are shown at the top of the list and the most recent at the end. You can switch on the Descending order box if you want to see a list that places the most recent files at the start. A list in date order is often useful to decide which files should be backed up, or in a search for files which need to be updated. Look in particular with the Hidden/System box selected to see if you have any old version of IO.SYS, MSDOS.SYS or COMMAND.COM lurking on your hard disk. If anything happened to wipe out a current version of such a file, you would be puzzled by the error messages (Wrong MSDOS version) that appeared if an old version started to run.

Sort by size allows files to be displayed with the shortest at the start of the list and the longest at the end. You may be surprised to find several files with zero bytes or one byte each when you combine this option with the All-Files list. Never erase zero-length or one-byte files, because these are used by programs to identify a version, a directory, or as a license ID, and erasing such a file may make a program unusable. You can create such files for yourself, using an editor to create a filename but with nothing typed. A common use for such a file is in identifying a floppy disk.

■ If you find batch files with only one byte, it is certain that these are editing mistakes and can be erased.

At the other end of the list, you may find program files of remarkable length, 900,000 bytes or more. You may also find temporary files made by programs such as Windows, which are read-only and of large size, 500 Kbyte or more. Sometimes you will find a collection of such temporary files taking up several Mbyte of your hard disk. You will have to check with the manuals for the software that produced the files to see if they can be deleted - very often they are deleted automatically the next time the program runs.

■ Remember that you can always find the directory that owns a file by selecting the file name on the All-Files list and looking for the Directory entry on the left hand side of the screen.

The remaining sort order is disk order, the order in which files appear from the first usable sector of the disk onwards, and this can often be very revealing. If you find that this order produces a list in which files from different directories are mixed, it is an indication that your hard disk needs re-organising. In the course of using a hard disk, many files are deleted, allowing the space that they have occupied to be re-used. This leads to fragmentation, with a file often being stored in pieces on several different locations on a disk. This is why a file from another directory can appear in the middle of a set of files that all belong together. At some stage, a file, usually a data file, has been erased, and its space has been taken up by another file or, more usually, part of another file which belongs elsewhere. This indicates the need to use DEFRAG, see Chapter 4.

■ Note that on a disk order list, the files IO.SYS, MSDOS.SYS and COMMAND.COM should normally appear first. The first two SYS files may be differently named (such as IBM.SYS) on some machines. The last files on a list of this type will not necessarily be the last files that were saved, because these files may have occupied the space of an earlier file that was erased.

All of the sort orders have their uses, but there is no way of combining sort orders, so that in a date sort, for example, all files of the same date were also sorted into alphabetical order.

Selecting files

A file is selected when its name is shown with a shaded or coloured bar. To select a single file, the cursor must be in the files window, and by far the easiest method is to move the mouse cursor over the file name and click. There will always be at least one file selected when the mouse cursor is in the files window.

■ Do not double-click on a data file name unless you have associated the file with a program, see later. Double-clicking on a data file which has not been associated with a program will produce a Bad command or filename message. If the file has been associated, the associated program will run and will make use of the data file.

The more useful actions, however, concern sets of files selected as a block. The simplest methods involve using the mouse along with other keys, and in this book

Figure 8.10
A complete block marked using the mouse and the SHIFT key together, as described.

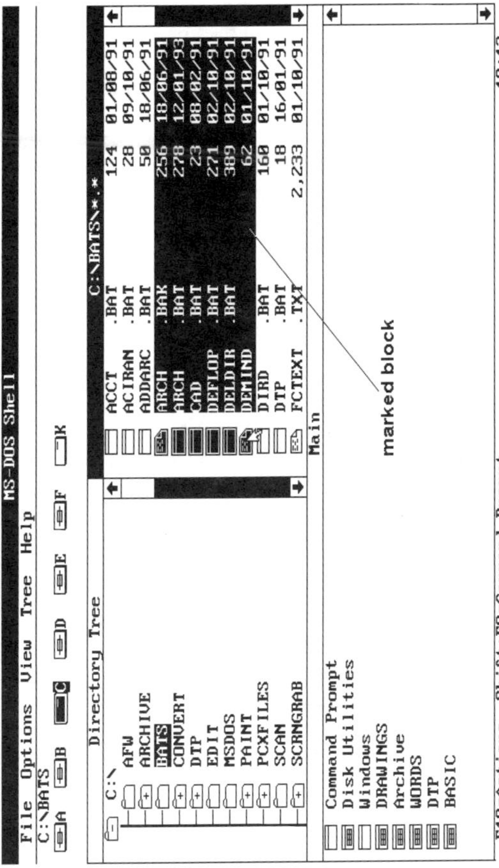

methods requiring the keyboard alone will be ignored - the mouse is by far the most effective method of using these commands.

The simplest marking system involves a set of consecutive filenames. To mark such a set as a block requires you to place the mouse cursor on the first of the files and mark it by clicking the mouse button. You then hold down the SHIFT key, move the mouse cursor to the last name in the set, and click again. This will mark the whole block, Figure 8.10.

If you need to scroll down the list, use the scroll bars and mouse, NOT the cursor arrowed keys (which will clear the markings). You can scroll in either direction to mark a block, so that the block can be marked starting at the lower item and ending at the upper.

In some cases, all the files you want to place in a block have some common characteristic, such as the same extension name, or the same main name, or with part of the main name being the same. This can best be dealt with by using the File Display Options from the Options menu, and filling in a suitable name line, such as *.TXT, CHAP?.TXT, 123.* or whatever will specify the files you want to use.

This will result in the Files display showing only the filenames that fit the pattern you have specified, such as all TXT files or all files starting with CHAP, in that directory. With this done, you can click over the Files menu name, and from this menu, click on Select All. This will automatically select all of the files that are displayed. Remember that Select All will not be available unless you have clicked on a file name.

■ Making a set like this is often easier if you use a sort order other than by name. Remember that you can switch to the All Files window if you want to select files from different directories. For many purposes, selecting all of the files that conform to a specification like this and then deselecting a few, is faster than picking files from a list to select.

If your selection of files does not conform to a pattern or consist of a set that are arranged in sequence, you will need to select files individually. This is not quite as easy as it sounds, because clicking the mouse button by itself will only ever select the filename on which the mouse cursor is resting; any previous selection will immediately disappear. Adding to a selection requires the Ctrl key to be held down while the button is being used.

Click on the first filename that you want, then hold down the Ctrl key while you click on the other names. Do not release the Ctrl key until you have finished the selection action. If you click the mouse button again after releasing the Ctrl key you will cancel all of your selection except the last file on which you clicked. Remember that if the list needs to be scrolled, this should be done using the mouse and the scroll-bars.

Deselecting is the action of removing the selection bar from a filename, so that file actions do not affect that file. Remember that any file action such as deletion or copying acts on whatever file is selected, or on a selected block of files. You need to be careful to ensure that the selection has not changed because of careless clicking.

1. For a single file, selecting another file name will automatically deselect that file.

2. Deselecting blocks of files can be done in ways that are very similar to those used to select blocks. All of the selected files in a directory can be deselected by using the Deselect option from the Files menu. This should always be done after a file action has been carried out on a block of files unless another block action is needed.

3. When a block of files has been selected, some files can be deselected from the end of the block. Place the mouse cursor on the last file you want to de-select and hold the SHIFT key down, then click. This will deselect all the files from the cursor position to the end of the block.

4. You can deselect files at random by holding down the Ctrl key and clicking on the files that are to be deselected. The display can be scrolled by using the scroll bars while this is being done, so that deselection can be carried out over a large range of files.

■ When a file is deselected from a block, the arrowhead will disappear, but the colouring/shading will not change until another file is also deselected. This can lead you into thinking that the deselection has not been carried out.

Range of selection

DOSSHELL allows you to select files from different directories that can extend over the whole of the hard disk. There are several methods that can be used.

1. Use the All Files list and carry out File Options specifications (such as *.TXT or 123.*) to restrict the display to a set of files that you want, taken from any set of the disk directories. You can then use the Select All option from the Files menu to select these files.

2. Again, using the All Files list, you can mark using the SHIFT or Ctrl keys in conjunction with the mouse cursor as described earlier. You can also use these mouse and key methods on a full list, in which the specifier name is *.* and all files are displayed. A selection of this kind can be carried out more quickly than you might expect because the files are arranged in order. Remember that you can determine for yourself the order in which files are displayed; by Name, Extension, Date, Size or Disk order.

3. Use the Select Across Directories option in the Options menu. This is an on/off switch item, and is marked with a dot when it has been switched on (click again on the name to switch it off and make the dot disappear). When Select Across Directories has been switched on, you can make selections as described earlier using the mouse along with the SHIFT and Ctrl keys as you wish. You can, for example, click on a single file name in one directory, then change directories and use the SHIFT key along with the mouse to mark out a consecutive set of files. You can then change directory again and pick out some scattered filenames to mark, using the Ctrl key along with the mouse button.

All of the names that are marked in this way will remain marked unless you return to a directory and mark some other name(s). When a set of files in different directories has been marked like this, all of the usual file actions can be applied, as listed later in this Chapter.

■ Select Across Directories must be used with some care. If it is left on, it is only too easy to move from one directory to another leaving a trail of selected files behind you. If at some stage you decide to delete a file you are liable to delete the whole set of files you have marked. For safety, use Select Across Directories only when you need to; always switch it off when you have finished using it, and keep the Confirmation options switched on. This ensures that you will be notified of each file that is to be affected, and you will know if a file appears from a different directory.

View file contents is an action that is available only when a single file has been selected, and the option is not visible in the File menu if a block of files has been marked. Any attempt to use the action by the alternative method of pressing the F9 key will cause a beep on the loudspeaker, and nothing will happen.

When only one file has been selected, the View File option can be used, either by selecting this from the Files Menu or by pressing the F9 key. The F9 key is also used to alter the way in which the file is displayed, see later. This is an excellent way of displaying batch or other text files, whether from a text editor or from a word-processor. Word-processor files will often contain characters other than those obtainable from the keyboard (these are the codes that control actions such as margin size, bold print, line spacings etc.), but these can be ignored except for WordStar files which use a changed character at the end of each word.

Figure 8.11
A batch file displayed using the F9 key. Scrolling can be done by clicking on the PgUp, PgDn or arrow signs at the top of the screen or by pressing these keys.

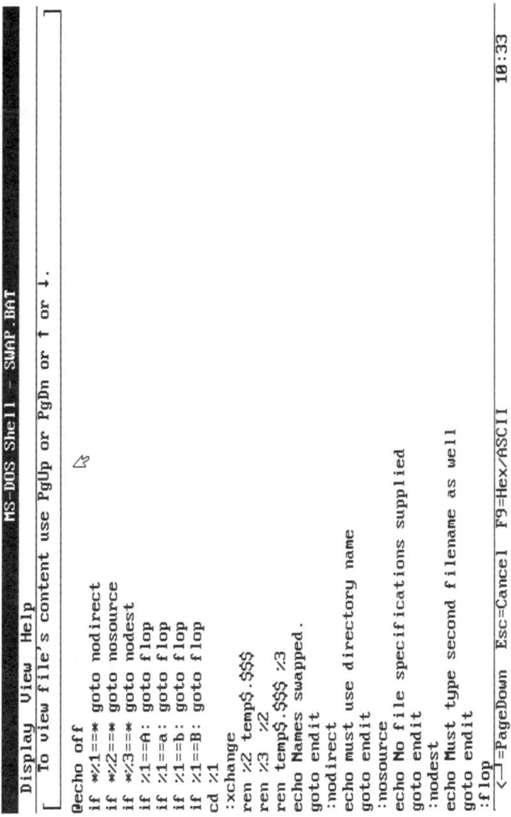

MS-DOS Shell - SWAP.BAT
Display View Help
To view file's content use PgUp or PgDn or ↑ or ↓.
@echo off
if *%1==* goto nodirect
if *%2==* goto nosource
if *%3==* goto nodest
if %1==A: goto flop
if %1==a: goto flop
if %1==b: goto flop
if %1==B: goto flop
cd %1
:xchange
ren %2 temp$.$$$
ren %3 %2
ren temp$.$$$ %3
echo Names swapped.
goto endit
:nodirect
echo must use directory name
goto endit
:nosource
echo No file specifications supplied
goto endit
:nodest
echo Must type second filename as well
goto endit
:flop
=PageDown Esc=Cancel F9=Hex/ASCII
10:33

This viewer is particularly useful for looking at batch files and the CONFIG.SYS files, also for the INI files of Windows programs and the DOSSHELL.INI file. Note that this is a viewing utility, not a text editor, and you cannot alter the files in any way with this action.

Unlike some File View utilities, you are not confined to text files. If you use the F9 key to look at a program, you will see the program either as a mass of character symbols, or (by pressing F9 again) as a set of numbers in hexadecimal scale.

The display switches over each time the F9 key is used, so that you cannot be certain in which mode it will start when you use File View on a new file. If you see mainly a set of hexadecimal numbers when you want to view a text file, press F9 to restore the full character display.

The File View utility will scroll in the usual way with the cursor arrowed keys or the Page Up, Page Down keys. You can also use the ENTER key as a Page Down key. You can also click with the mouse on the words PgUp and PgDn or the arrows at the top of the screen, Figure 8.11.

To leave the File View utility, press the Esc key, or, using the mouse, select the Restore View from the little View menu. The use of the Esc key is quicker and simpler.

The Search action

DOSSHELL contains, in its Files menu, a Search action which is used to find a file, either in a selected directory or using a search of the entire disk. You have to specify what you are searching for, and supply a valid filename. The cursor must be placed in the Files window to allow this option to appear in the Files menu - it is not available from other windows.

Selecting Search brings up the Search Form, Figure 8.12, in which you are asked to type the name of the file and indicate whether the search is to be over the whole disk (the default) or in the selected directory only. Only a file can be searched for, not a phrase or word within a file, so that the name that you supply must take the form of a valid file name (8 characters maximum in the main name and up to three in the extension). When the file is found, its name will be printed on a report form. If the name contains wildcard characters, several names will be printed which match the pattern you have typed.

Part of the Files menu contains a set of file actions which can be carried out either on individual files or on blocks of files selected by any of the methods that were described earlier. The list is:

Move
Copy
Delete
Rename
Change Attributes

Figure 8.12
The Search form which allows you to find your specified file in a selected directory.

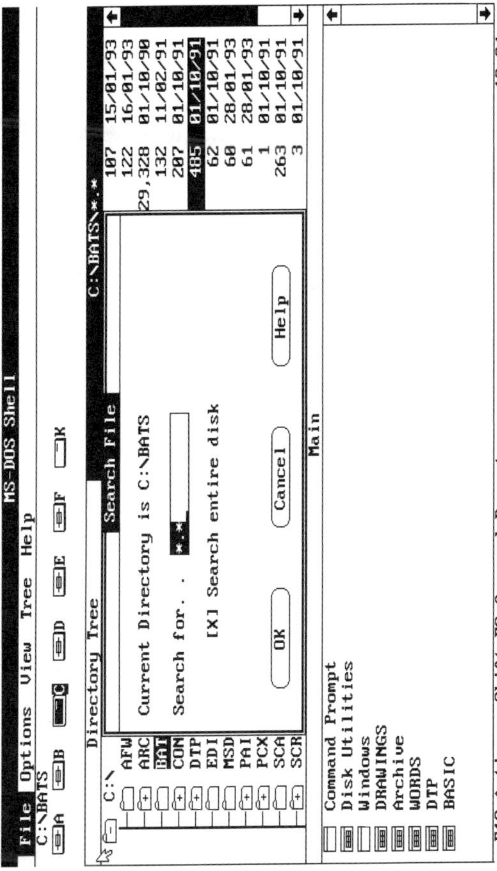

The most straightforward of these is to delete the file(s) by pressing the Delete key. This is much faster than selecting Delete from the Files menu and applies to a single selected file or to a block equally.

If Confirmation on Delete has remained ticked (in the Options menu), each deletion will require you to confirm by clicking on the Yes answer box in the window that appears. If you have opted for no confirmation, the deletion will be carried out as soon as you have pressed the key for an individual file.

If you have cancelled Confirmation, pressing the Delete key when a block is selected will bring up a single confirmation window for the whole block. Once you answer Yes in this window, all of the files of the block will be deleted.

The Rename action is oddly restricted in a way that does not apply when a set of files is renamed by using MS-DOS commands directly. For a single file, the method is straightforward - the file is selected and Rename is chosen from the Files menu. This brings up a Rename box into which you type the new name and selecting OK will cause the rename action to work. If you need to rename a whole set of files, such as CH1.TXT, CH2.TXT, CH3.TXT etc. to CH1.DOC, CH2.DOC, CH3.DOC and so on, you can select all of the files that need to be changed and start the Rename action as before, but you will prompted to type the new name for each file individually.

This is tedious, and the old-style MS-DOS command is much faster. Select Command Prompt from the Program list (with Program/File list displayed), or use Run from the File menu, and type a command such as:

REN *.TXT *.DOC

and press ENTER to carry out all of the changes in one action. This is possible using MS-DOS directly because all the changes are of the same type, altering TXT to DOC. The * is the wildcard which can be used to mean any set of characters. To return to the DOSSHELL when this is complete, type EXIT and press the ENTER key.

Use the DOSSHELL Rename for single files, and groups of files for which each new name differs completely from the old name. Use the MS-DOS REN command when the old and new filenames differ only in a straightforward way such as DOC for TXT, ART1 for CHAP1 and so on. Oddly enough, although the Rename command of Windows File Manager appears to work in the same way as that of DOSSHELL, it **will** accept wildcards, so allowing a group of files to be renamed.

Changing the attributes of files can also be done very easily from DOSSHELL, more easily than from MS-DOS commands. You should use this very sparingly, and mainly for making files read-only. Do not use the hidden or system attribute changes unless you know what you are doing, and never remove the hidden or system attribute from a file such as MSDOS.SYS or

IO.SYS. You seldom need to alter the archive attribute, since this is usually done automatically by actions, such as XCOPY, that make use of this attribute.

Copy and Move are the actions which, apart from Delete, are likely to be the most useful and most used of all the file actions. DOSSHELL provides for these to be controlled completely by mouse actions, so that working with single or multiple file copying or moving is fast and easy compared to the use of MS-DOS direct commands. A Move action is simply a Copy action followed by deleting the original file. Use Copy rather than Move if you are in any doubt - it is harmless to have a redundant file in a directory, and you can always delete the marked files later, after you are sure that you have copied them safely.

The simplest and most consistent methods for Copy and Move involve holding down a key while using the mouse to drag files from one place to another. The method sounds complicated to describe, but is very simple to use once you have practised using some unwanted files for which you have backup copies on floppy disks.

A Copy action starts by switching to a view that allows you to see both source and destination drive and directory, using the Dual Files list. With the cursor in the Source directory (which can be either window - whichever directory you are copying from), select the single file or block of files which must be copied.

Now hold down the **Ctrl** key, place the cursor on any marked file in the source set, and hold down the mouse button. Move the mouse until the cursor is over the destination directory. This must be on the left-hand side of the destination display, over the directory name and not over any filename on the right-hand side. Release the mouse button, then the Ctrl key. The files will then be copied and you will see the directory contents alter.

- You must be careful that you select the correct destination directory. If you release the mouse button while the cursor is over another directory the copying will be done to that directory. Always check the destination directory before you release the mouse button, particularly if the Confirm on Mouse Action option is cancelled.

The Move action is carried out in a way that is almost identical to the Copy action, but the **Alt** key is held down in place of the Ctrl key. Remember when you use Move that the source files will be deleted after copying.

This is automatic and cannot be interrupted. There should be no risk of losing files in the event of a power-failure, however, because the deletion is not done until the copy action is complete.

Both Copy and Move will require you to confirm for each individual file in a selected block unless you have turned off the Confirmation messages in the Options menu. While you are learning to use these commands, it is better to keep the confirmation messages in place, but you can cancel the confirmation when you are more sure of the actions. This will make the actions very much faster.

■ If you drag files from one directory of the hard disk to another, with no keys held down, a Move action will be performed. Dragging files from one disk to another (between a hard disk and a floppy usually) carries out a Copy action only. You can make this into a Move by holding down the Alt key as you drag the files.

Associating data files

A data file, whether it is a text file or one that has been produced by a spreadsheet, a database or graphics programs such as CAD or Paint programs, cannot be run - it is useful only when loaded into a running program of the correct type. DOSSHELL provides for any data file to be associated with a program, and when this is done, double-clicking on the data file will start the program and read in the data, just as if you had double-clicked on the program name and then opted to read the data file from the program. This facility exists also in Windows.

■ Not all data files can be Associated. Association can be used only for programs which, when used from MS-DOS directly, allow a data file name to be typed following the program name so that the data file can be loaded into the program. If the program does not permit this use (many insist on loading files by way of a menu when the program is running) then the Associate option cannot be used with that program.

Associating data files provides you with a timesaving way of working with your data files, since you do not need to locate the program file in order to make use of the data file once the association has been made. You can specify association either for a program file or a data file.

If you select a program file, you will be asked, Figure 8.13, what extension letters to look for. Data files with these extension letters will be associated with the

Figure 8.13

The Associate File option being used on a program name, requiring you to type in the extension letters that the program uses for its data files. You can use more than one extension.

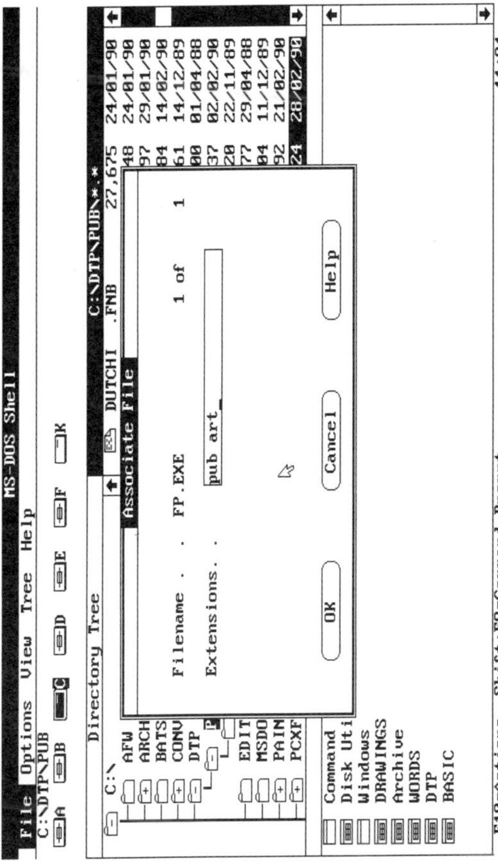

program file. You can type several sets of extension letters separated by a space. In future when you double-click on such data files the program will start and load the data file you have selected.

■ In this respect, a batch file is counted as a program file, but you should not associate data files with a batch file.

Figure 8.14
Associating a data file with a program - you can associate with only one program.

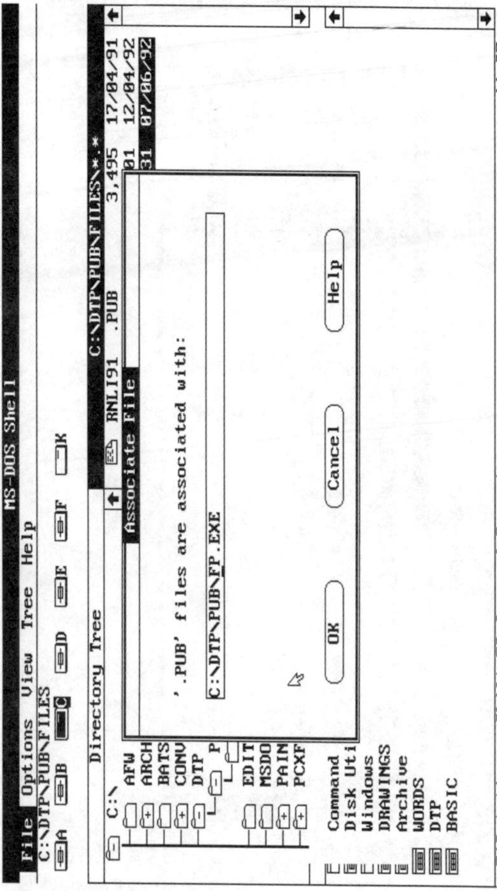

If you select a data file, you will be asked to type a program name in the form of Figure 8.14. You must provide the full path to the program file so that it can be located from any directory of the hard disk.

■ Note that a batch file is treated as a program file, not as a text file, because double-clicking on a batch file will run the batch file. You should not attempt, therefore to associate batch files with any text-editor program to allow you to edit them more easily.

- You cannot successfully associate one type of data file with more than one program. Be careful also of creating conflicts by using one association in a program file and a different one in a data file. You can remove an association by selecting the file, using the Associate option, and deleting the name(s) from the list.
- If you want to use a data file along with another unassociated program, use the Run command from the File menu, and specify the data file in the command line.

Using Open and Run

The Files menu of DOSSHELL contains the Open and Run options, which are used to a much lesser extent than the other commands. Open is the equivalent of double-clicking on a program name; it will run that program with no provision for adding parameters. Run is more useful - it provides a small panel in which you can type the program name and any parameters that are associated with it.

For any programs that you run frequently it is much more useful to set up a **Group**, see later, so that the program and any associated batch files can be run by double-clicking. Run is useful for programs that you might want to run every now and again.

The Group system

DOSSHELL can deal with programs in a way that will be unfamiliar to many new users of MS-DOS 6.0 unless they have already become familiar with MS-DOS 5.0 or MS Windows 3.0 or 3.1. The idea is that programs which belong together can be placed into Groups, displayed separately in DOSSHELL, and each program in a Group can be started by double-clicking on its name. More importantly, the way that a program runs can be controlled by setting up some items, rather in the way that a batch file is set up, when the Group is created or at any later time. Programs placed in Groups can be very easily task-swapped (see later) using a simple key combination for each program.

- One particularly useful aspect of Group action is that it allows existing batch files to be used. It also permits you to program all the actions of a batch file in a different way.

The use of Groups is a convenience - it does not replace any earlier methods, but it is a considerable improvement on them, and is superior to most of the alternatives, including other shell types of programs. It is, for example, very much more satisfactory than the use of Run or Open from the File menu of DOSSHELL. The main advantage of using Groups is that they avoid the need to search for frequently-used programs in directories. Instead, you simply double-click on the Group name and then on the program name. You can place any program you like in one or more Groups. The work of specifying directories is done once when the Group is set up, as it would be in a batch file.

You do not need to have a large numbers of Groups. The Main and Disk Utilities Groups exist ready-made for you, and you can add a Group for each distinct activity. You might, for example, have a Group called WRITING which contains a word-processor, an editor and some file utilities, and another called ACCOUNTS which contains a spreadsheet, an accounts program and some file utilities. This might be as much as you need. It is unlikely that you would need a very large number of Groups, certainly not as many Groups as you have directories on a hard disk.

Existing Groups

When you start DOSSHELL for the first time there are some ready-made Groups and of these the Disk Utilities Group is the obvious one to select as an example, since everyone will need to use some of some programs in thisGroup at some time. Double-clicking on this name will bring up the list of programs covered by this Group, Figure 8.15, and also the name Main which allows you to get back (by double-clicking on Main) to the original list.

Each line in the list of Disk Utilities can be used to summon up a program. This in itself is straightforward, and in some cases is no more than could be done by double-clicking on the program name in the Files list. The difference is that you do not have to search through directories to find the program, and you can specify how you want to make use of the program in a way that is not possible when you simply double-click on the name from the Files list.

- When you start a program by double-clicking on its name in the Files list, you cannot type options. For example, double-clicking on UNFORMAT will fail, because you cannot type the drive letter A:, B: or C: following the command. This has to be done by using

Figure 8.15
Programs in the Disk Utilities Group - these are set up ready for you and are used here as an example of Group structure.

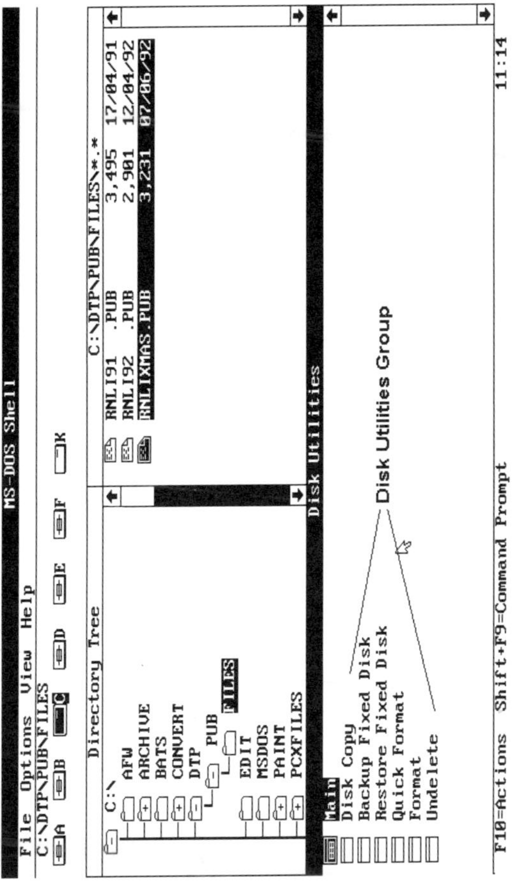

the RUN command, making the action longer. Using a program in a Group allows you to use options but without the need to specify the program directory, as is required for the Run command, each time you use the program.

Select the Quick Format program by a single-click (NOT a double-click) on its name. You will see the name change colour and an arrow will appear to its left. Now select the File menu, and click on Properties. This will

Figure 8.16
The Program Items Properties window. This allows you to alter the way a program is used from its Group. The example shows the PIP for the Quick Format command, with FORMAT %1 /q *used as the command.*

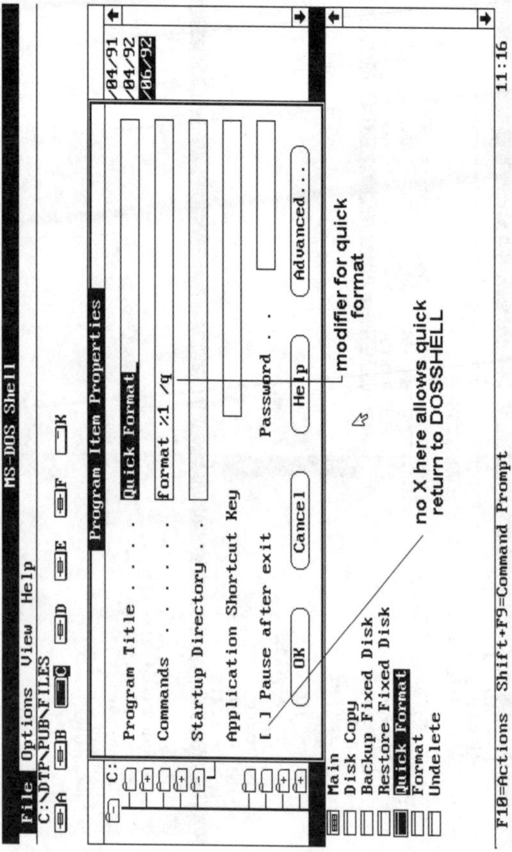

bring up the Program Item Properties window, Figure 8.16. This is the format that allows options to be selected, and in this case, some of the form has been used (as much as is needed in this case). Each line can be edited while the form is in use, but in this example you should not alter the information.

The Program Title line is for information only - it decides what will appear in the Group as a title. This need not be the same as the filename for the program, and it can take up more space, allowing you to use a longer description, up to 36 characters if need be.

The Commands line contains the commands as they would be typed if you were using Run. In this case, the command is FORMAT %1 /q, and the form of command is very much the same as you might use in a batch file. In this example, the %1 is a placeholder for a drive letter, and the /q option makes the format of the Quick variety, since Quick Format is only a variation of the ordinary Format command.

■ The directory path for FORMAT has not been used in this example, because FORMAT is in the MSDOS directory and the PATH line in AUTOEXEC.BAT specifies MSDOS as a directory that should be searched. If you were specifying a program in some other directory you would need to use a complete path and file name.

The Startup Directory line is not used in this example. It allows you to specify a directory, usually one that holds data files, from which the program will be started. If you were using a word-processor, for example, you might want the Startup Directory to be the one that contained the text files. This allows the program instant access to those files when it starts running. Not all programs can use this facility.

The Application Shortcut Key is also left blank in this example. Specifying a shortcut key allows program switching (see later, this Chapter) to be done rapidly by pressing key combinations such as Alt-A, Alt-B and so on. A Shortcut key can be specified only for a program in a Group.

The Pause after Exit box is not marked with a cross in this example. When this mark is made (by clicking on the box) it will prevent an automatic return to DOSSHELL, and you will be asked to press any key to return to DOSSHELL. Clicking again on this box will remove the cross, and make the return to DOSSHELL automatic. Cross this box if you need to read any messages that the program ends with.

The Password space allows you to type a password of up to 14 characters. If you use this option, you will have to remember the password - you must make a note because it will not appear again anywhere. You cannot read back your password from the Properties window once you have left the window. The Password can use upper and lowercase letters, and these are distinguished -qwer is not identical to QWER.

- Do not use passwording unless you really need to, and take great care of security of passwords if you need to use them. A password that is easy to remember is generally an insecure password, but if you forget a password and have no note of it you may lock yourself out of the system. You can read your password from the DOSSHELL.INI file if you have forgotten it. Anyone wanting to use your password might also know how to do this.

After the first Program Item Properties window has been examined (remember that it is seldom necessary or useful to fill in every line) you have the option of looking at the Advanced Properties. Using the Advanced Properties is not essential, but since we are looking at an existing set it helps to see how this window is used. Select Advanced by clicking on the name. The Window now looks as illustrated in Figure 8.17.

Of the items shown, the most obviously useful is the Help Text line. This is what you will see if you take the Help option when using a program, and in this case the Help Text has been provided. This text takes up more space that is provided in the line, but you can scroll it sideways with the left and right arrowed keys, and with the Home (start of text) and End (end of text) keys.

- When you place a program into a Group for yourself, you can use this line to write your own Help messages, which can be as brief or as detailed as you like. It is always useful to type some Help text, because you tend to forget precisely what you must do when running a program, and this text, together with the prompts that can be added, assists you greatly. In these Help lines, Ctrl-M produces a new line. You can also refer to pages in the DOSSHELL Help files.

There are lines in the Advanced options which deal with reserving memory, but you should not make use of these until you know a considerable amount about the programs for which you are creating a Group. The Quick Format example makes no use of these lines, and they are very seldom needed - never assume that you have to fill in anything into these lines, see later.

The sections, other than the Help line, that you are more likely to need to deal with are the Video Mode, Reserve Shortcut Keys and Prevent Program Switch. These are all 'special situation' sections, and for a large number of programs that you might add into a Group you would not need to make any use of these lines and options.

Figure 8.17
The Program Items Advanced Properties window with its Help text and specifying in this example the use of the Text mode screen.

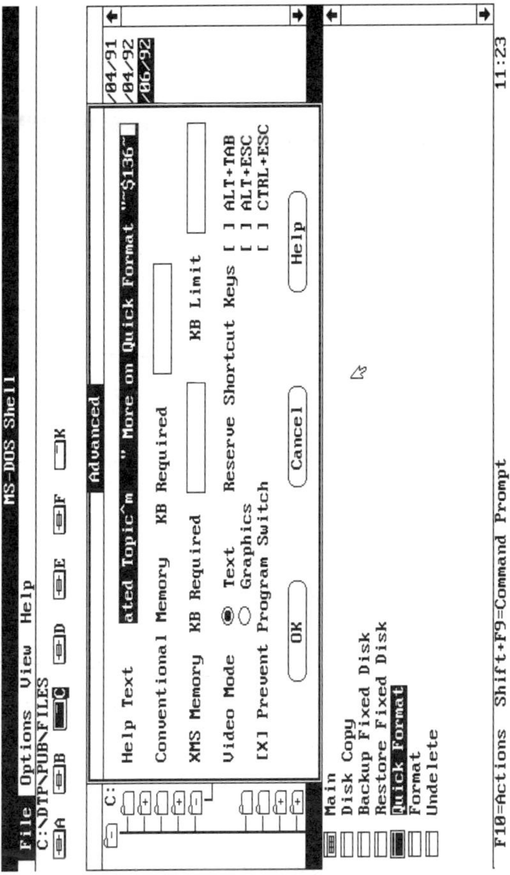

The Video Mode option allows you to specify the amount of memory needed for machines that use the CGA video card. In other words, if you use EGA, VGA or Hercules monochrome, you can leave this at the default setting of Text. Only if you use a CGA type of screen adapter, in colour, would you need to alter this setting. Since so few computers use CGA nowadays it is most unlikely that you would ever have to change the default setting of Text.

The Reserve Shortcut Keys boxes are more likely to be useful. The action of program switching makes use of three key combinations of Alt-Tab, Alt-Esc and Ctrl-Esc. Each of these carries out a switching action (if enabled), and the actions overlap to a considerable extent. Some programs, however, use one or even two of these key combinations for their own purposes. Normally, DOSSHELL will over-ride the program's use of such keys but you may find that your program must use one or more for actions that cannot be carried out by any other way. Once again, this is quite unusual - most programs do not use such combinations, or use them only as an alternative to the use of the mouse.

If you find that a program is crippled because you cannot make use of one of these key combinations in the program (meaning that the DOSSHELL action is carried out rather than the program action), you can opt to reserve any of the key combinations for the program. To do this, click on the box next to the key combination in the Advanced form. This will reserve the key combination(s) for the program, and will restrict your range of program swapping commands. If only one key combination needs to be reserved, the effect is not serious because of the overlap of DOSSHELL actions.

In some cases, swapping from a program may be undesirable. The normal swapping action of DOSSHELL is to keep the program in suspended animation, frozen in the state it had when you swapped. Some programs do not tolerate this, particularly communications programs which send and receive messages over the telephone lines. These programs need to remain working at all times, and they provide for working in the background, meaning that you can leave them running in a part of the memory, and run another program in the meantime.

■ This is not the same as swapping, because a swapped-out program is held on the hard disk and cannot run in this state. Unless you are informed otherwise, place a cross in the Prevent Program Switch box if you are setting up for a Communications program.

When you click on the OK (or Cancel) box of the Advanced form, you are returned to the ordinary Program Item Properties form, and at this point you would normally have filled in everything that was needed if you were adding an item. There will, however, be some further forms to fill in if you have opted for any parameter items in the Commands line, such as %1, %2 and so on. These %1, %2 represent items that have

Figure 8.18
The subsidiary form for dealing with a parameter. There will be one box of this type for each parameter, and you can enter reminders in the form of text in the three lines illustrated.

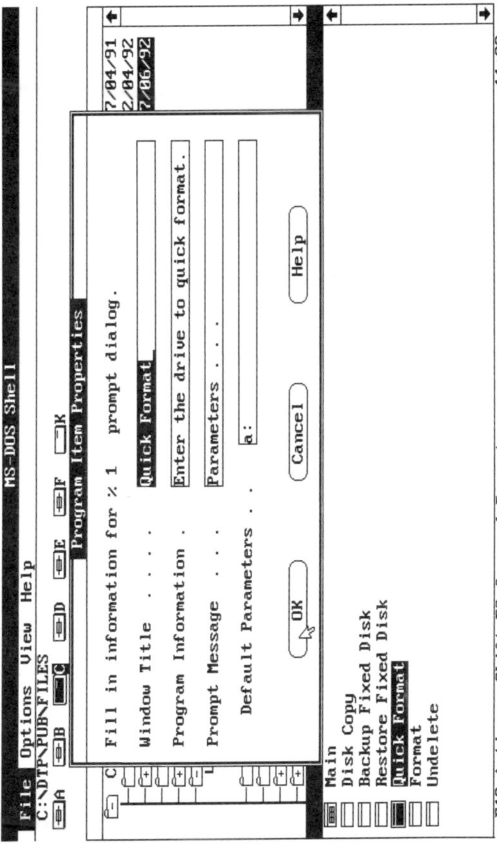

to be specified in order to run a program (such as filenames, directory paths and so on), and a separate form will appear for each of these. The syntax is exactly as it is for batch files.

In the Quick Format example, there is only one such item, so that when you click on the OK box of the main Program Item Properties form, the subsidiary form, Figure 8.18, appears. This uses four lines, and you would normally make use of all four as has been done in this example.

If you need to edit a line, be careful about your use of keys. When the line appears in inverse colours, pressing the backspace (delete) will delete the whole line. Pressing a left or right cursor arrow key will restore normal colours and allows you to delete or replace individual characters.

The Window Title is a reminder of what the program is called - you would normally use the same name (which will appear as a default) as you had used in the main Program Item Properties form, but if you want to use some other title you are free to do so. The Program Information line is the more useful one - you can type into this what information is needed. In this example of Quick Format, the drive name is required, and this is stated in the Information line.

The Prompt Message should be brief - it will appear on a line just ahead of the space where you will type the item, in this example the drive letter. In this example, the word 'Parameters' has been used, but you would probably want to be more specific. For any Format, remember, you can type a large number of parameter letters on one line.

The last line, Default Parameters, is very useful and important. In this example, you would certainly not want to carry out a Quick Format on the default disk, which would normally be the hard disk C:. By specifying A: in this line, you ensure that careless or unthinking use of the Quick Format command will result in the disk in the A: drive being formatted rather than the hard disk.

■ You will have to choose defaults which suit the program you want to run. In some cases, no default is really appropriate, and you would leave the line blank. Sometimes a default can be used to prevent a program from failing due to lack of a parameter; in other cases, as in this one, the default is a useful safety measure to ensure that you do not commit a terrible mistake by pressing the ENTER key without thinking.

On the Command line of the Program Item Properties form you can list programs, including batch files that need to be run both before and after the main program runs. This is the equivalent of batch file action, giving you all the powerful features of batch file use along with the easy and fast action of MS-DOS commands.

Creating a Group

The groups which exist when you first use DOSSHELL have been provided by Microsoft, and consist of Main, which contains the Command Prompt (temporary return to MS-DOS directly) and the Disk Utilities Group. Any other groups have to be created by you, using the procedures that will now be described. As with all other DOSSHELL actions of this type, you only have to specify what you want in a form rather than type an elaborate command.

You are not forced to place programs into a Group when you create the Group, and in most cases you will add programs to a Group later, and not necessarily in one operation. You will often find that in the course of using a Group you want to add programs, and this is provided for in DOSSHELL. The Program Item Properties item on the File menu also allows you to edit these properties, so that you can alter whatever you typed when a program was being added. It is likely that through experience you will want to modify these Properties fairly often in the lifetime of a program.

The creation of a new Group starts with the display of Program files - the most convenient option from the View menu is Program/File Lists.

1. Place the cursor on the word Main in the Groups list, or on any of the names in the window which is headed Main so that one of the items in this set will be highlighted. When this is done, the File menu will contain the item New which allows a new group to be created or a program to be added to a Group.

2. Selecting New brings up the New Program Object window, Figure 8.19, which allows you to choose Program Group or Program Item - the default is Program Item.

3. Change the selection to Program Group and click on the OK box. You will now see the Add Group window appear, Figure 8.20. This allows you to type a title for the new Group, and to add the optional items of Help and Password.

You need not fill in the Help portion, but it can be useful if you need to be reminded of the purpose of your Group and the programs that are contained in it. The Password can be used if you need to restrict access to the Group; the rules are the same as have been discussed earlier.

Figure 8.19
The New Program Object window. The default is a new Program Item, but in this example we need to click on Program Group.

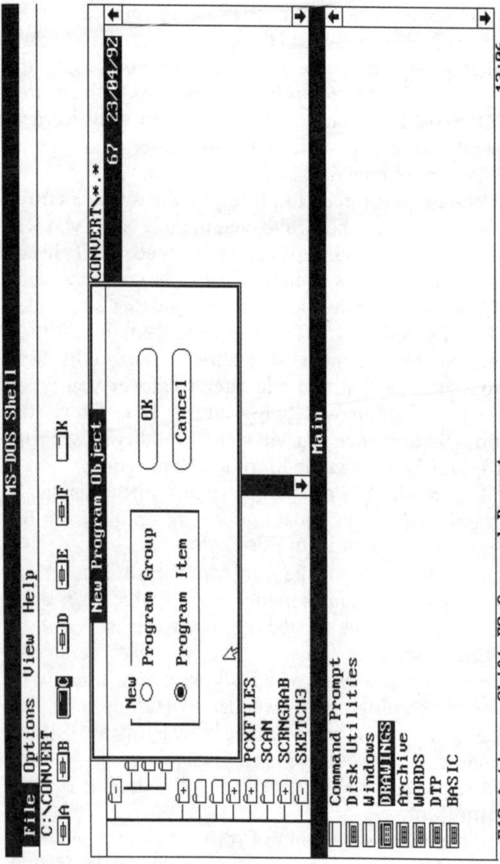

4. When the Title and Help lines have been filled in, click on OK to end the New Group creation. The Main display (bottom left-hand window) will now show the new Group and you can now place programs in it.

■ Placing a program in a Group does not involve making a new copy of the program (which would require substantially more disk space). It only places a directory path into a file called DOSSHELL.INI, taking very little extra space. This file is similar in its effect to a batch file, but is very different in format.

Figure 8.20
The Add Item window which requires a title line - the other lines are optional.

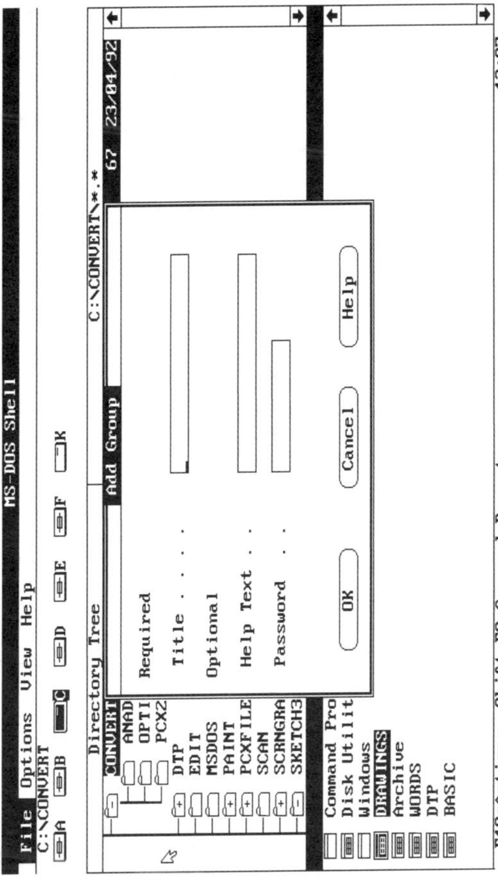

Adding a Program

Adding a program to a Group is done by selecting the Program/File view again, placing the cursor on to the Group that you have created, and using File, then New, once again.

1. Before you start this work, you must know the directory in which the program is located, and the commands that are needed to start it (at its simplest, just the program name).

Figure 8.21
The Add Program window which is the same window as is displayed when the Program Item Properties is selected.

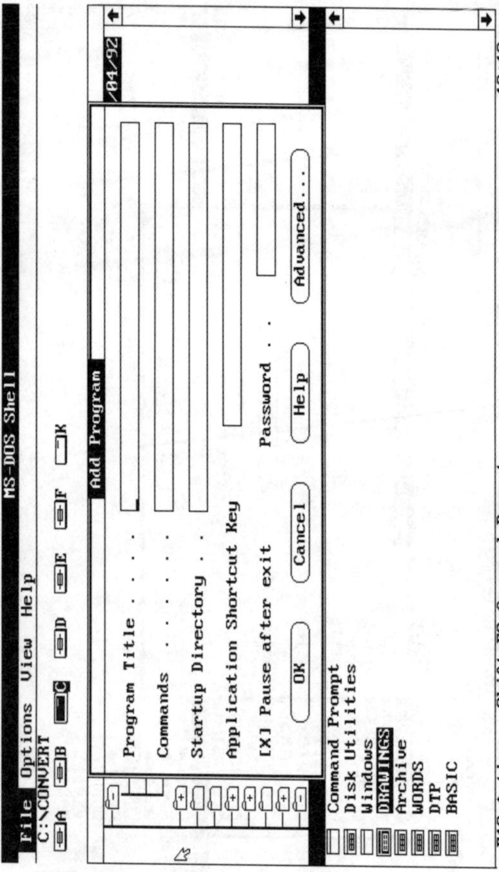

2. When the New Program Object window appears, use the (default) Program Item. When you click on OK you will see the Add Program window, Figure 8.21, which is identical in form to the Program Item Properties window of Figure 8.16.

The first line, Program Title, can be more descriptive than simply the name of the program file. If you are installing WordPerfect 5.1, for example, you can type the name WordPerfect 5.1 in this line rather than the name of the main program file, which is WP.EXE. You can elaborate the name - you might want to have one WordPerfect just for letters and another for writing magazine articles for PC Answers, so you might have a Program Title line such as WordPerfect for Letters or Wordperfect for PC Answers. What you put here should remind you of what the program is and what it does.

The Command line must contain the command that starts the program running. This might be a COM or EXE program file, in which case you would type the complete file name **with** the extension, not as you would when running the program from MS-DOS directly. For example, to run WP.EXE you would use WP.EXE as the command, rather than WP as you would use when running directly from MS-DOS.

- The Command line can also accept a batch file name, so that if you have a batch file called ARTICLE.BAT you can type the name ARTICLE in the command line provided that the path to the directory that contains the batch file is known (because of a PATH entry in AUTOEXEC.BAT), or by using the path in the Commands line, such as C:\BATS\ARTICLE. Note that you can omit the extension BAT when you want to run a batch file.

You will need, if you are using a batch file, to place the parameters used by the batch file into the command line so that it might read, for example:

```
WP %a %b
```

- and you will be prompted to specify prompts for the parameters in the usual way. Using a batch file in this way will produce the same effects as it normally would when the program is run from its batch file under MS-DOS directly, with the added bonus that you can swap in and out without losing the batch file actions.

The Commands line, however, is not restricted to single commands. You can treat the Commands line as if it were a batch file itself, so that entering a line such as:

```
dir ; \wp51\wp.exe ; dir
```

would produce a directory, start the WordPerfect 5.1 program running and after you had used WordPerfect 5.1, produce another directory listing. The commands must be separated by a space, a semicolon and another space - this is important. You can use more than one space, but you must not omit either space.

This structure allows the command line to produce the actions of a batch file, and you can even include PAUSE as a command to make sure that a directory listing is held on screen until you have had time to read it. You can also use other batch file commands such as FOR %%A IN (B:*.DOC DO DEL %%A and so on. You cannot, however, use label names in the Commands line, however, so that the GOTO actions of a batch file cannot be reproduced.

The Commands line can therefore replace some of the uses of a batch file, with the restrictions that it can accept only up to 255 characters and does not allow jumping to label names. For many purposes, the length is no real limitation, because many batch files will be considerably shorter than 255 characters (only 36 characters are visible at any one time). If you need batch-type actions that require much more space, you can overcome the problem by calling the batch file. For example:

```
call SETUP ; \wp51\wp.exe ; call ENDIT
```

would allow you to run large batch files, called, respectively, SETUP.BAT and ENDIT.BAT, before and after running WordPerfect 5.1. This also deals with any requirements for testing and branching using label names, because such sections can be contained in the batch files that are called. You cannot jump from a place in one batch file to a label name in another batch file, however.

The next line, Startup Directory, is used if data files are located in a directory which has to be notified to the program. This is not always necessary, because many programs contain their own internal methods for locating directories, and will not require this to be done. By setting up this directory, however, you can ensure that an automatic backup (using XCOPY) can be carried out after the program is run, and there are several programs that allow the data files directory to be set in this way. If in doubt, simple specify the directory in which the program itself is located.

- When a batch file is used, you might want to put the path to the directory that the program uses, particularly if all batch files start from a directory called BATS. This avoids the inconvenience of finding that the BATS directory is the current directory when your programs starts.

Specifying an Application Shortcut Key is not necessary unless you have planned to use this program as one you will be frequently swapping in and out of. It is usually better to leave this line vacant when you first place a program in a group, because you need to have your Group complete before you can plan what keys you will use. The normal entry will be something such as ALT A. (Press Alt key and A key; do not type the letters 'ALT A').

- You can use Alt, Ctrl and SHIFT keys in this specification, but since Ctrl and SHIFT actions are likely to be used in programs, and there are several combinations that are reserved in any case, you are recommended to stick with the Alt set. You can also use combinations of these keys with letter keys, so that Ctrl-Alt-A or Alt-SHIFT-A or Ctrl-SHIFT-A can be used.

The reserved combinations, which are not available as shortcut keys, are:

Ctrl-C Ctrl-H Ctrl-I Ctrl-MA Ctrl-[Ctrl-5

and the above set along with SHIFT (such as Ctrl-SHIFT-C). The Ctrl-5 and Ctrl-SHIFT-5 refer to the use of the 5 on the number-pad at the right of the keyboard, not the 5 above the letter keys.

The Pause after Exit box contains a cross by default, and you would normally remove this cross by clicking on it (click again to restore) to allow you to return to DOSSHELL automatically after a program has ended. If your program ends with information you want to read, or if you have commanded a directory display after a program ends, you will need time to read the screen, and placing the cross in the box will prevent a return to DOSSHELL until a key is pressed - any key can be used.

The Password use has already been discussed - use a Password only if you need to, because forgetting a password could lock you out of the use of a program until you remembered it or were able to read it from the DOSSHELL.INI file. This is not completely straightforward, as Chapter 7 shows.

Parameters in the Commands line

The Commands line can contain parameters such as %1, %2 etc. in addition to the program names and batch commands. A parameter is typed exactly as it would be for a batch file, that is with a space between the program name and the parameter. You can use up to nine parameters if you have any program that accepts such a large number. A program called NOTE.EXE for example, might be written so as to be used in the form NOTE MYNOTE.TXT so that a filename could be passed to it.

You would place this in the command line as NOTE.EXE %1, with a space between the program name and the parameter.

- When one or more parameters are included in a command line, the Prompt Dialog box will appear when you click on the OK box of the Add Program window.

You will be asked to supply, for each of the parameters, the information of Window Title, Program Information, Prompt message and Default Parameters. These pieces of information have already been mentioned, and in the following, a set is described for an imaginary program called NOTE. The Window Title should appear as a default. The Program Information line is edited, typing File Name in this line. This ensures that you see this heading when you start the program. The Prompt Message is a further reminder, and in this space you can type, for example, Please type name: (which is about as much as you are allowed).

- The beep will sound if you attempt to type too much into a space - the prompt message can be of up to 18 characters.

You can supply a default, such as TEST.DOC, using the last line of the form. Supply a default only if it makes sense to do so; this is a very useful provision, but in many cases there is no need for any default. When you select the OK box on this form the work of creating a Program Item is complete.

Running a Program - Advanced Setup

Running a program from a group consists of two main stages. You must first select the Group by double-clicking on the Group name when a program display is available. This will list the programs in the Group, along with the Main Group name to allow return to the other Groups. You then double-click on the name of the program in the Group that you want to run.

When this is done, you will be shown any parameter entry form, in the style that you have set up when you filled in the Parameters form. The prompts should help you to type the parameter that is required - you can, with some planning, ensure that you never at this point need to delve into the manuals for the program to find out what you need to type. When you type one parameter and click on OK or press ENTER, you will see the next parameter entry box, if there is a second parameter, or see the program start. If no parameters are specified, the program will start when you double-click on its name, with no parameters box appearing at all.

When you first add a program to a Group, ignore the Advanced section, because it is not needed initially. The Advanced section is designed to cope with special situations, and the most useful part of it for most purposes is the Help Text provision - study the Help Text for the existing programs to see just what can be achieved.

The only other requirement for the Advanced form arises if a program does not run smoothly. You need, of course, to be able to recognise that a program is not running smoothly, and in this respect you should not add a program to a Group unless you have already had some experience of the program running outside DOSSHELL. If you have no experience of the program, you cannot tell what is normal for it, and what constitutes a problem. If you know what a program does when used outside DOSSHELL, and you see notable differences and limitations appearing when you are running under DOSSHELL control this is what constitutes a problem that might be solved by using the Advanced form.

What makes this part of the form *Advanced* is that its lines can confuse you unless you know how the machine makes use of its resources such as memory. Never fill in quantities unless you know what you are doing - if in doubt, leave it alone. Very few programs require the use of the Advanced Form.

The first line is Conventional Memory KB required. To start with, this line is irrelevant unless you are using Task Swapping (see later), and if you don't swap programs any entry in this line has no effect. The conventional memory of a PC machine is the first 640 Kbyte, of which you have a considerable chunk free if you are using MS-DOS 6.0 correctly set up (with a LOADHI command in the CONFIG.SYS file) on a 386 or 486 machine.

When you run a program, it will normally take as much of this space as is available. If no other program is contained in the memory, this will be the usual amount that is available when the machine is booted up. Sometimes when programs are bring swapped around, there will be less memory available, and if a program (such as Lotus 1-2-3, for example) requires a lot of memory, it will refuse to run and may cause problems. The Conventional Memory KB required allows you to specify for the program you are adding to a Group how much memory must, as a minimum, be available. This will prevent the program for starting if this minimum amount of memory is not available. If more than the minimum is available, the program will run and take all of the available conventional memory.

The XMS Memory line refers to Extended Memory for an AT machine, and, like the other memory line, is applicable only if program swapping is to be used. This is an even more rarefied case, because very few programs make use of this part of the memory, and the instructions for using this part of the form will depend on the program that requires it.

■ Unless you are using a machine with at least 2 Mbyte of RAM, and a program that specifically states that it uses Extended memory to XMS specifications, ignore this part of the Advanced form.

In general, the KB Required section is filled in only if a program must be provided with a stated amount of Extended memory in order to run. Of the small number of programs that use XMS memory, only a few will need this to be specified, and this line will usually be blank. Program swapping is slower when a minimum memory size is specified here.

The KB Limit section is used when a program must be prevented from taking all of the available extended memory. Leaving this blank will prevent a program from using extended memory - and cause problems if the program needs to use extended memory. A setting of -1 will allow the program to take as much of the extended memory as it needs, subject to the amount actually installed.

The use of Video Mode and Reserve Shortcut Keys has been dealt with already. The Video Mode should be altered only in the unlikely event of your machine using a CGA graphics screen. The Reserve Shortcut Keys entries are used to prevent conflicts between program use of these key combinations and DOSSHELL program swapping uses. The Prevent Program Switch box should be ticked only if the programs being installed is a communications programs which must remain working 'in the background' when other programs are in use.

Switching Programs

Switching programs, or Task Switching, is a feature which is provided by Windows, but DOSSHELL treats the switching action in a comparatively simple way by storing all of a working program and its data on the hard disk in a temporary file, clearing the available memory and running another program. The number of programs that can be kept in limbo in this way is limited only by the hard-disk space that is available, and programs that are swapped out of use are frozen, they are not running. Only the program that is currently making use of the screen is running (apart from programs that can be left running in the background). The screen shows nothing of any programs that are swapped out, and their names appear on the Active Task List portion of the Programs window. Because swapping is to and from the hard disk, it is much slower than Windows swapping which is to and from extended memory.

When a program has been swapped, you can swap back to it in several different ways, some of which involve using the Alt-key with other keys. You can also end the program, return to DOSSHELL and then recover the other program. DOSSHELL keeps a list of programs that have been swapped out, the Active Task List, from which you can select a program to use by double-clicking on its name.

The alternative is to assign to every program in a group a short-cut key, such as Alt-A, Alt-B, Alt-C and so on. This allows you to run these programs by using these key combinations, either from an existing program or from DOSSHELL.

No swapping is possible at all unless it has been enabled. To enable swapping, select the Enable Task Swapper line in the Options menu. A dot will appear against this line when swapping is enabled. If swapping is not enabled, none of the swapping commands will have any effect, and program names will not appear in the task-swapping list.

Assuming that swapping is enabled, there are several methods that can be used to start a program and to swap out of it. The most straightforward is simply to start the program running in the normal way, but you have the alternative of placing one or more program names in the Active Task List, Figure 8.22, without running any of the programs.

Figure 8.22

The Active Task List contains the names of suspended programs. In this pair of suspended programs. De-Luxe Paint can be selected by pressing Alt-P as well as by double-clicking on the name.

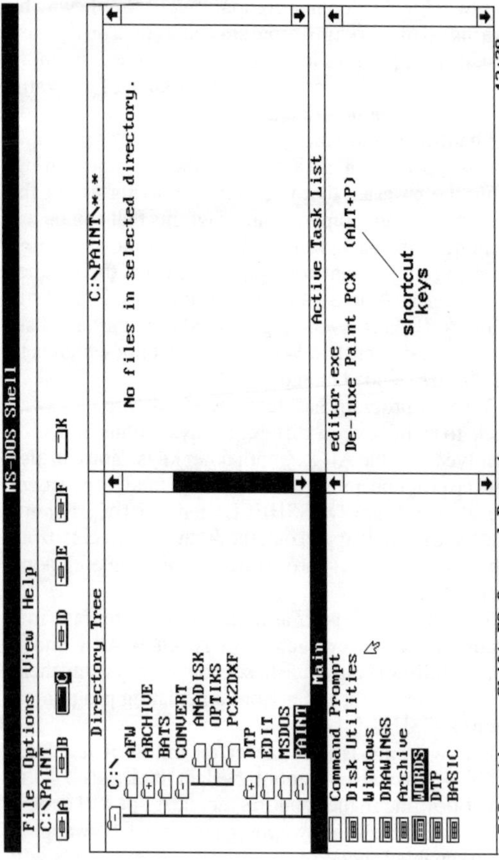

You can run any program whose name appears in the Active Task List by double-clicking on the name, just as if the name were in a Group list. Programs placed into the Active Task List need not all belong to one Group, but if they use Short-cut keys you need to be sure that no two use the same short-cut key. You also need to be careful that you do not start more than one copy of the same program by forgetting that you have a program suspended.

Running and swapping

To use running and swapping, make sure that Task Swapping is enabled from the Options menu, so that the Active Task List (initially empty) appears. Start and make use of the program in the usual way, but do not quit the program. Instead, use one of the following key combinations:

Ctrl-Esc

Alt-Tab

Alt-Esc

which, when you are starting a task list, will return you to DOSSHELL.

- The key combinations of Alt-Tab and Alt-Esc will have different effects when two or more programs exist in the Active Task List and you press the keys while you are using DOSSHELL.

While swapping is being done, the screen will be blanked out. Do not assume that something has gone wrong unless the blanking lasts for an unusually long time. This is done while the program is being stored on the hard disk. If you start a program and quit in the normal way by selecting a Quit option, the program is not put into the Active Task List, and you cannot swap directly between it and any other program.

- Some programs, such as large CAD and DTP programs will not swap because their memory requirements are too large and the portion of DOSSHELL that deals with swapping takes up enough space to prevent the program running.

- DOSSHELL allows you the option of creating your Active Task List without actually starting any of the programs. This is done by holding down the SHIFT key while you double-click on the program names. Each name will be added to the Active Task List and can be started from the list by double-clicking on the name in the normal way.

When an Active Task List exists, you have several options for running programs in the list. You can double-click on the program name in the usual way, or you can hold down the Alt key and press the Tab key. This will bring up a program name at the top of the screen and if this is not the program you want you can press the Tab key again, repeating until you see the program that you want. Release the Alt key to run this program.

When you are using DOSSHELL, the Alt-Tab combination cycles from one program in the Active Task List to another. When you are using one of the programs in the Active Task List, using Alt-Esc will cycle to the next program in the list until the DOSSHELL appears.

- These key combinations are the same as are used in Windows 3.1

The best method of program swapping is the use of short-cut keys, because this allows you to swap from any program to any other in the Active Task List without needing to cycle through the other programs in the List nor to return to the DOSSHELL. To make use of short-cut keys you must have designated a short-cut key for each program you are using (which implies that each program is one of a Group) and you must know what short-cut keys are used for each program. The Active Task List will show the programs which have such keys assigned, and what keys are used.

Leaving a program

A program which is currently running can be left by using its Quit option in the usual way. When this has been done, the name will no longer appear on the Active Task List. Leaving other programs on the Active Task List must be done by running each program and using its Quit option.

- You must not simply exit from DOSSHELL leaving programs in limbo - you must make each program active and then quit it. If you simply switch off the computer you risk losing data from the programs in the Active Task List.

Unless you use the Quit option, you should be able to swap from one program to another indefinitely, using programs in any sequence. You can also return to DOSSHELL and add other programs to the Active Task List. If you make use of the Command Prompt from DOSSHELL to run MS-DOS, you can put MS-DOS into your Active Task List by using Ctrl-Esc (or any other of the set); but if you want to quit Command Prompt you must type EXIT and press the ENTER key.

- If a program locks up while being used with swapping, DOSSHELL provides for a way out. The Ctrl-Esc key combination should allow you to return to the DOSSHELL, and once back, you must delete the offending program by selecting its name on the Active File List and then pressing the Del key.

It is always better to restart the computer after a program has caused a lockup. This is the only exception to the rule that you always quit each program in turn, because attempting to use the other programs might cause a further lock-up. Be careful, in such an emergency, to remember to select the program name on the Active Task List and not in the Files list or the Programs list - using Del on these names would delete the programs from the disk.

- The MS-DOS manual advises any user who uses both DOSSHELL and Windows to run DOSSHELL from Windows rather than to run Windows from DOSSHELL. I have never experienced any problems in running Windows from DOSSHELL, and you, like me, may find that there are advantages to working this way round.

9 The anti-virus software

Viruses

Hard disk viruses are a menace which affect very few hard-disk users, but which, like some other crimes, cause more worry and expense than real damage. A virus is, strictly speaking, a piece of code which can attach itself to a program and copy itself so that it can be transmitted to other programs and also from one computer to another. The term is also used of other unwanted codes which can be loaded into a computer and which from then on will cause problems to appear, whether these can be spread to further computers or not.

The main types of virus are the Boot Sector type which locates itself in the boot sector of the disk and loads in when the computer is booted, and the Parasitic virus, which is attached to a program file and is activated when that file is used. No problems have yet been reported of a virus infecting CMOS RAM, so that all viruses 'die' when a machine is switched off. There is also a 'Trojan Horse' which is not really a virus, but it can cause just as serious problems. It takes the form of a program with an interesting title. When the program is loaded and run, it carries out the damage.

The Worm is also not really a virus but a piece of code that reproduces itself continually within the computer that it affects until so many copies have been made that there is no further room on the hard disk. It also has a serious effect on networks. Bombs, also not necessarily viruses, come in two forms, time bombs and logic bombs. A bomb program, once loaded, saves itself on the disk and does nothing until some condition is met. A time-bomb will be activated by date (like Friday 13th) or time (like midnight) and will carry out its action if the computer is running at this time. A logic bomb will operate when other some conditions, such as 65% or more of the disk being used, or a copy of some well-known program being installed. The true virus will attach itself to programs, and if these programs are copied to other computers this will allow the virus to be spread.

The problem is not one that affects machines that run only floppy disks, because a disk with a virus can be thrown away. You can hardly throw away your hard disk if it is infected. In addition, viruses are not so effective on data files, because data files are not composed of instructions, so that the virus instruction cannot be executed. The data files can, however, be corrupted by the virus.

- A virus can affect your computer only if you load and run a program from a disk that contains the virus, or load software of unknown origin over the telephone lines by way of a modem. Millions of computer users who do not use a modem and are careful about where they buy software are at no risk of virus infection. Bombs most commonly appear in commercial systems after a programmer has been sacked.

Many viruses are, like graffiti, comparatively harmless and have been devised by programmers wishing to demonstrate their skills. A virus may simply put up a message of the Kilroy was here variety on your screen, but at the other end of the scale it may cause files to vanish from your hard disk directory. This damage is not necessarily irreversible, but even if it is not it can take a long time to sort out. The really destructive viruses are fortunately rare on well-kept systems.

- Always be suspicious about unsolicited gifts of disks such as demonstration disks. If in doubt, try them on an old floppy-only machine. Disks that have been run in a large number of machines are also suspect, as they could have picked up a virus from an infected machine. Free disks issued with magazines are usually checked, but mistakes can happen, and it would be foolish to accept such a disk unless you had unwrapped it yourself from its original container.

The earliest types of virus programs were comparatively simple, and their attachment to program files, particularly to the usual target, COMMAND.COM, could be counteracted by checking the size of such files regularly, by making all program files read-only, or by setting the archive bit and checking for any change before using a program. In all cases, these viruses show up as an increase in the length of a program file. Later types (like STEALTH) are much more ingenious, using a variety of techniques to conceal their presence and to evade virus-detecting software.

1. Some intercept the DIR command so as to show the original length of an infected program, and this interception can be used to affect any program that checks file length. These methods cannot conceal the amount of memory that the infected program takes up in the memory, and this is one of the methods that is used by virus-detecting programs which will compare the length from a DIR reading with the length of the file in the memory.

■ Such a virus, like the well-known Tequila, can cause CHKDSK to report a large number of errors, following which CHKDSK /F will scramble the files. The remedy is always to boot (as recommended earlier) from a floppy which is known to be virus-free, and then use CHKDSK. If this results in fewer errors being reported, it suggests that a virus is present on the hard disk.

2. The sequence of bytes (signature) that is used by each virus can often be used to detect a virus, and some now use code that is varied each time the virus reproduces. A few portions, however, need to be kept in sequence and can be detected.

3. A few rare viruses can make use of features that are built into the processor and which can by-pass any detecting software.

Dealing with viruses

The best method of dealing with viruses is not to become infected.

1. Beware of gifts of disks. Obtain programs only from reputable suppliers, whether these are commercial programs or shareware. Never run games programs that are passed on from another user.

2. Beware of demonstration disks or system checking disks that have been inserted into a large number of computers.

3. Try out suspect disks on a floppy-only machine. There's a place for that old Amstrad PC1512 after all......

4. Keep adequate backups of all program and data files on floppy disks

5. Do not leave your PC running unattended if there are people around who might be tempted to try a floppy disk on it.

6. If your shared PC permits password protection, make full use of it.

7. Install the MS-DOS 6.0 anti-virus software.

Virus problems

One possible sign of a virus infection is disk activity when you would not expect it. This is not always easy to detect, because many viruses are introduced at the time of booting the computer when the hard disk is working anyway. In addition, several programs will make automatic backups at intervals, causing disk activity, and when you use SMARTDRV in read/write mode you will often have disk writes at quiet times.

Some viruses signal their presence by messages, by bizarre behaviour (letters on screen messages suddenly drop down the screen, one by one) or by the appearance of graphics on a text-based program. If a program whose behaviour you know well by experience suddenly starts to behave in a peculiar way, virus infection is one possible cause. Deal with it as follows:

1. Shut down the system as soon as possible. Save your data in the usual way - if you are worried about the data being in good condition, use a fresh disk to save the data and label this disk so that you know it might be suspect.

2. After a few minutes, boot the computer from one of your write-protected copies of a System disk. This, unless you have been very careless or unlucky, should be free of any virus.

3. Re-install on to the hard disk the program that gave trouble, using a copy of the original floppies. Take the floppy out of its drive.

4. Run the program again from the hard disk.

5. If the trouble has ceased you may have eliminated the virus, but if it recurs after booting from the hard disk, try the preceding steps again, and following step 3, copy COMMAND.COM from a system floppy to the hard disk

6. If you have not eliminated the trouble, use the anti-virus software of MS-DOS 6.0 as described below.

■ Anti-Virus software is not a cure-all. It will not necessarily detect all forms of virus nor remove them, so that your main efforts should always be directed to prevention rather than cure. Because new viruses are being written, any anti-virus system needs to be updated regularly.

■ You should keep a set of write-protected floppy disks which contain the MS-DOS System tracks with the IO.SYS, MS-DOS.SYS and COMMAND.COM files. These floppies should be prepared directly from the MS-DOS 6.0 installation disks, or on a machine with no hard disk, so that they can be guaranteed free from infection. These can be used to boot up your computer if you think the hard drive may be infected. They are also valuable in the event that any damage occurs to the boot tracks of the hard disk.

The MS-DOS 6.0 Anti Virus System

The MS-DOS Anti Virus system consists of software that will scan the hard disk (or a floppy) for signs of a virus and which will report or destroy the virus. In addition, there is a memory-resident program which will detect when any program tries to carry out actions that are associated with virus activity. These are:

1. Starting a low-level format, which totally erases any data on the hard disk

2. Attempting to stay resident in memory using normal MS-DOS methods (other methods are not easily detected).

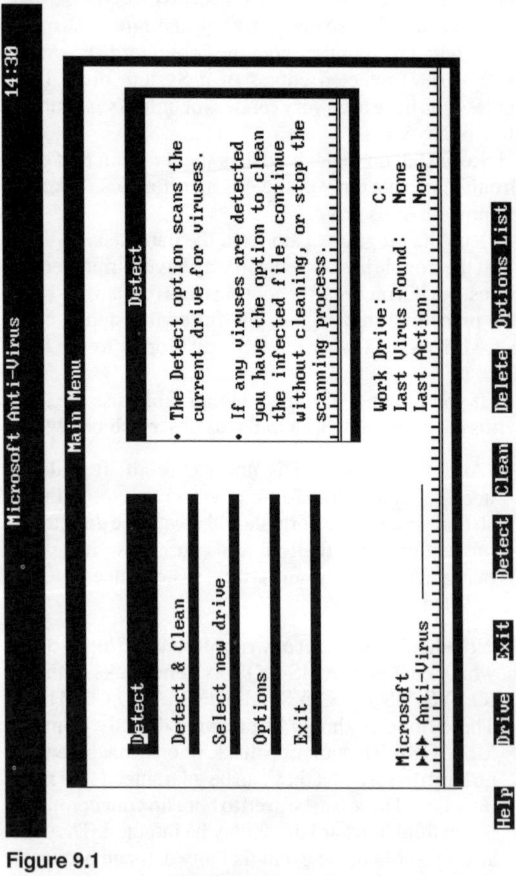

Figure 9.1
The main menu of MSAV, the anti-virus scanner.

Figure 9.2
A memory scan in progress, the first MSAV action. The thermometer scale shows how far the scanning has reached.

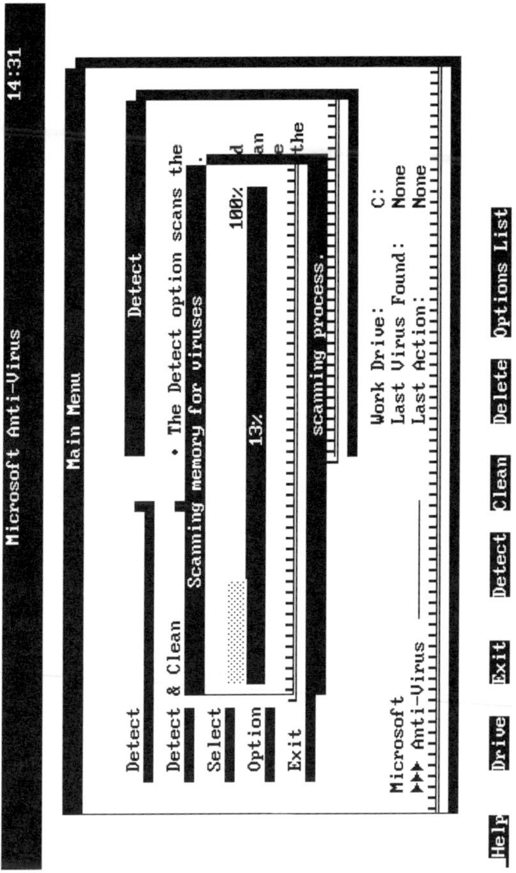

No program other than FDISK should carry out a low-level format, but there are many programs that will make themselves resident in memory (the VSAVE anti-virus program of MS-DOS 6.0 included), so that the second action should cause concern only if it is unexpected.

This software exists in two version, DOS and Windows, and in this Chapter, only the DOS version is discussed - see Chapter 10 for the Windows versions of Anti-Virus, Backup and Undelete.

Figure 9.3
Scanning the files and directories. This is an action that can take a fair time on a well-populated large disk.

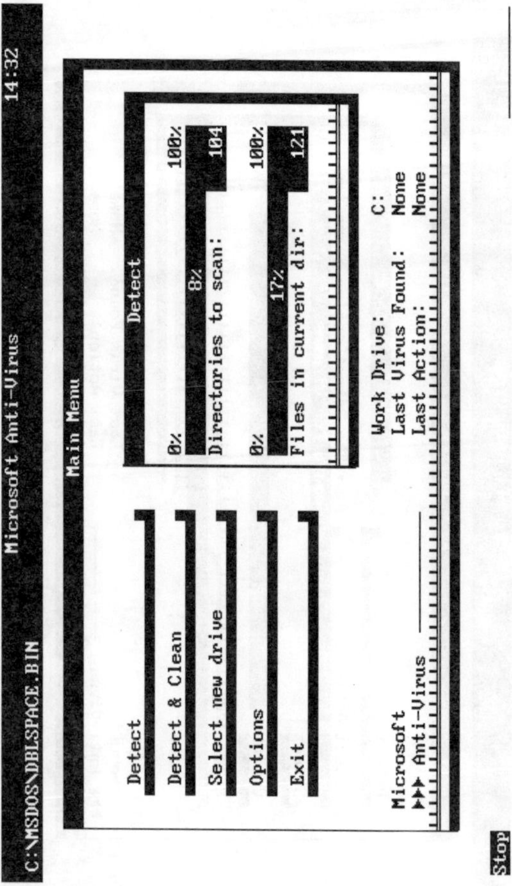

To check for existing virus infection:

1. Start up the program called MSAV.EXE, which should be located in the C:\MSDOS directory. This brings up the Main Menu, Figure 9.1, and there will be a pause while the hard disk directories are checked.

2. Unless you know that there is a virus infection, click on the Detect option. You can use Detect and Clean if you are sure that an infection is present.

3. The memory will be scanned, Figure 9.2, followed by each file in each directory, Figure 9.3. This takes time.

Figure 9.4
A report from MSAV showing, in this example, no detected virus problems.

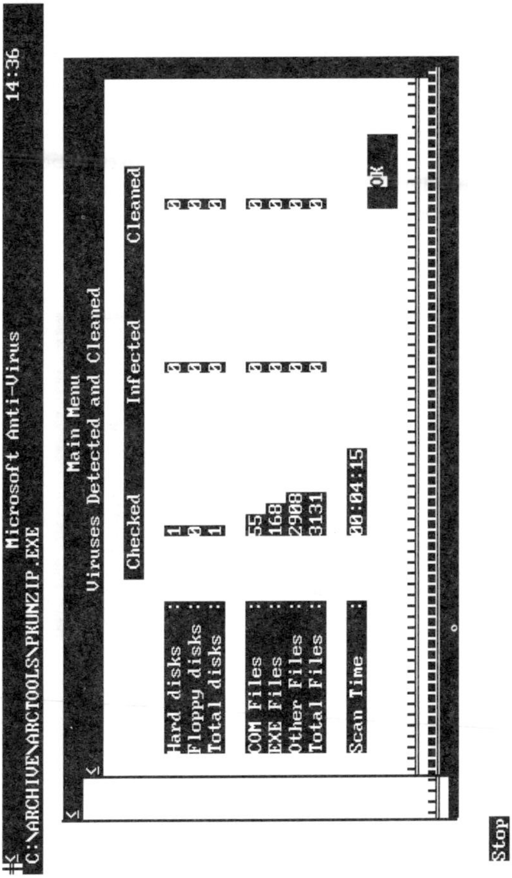

4. When scanning is completed, a report such as that of Figure 9.4 will be issued.

In this example, no virus have been found, and because this machine is never connected to a telephone line nor used with games software or unsolicited disks the conclusion is hardly surprising. Remember, however, that a clean report from an anti-virus scan is not an absolute discharge - there are viruses that may be present yet not detected. If you see no traces of virus activity in your day-to-day use of the computer (see above) and the anti-virus scan also shows no viruses you can be reasonably certain that there are no problems. Before you congratulate yourself too much, make sure that you can maintain this situation.

- You can get virus reports as a result of damaged programs, from some memory-resident programs, and from conflicts between device drivers (SYS files). Use CHKDSK to clean up damaged program files, re-install suspect programs, and alter relative position of driver lines in the CONFIG.SYS file before deciding to go on a full virus-buster rampage.

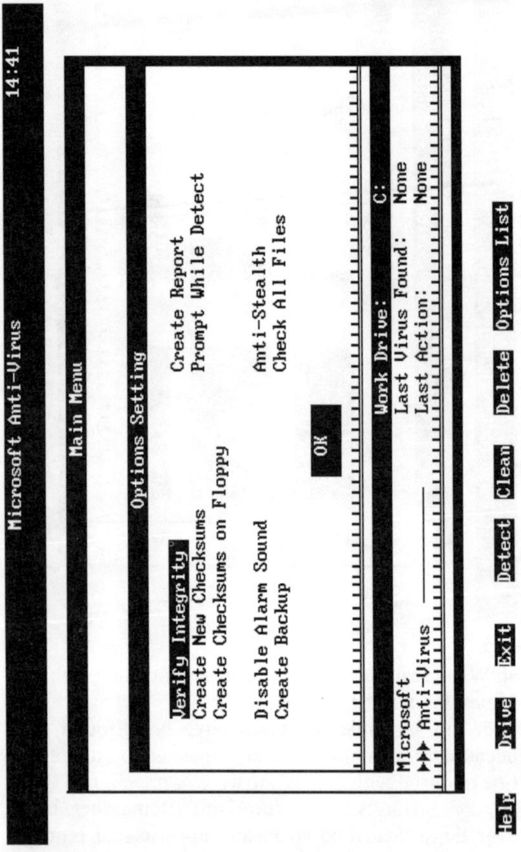

Figure 9.5
The Options menu of Anti-Virus, showing the eight choices.

Anti-Virus Options

The Main menu of Anti-Virus contains an options section which, when clicked, produces the menu shown in Figure 9.5. The sections of this menu are:

1. Verify Integrity. This is ticked as a default, and it looks for changes in files, using a Checksum (a number based on adding the number-codes of a file). The checksums for your files are created by the second option, also by default. This action can help to detect new viruses which use methods as yet not known.

2. Create New Checksums. This option, switched on by default, creates a file called CHKLIST.MS that consists of a checksum for each file. There is a separate CHKLIST.MS for each directory on the hard disk, and when new files are placed in the directory each Anti-Virus scan will add data for the new files. These files are used in the comparisons made using Verify Integrity.

3. Create Checksums on Floppy will carry out the creation of a CHKLIST.MS file for a floppy disk if Create New Checksums is also selected for use. After this has been done for a floppy, the disk should be write-protected. The option is off by default.

4. Disable Alarm Sound is normally off. When ticked it allows the normal sounds to be disabled so that only the screen warnings remain.

5. Create Backup needs to be used with care - the default is to turn this option off. When on, its effect is to make a backup of any infected file before attempting to clean the file. This is a desperate measure for a program which is precious because you have no other backup, and the backup should if at all possible be put on to a floppy. It will carry the VIR extension. Using this option means that when the virus has been removed from the original there will still be an infected copy.

6. Create Report is also switched off by default. When switched on it creates an ASCII text file placed in the root directory and containing a dated and timed report of all viruses found and removed.

7. Prompt while Detect is normally switched on, and produces three options in a dialogue box when a virus is found in a file. The options are to repair the file, continue scanning without repairing, or the stop scanning. With this option off, the scan detect and/or clean actions do not provide any messages until the end of the scan.

8. Anti-Stealth is normally switched off. It is an alternative to the checksum methods, devised because of the invention of viruses which infect files without

making any changes that can be detected by simple checksum methods. Anti-Stealth is normally switched off because its action is slower, since it has to check files more thoroughly, but it can be used if you have used Verify Integrity without finding a virus but you have reason to suspect that a virus is still present.

9. Check all Files is normally on, so that both data and program files are checked. When this option is switched off, only files with the extensions EXE, COM, OVL, SYS, BIN, APP and CMD are checked. These, however, are the files that are most likely to be infected. When the option is switched on, files with extension 386, DOM, DLL, DRV, FON, ICO, OL*, PGM, PIF, PRG are also checked.

- The settings that you make in the Options can be saved as a configuration file when you leave Anti-Virus. This ensures that the same settings will be used next time.
- There is a set of command short-cuts also listed at the foot of the screen.

While Anti-Virus is running, you can look at a list of viruses. This is also used when a virus is reported so that you can see what effects are reported and compare these with your own experiences. To see the list, press the F9 key, or click the List option at the bottom of the screen.

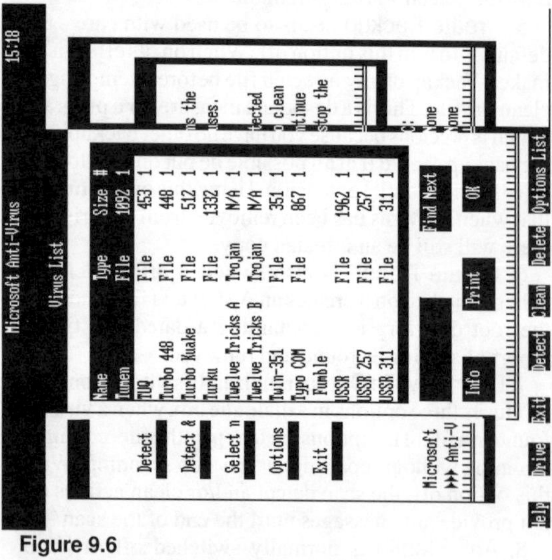

Figure 9.6
Part of the file of known viruses with their alias names and number of known aliases.

Figure 9.7
The further report on a particular virus.

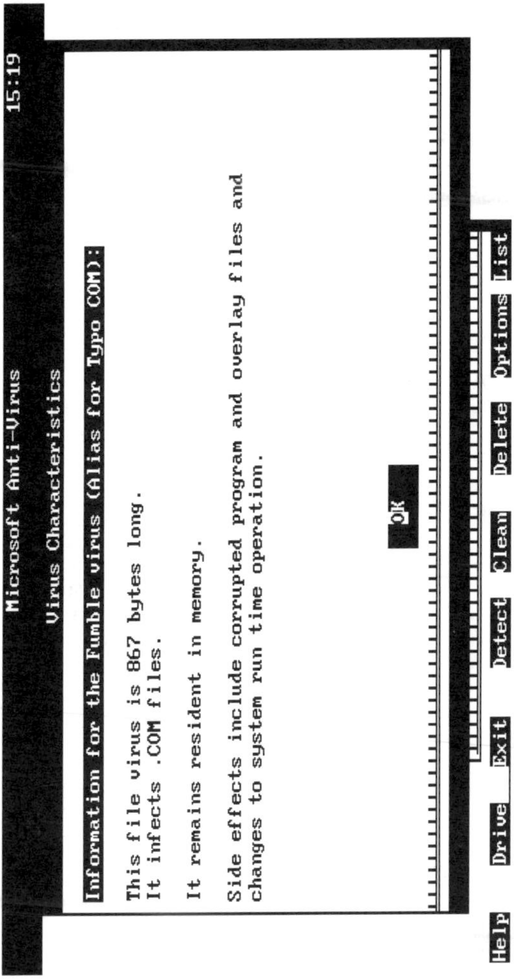

Figure 9.6 shows part of the (very large) list of known viruses. On a colour display the names are in blue, with alternative names in black. Clicking on a name will produce a detailed note, Figure 9.7, for that virus, showing size, what files are infected, whether or not there is any memory-residence, and the effects. The list window also provides for printing information.

If your system is vulnerable to virus infection you can install a scan for viruses in the AUTOEXEC.BAT file. This will carry out a scan each time the computer is switched on, and requires you to add the line:

```
MSAV C: /n
```

- the /n option avoids the use of the display that you get when you run the MSAV program normally, and puts the results into a file. The MSAV command word can be followed by a drive letter with its colon. The full set of MSAV command options are:

/S	Scan the drive and report, but do not remove
/C	Scan, report and remove.
/R	Create an ASCII file of scan action, MSAV.RPT, in the root directory of the drive.
/A	Scan all drives except A: and B:
/N	Scan without using the full-screen display and place results into the MSAV.RPT file.
/P	Use normal MS-DOS command line rather than graphical display.
/F	Turn off the display of filenames - use only along with /N or /P.
/VIDEO	List the MSAV video options, consisting of:
/25	25-line text screen display (default)
/28	28-line display (use on VGA only)
/43	43-line graphics display, EGA & VGA only
/50	50-line graphics display, VGA only
/60	60-line graphics display, Video-7 adapters only.
/IN	Use a colour display even if a monochrome type is detected.
/BW	Use a monochrome display.
/MONO	Use a monochrome display.
/LCD	Use an LCD type of display
/FF	Use fast-screen methods, for CGA only.
/BF	Display video using BIOS calls only
/NF	Disable use of alternate fonts
/BT	Allow use of graphics mouse in windows.
/NGM	Use alternative non-graphics mouse cursor.
/LE	Interchange left and right mouse buttons
/IM	Disabled mouse use
/PS2	Restore mouse if the cursor disappears or no longer moves when the mouse is moved.

Using VSafe

Another line of protection is to try to detect when a virus is starting its activity. This can be done by using a memory-resident program called VSAFE, which would normally be added as a line in the AUTOEXEC.BAT file. When VSAFE is installed, it will print a brief message, Figure 9.8. Note that some XMS (extended) memory is used, so that very little conventional memory is needed. The message shows that the Alt-V key combination will bring up a menu.

```
            VSafe (tm)

     Copyright (c) 1991-1992
   Central Point Software, Inc.
        Hotkey:   <Alt><V>

VSafe successfully installed.
VSafe is using 23K of conventional memory,
               23K of XMS memory,
                0K of EMS memory.

Press any key to return to MS-DOS Shell....
```

Figure 9.8
The VSafe installation notice.

■ This 'hotkey' action cannot operate if you are using DOSSHELL - exit from DOSSHELL before using VSAFE options.

VSAFE can be used with a set of options, see below, that can be set from within a menu system, or by option numbers when VSAFE is loaded. The numbers are used in a form such as /1+ (turn on 1) or /2- (turn off 2) following the VSAFE command.

There are also options that can be used following this set, each preceded by a slashmark.

/NE	Do not use expanded memory
/NX	Do not use extended memory.
/Ax	Use Alt-x as hot key combination, where x means a notified letter key.
/Cx	Use Ctrl-x as hot key combination, where x means a notified letter key.
/N	Use VSAFE to check network drives.
/D	Turn off checksum actions
/U	Remove VSAFE from memory residence (remove after quitting).

The options list that appears when you use the Alt-V keys is illustrated in Figure 9.9.

	Warning type	ON
1	HD Low level format	X
2	Resident	
3	General write protect	
4	Check executable files	X
5	Boot sector viruses	X
6	Protect HD boot sector	X
7	Protect FD boot sector	
8	Protect executable files	

Press 1-8 toggle ON/OFF
Press ESC to Exit
Press ALT-U to unload from memory

Figure 9.9
The options list for VSafe, visible when the Alt-V keys are pressed.

The items that are marked with crosses are normally switched on and consist of:

1. Warning of any attempt to carry out a low-level format (option 1)

2. Check any program that MS-DOS sets running (option 4)

■ Remember that there is a separate Anti-Virus for Windows.

3. Check each disk for any boot-sector virus (option 5)

4. Warn of any attempt to write to the boot sector of the hard disk (option 6)

The other items are not normally on, because they are either seldom needed or can give ambiguous reports.

1. Checking for memory-residence will warn you each time a program attempts to become memory-resident, (option 2). If you place VSAFE as the last line in your

AUTOEXEC.BAT file, so that it does not report on other memory-resident programs in AUTOEXEC.BAT, and you do not use any other memory-resident software, you might find it useful to mark this option. It will, however, report each time you run any of your own memory-resident software.

2. General write protect prevents writing to any file and is not a step that you would normally want to take, (option 3). Use it only if you suspect that a virus is operating and you want to detect any unauthorised writing to files.

3. Protect FD boot sector should be used only if you are using floppy disks and suspect that there are attempts to infect them, (option 7).

4. Protect executable files, (option 8), warns of any attempt to write to program files. A few programs allow for writing to portions of the program file, and if you use such programs you might need to disable this provision temporarily.

■ You can alter the options while VSAFE is running and carry on with the new options, which will be maintained the next time you start the computer. If you want to use the memory occupied by VSAFE or to remove the program for any reason, bring up the options screen (Alt-V) and then press the Alt-U keys.

Living with Anti-Virus protection

If you practise safe computing, as outlined at the start of this Chapter, you need not bother too much with Anti-Virus protection, and 99% of suspected virus problems are due in fact to the well-known problem of the erratic digit. If you are exposed to virus infection, however, and you make intensive use of the MS-DOS virus software, you will need to remember a few important points.

When you upgrade software you are likely to get virus messages because the upgrading will itself involve actions similar to this carried out by a virus. You should therefore proceed as follows:

1. Scan the floppy disks from which the upgrade will be made before you start to install the upgrade.

2. When the disk are checked and reported clear, write-protect them.

■ A few manufacturers like you to type your name and company and save this information on one of the floppies. This is impossible on a write-protected disks, but the practice is less common on an upgrade.

3. Install the upgrade as instructed - this usually involves running a SETUP or INSTALL program.
4. Scan the directory on which the upgrade was performed so as to update the CHKLIST.MS file.

Sometimes a virus will have extensively damaged a file before it is detected. In such a case, AntiVirus will deliver a message to the effect that the file is damaged beyond repair, and ask you if it can delete the file in order to prevent further infection. The normal answer will be YES, because you should have adequate backups.

You may also get a message about an invalid signature. This is usually an indication of a new virus about which Anti-Virus has no information. The signature is a tell-tale set of numbers which are always present in a particular virus. You should register for regular updates to Anti-Virus.

VSAFE in particular will deliver messages that indicate attempted actions which can in some cases be caused by normal circumstances, and it is up to you to determine what are your normal circumstances.

1. If a network is loaded after starting VSAFE you are likely to find VSAFE warning you of attempts to modify system memory. If it is possible to load VSAFE after loading the network, do so. If you cannot do this, check with a virus scan the first time you are warned of memory modification. If no virus is found it is likely that the normal action of the network software is the cause of the message. You can use the Continue option of VSAFE in future.
2. A warning of a program becoming memory resident should be treated as suspicious if you are not loading a memory-resident program. Make sure that all the memory-resident programs you need are loaded before VSAFE, and make a note of any other memory-resident programs that you know you are likely to use.
3. Writing to a disk when you are not saving data is not always suspicious. When you use SMARTDRIVE, writing is usually carried out shortly after a save action, and some programs, notably word-processors, save their text file(s) automatically every ten minutes or so.
4. You will encounter problems if you have loaded other memory-resident programs following VSAFE, and you then remove VSAFE from memory. This will unload the programs that were loaded subsequently.

10 The Windows utilities

Introduction

MS-DOS 6.0 breaks new ground by including three major Windows utilities, intended for Windows 3.1, plus the SMARTMON accessory for SMARTDrive. This Chapter consists of a brief description with illustrations, and it assumes that you have experience of using Windows 3.1.

- The MS-DOS manuals mention that Windows should not be started from DOSSHELL, and prefer you to start DOSSHELL, if required, from Windows. Since Windows 3.1 became available I have been starting it from DOSSHELL without problems in either, and I have not detected any differences with MS-DOS 6.0. I can only recommend that if you have problems in running Windows from DOSSHELL you should stop doing so and change to running DOSSHELL from Windows as recommended.

When MS-DOS 6.0 is installed on a computer, the hard disk directory is searched for a copy of Windows. If this is found, the Windows versions of Anti-Virus, Backup and Undelete are installed in place of the DOS versions. These versions are differentiated by using filenames that start with MW rather than MS. If you want to have both Windows and DOS versions on your disk you will need either to make this decision when you install MS-DOS 6.0 or to install the other set manually, using EXPAND for the files that are compressed.

When the Windows versions are installed, MS-DOS 6.0 setup also creates a new Windows Group called Microsoft Tools, Figure 10.1. This allows space for

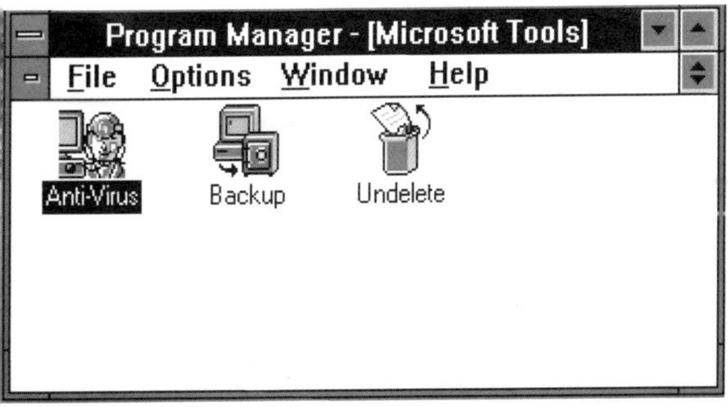

Figure 10.1
The Microsoft Tools group in WIndows 3.1, as installed by MS-DOS 6.0.

Figure 10.2
The opening menu of Anti Virus for Windows. When this is used for the first time, the Status report will not be filled in - and with some care, you can keep it that way.

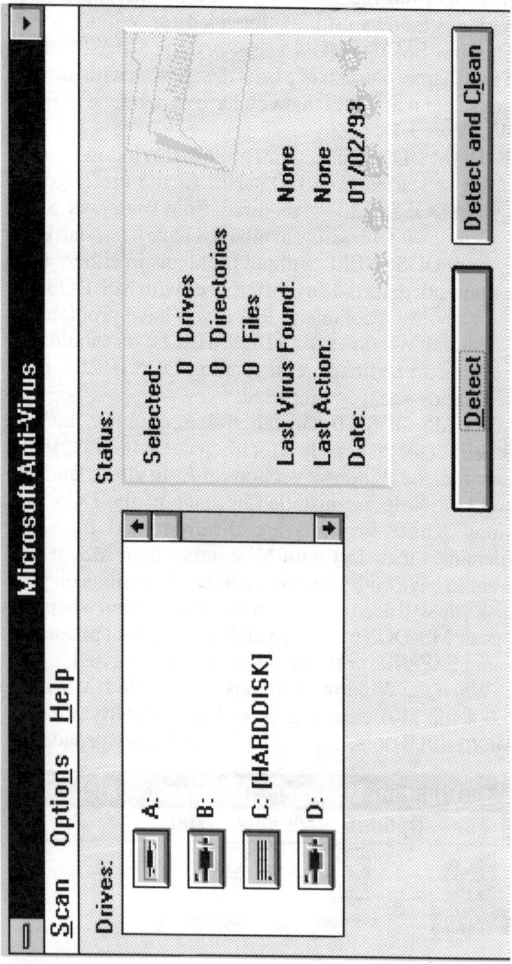

more utilities to be added at later dates. Each utility can be started by double-clicking on the appropriate icon. The File Manager of Windows also contains a new menu entry of Tools (between Options and Windows), containing the same set of actions.

Figure 10.3
The initial report of WIndows Anti-Virus which indicates the number of directories and files that will be checked.

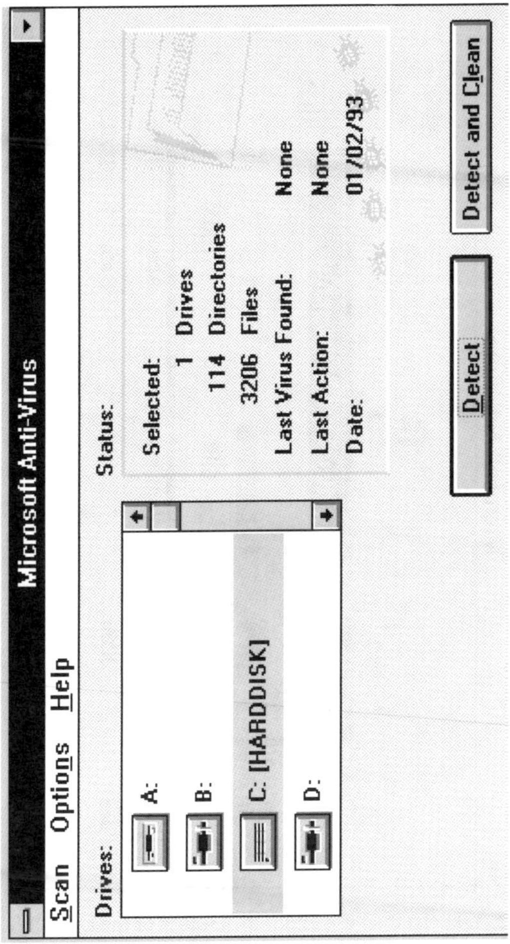

Anti-Virus for Windows

When the Anti-Virus icon is double-clicked, the opening menu is as shown in Figure 10.2. The procedure for using this is:

1. Click on the disk drive you want to scan - this will usually be C: This drive is rapidly checked for directories and files, and a report issued, Figure 10.3.

Figure 10.4
The progress of a scan is marked on the thermometer display.

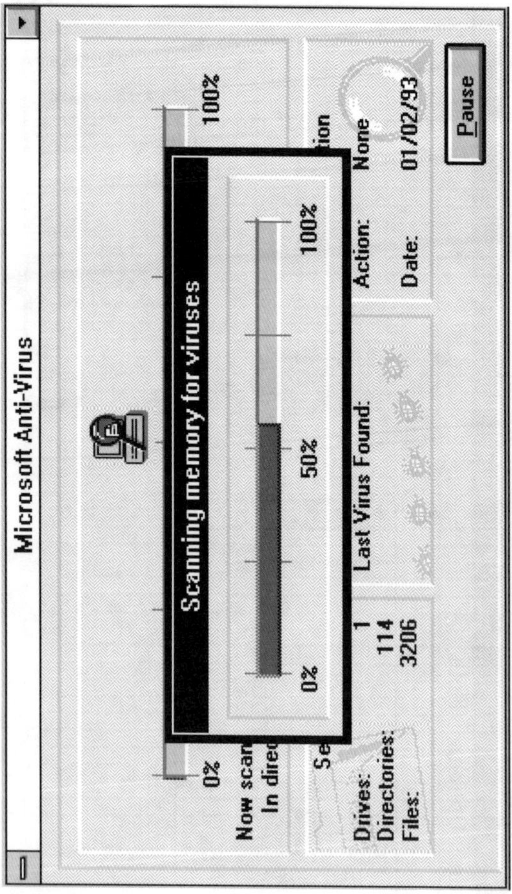

2. You can then use either the Detect or the Detect & Clean option buttons - click on either to start the action. The progress is indicated on a thermometer type of display, Figure 10.4, and the first scan is just a preliminary one - the main one follows and takes considerably longer (go for a coffee).
3. The final report is as shown in Figure 10.5. The time indicated is reasonable for the number of files that have been scanned.

Figure 10.5
The final report after a scan also shows the number of files arranged in categories with a health report for each and the total time taken.

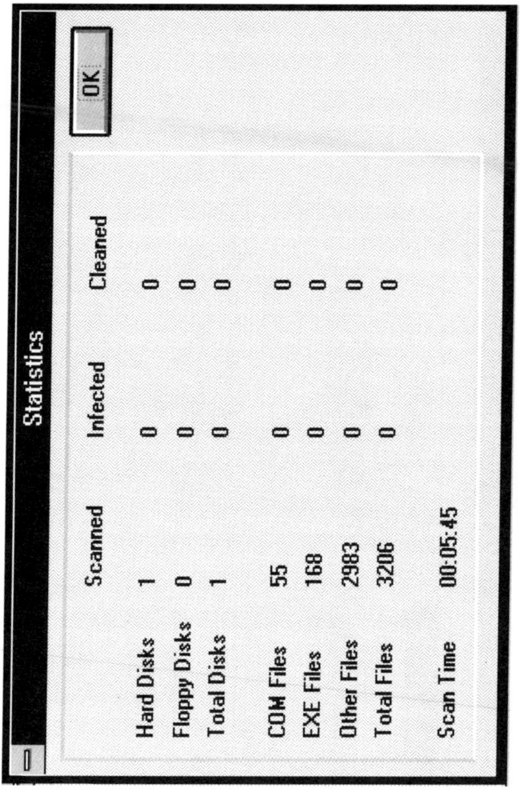

Statistics
OK
Scanned
Infected
Cleaned
Hard Disks 1 0 0
Floppy Disks 0 0 0
Total Disks 1 0 0
COM Files 55 0 0
EXE Files 168 0 0
Other Files 2983 0 0
Total Files 3206 0 0
Scan Time 00:05:45

The Menu line of Windows Anti-Virus contains, in addition to the usual Help, the Scan and Options set. The Scan set is illustrated in Figure 10.6 - it contains the Detect and Clean actions which can also be started from the buttons (as noted), and also contains the provision to Delete CHKLIST files and to display the Virus list with details.

- You should not delete the CHKLIST files in the normal course of using Anti-Virus. The files are comparatively small and you would need to be very hard-pressed indeed for disk space to need to delete them. If you do, the Verify Integrity action of Anti-Virus cannot be used.

Figure 10.6
The Scan menu expanded - this offers the Detect and Clean choices again, along with deletion of CHKLIST files and the display of the known virus list.

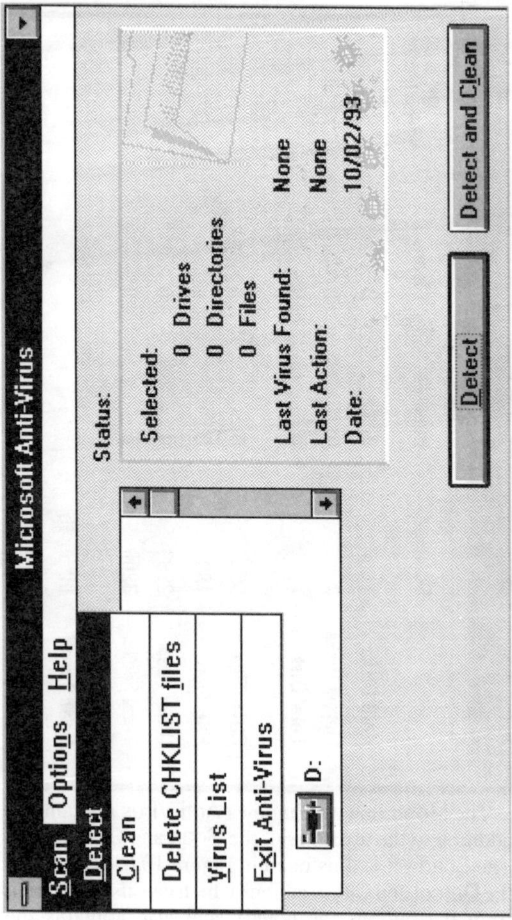

The Virus list is, of course, the same as that of MS-DOS, as is the information on each virus. The Options list is also identical; and you do not need a separate Windows version of VSAFE.

■ An enhanced feature of Windows Anti-Virus protection is drag and drop checking. Dragging a file from the File Manager entry to the MWAV.EXE file on the C:\MSDOS directory will carry out a scan for that file.

Figure 10.7
The Configuration reminder when WIndows Backup is first used. This will be delivered even if MS-DOS Backup has previously been used.

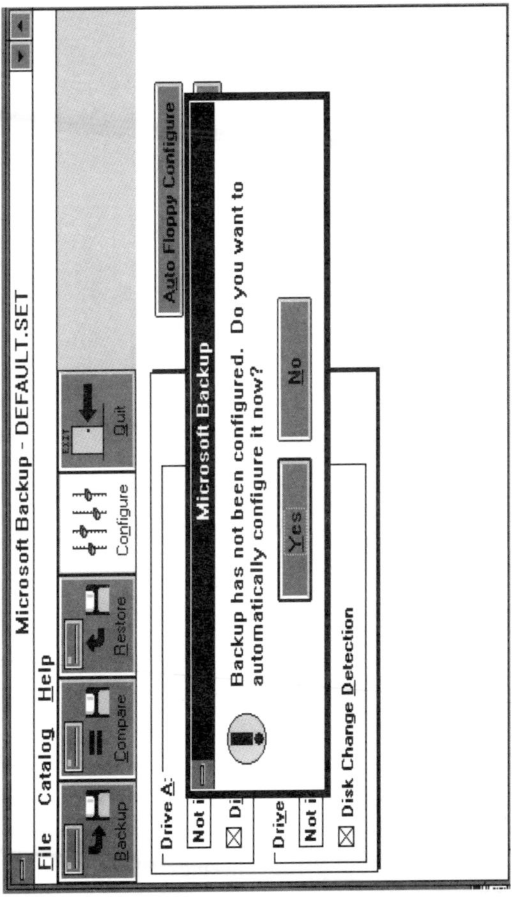

Windows Backup

Backup for Windows is started by double-clicking on the Backup icon. This brings up a Backup menu, and if Windows Backup has not been configured, a message about configuration, Figure 10.7.

■ Note that if you have configured and used DOS Backup this does not affect Windows Backup - you will be asked to make a separate configuration.

Figure 10.8
Starting the Compatibility test. You may need to select which floppy drive to use if you have more than one.

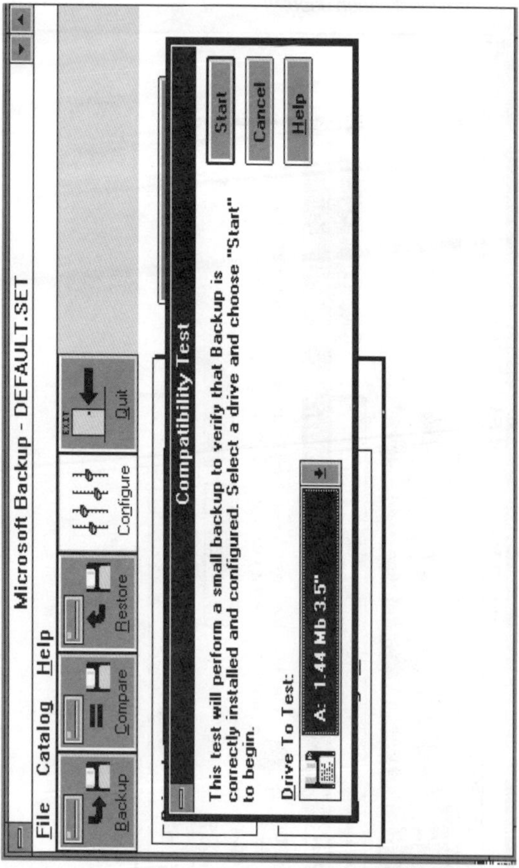

If you opt to configure by clicking on the Yes button, you will be asked to remove all floppies (diskettes) from their drives and confirm this by clicking on the OK button. This is used to check that a disk change can be detected. The Compatibility test, Figure 10.8, then starts. You can select which floppy drive to use if you have more than one.

When the Compatibility test starts you will be asked to insert a floppy disk into the selected drive. If the disk is unformatted it will be formatted as the data is backed up, as will the second disk you will be asked to use.

Figure 10.9
The thermometer scale for backup progress which is used for both formatting and backup in this example, where unformatted disks have been used.

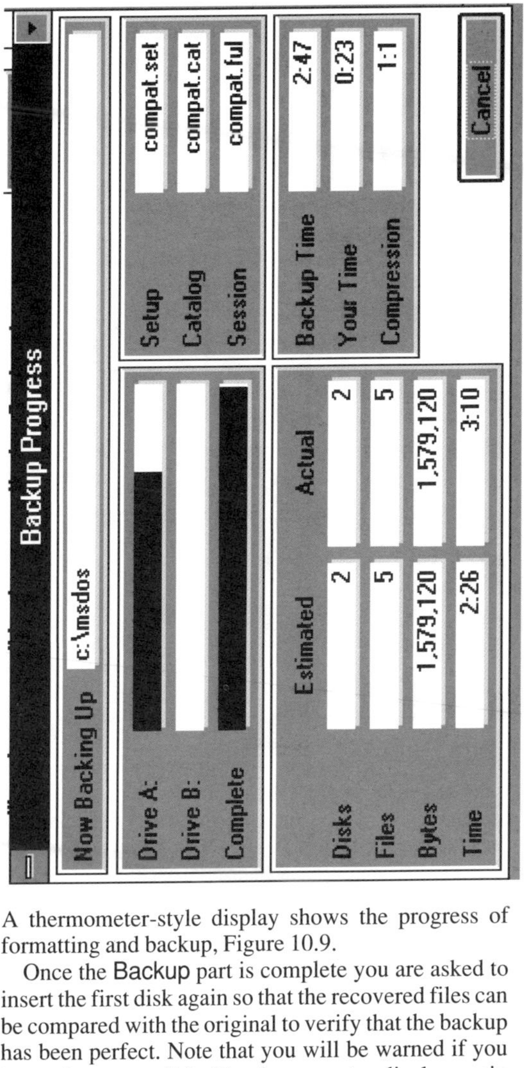

A thermometer-style display shows the progress of formatting and backup, Figure 10.9.

Once the Backup part is complete you are asked to insert the first disk again so that the recovered files can be compared with the original to verify that the backup has been perfect. Note that you will be warned if you insert the wrong disk. The thermometer display again shows the progress of the file recovery, and you will be warned by sight and sound when to change disks.

Figure 10.10
The Backup window showing the clear options for From and To drives, and the form of the report that will tell you how many floppies will be needed and how long the backup will take.

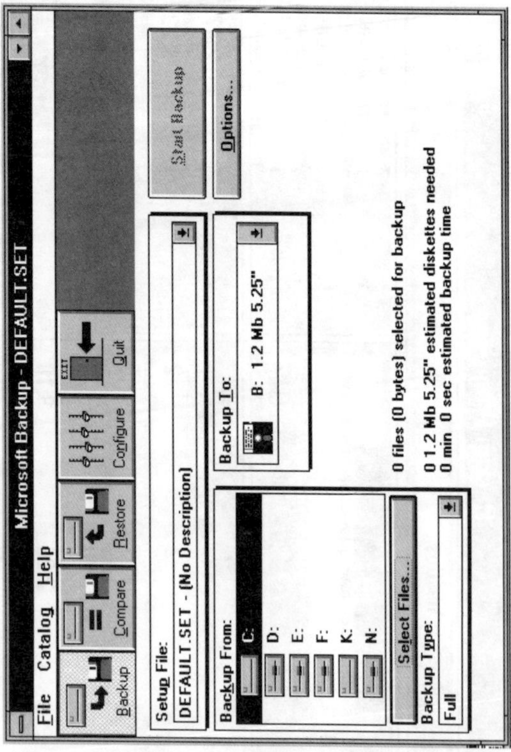

As for the DOS version, this checks that disk backup can be made reliably, and it ensures that configuration files are made which will guide the backup and restore processes for future use. The normal backup will use file compression similar to that used for Doublespace (though the files are not interchangeable). You cannot use File Manager to find the size of the file because the file is not a normal MS-DOS type and will not be listed. It is not listed by DOSSHELL either.

- You cannot use a floppy that has been compressed using DBLSPACE, because such a floppy has files on it and is seen by Backup as a used disk. If you opt to use such a disk the Doublespace files will be wiped and the disk will be treated as a normal disk.

Figure 10.11
The Backup Options. The items selected by a cross are sensible defaults.

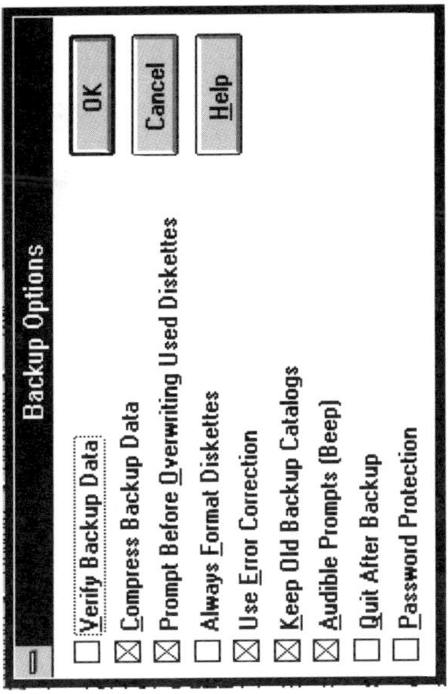

Other main options

Backup is started by clicking on the Backup icon. The Backup window, Figure 10.10 will appear. There are a number of choices to be made before Backup is started.

1. Select the source drive for the backup. This is normally the default C: but if you have more than one hard drive you will need to alter the setting.

2. Select the drive which is to be used for backing to, normally a floppy drive. If you have two identical floppy drives you can use both, making backup faster because one disk will be used while the other is being replaced. The MS-DOS Path option allows you to use external floptical drives, external floppy drives, network drives, any compatible tape drive; any device, in fact, which can be allocated a drive letter.

■ Backup allows the use of 360 Kbyte disks in a 1.2 Mbyte drive solely to permit files to be moved between AT and XT machines. Do not use 360 Kbyte disks in a 1.2 Mbyte drive as a normal backup system. There are no restrictions on the use of 720 Kbyte disks in a 1.4 Mbyte drive.

Figure 10.12

The Selected Files option produces this directory tree and files list for a selected directory.

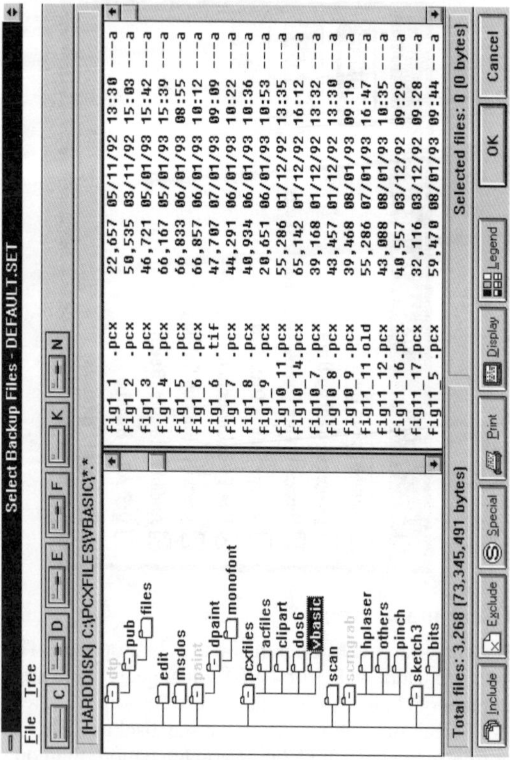

3. Check that the Options, Figure 10.11, are as you want them. The items that are marked by default are sensible options that you will in all probability want to use. Verification is usually off in order to save time, and you would select Always Format Diskettes only if you always backed up on new floppies.

4. Unless you intend to back up the whole disk (subject to the Backup Type settings), you can click on the Selected Files option. This brings up a Directory tree and files list, Figure 10.12, with a set of icons and a menu line. Dealing with these in order:

a. Include/Exclude allow you to specify directories and files for inclusion or exclusion if you find this more satisfactory than using the mouse. Files can be specified using wildcards such as *.PXC or TOPIC.* , and the

Figure 10.13
The Include/Exclude list, showing a file specification typed into the list. You can add other specifications so as to select the range of files you particularly need to back up.

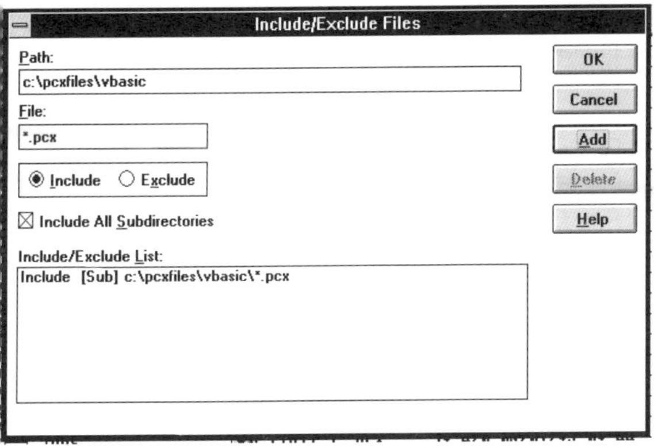

affected files will be placed in the Include/Exclude list when you click on Add, Figure 10.13. The mouse alternative is to select one by one, or to display all files of a selected type (like *.PCX) and use Select All or Deselect All from the File menu. Selected files are marked with a black square.

b. Special Selection can be clicked to bring up the menu of Figure 10.14. The Apply Range option can be used to set a range of dates for acceptable files but this does not constitute a selection method, and you still need to select files in the usual way.

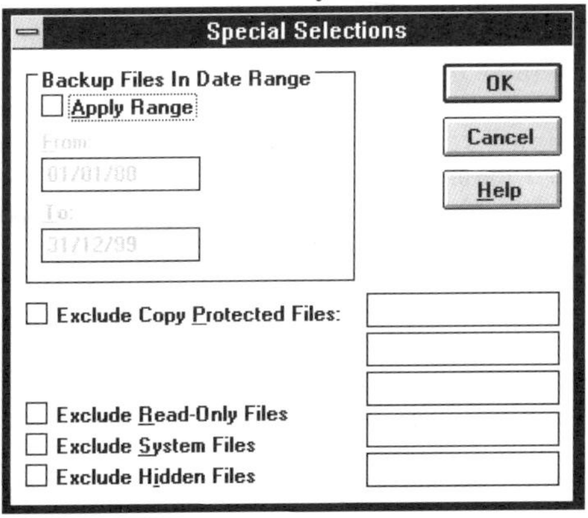

Figure 10.14
The Special Selection list has the valuable feature of a date range as well as the options to exclude some types of files.

Figure 10.15
The Display options are intended to make it easier for you to select the files you want to back up.

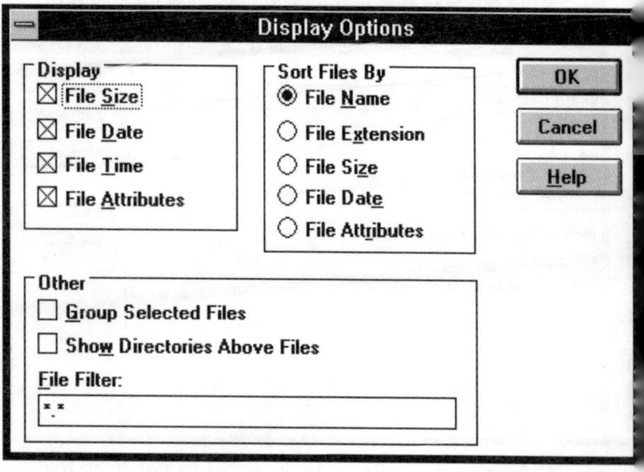

The Range action will then pick from your file selection the files that fall within the date range. You can also opt to exclude Copy-protected files, Read-only files, System files or Hidden file (in any combination).

c. The Print icon allows you to print a list of your backup selections as a permanent reminder of what you have backed up. This is useful because it supplements disk labelling and provides you with a full listing of what you have done.

d. The Display Options icon brings up the window of Figure 10.15. This allows you to determine what file data will be displayed (or printed), how files will be sorted into order, and the options to group files and show directories. The File order options can be particularly useful if you are carrying out a differential or incremental backup. Grouping allow a few selected files from a directory to be shown together at the top of the directory so that you do not need to hunt for the names. You can also specify a file filter such as *.PCX that will cause only one particular type of file to be displayed.

e. Legend provides an explanation of the markings that appear in file lists, Figure 10.16. This marking system allows you to see which files are selected and which will be backed up, and using the Legend option reminds you of the system.

Figure 10.16
The Legend display of markings on files and directories. You can hardly be expected to remember these, so that this display can be useful - a paper copy is even better.

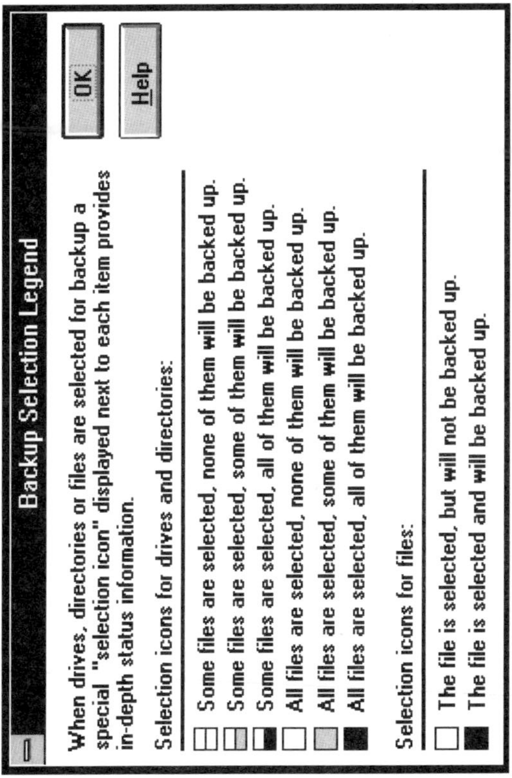

5. Your final options are for Backup, as Full, Differential or Incremental, irrespective of any File selections. A Full backup will backup all of the files that you have selected, whether they have changed or not since any previous backup, and the archive bit is reset on each file. An Incremental backup will backup only the files that have changed since the last backup, resetting the archive bit on each file so that it will not be backed up again by an incremental backup unless the file is changed. A Differential backup will backup all files that have changed since the last backup, but does not change the archive bits, so that the same file will be backed up again for the next backup of this type.

6. If you have made a file selection you can save this as a Setup file. Click on the File menu and select Save Setup or Save Setup As, name the file and save it. The DEFAULT set is used if you do not specify a set. This avoids the need to specify files for restoration and to go through the selection process each time you want a similar style of Backup.

- A full backup will be used when you need to backup a large set of files that have been created. Use incremental backups if you work with a variety of files each day - you will need to save all the incremental backups along with the main backup. Use a differential backup if you work with the same set of files each day, so that this single backup along with the main backup will restore all files if necessary.
- The Start Backup button will always be 'greyed out' (in dim print) until the backup selections have been appropriately made - you may, for example, have omitted to mark all directories and files if you want to back up the whole disk.

Compare

The Compare option allows you to compare the backup with the original files, or a selection from the original files. Unless you opted for a full backup of all files, you will need to select the files in the same way as you did for backup. You will be informed when the action is completed and all the backup disks inspected, if the backup files match the originals.

Restore

The Restore icon brings up the Restore window, Figure 10.17. A restore action is done as follows:

1. Select the drive, usually a floppy drive, from which the restorations is to be carried out. You have the usual options of floppy drives or MS-DOS path as for Backup. You can opt to use a Setup file if you have created one.

2. You can opt to restore files to the original directories (the usual default) or to other directories or other drives. These latter options allow for restoration of files when the original directory has been deleted. 'Alternate drives' in this sense means a hard drive - you will get an error message if you select a floppy. The actual selection of drive is done just before backing up, and the C:\drive is used as a default. Selecting Alternate Drives does not therefore commit you at this stage.

Figure 10.17
The window that appears when Restore has been selected.

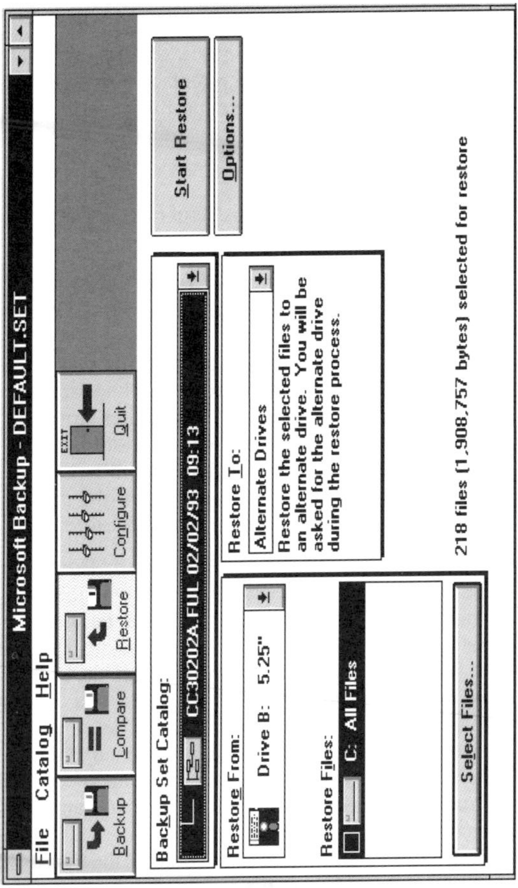

3. If there is more than one Backup Set Catalogue you can choose which one you want. The catalogue name provides clues to the contents. For example, the catalogue name of CC30202A.FUL signifies a full backup (alternative extensions are INC or DIF for an incremental or differential backup respectively). The first two letters indicate the first and last drives that were backed up - in this CC because only the C: drive was used. The figures show year, month and day numbers, using a single digit for the year (1993 in this example). The final letter in the main name indicates the sequence of backing up when more than one disk is used.

4. You must also select files, using the same basis is when you backed them up. The Start Restore option will not become available until you do this.

5. You will be prompted to insert the floppy which carries the backup files, and to replace this floppy as required. You will see a notice appear when the backup has been completed.

The Menu line

The menu line for Backup consists of File, Catalog and Help.

The File menu set consists of Load Setup, Save Setup, Save Setup As, Delete Setup, Print, Printer Setup and Exit.

1. The Setup actions allow you to save and load files of settings which perform a standardised backup or restore action, such as backing up all *.PCX files from/to a specified directory. You can also use Delete Setup to erase a setup file that is no longer required.

2. The Print actions allow you to print the current settings that will be used for Backup or Restore.

The Catalog section consists of Load, Retrieve, Build and Delete. These options are clearly visible only when Retrieve has been selected for use, because the Catalog is the file that is created when a backup is made. This file indicates where files are stored on the backup disk, and files cannot be retrieved unless this data is available.

1. Normally the catalogue will be obtained from the hard disk, and you can recover it using the Load instruction. See earlier for the format of the catalogue filename which indicates the contents.

2. If the catalogue has been removed from the hard disk it can be retrieved from the floppy disk by using the Retrieve instruction.

3. If the catalogue is not on the hard disk and cannot be retrieved from the floppy disk, it can be rebuilt from the floppy disk data, using the Rebuild option.

4. The last option is to delete a catalogue file. You would use this only if the data has been restored and the backup is not longer required.

Figure 10.18
The Windows Undelete main menu as it first appears when used on a disk that contains no deletions.

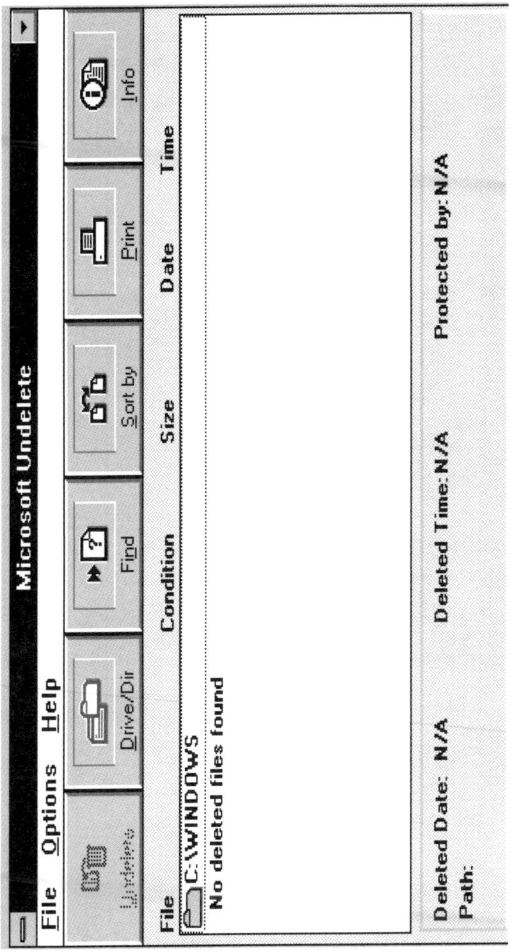

Windows Undelete

Windows Undelete is started by double-clicking on the icon, and it brings up a window, Figure 10.18. The icons at the top control the main actions:

1. Undelete is used to carry out the Undelete action when a deleted file has been found

Figure 10.19
The Undelete menu when there are deleted files on a disk. Note that the message for each is 'Destroyed', meaning that these files cannot be recovered even though their names are partly recovered.

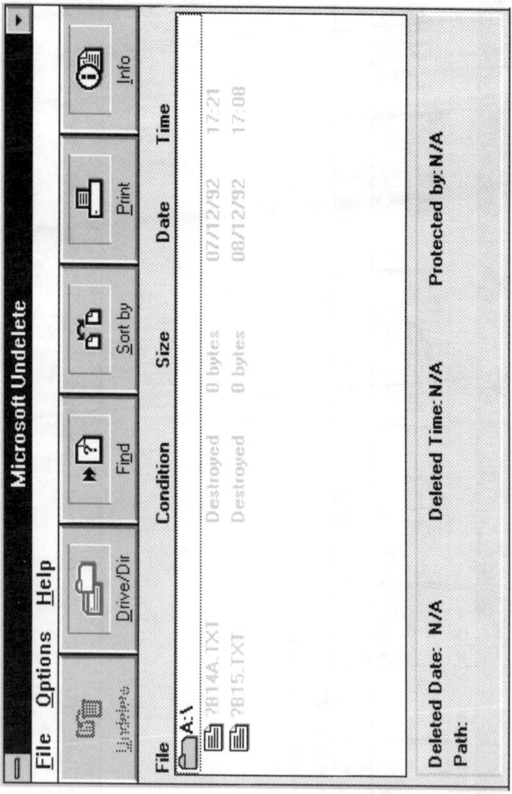

2. Drives/Dir is used to change to any drive and/or directory that is available on your system. The illustration, Figure 10.19, shows some deleted files detected on a disk in the A: drive.

3. Find is used to specify deleted files in terms of a wildcard such as *.PCX, or a full or partial name. For deleted text files you can search for words specified in the Containing box, and you can choose Ignore Case and Whole Word to tighten the selection. Search Groups can be used to confine the search to groups of directories.

4. Sort By allows the file list to be sorted by the usual headings of name, extension and size, plus date/time of deletion, date/time of modification, and file condition (Perfect, Excellent, Good, Poor, Destroyed).
5. Print allows the deleted file list to be printed. This is useful for a long list if you want to select specific files for undeletion.
6. Info provides information on a deleted file, showing its name, size and condition among other information.

The display of deleted files will include descriptions that tell you the likelihood of file recovery, and this varies depending on the file protection methods you have used - see Chapter 4 for details of Sentry and Tracker systems.

Perfect is used only of a file that has been protected by the Sentry system, meaning that it can be completely recovered. A program file in Perfect condition can be undeleted and run, for example.

Excellent is used only of a file that has been recovered by the Tracker method. Such a file can be recovered and is almost certain to be complete so that even a program file can be used.

Good is used of files that have not been protected by Sentry or Tracker but which seem to be recoverable. A program file might have suffered corruption that prevents it from running perfectly, but a data file can usually be trusted.

Poor means that the file cannot be undeleted by Windows Undelete. If this was a program file, forget it. If it was a text file you may be able to recover a corrupted version by using MS-DOS Undelete (leave Windows in order to use this).

Destroyed indicates that absolutely no recovery is possible, even though some of the file name may be visible.

The menu line of Undelete offers a set of items, many of which duplicate the items that are chosen by using the icons. The File menu contains Undelete, Undelete To, Change Drive/Directory, Find Deleted File, File Info, Purge/Delete Sentry File, Print List, Printer Setup and Exit.

The Undelete and Undelete To options allow a file to be recovered either to their original locations on the disk or to another specified location which can be on a different drive and/or directory.

Figure 10.20
The Configure Sentry form which allows you to specify which deleted files Sentry should save.

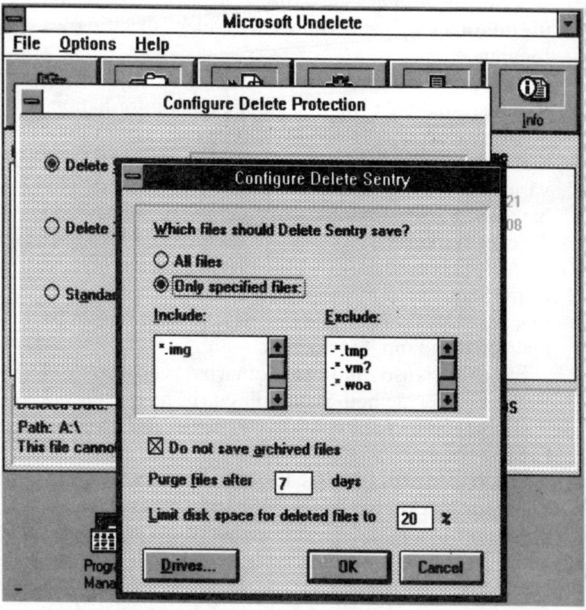

The Change Drive/Directory, Find Deleted File, File Info and Print List actions provide an alternative to icon selection for these items.

The Options menu consists of Sort By, Select by Name, Unselect by Name, and Configure Delete Protection.

The Sort By options allows the deleted files to be sorted into order, an action that is also available from the Sort By icon. The Select and Unselect by name items allow you to specify the files that you want to undelete by using names, including wildcard names of the *.PCX format.

The most important option in this set is Configure Delete Protection. This brings up a window that allows you to specify Sentry, Tracker or Standard (see Chapter 4.) Clicking on one of the higher options produces a form as illustrated for Sentry in Figure 10.20.

1. You can opt for All files or Specified files. Since your data files are the most precious (you will still have the original distribution disks for program files) it makes sense to protect these rather than all files
2. You can make an inclusion/exclusion pair of lists of file extensions to specify the file you want to safeguard.
3. You can opt whether or not to save archived files for which other backups must exist.
4. The Purge time is, by default, 7 days. This is more generous than it seems because you can usually reckon that if you have not recovered files in 7 days they will have been over-written by new files.
5. The default disk space for deleted files is shown as 20% which is rather generous, even taking into account that Sentry stores the whole of a 'deleted' file.

When you leave the Configure Protection window you are reminded that you have to alter the AUTOEXEC.BAT file. You have to do this for yourself.

SMARTMON

This program can be run by double-clicking its name in the File Manager list for the MSDOS directory. The monitor will remain on screen until you cancel it or minimise it. In minimised form it will continue to show the cache success rate as a percentage. The report covers all drives and shows the cache format used and the success of caching. Figure 10.21 shows the cache report for drive K, the host for the Double-spaced C drive.

■ Note that when your main hard disk uses DBLSPACE, the system regards the host, in this case K:, as the drive that is actually cached and C: will be shown as not cached. If you use DBLSPACE, do not try to alter the cache status of C:. This is important.

The buttons of SmartDrive Monitor, apart from Help, are used as follows:

Commit is used to force SmartDrive to write its cache back to the disk. This should never be needed, because write-back is automatic after five seconds.

Reset is used to write back the cache, clear the cache buffer and start again on the cache reporting.

Options allows you to select sampling frequency in the range 50 milliseconds to 10 seconds. The default is 0.5 seconds (500 milliseconds). The histogram (bar) display intervals can also be changed from their default of 30. You can type a name for a log file (default is SMARTMON.LOG) and determine the time after which

Figure 10.21
The SmartDrive Monitor window, which will remain on screen in front of other Windows until you dispense with it. Even when reduced to an icon this will still show the efficiency of SmartDrive. The spelling of 'Frequency' should be corrected by now.

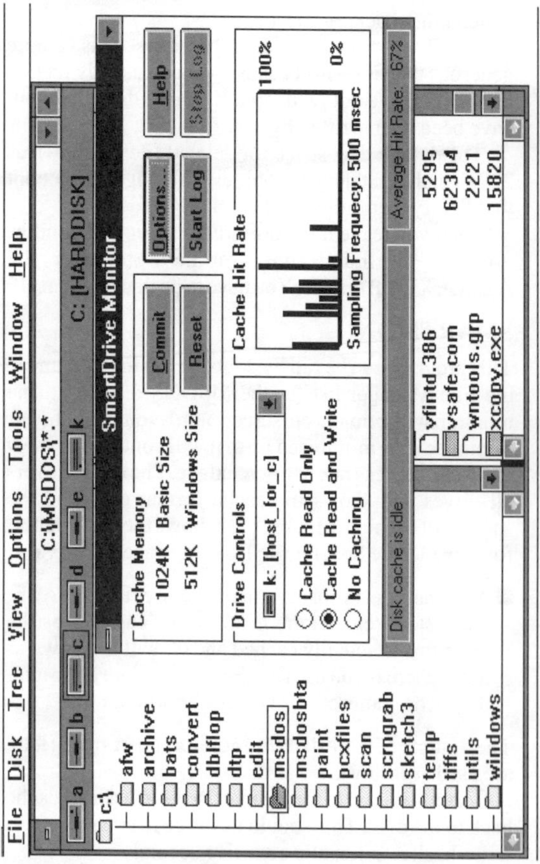

the log stops - the default is 2 hours (120 minutes). The automatic stop can also be disabled or enabled in this section. Settings made by SmartMon can be saved so as to alter the SmartDrive line in AUTOEXEC.BAT so that a different drive-caching setup will be made when the computer is re-started.

11 DOS Sundries

Interlnk

Interlnk is intended as a simple utility for connecting a laptop to a desktop computer, but it can be used as an elementary form of network system for two computers, using either parallel or serial ports. Most computers possess only one parallel port which is used for the printer, but it is quite common to fit two serial ports and even if one of these is used for a serial mouse this leaves one spare for Interlnk connection.

■ As a simple networking system, Interlnk is not quite so versatile as the well-known $25 Network, but it is supplied as part of MS-DOS 6.0. These simple interconnections do not rank as a network for the purposes of WorkGroup Connections, Mail or Micro.

Since the use of serial links is much more common, this will be described. Serial links allow transfer rates of just over 115,000 bits per second, which is considerably slower than can be achieved with parallel ports, but fast enough for printing or file copying. The hardware consists simply of a seven-core serial non-modem cable terminated in the type of plugs that the machines use - either a 25 pin or a 9 pin type.

■ Serial cables intended for printers or external modems are useless - their connections are not suitable. You should specify that you want a non-modem connected cable for linking two computers together. If a parallel cable is used it must be of the bidirectional machine-to-machine type - these are unusual.

With INTERLNK in use two machines can share drives and printers. One machine is designated as the server and the other as the client. The Client can be used normally, with the drives and printer of the server at its disposal. During this time the server is immobilised - you cannot use it normally. This is one major difference between Interlnk and The $25 Network.

Interlnk can be used in a variety of configurations, and you need to decide for yourself, after trying some out, what will be best suited for your own uses. Interlnk can be used along with Windows and DOSSHELL on either machine, though task switching on DOSSHELL cannot be used while the machine is being used as a server.

The minimum requirement to use Interlnk is to add INTERLNK.EXE in a CONFIG.SYS line of the machine you will use as a Client. You might want to use this line in the CONFIG.SYS files of both machines to allow yourself some flexibility. A typical CONFIG.SYS entry is:

device=c:\msdos\interlnk.exe

which will install Interlnk (whose files are, in this example, in the MSDOS directory) and look for a connection as the computer is starting up. This connection need not exist at that time and can be started at any time later by using INTERLNK or INTERSVR, see later.

The options that can be used following INTERLNK.EXE are:

/DRIVES:n Interlnk assumes three drives. If you have fewer or more on the other computer you can specify them as /DRIVES:2 or /DRIVES:4 for example. If you use /DRIVES:0 no drives will be shared, only printer connections.

/NOPRINTER Ensures that the printer is not shared. Remember that if a printer is shared both machine must be switched on and running Interlnk before printing can be done from the machine which does not have the printer connected.

/COM Can be used in the form /COM:1 or COM:2F8 - the first form is more useful and intelligible. This allows you to specify a serial port (usually in the range of COM:1 to COM:4) rather than have Interlnk find it for itself.

/LPT Can be used in the forms /LPT:1 or LPT:378 - the first form is more useful and intelligible. This allows you to specify a parallel port for data transfer (NOT for the printer).

/AUTO Creates a link only if the server is active, otherwise does not load Interlnk into memory.

/NOSCAN Installs Interlnk in memory, but does not attempt to link with the server.

/LOW Installs Interlnk into conventional memory rather than the default upper memory.

/BAUD Used to specify a serial transfer rate if for some reason the normal rate of 115200 cannot be used. The slower rates are 57600, 38400, 19200 and 9600 and they will make access noticeably slower.

/V Prevents timer conflicts - use this if, for example, a serial mouse stops working when Interlnk is running.

When the INTERLNK.EXE line runs in the CONFIG.SYS file it establishes a set of new drive letters, equal to the number of drives on the other computer that can be shared. If the number of drives on the other machine is not the default 3, you should use the /DRIVES option to correct this. It is also useful to add the /NOSCAN option if you often start one machine alone or at a different time from the other. If you do not share a printer then add the /NOPRINTER option because this reduces the memory requirements of INTERLNK.

The /COM option can also be useful, particularly if you use a serial mouse on the COM1 port. Using /COM:2 in INTERLNK.EXE prevents the program from checking COM1 and possibly interfering with a serial mouse action.

The normal use of Interlink involves starting the INTERSVR program on the Server machine and INTERLNK on the Client. There is an option which allows INTERSVR on one machine to copy the INTERLNK files to a machine which is not equipped to load files from a disk, such as a diskless laptop machine which retained files in its memory. Only machines that use MS-DOS compatible files can be used in this way. In this Chapter we shall concentrate on the more normal method in which one machine runs INTERSVR and the other runs INTERLNK.

1. On the server machine, run INTERSVR, either direct from DOS or by way of DOSSHELL or Windows. This will show only the outline window when the other machine is not yet activated, Figure 11.1

```
Microsoft Interlnk Server Version 1.00
This Computer          Other Computer
(Server)       (Client)
A:
B:
C: (229MB)
F:
G:
H:
I:
J:
K: (130Mb)
D:
E:
LPT1
```

Figure 11.1

The INTERSVR screen as it appears before a connection is made.

2. On the Client machine, start INTERLNK either at the MS-DOS command line or by clicking on the command in DOSSHELL or Windows. If you are running DOSSHELL or Windows you can click on a drive letter that is linked to the other machine instead of running INTERLNK.

■ If you have previously used INTERLNK under DOSSHELL there may be remote drive information held in memory, so that clicking on the remote drive letter produces an old directory. Use the F5 key to refresh the display.

3. The screen of the client machine will show a list of equivalent drive letters and the display on the server machine will change to reflect the connection. The connection remains in use until it is broken by pressing Alt-F4 at the server.

4. The server diagram remains on screen as a reminder of the connections. In the example, the C:\ drive of the server machine is referred to as F: on the Client machine, so that a command such as:

COPY F:\words*.TXT C:\text

can be used. For most purposes it is easier to use DOSSHELL or Windows File Manager to carry out such actions.

■ Running INTERLNK from DOSSHELL or Windows presents no problems, but when INTERSVR is run the INTERSVR menu remains on screen. You cannot make use of DOSSHELL actions like task switching while INTERSVR is running, and the same applies to Windows. A message will appear to remind you of this.

INTERSVR offers a similar range of options, adding the /X=B: type of option to specify a drive letter that will not be linked. The /LPT, /COM, /BAUD and /V options are as for INTERLNK. The /B option allows the INTERSVR screen to be seen in black and white if you have any problems with the colours. /RCOPY is used to copy the INTERLNK files to a Client which cannot load them in any other way.

■ To use /RCOPY to copy the INTERLNK files to a diskless laptop, start your main machine running INTERSVR /RCOPY and follow the instructions that appear on the screen. On the laptop you need to type MODE COM2:2400,n,8,1,p (ENTER) followed by CTTY COM2 (ENTER) - this assumes that the COM2 port is being used.

There are some variations on the Interlink theme:

1. You can force a drive on the client to be equivalent to a drive on the server by using the command INTERLNK clientdrive: = serverdrive: such as:

INTERLNK E:=A:

- you must use the drive letters that are shown as equivalent when the INTERSVR program is running on the server machine.

2. You can cancel a link by using INTERLNK Clientdrive:= with nothing equated, such as:

INTERLNK F:=.

3. You may have problems in some cases with different MS-DOS versions. Normally, provided that one machine is using MS-DOS 6.0, the other can be using any version from 3.0 onwards. This is not true if the Server machine uses a single large disk partition, as is normal, and the Client is using MS-DOS 3.0 to 3.4, because these versions cannot make use of large disk partitions.

4. If you use the Client machine to run a program that is located on the disk of the Server you need to be sure that the program is one that could run on the Client (not configured for a different video system, for example).

5. You cannot use the commands:

CHKDSK DEFRAG DISKCOMP FDISK
FORMAT SYS UNDELETE UNFORMAT

6. Drives created by a Network are not handled by Interlnk.

Code page settings

The Code Page system is the third part of the MS-DOS provision for international use, of which the other two are the use of COUNTRY.SYS and KEYB in the CONFIG.SYS file. For most users these provisions will be enough, and if your use of characters from other languages is confined to word-processed documents it is usually possible to obtain the characters from the software of the word-processor. By doing this you can be assured that your printer will be able to print these characters. By specifying Code Page 850 in the KEYB command and using a word-processor (such as WordPerfect) that can cope with a huge range of characters, you can deal with practically all requirements for documents in other languages.

Code pages are intended to allow the use of more than one character set, and the system was initially set up to work with the EGA video system and a few IBM printers. They are needed if you permanently need to use different alphabets for all of your work (not just word-processing) and if your hardware is equipped to deal with code pages. One set of code-page characters, code page 437, is built in and always available - the hardware code page. Each other code page is created by using a character-set file (with a CPI extension) of which the most useful general-purpose one is 850.

If you need to change to a different character set, the steps are:

1. Use a device line in the CONFIG.SYS file which will load the DISPLAY.SYS driver. This will cope with LCD, EGA or VGA screen types, using EGA to cover VGA also. You have to specify the hardware code page (437) and the number of software code pages you want to use (up to 6 for EGA or VGA, only 1 for LCD). A typical line for a VGA monitor would be:

```
DEVICE=C:\MSDOS\DISPLAY.SYS   CON=(EGA,437,1)
```

to load one additional software page. A further number can be used following the number of software code pages to specify the number of sub-fonts if this is known. The default is 2 for EGA and 1 for LCD.

2. Place in the AUTOEXEC.BAT file the NLSFUNC command line. This can alternatively be placed in the CONFIG.SYS file by using INSTALL. No parameters are needed with NLSFUNC unless you have a language file other than COUNTRY.SYS.

3. Place into the AUTOEXEC.BAT file the MODE COM CP PREP command which will load in the CPI character set file. This command needs parameters which will show the code page or pages you need and a path to them. A typical line is:

```
MODE CON CP PREP=((850)C:\MSDOS\EGA.CPI)
```

Note that it would be very unusual to need more than code page 850 because so many languages can use this page.

4. Following this, also in AUTOEXEC.BAT, use CHCP to make the page active. In this example you might use:

```
CHCP 850
```

■ You need not put CHCP in the AUTOEXEC.BAT file. By using CHCP as a direct command you can switch from one character set to another as and when you please, provided that the preceding steps have been correctly carried out.

Remember that if you change character sets you might also want to change keyboard, keyboard layout and Country number. Character sets other than 850 are likely to be limited- you cannot, for example, use 437 with Polish.

The DOSSHELL.INI file

The file called DOSSHELL.INI is used to keep a record of the settings of DOSSHELL, and each time you use DOSSHELL and change settings this will cause a change to DOSSHELL.INI. This file will then ensure that DOSSHELL starts up next time in the same configuration as it had when shut down. You can look at DOSSHELL.INI using a normal text editor, but you should not try to alter the file and there is no point in doing so. If there is a particular (unusual) configuration that you sometimes use, you can save the DOSSHELL.INI file that it produces so that you can return to it by renaming the current DOSSHELL.INI and loading in the alternative one. As an alternative, you can put your different DOSSHELL.INI files in different directories and direct DOSSHELL to use a specific file by using the environment variable dosshell in AUTOEXEC.BAT, such as:

```
dosshell=C:\MYSHELL
```

Note that if you change to a different video system this requires DOSSHELL to create a different DOSSHELL.VID file - unless the DOSSHELL.VID file matches the video system DOSSHELL will lock up when you try to use it. The DOSSHELL.INI file should also be replaced if your new monitor can handle a large range of colours or if you are changing from a mono to a colour monitor.

There are three files supplied (except for IBM Mono) for each of the seven monitor systems that DOSSHELL supports, and their extensions are VID, INI and GRB. In the course of installation for DOSSHELL, each main name is changed, so that VGA.VID becomes DOSSHELL.VID and VGA.GRB becomes DOSSHELL.GRB and so on. Changing video systems requires you to select the correct set of files and rename them. The file sets are:

IBM MONO	(no VID file)	MONO.INI	MONO.GRB
CGA	CGA.VID	CGA.INI	CGA.GRB
EGA (Colour)	EGA.VID	EGA.INI	CGA.GRB
EGA (Mono)	EGA.VID	MONO.INI	EGAMONO.GRB
VGA (Colour)	VGA.VID	EGA.INI	VGA.GRB
VGA (Mono)	VGA.VID	MONO.INI	VGAMONO.GRB
Hercules	HERC.VID	MONO.INI	HERC.GRB

-and on the distribution disk these files are in compressed form, using extensions IN_, VI_ and GR_. You need to use EXPAND to decompress and place the files in the correct hard disk directory, usually \MSDOS. Once you have the files expanded in the directory you can make the change as follows:

1. Move the existing DOSSHELL.VID, DOSSHELL.GRB and DOSSHELL.INI files to another directory, or back them up and delete them from the hard disk.

2. Rename the VID file you have just imported to DOSSHELL.VID

3. Rename the GRB file you have just imported to DOSSHELL.GRB

4. Rename the INI file you have just imported to DOSSHELL.INI

5. Start DOSSHELL and set it up the way you want it (including colour scheme if applicable) so that your DOSSHELL.INI file will be updated to your current preferences.

Handicapped users

The Microsoft Supplemental disk, which can be downloaded from some on-line services, contains ACESSDOS which is a set of utilities that can provide actions suited to handicapped users. These include:

1. Sequential use of Ctrl, Shift and Alt keys so that Alt-A can be typed in sequence (one-fingered) rather than as two keys pressed simultaneously.

2. Ignoring accidental key presses

3. Adjusting or removing the typematic repeat rate

4. Mouse cursor control from the keyboard

5. Control of keyboard and mouse actions from other input devices (pucks, pens, graphics tablets etc.)

6. Adding on-screen signals to sound warnings

There are also keyboard files to allow the use of the more logical Dvorak type of keyboard to replace the standard QWERTY type. As well as the normal two-handed Dvorak layout, this can cope with single-handed, left or right, keyboards.

Appendix A

Error and Information messages

These are taken from the MS-DOS 6.0 list, so that some will not be applicable to earlier versions. Brief meanings have been included for guidance, but unless the error is obvious you may need to seek further information. Some of these messages are *very rarely seen* because they indicate problems that are seldom encountered; such problems may require expert attention. Other messages can be missed - when a command is used in the AUTOEXEC.BAT file its messages may be on the screen for only a fraction of a second before the next line is executed and prints its own messages.

Error messages for utilities such as APPEND or JOIN, which should no longer be in use, have been omitted, as have error messages from DEBUG and EXE2BIN. A large number of error messages originate from FDISK, and since modern IDE hard disks are ready-formatted and do not require FDISK this utility can be removed from the hard disk.

A large number of error messages concern files that cannot be found, and the simplest way to deal with this is to place ALL of the MS-DOS utility files into a directory called MSDOS, and use this in a path statement such as:

```
PATH C:\;C:\MSDOS
```

in the AUTOEXEC.BAT file.

All SYS files should be placed in the root directory, because they will be looked for **before** the AUTOEXEC.BAT file runs, so that the PATH command has not yet been executed. The alternative is to use a full path to each of these files in each line of CONFIG.SYS where they are needed.

■ If you hear a lot of disk drive activity when a floppy is being formatted unconditionally it indicates some poor sectors which have to be written several times before giving a satisfactory check. Either throw out the disk or label it and keep it apart from others. Never use such a floppy along with DBLSPACE.

Where networks are used, several messages relate to attempts to perform actions that must be prohibited to avoid damage to the network server files. The many messages concerning the use of Code Pages can be avoided simply by ignoring the use of Code Pages unless they are essential to your work. Very few users of PC machines in the UK need Code Pages.

- References to 'device' mean letters such as PRN, CON, COM1 etc.

Remember that when a fault is due to the CONFIG.SYS entry, changing the entry has no effect until the computer is rebooted. When a fault is corrected in the AUTOEXEC.BAT file, this can be run by typing AUTOEXEC directly. Some care may be needed if this might result in making multiple copies of a memory-resident program.

The order of lines in the CONFIG.SYS file is important, because one line often depends on another having been carried out earlier - you cannot install a device that uses extended memory, for example, until you have installed an extended memory manager driver. Other lines can cause less obvious interference effects, and the suppliers are often aware of these problems - look for a README type of file, or contact the suppliers if you have traced the problem to a specific non-Microsoft device.

Problems with extended memory often arise if a computer uses a chip set that copies ROM contents into RAM (a 'shadow' RAM) for speed. This action can usually be turned off in the CMOS SETUP procedure, but if it is retained you will not be able to use the memory affected by this shadowing action, and such memory is usually reported as available by memory utilities.

10 Mismatches - ending compare Files compared using COMP have 10 or more mismatches and can be regarded as different.

Access denied A file is read-only; attempt to use TYPE with a directory name; attempt to use CD with a filename. Note that SENTRY and some other files will give this report but access cannot be gained in any ordinary way. Sentry files in particular will survive a FORMAT A: /U command, and can be deleted only if the first 256 bytes of the disk data sector are set to zero, using DEBUG, followed by a format /U.

Active code page *nnn* The number is that of the code page in use.

Active code page for device *ddd* is *nnn* The number is of the code page being used by the device.

Active code page not available from CON device The code page that has been selected is not usable by the screen type you are using.

All available space in the Extended DOS Partition is assigned to logical drives You are trying to create another drive (partition letter) with FDISK and no more disk space is available.

All files cancelled by operator You have used the /T option with PRINT so that there is nothing more to print.

All files in directory will be deleted! Are you sure (Y/N)? You have used DEL *.* to delete all files, and you are being asked to confirm.

All logical drives deleted in the Extended DOS Partition Issued from FDISK when you have removed an extended partition, deleting any files that existed on that partition.

Allocation error, size adjusted There is a discrepancy between the amount of data in a file and the file size as recorded in the directory. Use CHKDSK /F to find any stray pieces of the file. If these pieces are of text you can make files of them and read them.

All specified file(s) are contiguous Your disk is well-organised, no compression needed because all files follow each other with no gaps.

ANSI.SYS must be installed to perform requested function You have tried to use a screen action that needed the DEVICE=ANSI.SYS driver in CONFIG.SYS.

Attempting to recover allocation unit Message from FORMAT when a bad allocation unit has been found. This points to a serious disk problem.

/B invalid with a black and white printer You have used GRAPHICS/B to specify background colour, but your printer cannot deal with colour.

Bad command or file name Check your typing using F3 (or DOSKEY commands) - there is something wrong (spelling, syntax) with the command.

Bad or missing *d:path* SMARTDRV.EXE You have opted to use SMARTDRIVE but the file is missing or is in a path not named in the line that loads SMARTDRIVE.EXE.

Bad or missing Command Interpreter The COMMAND.COM file cannot be found. On a floppy-only machine, insert the system disk into drive A. On a hard disk machine, check directories (and look for your backups!) - absence of COMMAND.COM may mean severe disk corruption or lack of a SHELL statement in CONFIG.SYS. You may be able to boot from a system floppy and gain access to your hard disk to copy COMMAND.COM back on to it.

Bad or missing filename A line in the CONFIG.SYS file is incorrect. A device name may be mis-spelled or its SYS file missing.

Bad or missing Keyboard definition file The KEYB command has specified a KEYBOARD.SYS file that cannot be found - check the directories and/or path in use.

Bad partition table No DOS partition can be found on the hard disk, usually because FDISK has not been used.

Bad unit error reading drive *x:* Incorrect identification codes have been used - check that the drive is correctly installed.

Batch file missing The batch file you have called cannot be found in the current directory or any specified path.

Baud rate required You have used a MODE COM command without specifying a serial baud rate.

BREAK is off/on Displays the current setting of BREAK.

Cannot CHDIR to path - tree past this point not processed Delivered when CHKDSK is running and cannot find a directory. Run again using CHKDSK/F.

Cannot CHDIR to root During use of CHKDSK the root directory could not be found again. Reboot and try again. If the same message appears, the disk is seriously corrupted and must be reformatted (but try the UNDELETE utilities first). This is when you wish you kept good backups.

Cannot CHKDSK a network drive CHKDSK cannot operate on a drive that is accessed over a network - use CHKDSK locally on the computer that possesses the drive.

Cannot create a zero-size partition You cannot specify a partition with 0% or 0 Mbyte size using FDISK. Minimum is 1% or 1 Mbyte.

Cannot create extended DOS partition without primary DOS partition on Disk 1 You are using FDISK and have not yet created a primary DOS partition for MS-DOS. No other partition can be created until this is done.

Cannot create Logical DOS drive without an extended DOS partition on current drive You are using FDISK and trying to create a new drive letter before creating the DOS partition.

Cannot delete Extended DOS partition while logical drives exist You are using FDISK to delete a partition without first taking the option to delete the logical drive letter (D, E etc.) assigned to the partition.

Cannot DISKCOMP to or from a network drive DISKCOMP cannot be used on a drive that is accessed over a network, only on local drives.

Cannot DISKCOPY to or from a network drive DISKCOPY cannot be used on a drive that is accessed over a network, only on local drives.

Cannot do binary reads from a device You are using a command to copy from a device (CON, COM1 etc.) with the /B option. Omit this option or use /A instead.

Cannot edit .BAK file — rename file The editor will refuse to alter a BAK file unless you rename it with another extension.

Cannot find FORMAT.EXE You have tried to back up to a disk that is unformatted, and the FORMAT.EXE file is not in any searched path, or is missing.

Cannot find GRAPHICS profile The GRAPHICS.PRO file is not in the current directory or in any searched path.

Cannot find system files The main IO.SYS and MSDOS.SYS files cannot be found. On a floppy-only machine, insert the system disk and try again. On a hard disk machine, check for serious disk corruption. You may have to re-install MS-DOS 6.0.

Cannot FORMAT non-removable drive *X:* You are using a backup command with /F to specify a fixed disk target. This cannot be done if only one hard disk is in use, and if a second hard disk can be used, it must already be formatted.

Cannot LABEL a network drive The LABEL command cannot be used on a drive that is accessed over a network.

Cannot load COMMAND, system halted COMMAND.COM cannot be found. Use a system disk and reboot. If COMMAND.COM has disappeared from the hard disk check for serious disk corruption.

Cannot perform a cyclic copy Using XCOPY /S, you are not allowed to specify a sub-directory of the directory you are copying from.

Cannot read file allocation table The disk is seriously corrupted - you may be able to use the SENTRY UNDELETE utilities to rebuild the table, but this does not solve the problem of why the corruption should have happened. Check the disk surface using a suitable utility.

Cannot recover . entry, processing continued The current directory entry (shown as a single dot in the DIR listing) is defective and cannot be recovered.

Cannot recover .. entry, Entry has bad attribute/link/size The previous directory (shown as a double dot in the DIR listing) is corrupted and cannot be recovered. Use CHKDSK/F to attempt correction.

Cannot setup expanded memory The EMS (expanded memory) card in your computer is not working or is absent.

Cannot specify default drive You have tried to use the SYS command on the drive you are currently using - another drive must be specified.

Cannot start COMMAND, exiting Possible causes are too low a value for FILES= in CONFIG.SYS, path to COMMAND.COM incorrect (put into MSDOS directory and ensure correct path) or insufficient memory to load COMMAND.COM (very unusual).

Cannot SYS to a network drive You cannot copy system files to a drive that is accessed over a network.

Cannot use FASTOPEN for drive *X:* FASTOPEN cannot be used on floppy drives, on a networked drive or with more than four hard disks at a time.

Cannot use PRINT - use NET PRINT You are trying to print files over a network with no local printer - use the NET PRINT command, not PRINT.

Cannot XCOPY to a reserved device The XCOPY command must specify a suitable device (disk drive, tape backup etc.), not NUL.

CHDIR failed, trying alternate method CHKDSK has been checking the directory tree and has been unable to return to a parent directory. It will return to the root and try again.

CHKDSK not available on drive *X* You are trying to run CHKDSK from a disk which does not contain CHKDSK nor any path to CHKDSK.

***nnnnnnnn* code page drive cannot be initialized** Either DISPLAY.SYS or PRINTER.SYS cannot be started, usually because of an incorrect line in CONFIG.SYS (usually an incorrectly specified parameter, such as a non-existent code page).

Code page not prepared You have selected a code page with CHCP that is not available until you use MODE CP PREP.

Code page *xxx* not prepared for system You have used CHCP without NLSFUNC or MODE CP PREP.

Code page operation not supported on this device Code paging is available on some hardware - not yours!

Code page requested *xxx* is not valid for given keyboard code You have used a KEYB command with the wrong keyboard code/ code page combination.

Code page specified has not been designated You have used KEYB with an option that is not available.

Code page specified has not been prepared You have used KEYB with a code page option that needs MODE CP PREP to be used first.

Code page specified is inconsistent with invoked code page The KEYB option for the keyboard does not match the code page; use MODE CP SELECT to change the code page for the CON device.

Code page specified is inconsistent with selected code page The KEYB command option is not suited to the code page selected for CON; use MODE CP SELECT to change the code page.

Code page *xxx* Notifies current code page.

Code pages cannot be prepared You have specified a duplicate code page number or tried to prepare too many code pages (see the DEVICE line in CONFIG.SYS), and use MODE /STATUS to check which pages have been prepared already.

Compare another diskette (Y/N)? DISKCOMP has completed a run, allowing you to exit or make another comparison.

Compare error at OFFSET *X* COMP has found a difference between two binary files. The offset number (position in file) will be in hexadecimal.

Compare error on disk side *s*, track *t* DISKCOMP has found a difference in a file, showing location on the disk.

Compare more files (Y/N)? COMP has finished, allowing you to exit or run another comparison.

Compare OK DISKCOMP has found two files identical.

Compare process ended A fatal error has occurred during DISKCOMP use.

Comparing *t* tracks *n* sectors per track, *s* sides You have started DISKCOMP, and this message confirms the format of the disks that are being compared.

***X* Contains *N* non-contiguous blocks** There are fragmented files in the named disk. This is harmless, and a copy can be made using COPY or XCOPY that will not be fragmented.

Content of destination lost before copy The file being copied has been overwritten before the copying could be completed - usually because of incorrect use of the COPY command. Always label your disks as source and destination to avoid confusion.

Convert directory to file (Y/N)? A directory has been found to be corrupted, and can sometimes be recovered by replying Y and using DEBUG (if you know how).

Convert lost chains to files (Y/N)? CHKDSK has found pieces of stray files. Answer Y to assign file names, so that if any text is on these fragments it can be recovered. Answering N will release the disk space for re-use.

Copy another diskette (Y/N)? DISKCOPY has completed its action, and you can exit or make another copy.

Copying *t* tracks *n* sectors *s* sides Message from DISKCOPY during its normal action.

Copy process ended DISKCOPY could not copy the entire disk (problems with disk sizes?). Use COPY or XCOPY to copy other files.

Corrections will not be written to disk CHKDSK has found errors on a disk but because you did not use /F it will not correct them.

Current code page settings Indicates what codes are in use and prepared.

Current date is *mm-dd-yy* Enter new data (mm-dd-yy): Message from the DATE command - if correct, press ENTER, otherwise enter correct date and press ENTER. Check your CONFIG.SYS file for the Country line - you should be using dates in UK format.

Current drive is no longer valid You are using either a network drive, a spare un-allocated drive letter, or a empty floppy drive (no disk, or door not closed).

Current keyboard code: *xx* code page: *yyy* Current CON code page *zzz* Displays the current code page settings for keyboard and screen.

Current keyboard does not support this code page Incorrect code page selected, not machine KEYB setting. One or other should be altered.

Current time is *hh:mm:ss.dd* Enter new time: This is the message from the TIME command, press ENTER to confirm, or type new timed (ignoring fractions of a second) and press ENTER. Check time frequently (at least once a week) because the timekeeping of a PC is notoriously poor.

Data error reading drive *X:* Defective disk, often unformatted or created by an incompatible machine. Applies also to disks created by backup programs, which are formatted in a special way, or to network disk drive letters when the network is not running.

***filename*, Delete (Y/N)?** Requires you to confirm that the file is to be deleted; message delivered when DEL /p has been used.

Delete current volume label (Y/N)? You have used LABEL to enter a new label name.

Device error during status Usually a code-page incompatibility error -check the CONFIG.SYS file, also ability of devices to support code pages.

Device error during prepare Usually a code-page incompatibility error -check the CONFIG.SYS file, also ability of devices to support code pages.

Device error during select Usually a code-page incompatibility error - check the CONFIG.SYS file, also ability of devices to support code pages.

Device or code page missing from font file Code page not available for specified device, use MODE to alter code page.

Device *ddd* not prepared No code page prepared for this device.

Directory already exists You have used MD (MKDIR) with the name of a directory that has already been created.

Directory is totally empty, no . or .. The directory is faulty, with no references to current or parent. Delete and create again.

Directory not empty You can use RD (RMDIR) only on an empty directory. Use DELTREE to delete a directory and all of its files.

Disk error reading/writing drive *X:* Defective, unformatted or incorrectly formatted disk.

Disk error reading/writing FAT *X* Defective file allocation table, MS-DOS is using spare table. Copy files to another disk as soon as possible and run CHKDSK/F on the faulty disk.

Disk full error writing to BACKUP Log File The disk being used for backup is full, change disk and press any key to restart.

Do not specify filename(s) Command format: DISKCOMP d: D:[/1][/8] DISKCOMP has been used with incorrect options or with a filename in addition to a disk drive letter.

Do not specify filename(s) Command format: DISKCOPY d: D:[/1] DISKCOPY is being used with incorrect options, or with a filename in addition to disk drive letter.

Do you see the leftmost 0?(Y/N) MODE is being used to display pattern - use N if the pattern needs to be shifted to the right.

Do you see the rightmost 9?(Y/N) MODE is being used to display pattern - use N if the pattern needs to be shifted to the left.

Do you wish to use the maximum available size for a primary DOS partition and make the partition active (Y/N)? Message from FDISK which allows you to use all of your disk space for one active DOS partition (normally desirable if you are using only MS-DOS); check the maximum size that your MS-DOS version allows. Note that you should never need to use FDISK on an IDE hard disk.

Does name specify a file name or directory name on the target (F=file D=directory)? A message from XCOPY if the target directory does not exist; select to create new file/directory.

Drive *X* already deleted You have tried to delete a drive letter that has already been deleted.

Drive deleted You have deleted a hard disk drive letter.

Drive letters have been changed or deleted A hard disk drive letter has been changed or deleted.

Drive types or diskette types not compatible DISKCOMP or DISKCOPY has been used with incompatible disks (one 3.5", one 5.25, for example).

Duplicate file name or file name not found You cannot rename a file to a name that already exists, and you cannot load or copy a file that does not exist.

Duplicate parameters not allowed You cannot repeat parameters in a command line.

ECHO is off/on Displays current status of ECHO.

End of input file The file has been completely read into memory; this is the last section.

Enter current volume label for drive *X:* You have requested to FORMAT a hard disk; this is a way of checking that you actually want to do something so drastic. Use VOL to find the volume label if you do not know it.

Enter new date (mm-dd-yy): You have used DATE - type ENTER to accept date shown, or type new date and press ENTER.

Enter new time: You have used TIME - type ENTER to accept date shown, or type new date and press ENTER.

Entry error The last typed command contains a syntax error. Retype or edit with F1/F3 or DOSKEY commands.

Entry has a bad attribute/link/size Use CHKDSK/F to correct error in directory (message may show . or .. as an indicator).

Error during read of font file Error in reading font file for specified code page.

Error in COUNTRY command Incorrect syntax in COUNTRY line of CONFIG.SYS.

Errors found, F parameter not specified. Corrections will not be written to disk. CHKDSK has been used, but without /F. Run CHKDSK/F to make the corrections.

Error in EXE file Corruption of a program file - possibly because it cannot run under the current DOS version (see SETVER if you are using MS-DOS 6.0).

Error loading operating system Boot from hard disk is faulty. If this persists, boot from a floppy (you do have several spares, don't you?) and use SYS to put a new copy of MS-DOS on the fixed disk (this is relatively easy with MS-DOS 6.0).

Error occurred in environment variable Check your use of the SET DIRCMD variable in MS-DOS 6.0.

Error opening log file The backup log file cannot be opened - it may have been on the wrong drive.

Error reading directory Bad sectors on disk affecting directory or file allocation table. Discard a floppy disk with this error, re-format a hard disk with this error.

Error reading fixed disk Message from FDISK - often because the interleave number (for MFM or RLL) is too small for the computer to use.

Error reading GRAPHICS profile GRAPHICS.PRO file cannot be read - check for presence of file, path, or presence of floppy disk with file.

Error reading MS-DOS system file No system file on disk, or corruption of system files. Boot from another disk, and check suspect disk.

Error reading/writing partition table Message from FORMAT, indicating partition trouble. Use FDISK again.

Error writing MS-DOS system file Faulty disk sectors. Use another disk.

Error writing directory (FAT or fixed disk) Faulty disk sectors. Discard a floppy disk with this error, re-format a hard disk with this error.

Error writing to device Printer switched off, or too much data sent.

EXEC failure Possible error in reading a command, or FILES= line in CONFIG.SYS set to too low a value.

Extended DOS partition already exists You cannot use FDISK to create another DOS partition when one already exists.

Extended DOS partition created FDISK has created a partition successfully.

Extended DOS partition deleted FDISK has deleted a partition.

Failure to access code page font file Font pathname incorrect, device driver in CONFIG.SYS incorrectly installed.

Failure to access device: *xxx* Code page has been specified for device which is not connected, or name incorrect.

Fastopen already installed You have tried to re-install FASTOPEN.

Fastopen installed You have successfully installed FASTOPEN.

FCB unavailable reading/writing drive *X:* An old program is running and has been corrupted. Requires expert attention.

fc: cannot open *filename* - No such file or directory You have used the FC command with a file or directory name that does not exist.

fc: Incompatible switches The options you have specified for FC conflict -usually because you have specified both binary and ASCII comparisons.

fc: No differences encountered The files are identical.

fc: out of memory Lack of memory prevents further comparison.

File allocation table bad Defective disk Use CHKDSK/F

File allocation table bad drive *X:* Disk not formatted or incorrectly formatted (or not using MS-DOS). Try CHKDSK/F, or reformat.

File name cancelled by operator You have used PRINT/t to cancel PRINT queue.

File cannot be copied onto itself You cannot use any copy command that specifies the same names on the same disk or path.

File creation error Root directory full, too many files, filename unsuitable (same as directory, volume or hidden file name).

File is READ-ONLY File cannot be changed until READ-ONLY attribute is altered.

File MSDOS.SYS not found on specified drive The disk which is being used as a system disk lacks this essential file.

File not found Requested file does not exist, or file renamed with existing name.

File not in PRINT queue You cannot remove from the PRINT queue a file that is not in the queue.

FIND: Access denied The file is not available (hidden or system file).

FIND: File not found Filename incorrect, wrong path.

FIND: Invalid number of parameters Incorrect number of options in FIND command line.

FIND: Invalid parameter An option is incorrect.

FIND: Read error in filename The FIND command could not read the file (corrupted file, perhaps).

FIND: Syntax error You have typed the command incorrectly.

First allocation unit is invalid, entry truncated File directory entry is incorrect. Using CHKDSK/F will remove this file.

FIRST diskette bad or incompatible DISKCOMP is being used, and the source disk has an unrecognised format. Use CHKDSK on the disk to see if the fault can be identified.

Fixed backup device *X* is full A device (such as a tape streamer) is full and cannot be used for further backups.

Fixups needed - base segment hex: Expert help needed to locate file correctly into memory by specifying absolute segment address.

Font file contents invalid Specified font file is faulty - or name incorrect. This can also damage code pages which will need to be prepared again.

FOR cannot be nested A batch file cannot contain one FOR line inside another- each FOR must end before another one is started.

Format another (Y/N)? FORMAT has completed its work on a disk and you can exit or repeat the action on another disk.

Format complete The disk is now formatted.

Format not supported on drive *X:* This drive does not allow formatting of disks - check that the drive is correctly installed. You may get this message if you try to format on drive letters that do not correspond to physically-present drives.

Formatting while copying DISKCOPY is copying to an unformatted disk.

Function not supported on this computer - *X* Your computer cannot carry out an action (missing display card or other adapter).

General failure reading/writing drive *X:* Incorrectly formatted disk, or failure of drive. You will also get this message if you try to use drive letters that do not correspond to physically-present drives.

Hardware code pages: Prepared code pages: List of current code pages.

Has invalid allocation unit, file truncated Error in data file, use CHKDSK/F to remove.

HMA not available: loading DOS low CONFIG.SYS contains DOS=high, but no high memory is available. Check that device=himem.sys is used before dos=high, and that memory is not allocated to shadow RAM.

Illegal device name MODE has been used with a name other than PRN, LPT, COM, etc.

Illegal device name - COM*x* The COM port number is invalid.

Incorrect DOS version You need to use the version of DOS for which the program was created (see SETVER for MS-DOS 6.0).

Incorrect DOS version, use DOS 2.00 or later You are trying to use a very old DOS version (most unlikely nowadays).

Incorrect number of parameters The command line for a command contains too many or too few parameters.

Incorrect parameter You are using FASTOPEN with an incorrect option.

Infinite retry on parallel printer timeout Printer offline, out of paper, not ready or working very slowly. This may hang up the computer unless the software allows some way of releasing it.

Infinite retry not supported on network printer The network does not allow printer errors to be sensed. Use a local printer or do not specify RETRY.

Insert backup disk *n* into drive *X:* Change backup disks, remembering to label the number of each disk used.

Insert backup source disk in drive *X:* Restore message prompting you to put in the backup disk.

Insert disk with COMMAND.COM in drive *X:* Put system disk in drive- this should never be seen when a hard disk is being used.

Insert disk for drive X: and strike any key when ready During COPY or FORMAT, asking for disk to be inserted.

Insert disk with batch file and press any key when ready A batch file has been started from a floppy, but the floppy is no longer in place when the next command of the batch file is ready to run.

Insert DOS disk in drive *X:* and strike ENTER when ready You have used FORMAT/S, but the disk in the current drive does not contain system tracks.

Insert FIRST disk into drive *X:* DISKCOMP requires you to put the first of the disks to be compared into the drive. Make sure that the disks are labelled.

Insert new disk for drive X: Put disk in drive for FORMAT action.

Insert SECOND disk in drive X: Using DISKCOMP, asks for second of the two disks that are being compared. Check disk label.

Insert source disk Put COPY source disk into drive.

Insert SOURCE disk into drive *X:* Put COPY source disk into specified drive.

Insert system disk in drive *X:* and press any key when ready Message delivered when using SYS, requesting a system disk from which these files can be read.

Insert TARGET disk into drive X: Message from DISKCOPY requiring you to place target disk into drive.

Insufficient disk space No room for files to be copied.

Insufficient memory No memory space for program to run - it may be possible to free enough memory by deleting unwanted resident files (like GRAPHICS). MS-DOS 6.0 releases enough memory to make this message less frequent.

Insufficient room in root directory Erase some unwanted files from the root and repeat CHKDSK. CHKDSK cannot rescue files because the root directory (where it puts rescued files) is full. Move files to another directory or disk. You should never have more than a few essential files (the SYS files and AUTOEXEC.BAT, for example) on the root directory.

Insufficient space in version table for new entry Version table is full - delete some of the entries that you do not need and then try again.

Intermediate file error during pipe Error in a temporary file created in a pipe action, often because of lack of disk space, or a write-protected disk. MS-DOS 6.0 allows a TEMP environment variable to be used for this purpose; typically SET TEMP=C:\TEMP.

Internal error Usually an error within a utility, no simple cure. Try another copy or version. Sometimes a CONFIG.SYS line associated with the program or device has become corrupted.

Internal stack overflow System halted Unusual fault caused by a lack of memory stacks - use the STACKS command in CONFIG.SYS to allocate more stacks.

Invalid argument Incorrect command line argument (filename etc.)

Invalid baud rate specified Incorrect rate, or badly specified in MODE.

Invalid characters in volume label Up to 11 letters or digits can be used.

Invalid code page specified Repeat command using correct code page number.

Invalid COMMAND.COM Insert COMMAND .COM disk in driver and strike any key when ready. A program run from a floppy has used most of the memory, and COMMAND.COM has to be reloaded - insert a system disk and press any key. This message should never appear when using a hard disk. The version of COMMAND.COM must match the other system files.

Invalid country code of code page Check the CONFIG.SYS file for the COUNTRY command line.

Invalid current directory Corrupted disk - some files may be recovered by using COPY to another disk.

Invalid date Incorrect entry to DATE command.

Invalid Date/Time Incorrect date or time specified in a BACKUP option.

Invalid device Device was not AUX, CON, NUL or PRN

Invalid device parameters from device driver FORMAT problem, usually caused by an incorrect DEVICE or DRIVPARM command in CONFIG.SYS, or attempt to format an old hard disk without having used FDISK first.

Invalid directory Mis-spelled directory name, or directory does not exist.

Invalid disk change reading/writing drive *X:* A disk has been changed without any prompt asking for a disk change. Replace the disk, press (R)etry.

Invalid drive in search path Drive letter for non-existing drive in PATH.

Invalid drive or filename Incorrect entry of drive/file name.

Invalid drive specification Drive letter does not correspond to a drive.

Invalid entry, please enter *X* FDISK value within correct range must be used

Invalid entry, please press ENTER Edit the entry and use acceptable characters.

Invalid environment size specified Use of /e with a number outside the acceptable range of 160 to 32768.

Invalid file/directory entry In a FASTOPEN cache, the number of filenames must be between 10 and 999, with a default of 34.

Invalid filename You have used a reserved name, or a name that does not follow filename conventions.

Invalid keyboard code specified The KEYB command specified an incorrect code - alter the KEYB command.

Invalid keyword Check with the command name followed by /? to display correct syntax.

Invalid number of parameters Option not specified, or wrong number of options.

Invalid parameter Edit command line, checking syntax.

Invalid parameter combination Edit command line, checking syntax.

Invalid parameter (or parameter combination) Options wrongly typed.

Invalid partition table Fault in partition table - you might be able to use UNFORMAT, otherwise use FDISK to re-partition (losing all files).

Invalid path Pathname incorrect, or more than 63 characters used.

Invalid path, not directory, or directory not empty You are trying to use RD on a directory that contains files or is incorrectly specified.

Invalid path (or file not found) Path name or filename does not exist.

Invalid path or parameter File or directory does not exist.

Invalid profile statement on line *X* Check numbered line in profile statement.

Invalid STACK parameter STACK command in CONFIG.SYS used incorrect syntax.

Invalid sub-directory entry Check spelling of name.

Invalid switch Check options on command line. Use command name with /? to find correct options.

Invalid switch type Option in wrong place or duplicated.

Invalid syntax Command syntax wrong.

Invalid syntax on DISPLAY.SYS code page driver A DEVICE line in CONFIG.SYS file uses incorrect syntax.

Invalid syntax on PRINTER.SYS code page driver Incorrect line in CONFIG.SYS file.

Invalid time TIME command used with incorrect entry.

Invalid version number format must be 3.20 - 9.99 Version number of DOS incorrectly specified.

Invalid volume ID Message from FORMAT if volume label for hard disk does not match, format will be abandoned.

Is cross linked on allocation unit *X* Two files are using the same directory entry, use CHKDSK/F to separate, with some loss of data.

***X* is not a choice, please enter ...** FDISK has been used with an incorrect option.

KEYB has not been installed No alternate keyboard code other than US available (no change needed if you are using a US keyboard).

Label not found A batch file contains a GOTO command, but the label name does not exist.

Last backup disk not inserted Insert last backup disk in drive *X:* Strike any key when ready Prompts for the last backup disk.

*****Last file not backed up***** Backup of last file failed because of lack of disk space or file error.

List output is not assigned to a device PRINT has prompted for a printer device name, but the device does not exist.

Lock violation reading/writing drive *X:* A requested file used on a network is already in use by another program.

***X* lost allocation units found in y chains Convert lost chains to files (Y/N)?** Message from CHKDSK when fragments of files are found. These can be converted into files if CHKDSK/F has been used and the Y answer is used.

Logging to file *X* BACKUP is writing a backup log file on the specified drive.

Logical DOS drive created, drive letters changed or added Addition or revision of logical drive letters.

LPT*x:* not rerouted MODE used, but cannot reroute parallel printer output; check for incorrect options in MODE.

LPT*x:* rerouted to COM*x:* Parallel printer output sent to serial port.

LPT*x:* set for 80/132 Parallel printer port set for 80 or 132-column output.

Maximum number of logical DOS drives installed No more logical drives can be created (see LASTDRIVE).

Memory allocation error. Cannot load MS-DOS, system halted. Try to restart. If this persists, boot from a floppy or a different copy of MS-DOS.

Missing parameter Need version number or /delete option.

Mode *fff* code page function complete MODE has correctly terminated.

—More— Press any key (preferably spacebar) to see more of a text file.

MORE: Incorrect DOS version The MORE command does not run on old DOS versions.

Must enter both /T and /N parameters FORMAT has been used with one option without including the other.

Must specify COM1..COM4 Serial port number must be entered.

Must specify ON or OFF Command requires ON or OFF argument.

Name of list device [PRN]: PRINT is being used without the /d option - the default is PRN, but you can type LPT1, a serial printer would use another name such as AUX or COM1.

NLSFUNC already installed NLSFUNC remains in memory after being invoked, and it cannot be re-invoked until you re-boot.

No code page has been selected No code pages exist, use CHCP if needed.

No drive specified DEVICE line in CONFIG.SYS lacks drive number.

No extended DOS partition to delete FDISK in use, wrong option selected.

No fixed disks present Fixed disk not installed, not connected, controller faulty.

No free file handles. Cannot start COMMAND.COM, exiting. Increase the FILES= number in CONFIG.SYS and try again.

No logical DOS Drive(s) to delete Partition information, no DOS drives present.

No logical drives defined No drive letters allocated in your system.

No paper error writing device *XXX* Printer out of paper or off-line.

No partitions to delete FDISK options incorrect.

No partitions to make active Incorrect use of FDISK.

No path Response to PATH command when no paths have been specified.

No primary DOS partition to delete FDISK being used to delete a primary DOS partition which does not exist.

No room for system on destination disk Trying to transfer system files to a disk with no available space - better to reformat using FORMAT/S.

No source drive specified A source for copy or backup files must be given.

No space left on device Target disk for BACKUP or RESTORE is full, may have to delete some files.

No space to create a DOS partition The hard disk has not enough space for a DOS partition because the other partition is too large. Use FDISK to re-organise the partition allocations.

No space to create logical drive There is no further space on the hard drive for another logical drive to be allocated.

No sub-directories exist The /S option has been used, but the directory does not contain any sub-directories.

No such file or directory You have typed a file or directory name that does not exist.

No system on default drive A system disk must be put into the drive.

No target drive specified BACKUP requires a drive to be nominated.

Non-DOS disk error reading/writing drive *X*: The disk format is incorrect. If CHKDSK/F does not help, re-format the disk (destroying the files). If the disk is from another type of machine there are utilities (such as the shareware ANADISK) which can allow a PC to read text files from it.

Non-system disk or disk error Replace and strike any key when ready Put a system disk onto the drive and press any key.

*****Not able to back up (or restore) file***** Error in source or target disk - use CHKDSK/F on source disk and try again.

Not enough memory Command cannot be run, insufficient space in conventional memory.

Not ready error reading/writing drive *X*: Disk drive door open or printer offline.

One or more CON code pages invalid for given keyboard code KEYB has found an incompatible console (screen) code page. Not necessarily a problem.

Only non-bootable partitions exist Remaining hard disk partitions cannot contain MS-DOS system tracks.

Only partitions on drive 1 can be made active FDISK is being used to create an extra active partition.

Out of environment space No more SET commands can be used because of memory restrictions. Use /E with COMMAND to create more space, or edit out excessive SET commands.

Parameter value not in allowed range Check for correct syntax.

Parameter value not allowed Check for correct syntax.

Parameters not compatible Selected options cannot be used together.

Parameters not compatible with fixed disk An option has been chosen that applies to floppy disks only.

Parameters not supported MS-DOS does not allow these parameters to be used.

Parameters not supported by drive A FORMAT message when the drive type conflicts with formatting requirements.

Partition selected (*x*) is not bootable, active partition not changed FDISK being used to change partitions, but chosen partition cannot be used to boot MS-DOS.

Parse error *xx* Command line error, and COMMAND.COM not available for more detailed error message.

Path name too long Path name must be of less than 63 characters.

Path not found Invalid path name typed.

***X* percent of disk formatted** Information from FORMAT.

Press any key to begin copying file(s) Message from XCOPY to allow for changing floppy disks during a backup.

Press any key to begin formatting FORMAT message, giving you time for second thoughts.

Press any key to continue Prompt issued at a pause.

Press any key when ready.. Prompt intended to provide time to change disks during DISKCOMP or DISKCOPY.

Previously prepared code page replaced MODE has been used to replace one code page by another.

Primary DOS partition already exists FDISK cannot create a primary DOS partition if one has already been created - create an extended DOS partition if there is room.

Primary DOS partition created Message from FDISK indicating success.

Primary DOS partition deleted Message from FDISK indicating deletion.

Printbox ID not in GRAPHICS profile You need to use /PRINTBOX:ID option of GRAPHICS to match PRINTBOX in GRAPHICS.PRO file.

Printer error Printer off, off line, out of paper etc.

Printer lines per inch set MODE has set printer parameters of lines per inch.

PRINT queue is empty No files awaiting printing.

PRINT queue is full No more files can be added, limit of 10 files exists. Use /q option to increase maximum to limit of 32.

Printer type not in GRAPHICS profile Printer not supported by MS-DOS GRAPHICS command.

Probable non-DOS disk Continue (Y/N)? Disk may have been created by another version of MS-DOS or a different type of DOS. Disk probably unusable, though the shareware utility ANADISK can read text files prepared on other machines.

Processing cannot continue CHKDSK is being used, but there is not enough memory to continue.

Profile statement out of sequence on line *x* Indicates where correction of profile statement should be made.

Program too big to fit in memory Delete memory-resident programs (might have to alter AUTOEXEC.BAT) and try again after rebooting.

RAMDrive: Bad extended memory manager control chain Problems with memory management, due to a line in CONFIG.SYS ahead of RAMDRIVE.SYS. Try removing device drivers that are not concerned with HIMEM.

RAMDrive: Error in extended memory allocation Use diagnostic software to determine source of allocation problem.

RAMDrive: Expanded memory manager not present Using /A in RAMDrive requires a line in CONFIG.SYS to install an expanded memory driver, and this line must be ahead of the RAMDRIVE.SYS line.

RAMDrive: Expanded memory Status shows error Problems with expanded memory board or driver.

RAMDrive: Extended Memory Manager not present No HIMEM.SYS line in CONFIG.SYS (ahead of RAMDRIVE.SYS line).

RAMDrive: Incorrect DOS version RAMDRIVE.SYS could not be installed because the DOS version is earlier than 3.0

RAMDrive: Invalid parameter Incorrect RAMDRIVE.SYS line in CONFIG.SYS.

RAMDrive: I/O error accessing drive memory Fault in the memory on which RAMDrive is being installed.

RAMDrive: No extended memory available No extended memory free - not present, or being used in some other way such as Shadow RAM.

RATE and DELAY must be specified together RATE=*X* DELAY=*X* You have used MODE to alter keyboard rate or delay; both must be specified.

Read error, COUNTRY.SYS The COUNTRY.SYS file cannot be read. File may be corrupted (try another copy).

Read error in *filename* The file could not be completely read due to error - try a backup copy.

Read error, KEYBOARD.SYS File unreadable, replace with backup copy.

Read fault error reading drive *X*: Device, usually floppy drive, cannot be read - remove and replace disk and try again.

Reading source file(s) XCOPY message to show that copying has started.

Re-insert diskette for drive *X*: FORMAT message to re-insert disk.

Replace the file (Y/N)? A file being restored from a backup disk already exists on the hard disk. Press Y to overwrite, N to skip this replacement.

Requested logical drive size exceeds the maximum available space You are trying to create a drive size that is impossible - like making a 24 Mbyte partition in a disk with only 10 Mbyte remaining.

Requested partition size exceeds the maximum available space You are using FDISK to create a partition that is larger than the space available on the disk.

Requested screen shift out of range The display cannot be shifted any further to left or right.

Required font not loaded Check the DISPLAY.SYS line - the number for subfonts may be too small.

Required parameter missing The command is not complete because a parameter such as a filename was not supplied.

Required profile statement missing before line *X* A profile statement is needed, and should be placed before the numbered line.

Resident part of PRINT installed The PRINT command has been activated, and is taking up some of the memory ready for use.

Resident portion of MODE loaded The MODE command has been used and is taking up some memory.

Resident portion of NLSFUNC loaded NLSFUNC has been loaded into memory, it cannot be re-loaded.

Resync failed. Files are too different The FC command is comparing files and too many differences have been found - the files are quite different.

Same drive activated more than once FASTOPEN has been reactivated on the same hard disk.

Same parameter entered twice Parameters such as /t, /n, /f, or /v have been entered twice in the same line.

SECOND disk bad or incompatible DISKCOMP has found that the second disk is of a different format.

Sector not found error reading/writing drive *X*: Defective disk - copy all files to another disk and reformat the defective disk.

Sector size too large in file filename A driver in the CONFIG.SYS file is trying to use a sector size larger than that of any other driver.

Seek error reading/writing drive *X*: A file cannot be located on the disk. Disk may be faulty, but check that it is in the drive correctly, then check it in another drive.

SHARE already installed The SHARE command can be used only once in a session.

Sharing violation reading drive *X*: Two programs on a network are trying to use one file. Use (A)bort, or wait and then use (R)etry.

SMARTDrive: Bad extended memory manager control chain Check the CONFIG.SYS file for a device driver ahead of SMARTDRIVE which conflicts with SMARTDRIVE.

SMARTDrive: Error in extended memory allocation Check the use of extended memory, using a memory-check utility.

SMARTDrive:Expanded memory manager not present SMARTDRIVE has been installed using /A but CONFIG.SYS does not contain an expanded memory driver.

SMARTDrive:Extended memory manager not present The CONFIG.SYS file does not contain an extended memory manager ahead of SMARTDRV.SYS

SMARTDrive:Expanded Memory Manager Status shows error Check the action of the expanded memory manager using a utility.

SMARTDrive:I/O error accessing cache memory Error in setting up SMARTDrive; probably no memory available.

SMARTDrive:Incorrect DOS version Cannot be used with DOS earlier than 3.0.

SMARTDrive:Insufficient memory No memory available - check your system.

SMARTDrive:Invalid parameter Incorrect option letter, or an impossible value (too large or too small memory size, for example).

SMARTDrive:No extended memory available No extended memory, or insufficient to install SMARTDrive. Check your use of extended memory (is it being used for Shadow RAM?).

SMARTDrive:No hard drives on system Cannot use SMARTDrive on floppy disk.

SMARTDrive: Too many bytes per track on fixed drive Unknown type of hard disk in use.

SORT:Incorrect DOS version Cannot be used on DOS earlier than 2.0

SORT:Insufficient disk space Disk full, clear out some files.

SORT:Insufficient memory Cannot use SORT until memory cleared (too many resident programs?)

Source and target drives are the same You cannot copy a disk on to itself.

Source disk is Non-removable Copying from a hard disk, not a problem.

SOURCE disk bad or incompatible Disk is in wrong drive (1.2 Mbyte disk in 360 Kbyte drive) or is wrongly formatted.

Specified COMMAND search directory bad An incorrect SHELL line in CONFIG.SYS.

Specified drive does not exist or is non-removable DISKCOMP and DISKCOPY cannot be used with a hard disk, only with floppies.

Specified entry was not found in version table SETVER is being used to delete an entry that did not exist - type SETVER to see the list.

Strike a key when ready Prompt which gives time for disk changes or second thoughts.

Syntax error A command is wrongly spelled or incorrectly used.

Syntax errors in GRAPHICS profile Check command for correct spelling and use.

System files on the specified drive do not support a version table The version of MS-DOS being use is earlier than 5.0.

System transferred A FORMAT/S or SYS command has put the system files on a disk.

Target cannot be used for backup Target disk for copy action has incorrect format or is corrupted. Use CHKDSK/F, or re-format.

Target disk bad or incompatible Target disk for copy action has incorrect format or is corrupted. Use CHKDSK/F, or re-format.

Target disk may be unusable Target disk for copy action has incorrect format or is corrupted. Use CHKDSK/F, or re-format.

Terminate batch job (Y/N)? You have pressed Ctrl-C while a batch file was running. Press Y to end the batch file, N to continue.

The current active keyboard table is *xx* with code page: *yyy* The current active COM code page is *zzz* Information on code page settings.

The last file was not restored Restoration incomplete because of lack of disk space or a bad file.

The only bootable partition on drive 1 is already marked active FDISK cannot change this active partition.

Too many drive entries FASTOPEN is working on four drives already, a fifth cannot be used.

Too many file/directory entries Trying to use more than 999 files or directories.

Too many files open Edit CONFIG.SYS to increase the number in the FILES= line, and try again.

Too many name entries The limit is 999

Too many open files Edit CONFIG.SYS to increase the number in the FILES= line, and try again.

Too many parameters Command has been followed by too many or options. Check the command syntax.

Top level process aborted, cannot continue The (A)bort option was used and the processing cannot continue.

Track 0 bad - disk unusable You are using FORMAT/S, and the disk has damaged sectors near the beginning. Scrap the disk.

Tree past this point not processed CHKDSK cannot continue because of a directory error.

Unable to access Drive *X*: FDISK cannot use the drive. Try again, checking that the interleave factor is correct.

Unable to create directory You used MD (MKDIR) with a name already in use, a reserved name, or on a full disk.

Unable to create KEYB table in resident memory KEYB table requires memory, insufficient available.

Unable to perform refresh operation No copy of code page for PRINTER.SYS. Prepare and select the code page ready for use.

Unable to reload with profile supplied GRAPHICS already loaded, not enough memory for a second set.

Unable to shift Screen MODE SHIFT is being used to test screen alignment and no further shift is possible.

Unable to write BOOT First track of disk is bad - use another disk.

Unexpected DOS error *n* Note the number - the error should be reported to Microsoft.

Unrecognized command in CONFIG.SYS Check the CONFIG.SYS file for an incorrect entry.

Unrecoverable error in directory Convert directory to file (Y/N)? CHKDSK cannot correct an error. Press Y will convert stray pieces into a file which you can examine and possibly use.

Unrecoverable read error on drive *X* side *S* track *T* Data cannot be read after four attempts. Copy all files to another disk and format or scrap faulty disk.

Unrecoverable read/write error on drive *X*: Disk cannot be used - check that disk is correctly inserted.

VERIFY is off/on Current setting of VERIFY command.

Version table is corrupt Error in version table, check with SETVER.

Volume in drive *X*: has no label Reminder only, no action required.

Volume in drive *X:* is *name* Reminder only, no action required.

Volume label (11 characters, ENTER for none)? LABEL command used, or FORMAT/V option. Type a label name, or just press ENTER to ignore.

Volume label does not match You cannot FORMAT a hard disk that has a label name unless you type the correct name (a form of passwording to deter mistakes).

Volume serial number is *n-n* Information only, no action required.

WARNING, ALL DATA ON NON-REMOVABLE DISK DRIVE C: WILL BE LOST! Proceed with format (Y/N)? You are using FORMAT on a hard disk which contains data, risking total loss of data (unless you have the UNFORMAT utility ready).

Warning - directory full The root directory of the hard disk is full and RECOVER cannot be used. This should never be allowed to happen; files will have to be deleted.

Warning! Disk is out of sequence Replace disk or continue if okay Strike any key when ready Disks are being used to RESTORE in wrong order.

Warning! File *filename* is a hidden (or read-only) file Replace the file (Y/N)? A file that is hidden should not normally be replaced, and a read-only file may not need to be replaced.

Warning! File *filename* was changed after it was backed up Replace the file (Y/N)? The version on the backup disk is an older version and you might not want to use it.

WARNING! File X is a read-only file Replace the file (Y/N)? A file is usually marked as read-only because you do not want to replace it.

Warning! Files in the target drive Backup (or root) directory will be erased. BACKUP is being used without /A to append, and there are files already present on the backup disk.

Warning! No files were found to back up BACKUP has been used, but no files have been found.

Warning! No files were found to restore RESTORE has been used, but there are no files on the backup disk.

Warning: Read error in EXE file A program file is not of the expected size - this may or may not cause problems; could indicate a virus.

Warning! The partition marked active is not bootable FDISK has made an active partition without making it bootable; this is forbidden.

Write failure, disk unusable SYS command has found that system tracks cannot be put one a disk. Scrap the disk.

Write fault error writing drive X: Disk or drive problem - check fit of disk in drive.

Write protect error format terminated FORMAT has been attempted on a disk that is write-protected.

Write protect error writing drive *X*: The disk is write-protected and cannot be written until the protection is removed.

Appendix B
ASCII codes in Denary and Hex

No.	Hex	Char	No.	Hex	Char
32	20	(space)	80	50	P
33	21	!	81	51	Q
34	22	“	82	52	R
35	23	#	83	53	S
36	24	$	84	54	T
37	25	%	85	55	U
38	26	&	86	56	V
39	27	‘	87	57	W
40	28	(	88	58	X
41	29	)	89	59	Y
42	2A	*	90	5A	Z
43	2B	+	91	5B	[
44	2C	,	92	5C	\
45	2D	-	93	5D	]
46	2E	.	94	5E	^
47	2F	/	95	5F	_
48	30	0	96	60	‘
49	31	1	97	61	a
50	32	2	98	62	b
51	33	3	99	63	c
52	34	4	100	64	d
53	35	5	101	65	e
54	36	6	102	66	f
55	37	7	103	67	g
56	38	8	104	68	h
57	39	9	105	69	i
58	3A	:	106	6A	j
59	3B	;	107	6B	k
60	3C	<	108	6C	l
61	3D	=	109	6D	m
62	3E	>	110	6E	n
63	3F	?	111	6F	o
64	40	@	112	70	p
65	41	A	113	71	q
66	42	B	114	72	r
67	43	C	115	73	s
68	44	D	116	74	t
69	45	E	117	75	u
70	46	F	118	76	v
71	47	G	119	77	w
72	48	H	120	78	x
73	49	I	121	79	y
74	4A	J	122	7A	z
75	4B	K	123	7B	{
76	4C	L	124	7C	|
77	4D	M	125	7D	}
78	4E	N	126	7E	~
79	4F	O	127	7F	

Appendix C
Using DEBUG

Of the programmer's utilities on the MS-DOS System, the one that you are most likely to need (or least unlikely to need) at times is called DEBUG. In programmer's language, a bug is a fault in a program, debugging is removing bugs, and the cause of the bug is called, of course, a programmer. Using DEBUG definitely requires some knowledge about the machine and how it is designed, which is why it isn't a utility that you can use as you would use DIR, COPY or DEL. When DEBUG is loaded and run, it loads into the machine, using the lowest part of memory that is available.

- DEBUG is not intended for the ordinary PC user but for the programmer with a knowledge of the internal design of the machine and the machine-code of its processor. This summary is provided as a reminder for someone with suitable experience whose use of DEBUG is not so frequent that the commands are easily remembered.
- DEBUG was written in the days when a large-capacity floppy meant a 360 Kbyte disk, so that its disk operations rely on reading data into memory and writing it out again. This is by no means easy if you want to change the contents of a complete 1.4 Mbyte disk, and the only practicable method is to deal with the disk in manageable chunks.

The memory of the PC type of machine is specified in the form of two numbers which are combined to make an address number, and each address number that can be formed in this way corresponds to an address at which one byte will be stored. Since the PC is a 16-bit machine, many of the commands make use of two bytes at a time, and the address numbers are changed in twos.

The standard form of address is written in the form:

```
2F65:0100
```

using hexadecimal (hex) notation. The address consists of two numbers, the first of which, 2F65 in this example is stored in a Code Segment (CS) register of the microprocessor, while the other is stored in the Instruction Pointer (IP) register. Many references to memory make use of the address numbers in this form, but the true address has to be calculated from this. The method is to add a zero to the end of the first number and then add the second, remembering that this is hexadecimal addition:

```
 2F650
  0100
 -----
 2F750
```

- so making the actual address 2F750H, where the H is a reminder that this is a hex number. This number corresponds to the denary number 194,384.

This is fairly typical of the address number range that you will find when DEBUG has been loaded into an old XT machine. The memory starts at address zero, but it has been filled, as the machine started up, with the hidden files, part of COMMAND.COM, any SYS files that are used in CONFIG.SYS, and to this we have added DEBUG, so that it is hardly surprising that some 194,384 bytes have been used up out of the total, in a 640K machine, of 655360 bytes.

Note that this address could just as easily have been specified as:

2F75:0000 or as 2000:F750

because this would give the same final result. The reason that the figure 0100 so often occurs is that all COM programs start with 0100 as the value in the IP register. The way that the designers of the microprocessor interpreted these numbers was to use the CS number (the first one) to contain a number which is the number of 64K segments (memory blocks), followed by zeros. If this first number were 3000, for example, this would mean segment 3, if it were F0000 this would mean segment F (16 in normal numbering). By convention, a COM type of file starts at a number which is 0100 (hex) bites into a segment, so that a COM program located in segment 3 would start at address 30100. The EXE type of file can start at any number, because it is constructed in a way that allows the file to be relocated as it is being read into memory.

The reason for using this type of reference to memory is that it allows a 20-bit number (of five hex digits) to be stored in two 16-bit registers. For use with extended memory, the same two registers can be used to store a 32-bit number, and the differences in use are one reason for treating extended memory in a way that differs from conventional (20-bit) memory. The snag is that when a program like DEBUG is used, it will split a memory address number up rather arbitrarily, so that the start of the program that is loaded following DEBUG has 0100 as its second number of the pair. You will quite often find that this has been done, and it tends to conceal the true segment number from you. This, however, does not prevent you from using DEBUG to get to any part of the memory that you choose.

For many purposes, however, there is no need to specify addresses in this split number way, because you will very often only be working with addresses in one single segment, a relative address, so that the address that is of interest will be the second number, the number in the IP register. This is particularly true when you are using DEBUG, as you normally are, to sort out some feature of a file.

When you load DEBUG, you can specify also that the file that you want to work on will be loaded with it. For example, you can type DEBUG b:rped.exe so as to load in DEBUG, and also load in the program RPED for DEBUG to work on. You would do this only if you were a programmer wanting to check or alter some part of the RPED program, and if you are not a programmer it's more likely that you will not want to load in a file along with DEBUG, or if you do, it will be a modified text or other unusual ASCII file. There would be no point in using DEBUG to work on an ordinary text file, because any editor could do that, but if you wanted to alter a character in a text file to be a control character, for example, DEBUG is ideal. Working on program files definitely requires knowledge of the program, even if you are only going to alter a message on the screen to indicate that the program is your own property.

You may have found, however, advice in a magazine which shows you how to improve the action of a program by modifying part of the file, and you can use DEBUG to carry out this modification, and then save the modified version back to the disk (but only if you have another backup copy of the original). If, as is also likely, you want to use DEBUG only for investigating the contents of the memory of the PC, then all you need do is type DEBUG and press the ENTER key in the usual way.

Using DEBUG

NOTE: Where a number that is shown stored in the memory is composed of several bytes, these bytes are stored in reverse order. The number 2B7F, for example, would be stored in the order 7F 2B, because this is more convenient for the microprocessor to work with (in an addition, for example, the lower bytes are added first so that any carry can be added to higher bytes).

Once DEBUG is up and running, all you see to remind you is a 'prompt' that consists of a hyphen, -. When you see this reminder, you can give a command to DEBUG, consisting of a single letter (upper-case or lower-case) followed by pressing the ENTER key.

The letter commands that can be used are listed here.

A write in a simplified assembler language.
C compare two blocks of memory for mismatch.
D Dump memory. Show contents of 128 addresses in sequence.
E enter codes into memory directly.
F fill a block of memory with one byte repeated.
G execute a program at stated address. Breakpoints can be set at which the execution will stop.
H shows sum and difference of two hex numbers.
I input one byte from a specified port.
L Load, will load the file whose name has been typed in, see N. The filename can be specified when DEBUG is entered. Another form of Load will load specified sectors directly from the disk
M move a block of data to a new starting address.
N Name, specifies the name of a file to be loaded or saved. The full name, including extension, must be used. This allows a filename to be changed if necessary.
O output a byte from a specified port.
Q leave (quit) debug, return to MS-DOS.
R show the contents of the CPU registers.
S Search for a pattern of numbers of characters.
T trace instructions one at a time, showing the register contents at each step. The number of instructions per step can be altered.
U unassemble code, converting hex code into assembler language instructions (whether these make sense or not).
W write a named (with N) file (not a HEX or EXE file).

Memory Dump

From this list, you will see that the command that is most likely to be immediately useful is D, the memory dump command. A memory dump is a listing of each address in memory with the value of the code number that is stored in that byte. Obviously, a listing of the whole memory in this way would be impossibly large, because even the PC-XT can use over a million memory addresses, though only 655360 are available to be used for programs in conventional memory on the XT, and this allocation includes all of the system files. After a dump has been displayed, you can display another, or use any of the other commands, including Q to leave DEBUG.

The dump command therefore displays in pages, consisting of 128 bytes of data at a time. The big problem is how to find what you are looking for. If you have loaded DEBUG along with a file, the second number of the two used to set an address will be set so that it corresponds to the start of the file. For a file with a .COM extension, for example, the second address number will normally be 0100, which in hex does not mean one hundred but 256. If you have loaded DEBUG on its own, the number also starts off at 0100, and to read any data in the memory, you either have to reset it, or use D and keep pressing keys (any key) to display another 128 byte section until you get to whatever you want.

In the following example, DEBUG has been loaded and followed by a simple batch file, rather than a program file, so that it is easier to see the form of the display, Figure C.1.

Note the high value of the CS register number, the first half of the address that indicates the start of each line. This is because DEBUG and the batch file were loaded in following the word-processor which was being used to write this chapter. The other commands were DEBUG C:\WS.BAT >DB1.DOC (so that the results of DEBUG were dumped to a file that WordStar could then read), and when this had loaded, D for Dump and the Q for Quit.No prompt is visible when the file is being redirected in this way, and the letters D and Q are not visible either, so you need to know what you are doing if you use DEBUG in this fashion.

In this example, using D again will dump the next 256 bytes of data, but you might want to dump an entirely different part of the memory. This is done by specifying the address in the D command in more detail. If you are working in the same segment (first address number unchanged) you can use, for example, D 0150. If you want to move to an entirely different part of the memory, you can use D with an two-part address, such as D 2000:0100 .

The listing shows the second address number set to the conventional 0100, and the next 16 columns display

Figure C.1
A typical display from DEBUG using the D command. Note that you can also get this display by using the F9 key from DOSSHELL.

```
-d
7861:0100 65 63 68 6F 20 6F 66 66 - 0D 0A 63 64 20 63 3A 5C echo off..cd c:\
7861:0110 77 73 74 61 72 0D 0A 77 - 73 0D 0A 65 63 68 6F 20 wstar..ws..echo
7861:0120 57 61 6E 74 20 74 6F 20 - 73 61 76 65 20 74 65 78 Want to save tex
7861:0130 74 20 74 6F 20 41 3A 20 - 3F 0D 0A 79 6E 0D 0A 69 t to A: ?..yn..i
7861:0140 66 20 65 72 72 6F 72 6C - 65 76 65 6C 20 31 20 67 f errorlevel 1 g
7861:0150 6F 74 6F 20 67 65 74 6F - 75 74 0D 0A 63 6F 70 79 oto getout..copy
7861:0160 20 2A 2E 74 78 74 20 61 - 3A 0D 0A 3A 67 65 74 6F  *.txt a:..:geto
7861:0170 75 74 0D 0A 63 64 20 63 - 3A 5C 0D 0A 64 69 72 20 ut..cd c:\.dir
-q
```

the bytes of the file, with the hyphen separating sets of eight. The ASCII codes for these bytes are shown in the right hand side of the file, but only where the ASCII code is between 32 and 127 inclusive. The hex codes 0A and 0D are the line feed and carriage return, respectively. Not shown here is the end of file byte, which is 1A, denary 26, the Ctrl-Z character.

Position in memory

Whether DEBUG is operating on a file that has been left at the bottom end of the memory because of a problem with some other program, or is working on a file that was loaded along with DEBUG, the DEBUG program will normally be automatically loaded into the lowest part of the memory that is free. This is what makes DEBUG so very convenient as a rescue program. If, for example, your word-processor crashes so that the DOS prompt re-appears on the screen, any attempt to reload the word processor to recover text will wipe the text out of the memory. If you load DEBUG, however, it will invariably take much less space than a word-processor, and it can be used to search through the memory until the text is found, then it can be used to save a file of the text, specifying the addresses of the start and the end of the text.

If a file is specified to be loaded along with DEBUG, the file is then loaded into the next available part of memory above DEBUG. This is normal for MS-DOS, which can arrange for programs to load in where they can run, but allowing other programs also to load and run.

Either way, the data that you are working on will be in the memory addresses that it normally occupies. This allows us to do things like altering the codes in the memory, and saving the altered copy. This is one way of making a 'custom' copy of a program for our own purposes, but it is definitely not for the beginner or the user who feels that backing-up disks is a waste of time. You must never attempt any of these actions on any file or disk for which you do not have an adequate backup, preferably two backup copies.

Apart from the risk of losing a disk-full of data, there's nothing to prevent you from experimenting. It can't damage the computer, and if you lose a disk for which you have a couple of back-ups, then all you have really lost is time. On the other hand, you may very well have achieved something very useful that allows you to obtain considerably more from the computer in the future.

A Printer file

This example illustrates DEBUG being used to produce a file that when printed using PRINT or TYPE (with CTRL-P), will set an Epson RX or FX printer into bold face. This is done by sending the ASCII codes 27 and 69 (code for letter E) to the printer, in that sequence. At first sight this looks very simple, and all you have to do is create a file with these characters. The problem is that, as we have seen, very few file editors will allow you to enter the ASCII Esc code which is 27. The solution is to enter some dummy value, and then use DEBUG to change the file.

Start by calling up your text editor, specify a new file and name it BOLPRT, then make a file that consists only of a space and the letter E, whose ASCII code is 69. Now proceed as follows:

1. Enter DEBUG, using your filename. For example, use DEBUG b:BOLPRN if the printer file is on drive B.
2. Type d (ENTER) to see the file displayed. It should read: 20 45 0D 0A 1A 20 .. - with the rest of the file giving the 20 character code, which is the space.
3. The character 45 is E in ASCII code. This is 45 and not 69, because DEBUG always uses hexadecimal codes.
4. Type e100 (ENTER). You will now see the number 20 displayed with a dot following it.
5. Type 1B and press the spacebar. This has the effect of changing the 20 number to 1B, the Esc code. Now press ENTER.
6. Press d100 (ENTER) to check that the change has been made.
7. Type w (ENTER). This will return the file to the disk in its altered form, using the same filename.
8. Type q (ENTER). This gets you out of DEBUG and back to the normal DOS prompt.

If you have an Epson printer on line, you can now test the BOLPRT file. Switch the printer on, and select a short file, such as a batch file like AUTOEXEC.BAT. Type:

```
TYPE AUTOEXEC.BAT
```

- press CTRL-P, and then (ENTER). The printer should print out the file in ordinary type. Press CTRL-P again. Now type:

```
TYPE BOLPRT
```

- press CTRL-P, and then (ENTER). The printer will

take a new line, but probably won't print anything. Press CTRL-P again, and try printing the AUTOEXEC.BAT file again. This time it should be in bold type, indicating that your BOLPRT file did as it was supposed to.

Your printer manual will show details of all the codes that alter printer behaviour. Many of these will start with the Esc character, which is 1B in hex. code, so that you can write a string of codes in this way to set up whatever you want. The general method that has been illustrated here will work just as well for any sequence of codes. You create a file with an editor, and use a space or an unusual character (such as ~) for any character that you cannot enter, such as Esc. By using DEBUG with this file, you can then substitute these characters, and save the amended file. This file can then be printed as part of an AUTOEXEC.BAT sequence if you want your printer always set in this way, using the TYPE command in the AUTOEXEC.BAT file.

Floppy Disk Diagnosis

One particularly useful feature of DEBUG allows sectors of data stored on a disk to be loaded into the memory of the computer. This is one way in which data from a disk that has been damaged can be recovered, and it is the basis of the way in which a deleted file can be replaced. The problems of recovering a corrupted program file need very considerable knowledge of the system and of the program, but we can look in outline at how to recover deleted text files (ASCII files).

The trouble with this command, a variety of the Load command, is that it is never easy to work with, certainly not so easy as the disk utility programs that are sold specifically for the purpose. If you are concerned with the recovery of files from a hard disk, then a utility specifically designed for the purpose will be easier to use, though DEBUG can often prove to be more effective, given sufficient time. What follows, then, is a very brief description which is intended to be the basis for experiment rather than a do-it-yourself guide to any kind of file recovery from a damaged disk or deleted file.

To start with, the sectors on a 360 Kbyte disk are numbered starting with 0 and going up to 719. In hex, this latter number is 02CF. The number is not quite so straightforward as you might think, however, because of the way that the double-sided disks are used. Sector 0 is on the first side of the disk, and is the first sector of the first track. There are 9 sectors on each track, so that the numbering of sectors goes from 0 through 1, 2, 3..up to sector 8, which is the last sector (since we started at 0) on Track 0, first side.

The count then continues, but sector 9 is the first sector of Track 0 on the other side of the disk, and in this track we find sectors 9 to 17. Sectors 18 to 26 are on Track 1 on the first side, and sectors 27 to 35 on Track 1 of the second side and so on. The loading direct from sectors depends on making use of these numbers, but in the hex scale. The best way to experiment is on a copy of a disk that has been formatted with no System tracks, and has been used only for text.

The L command of DEBUG, when it is used for loading disk sectors, requires four numbers following it, all in hex. The first number is a starting number in memory, and a good choice is the usual 0100. The next number is 0 for Drive A, 1 for drive B, 3 for drive C or 4 for drive D. The third number is a starting sector number. DEBUG numbers sectors starting with the first sector of track zero, side 1, and the count moves to track 0 side 2, then back to track 1 side 0 and so on. For a disk of text, a good choice is 0C, because this is sector 12, the first one that is likely to be used. Sectors up to this are kept clear in case you want to add the system tracks. The fourth number is the number of sectors that you want to read. You can try 10 which is sixteen sectors (10 hex is 16 in normal numbering).

With DEBUG running, type:

```
L 100 0 C 10 (ENTER)
```

- and the disk will spin briefly, leaving you with the DEBUG prompt again.

Now type:

```
D 100 (ENTER)
```

- and you will see the start of the text on the disk.

You can now alter the text, using E as in the example earlier. For a text disk, this is hardly worthwhile, because you could do the same with less hassle by using an editor. The point, however, is to show that DEBUG can deal with anything, and that includes items that text editors cannot deal with, like the Esc character, and files that are on a disk and which might be corrupted.

The file can be put back on the disk in its altered form by using the W command. If, for example, you use DEBUG to replace one character in a file with the number 1AH, which is the end-of-file marker, the file can from then on only be read as far as this point. If a file cannot be read correctly by a text editor, it may be that some disk corruption has placed the 1A character on the disk at an unwanted point, and that you could find it and remove it.

■ You can remove SENTRY and other non-deletable files from a floppy by using L 100 0 0 0, followed by F 100 2FFF 0 and W 100 0 0 0. This places a set of zeros into the start of the disk, wiping the codes that specify that the data cannot be erased by a FORMAT. Follow this by a Format A: /U. Make sure that you are working on the floppy and not on your hard disk.

Register inspection

Register inspection with DEBUG makes use of the R command when DEBUG is working with a file loaded, or with its address changed to some part of the memory. The command is useful only if you have some experience of assembly language programming so that you know what the registers ought to be showing. The display is of the form:

```
-r
AX=0000 BX=0000 CX=5C3C DX=0000 SP=FFFE BP=0000 SI=0000 DI=0000
DS=787A ES=787A SS=787A CS=787A IP=0100  NV UP EI PL NZ NA PO NC
787A:0100 E9DD0B          JMP0CE0
-q
```

- which shows the content of each register at the address which is given at the start of the third line. Note that this address corresponds, as it ought to, with the contents of the CS and IP registers. This is a COM type of file which is being debugged, so that the starting address with 0100 in the IP register is genuine. The SP register shows the stack pointer at FFFE, the normal starting position before a program starts. There is a word of data in the CX register, but none in any of the other general-purpose registers, AX, BX and DX. The two index registers SI and DI are set to zero, as also is the base pointer BP.

The flag line shows the state of the flags which report the results of the action. Eight of nine flags are shown here, using two-letter codes to indicate the settings. The meanings of all possible two-letter reports (two for each flag) are:

OV Overflow occurred
NV No overflow
DN Direction down (decrement)
UP Direction up (increment)
EI Enable interrupt
DI Disable interrupt
NG result negative
PL result positive
ZR Result zero
NZ Result not zero
AC Auxiliary carry made
NA No auxiliary carry
PE Parity even
PO Parity odd
CY Carry took place
NC No carry

In the example, there is no overflow, and the direction flag shows UP (it usually does, and its setting is not used in any tests). The direction flag is used in connection with the index registers to show whether the register is being incremented (UP) or decremented (DN). Interrupts are enabled, and the command that has just been executed left a positive result, not zero. There was no auxiliary carry, parity is odd, and no carry was generated.

The left hand side of the last line in the register display shows the instruction that has been read from memory starting at the current address. This shows that at the address 787A:0100 the command in hex code was E9DD0B, a three-byte command, meaning JMP 0CE0. This assumes, as it always does, that the codes are genuine command codes and not simply stored data, because there is no simple way of distinguishing between the two if they are mixed up together.

The address 0CE0 is obtained by adding the address to which the program would normally go next (0103) to the displacement number shown in the JMP command (0BDD, written in reverse order as DD0B), because

0103 + 0BDD = 0CE0.

The alternative use of the R command is in modifying a register.

Example: R AX 0300

-will place the word 0300 into the AX register. To see that this has been carried out, you need to make use of R by itself again. Modification of registers can be used to change the IP number so as to look at another address. In the previous example, the jump to 0CE0 can be followed by using:

R IP 0CE0

-which will change the content of IP to this address and allow whatever is stored at this address to be viewed by using R or D.

Searching through memory

The S command allows the memory to be searched for a specified byte or group of bytes or for a string of characters. If the search is for a byte, then that byte can be specified in hex; for a group of bytes, the bytes are separated by spaces. When a string is to be searched for, it can be specified as character rather than as ASCII codes, such as 'BAT'.

A search will be made specifying a start address and an ending address, because it would be time-wasting to search all the way through memory. The addresses can be specified in three ways, following a pattern similar to the D command:

1. As an address in the current segment like CS:1CE4 (or just 1CE4)

2. As a complete address like 3000:1050

3. For the second number only, as a length like L200 - the length number uses the letter L to distinguish it from an address, and the number of bytes that follows the L is in hex.

Example: D F000:C0000 L60 'plc'

- will give the result F000:C033 which will be the address of this message, the start of the Resident Operating System (ROS) of the Amstrad PC, and a dump of this part of the memory shows that the search action was correct, Figure C.2.

An alternative would have been to type the search command as:

S F000:C000 C07F 70 6C 63

-using the absolute address for the first address, a relative address (IP register number) for the second, and the ASCII codes in hex for the required bytes. For searching through machine-code program files in which a set of instruction codes rather than a recognisable name is wanted, this second form is better, and can be used with all of the usual address methods, or with L marking the number of bytes which are to be searched.

Figure C.2
Dump from the start of the Resident Operating System of the Amstrad PC.

```
-d f000:c000
F000:C000 E9 D7 00 28 43 29 20 43 -6F 70 79 72 69 67 68 74 . . . ( C)  Copyr i ght
F000:C010 20 31 39 38 36 20 41 6D -73 74 72 61 64 20 43 6F 1986  Amstr ad  Co
F000:C020 6E 73 75 6D 65 72 20 45 -6C 65 63 74 72 6F 6E 69 nsumer  El ect r oni
F000:C030 63 73 20 70 6C 63 28 28 -43 43 29 29 20 20 43 43 cs  pl c( ( CC))   CC
F000:C040 6F 6F 70 70 79 79 72 72 -69 69 67 67 68 68 74 74 ooppyyr r i i gghht t
F000:C050 20 20 31 31 39 39 38 38 -36 36 20 20 41 41 6D 6D    11998866  AAmm
F000:C060 73 73 74 74 72 72 61 61 -64 64 20 20 43 43 6F 6F sst t r r aadd  CC oo
F000:C070 6E 6E 73 73 75 75 6D 6D -65 65 72 72 20 20 45 45 nnssuummeer r EE
-q
```

Example:

```
DEBUG COMMAND.COM
-S CS:0100 9000 A8 01 B0 01 74 02 B0 05
```

-will find where this set of bytes is stored in COMMAND.COM. Then by changing the B0 01 to B0 02, the DIR display of the computer is changed to double-column (and DIR/W to four column).

If you specify only a few bytes in a search, there is a chance that the combination will occur several times. If this happens, DEBUG will print a list of addresses, and you may want to redirect this list to a file or to the printer in order to make reference to it later.

The C command exists so that two blocks of memory can be compared, byte by byte, and any differences noted. The form of the display is to show only where differences exist, in the form of first address, byte, second byte, second address. The C command is followed by the starting address of the first memory block, then the number of bytes (using L to indicate length), then the starting address for the second block of memory. As usual, if the full address is not given, the number is assumed to be in the current segment.

Example: C 0200 L20 0300

-will compare 20H bytes (32 bytes) starting at 0200 in the current segment with the 20H bytes starting at address 0300 in the same segment. If these bytes were identical except for the corresponding addresses 021A and 031A, then the display would be:

```
2F65:021A 1A 3C 2F65:031A
```

-with the code segment being 2F65 in this example.

Changing Memory

While DEBUG is working on any part of the memory, including a program file stored in the memory, it can use the codes E and F to alter memory contents. The E command means enter into memory, and has to be followed by an address number of a point where you want to start making alterations. As usual, this address can be given in the forms:

0115	- a position in the current segment
CS:0115	- also in current segment
3000:0115	- the full address

and when the ENTER key is used, you will be shown the (full) address followed by the byte which is stored at that address and a full-stop, which is the entry prompt. You can then either:

- enter a new byte, as two hex characters, or
- press the space-bar to leave the byte unchanged.

and you will then see the next existing byte appear. Do not press ENTER, as this terminates the action. If you have altered a byte, you will see that byte, the full-stop and your alteration, followed by the next byte in the sequence.To edit an incorrect entry (before pressing ENTER), press the hyphen key. To end the entry of data, press ENTER without entering any data. The example is illustrated with a batch file for simplicity, but the E command would always be used for altering program files.

Example: DEBUG WS.BAT

```
-e 0100
6AF1:0100 65.68 63.64 68.
-q
```

- which has changed the start of the file, the word echo to hdho. The important point is that changes could just as easily be made to the file COMMAND.COM (try the wide-directory modification as outlined in the S command) or to any other file that you use. Never attempt such changes unless you have a backup of the file on another disk.

The F command will fill an area of memory with a byte or set of bytes, and the byte that is used is generally 00, since this is a way of indicating that the memory is cleared. Though the command does not have many uses, it is indispensable for the task it does, since no-one would want to use the E command to enter 8K of zeros into a block of memory. The fill character need not be a single byte, however, but can be a set such as 'ABCDEFGH', distinguished by the use of the single (or double) quote character at each end of the string. The start and stop addresses, or a start address and a length, must be specified, followed by the byte or string.

Example: F 0100 2FFF 0

-will fill from 0100 to 2FFF in the current segment with the byte 0.

Example: F 0000 L 500 'ABCD'

-will fill memory in the current segment from 0000, for 500H bytes (1280 bytes) with the repeating string ABCD.

The M command copies a set of bytes from one part of the memory to another, and can be used to make a copy in RAM of data that is normally held in the ROM. The starting address of the data and its ending address or length must be specified, followed by the starting address of the part of memory where the data is to be copied. As usual, if only a single address number is given, the current segment is assumed, but addresses can also be shown in full, either as numbers or in the form register:number. For example, if the ES register stores the number 3000H, then an address of ES:0100 is equivalent to an address of 3000:0100.

Example: M 0100 L4F 1FC4

- will move 4F bytes (79 bytes) starting at 0100 in the current segment to an address starting at 1FC4 in the same segment.

Example: M 2000:0100 L1000 ES:0100

- will move 1000H bytes (4096 bytes) starting at address 2000:0100 and shift them to an address ES:0100, whose exact value depends on whatever number is stored in the ES register at the time.

Inputs and outputs

The specialised uses of the L command for loading disk sectors, and W for writing the sectors back to disk have already been noted. These forms of the commands are used for inspecting disk contents as distinct from file contents, so that the inputs and outputs referred to here are for files and ports. Very often, the only way that you will need to get a file inspected by DEBUG is by typing the name of the file following the DEBUG name. The alternative is to enter DEBUG, and then use the Name command to enter a name for loading or saving. You can, of course, load a file under one name and the alter the name before saving again.

The N command is used only for naming a file and it has no visible effect. Once it has been used, however, the load and save commands will make use of that filename but with an important exception. Though you can read a file whose extension is .HEX or .EXE, you are not permitted to write a file with these extension names. If you need to read such a file, alter it and write it back, then you will have to change the name by using the normal REN command of MS-DOS before and after using DEBUG (an extension such as .BIT can be used).

The N command can be used after a file has been loaded in order to name any other files that will be loaded when that file is run. If, to take an example, you have a program RESTFILE.COM which can read and modify another file MYTXT.TXT, then you can load in DEBUG, load in the file RESTFILE.COM and then use N to name the file MYTXT.TXT. If the RESTFILE program is then run using DEBUG to inspect what happens during running (see later), then it will load MYTXT.TXT when it comes to the appropriate stage. The form of the N command is simply the letter followed by a space and then the name. The extension letters for the file must be included, unless there is no extension.
Example: N spoolit.com
- sets up the filename in the memory ready for loading or saving actions.

The L command will load a file whose name has been established using the N command. Precisely where in the memory the file is loaded depends on the type of the file, and for some types of file there will be a choice of address. If the file extension is COM, then the file will be loaded so that the first instruction in the file will be placed at the relative address of 0100 hex, with the segment address placed in the CS register in the usual way. The BX and CX registers are used to hold the number of bytes that have actually been loaded into memory.

This will be equal to file length for a COM type of file, with the BX register holding the fifth hex digit for a long file. For the EXE type of file, the starting address will have been held as part of the file and will not normally be 0100. In addition, the number of bytes that have been loaded (in the BX:CX registers) will be less than the file length. This is because the file holds data about how to make alterations in order that the file can be located starting at any specified memory location, and these relocation bytes need not be kept when the file has been loaded.

When the file is a text file, or any file which is not of the COM or EXE type (or the HEX type, an intermediate between assembly language and COM or EXE), you can use the L command along with an address (full or relative) to force the file to be stored starting at this address. The BX and CX registers will be set to show the length of the file, and the segment that is used will be the segment that corresponds to an address 100H bytes before the start of the file (following the same convention about COM and EXE files starting at 0100H). Remember that if you have loaded a file to some address other than CS:0100 that the D command will still display the bytes starting at CS:0100 unless you specify otherwise.

Example: N MYFIL.COM

L

-will load in this file at the lowest available address, with the relative displacement of 0100. The length of the file is equal to the number of bytes loaded and is shown in the BX:CX registers - for most practical purposes, this means the CX register alone.

Example: N MYFIL.EXE

L

-will load in the file at the lowest possible address and show the starting address in the CS:IP registers. The IP register number will not be 0100, and the number in the BX:CX register pair will not be as large as the size of the file as indicated in the DIR display.

Example: N MYFIL.DOC

L 0000

-will load the file at relative address 0000 in whatever segment is available at relative address FF00 (100H bytes before 0000).

The W command allows a file that is being worked on by DEBUG to be written back to the disk. In most ways, the W command is the opposite of the L command, and this includes the writing of disk sectors, but the important exception is that a file of the EXE (or HEX) type cannot be written unless its extension has been changed before loading. The amount of data that will be written is specified by the number in the BX:CX register pair, and the starting address will be CS:0100 unless another address is specified (which is why EXE files are excluded, because unless they are renamed, they will not load to CS:0100 and cannot be correctly saved from that address).

Example: W

-will write the file, using the filename specified by the N command, from addresses starting at CS:0100, and for a number of bytes specified by BX:CX.

The I and O commands are more specialised, and deal with the input and output ports. These ports are used to allow the computer to read in bytes from external sources (like serial input) and to send out bytes (to a loudspeaker, parallel printer, serial modem and so on). You cannot make use of the I and O commands unless you know the address numbers for the ports on your computer and how they are used. The standard port A, B and C address numbers are 060H, 061H and 062H, with serial ports at 03F8 to 03FF and parallel printer on 0378 to 037A, and for the use of these ports or details of other ports such as light- pen ports, you should consult the technical manual for your PC. Each bit is used for a different purpose, so that considerable care has to be taken when writing to a port (using the O command) that the correct bit is being changed.

The form of commands is that I is followed by an address, and O is followed by an address and a byte.

Example: I 062

```
23
```

displays output from Port C indicating in this case that 640K RAM is installed, and that there is a timer bit present.

Example: O 061 01

- sends a 1 to the XT machine's loudspeaker. If this command is use to send 0 and 1 alternately (in a loop) then a note will be sounded.

Go and Trace

The commands that display or alter the contents of file or memory are comparatively innocuous in the sense that though they can alter data they will not have any effect on the computer until the file is used. The G and T commands allow programs to be run under the control of DEBUG, and unless considerable care is taken, or the program is known to run without problems, it is possible that the computer could lock up. The G and T commands are normally used when testing a machine-code program that is suspected of being troublesome, so when these commands are to be used, backup copies must be made first of all. Never use G or T commands on a file that is not a program COM or EXE file.

The G command will start executing a program from any address and can allow up to ten stopping places (or breakpoints) to be specified. For a short program, or one which was though to be working normally, no break-points might be set and if the program ends normally, a message to this effect will be displayed. If another run is required the program will have to be reloaded first.

Example: G

```
Program terminated normally
```

- the program has run without problems and will have to be reloaded if another run is required. If the program has altered memory, then you can use the D command to check what has happened. Normal termination is no guarantee that the program has done what you expected it to do, only that it has ended without locking up the computer. If, as will certainly happen in the event of a fault in the program section or incorrect selection of starting point or breakpoint, the machine does lock up, you will have to restart. Make sure that you have backups of any files that might be affected, and always make a note of what you have done, so that you do not repeat mistakes.

When an address follows the G command, the execution will be forced to start from this address. When you start at the beginning of a program, there is no need to specify an address because this will be taken from the CS:IP registers, ensuring that the correct address is used for either a COM or an EXE file. The use of an address is a way of starting a program at some point other than the beginning, and requires you to know where suitable starting point are. Incorrect selection of a starting address will almost certainly cause a lock-up.

Example: G = 020C

- will start the program running at address CS:020C.

When an address is specified without the equality sign, this address is taken as being a breakpoint, a place where the program is forced to stop. In some programs, more than one breakpoint might have to be specified because there might be branching commands that could lead to any one of a number of addresses being used after a number of commands of the program have been executed. DEBUG allows up to 10 breakpoints to be entered, separated by spaces. Note that these do not imply that the program can be resumed after breaking at one point to be caught at another. Each time breakpoints are to be used, another G instruction must be typed along with whatever breakpoints are to be checked.

Example: G 3CF 5A2

- will start the program from its normal starting point (CS:IP address) and break at 3CFH or 5A2H, whichever is first used in the program. When the break occurs, the register contents will be displayed, and the DEBUG prompt, the hyphen, will appear to indicate that you can enter any valid DEBUG command. This allows you to resume, using G with an address following the breakpoint and specifying more breakpoints.

The use of T is a way of sorting out a small section of a program that is proving stubbornly troublesome. This command will trace what is happening, step by step, either one command for each T or a multiple, but whichever method is used, the full register contents will be shown for each step.

Example: T

- will execute the command at the address in the CS:IP registers, then display the register contents.

Example: T5

- will execute the first five commands, starting at the current CS_IP address, and displaying register contents at each step.

If the part of a program that is under investigation contains a loop, it is often better to use G with a breakpoint just following the loop, and the T to find out what happens next, rather than use T round each part of the loop in each run round the loop. You should not continue to use T to follow a call into MS-DOS or into the ROM BIOS.

Assembly and Unassembly

The A and U commands of DEBUG allow for a very limited form of assembly language working. The A command permits assembly language to be written and placed in memory, but without any editing facilities, so that you cannot slip in an extra command between two others. The U command allows an existing program to be unassembled (or disassembled), showing the assembly language lines that correspond to the machine-code bytes. This assumes that all of the bytes are genuine code, because the U command cannot distinguish between ASCII coded text and machine code instructions. Before the U command is used, then, the code should be looked at using the D command to see where the text, if any, has been placed. The address boundaries for the text should be noted, and these addresses not used along with the U command.

The A command permits limited assembly language facilities for very small-scale work only. The main limitations and differences are:

1. No address labels can be used, so that any reference to other positions in memory have to be made using the memory address.

2. No data labels can be used, so that bytes such as 0DH must be shown as such, and not as word labels like CR.

3. RET instructions must use RETF for a FAR return.
4. An address location is shown inside square brackets
5. MOVESB is used for moving a string byte into memory
6. MOVESW is used for moving a string word into memory.
7. The normal assembler use of a full address is modified so that in place of MOV AX,DS:012F, DEBUG uses DS:MOV AX,[012F]

The advantage of the A command is that it can be very quick to use for short routines, since no assembly time is needed - the code is placed directly into the memory. The form of the command is A followed by the starting address at which the code is to be written.

Example: A 0100

```
6AF1:0100 mov AH,02
6AF1:0102 mov DL,0f
6AF1:0104nt 21
6AF1:0106 int 20
6AF1:0108
-d 0100
6AF1:0100 B4 02 B2 0F CD 21 CD 20-00
```

- allows the lines of assembly language to be written, showing the full address for the first byte in each line. This does not show the actual bytes of assembly language, so that a D command has been used in this example, and only part of the first line is shown.

The U command allows for un-assembly of code, with the usual proviso that any bytes will be treated as code. If the start of the code is at the location given by the contents of CS:IP, then no address needs to be given in the U command, but normally both a starting address and a length (using L) will be specified. The result will be an assembly language version of the bytes in the memory, rather as they would be produced by the A command of DEBUG, with absolute memory addresses. If no length byte is specified, DEBUG will unassemble 20H (32 denary) bytes.

If ASCII text has been present, it will be interpreted as code, and the usual clues to this are jumps to impossible addresses, or the use of very rare and meaningless instructions. Similarly, if an unassembly is started at an address which is in fact the middle of an instruction, the results will be meaningless.

Example: DEBUG EXAMP.COM

```
-U cs:0100 L2B
6B09:0100  BA1801    MOVDX,0118
6B09:0103  B8013D    MOVAX,3D01
6B09:0106  CD21      INT21
6B09:0108  93        XCHGBX,AX
6B09:0109  BA1C01    MOVDX,011C
6B09:010C  B91000    MOVCX,0010
6B09:010F  B440      MOVAH,40
6B09:0111  CD21      INT21
6B09:0113  B8004C    MOVAX,4C00
6B09:0116  CD21      INT21
6B09:0118  50        PUSHAX
6B09:0119  52        PUSHDX
6B09:011A  4E        DECSI
6B09:011B  001B      ADD[BP+DI],BL
6B09:011D  4D        DECBP
6B09:011E  1B471B    SBBAX,[BX+1B]
6B09:0121  52        PUSHDX
6B09:0122  031B      ADDBX,[BP+DI]
6B09:0124  6C        DB6C
6B09:0125  0A1B      ORBL,[BP+DI]
6B09:0127  51        PUSHCX
6B09:0128  5A        POPDX
6B09:0129  1B4E02    SBBCX,[BP+02]
-q
```

- has unassembled the bytes of a short program, treating all of the bytes as code. In this example, the last 16 bytes are not program code but data to be sent to a printer, and the bytes following address 0117 must be treated as dubious. The sequence 50 52 4E when viewed with the D command gives PRN, the name for printer output.

Finally, the H command allows hexadecimal arithmetic to be performed while DEBUG is running, and is a useful way of checking jump number and other arithmetic. The H command is followed by two numbers, and will print the sum and the difference of these numbers, which can be of 1 to 4 hex digits.

Example: h 01f7 3cd6

```
3ECD C521
-q
```

- showing that the sum of the numbers is 3ECDH and the difference (meaning 01F7 - 3CD6) is C521.

DEBUG now contains some new sub-commands for programmers:

XA will allocate a specified number of 16K pages of expanded (EMS) memory

XD will de-allocate memory allocated by XA

XM will map expanded memory pages into a physical page

XS will display expanded memory status.

- DEBUG, used by an experienced programmer, is a superb tool for removing virus infection.

Appendix D
The Public Domain and Shareware Library

Programs, particularly utilities, in the PD and shareware lists are all available from:

The Public Domain and Shareware Library,
Winscombe House,
Beacon Road,
Crowborough,
Sussex TN6 1UL

Index